BBAC

THE
MILITARY
HISTORY
BOOK

BIG IDEAS

- THE ARCHITECTURE BOOK
- THE ART BOOK
- THE ASTRONOMY BOOK
- THE BIBLE BOOK
- THE BIOLOGY BOOK
- THE BLACK HISTORY BOOK
- THE BUSINESS BOOK
- THE CHEMISTRY BOOK
- THE CLASSICAL MUSIC BOOK
- THE CRIME BOOK
- THE DESIGN BOOK
- THE ECOLOGY BOOK
- THE ECONOMICS BOOK
- THE FEMINISM BOOK
- THE HISTORY BOOK
- THE ISLAM BOOK
- THE LAW BOOK
- THE LGBTQ+ HISTORY BOOK
- THE LITERATURE BOOK
- THE MATH BOOK
- THE MEDICINE BOOK
- THE MILITARY HISTORY BOOK
- THE MOVIE BOOK
- THE MYTHOLOGY BOOK
- THE PHILOSOPHY BOOK
- THE PHYSICS BOOK
- THE POETRY BOOK
- THE POLITICS BOOK
- THE PSYCHOLOGY BOOK
- THE RELIGIONS BOOK
- THE SCIENCE BOOK
- THE SHAKESPEARE BOOK
- THE SHERLOCK HOLMES BOOK
- THE SOCIOLOGY BOOK
- THE WORLD WAR I BOOK
- THE WORLD WAR II BOOK

SIMPLY EXPLAINED

THE MILITARY HISTORY BOOK

DK LONDON

SENIOR ART EDITOR
Nicola Rodway

SENIOR EDITOR
Victoria Heyworth-Dunne

EDITORS
John Andrews, Rose Blackett-Ord,
Tim Harris, Dorothy Stannard,
Rachel Warren Chadd

US SENIOR EDITOR
Jennette ElNaggar

ILLUSTRATIONS
James Graham

SENIOR CARTOGRAPHIC EDITOR
Simon Mumford

SENIOR PRODUCTION EDITOR
Andy Hilliard

SENIOR PRODUCTION CONTROLLER
Rachel Ng

MANAGING EDITOR
Gareth Jones

SENIOR MANAGING ART EDITOR
Lee Griffiths

MANAGING ART EDITOR
Luke Griffin

PUBLISHING DIRECTOR
Georgina Dee

ART DIRECTOR
Maxine Pedliham

MANAGING DIRECTOR
Liz Gough

DK DELHI

SENIOR ART EDITOR
Ira Sharma

ART EDITOR
Aanchal Singal

SENIOR EDITOR
Janashree Singha

PROJECT EDITOR
Nandini Devdutt Tripathi

MANAGING EDITOR
Soma B. Chowdhury

SENIOR MANAGING ART EDITOR
Arunesh Talapatra

SENIOR JACKET DESIGNER
Suhita Dharamjit

SENIOR JACKETS COORDINATOR
Priyanka Sharma Saddi

SENIOR PICTURE RESEARCHER
Aditya Katyal

HI-RES COORDINATOR
Neeraj Bhatia

DTP COORDINATOR
Tarun Sharma

DTP DESIGNER
Rakesh Kumar

PRE-PRODUCTION MANAGER
Balwant Singh

PRODUCTION MANAGER
Pankaj Sharma

CREATIVE HEAD
Malavika Talukder

SANDS PUBLISHING SOLUTIONS

EDITORIAL PARTNERS
David and Silvia Tombesi-Walton

DESIGN PARTNER
Simon Murrell

original styling by
STUDIO 8

First American Edition, 2025
Published in the United States by DK Publishing,
a division of Penguin Random House LLC
1745 Broadway, 20th Floor, New York, NY 10019

Copyright © 2025 Dorling Kindersley Limited
25 26 27 28 29 10 9 8 7 6 5 4 3 2 1
001–325108–Mar/2025

All rights reserved.
Without limiting the rights under the copyright
reserved above, no part of this publication may be
reproduced, stored in or introduced into a retrieval
system, or transmitted, in any form, or by any
means (electronic, mechanical, photocopying,
recording, or otherwise), without the prior written
permission of the copyright owner.
Published in Great Britain by
Dorling Kindersley Limited.

A catalog record for this book
is available from the Library of Congress.
ISBN 978-0-7440-4838-4

Printed and bound in UAE

www.dk.com

This book was made with Forest Stewardship Council™
certified paper—one small step in DK's commitment
to a sustainable future.
Learn more at www.dk.com/uk/
information/sustainability

CONSULTANT & CONTRIBUTORS

ADRIAN GILBERT—CONSULTANT

Adrian Gilbert is a military author and consultant, who has written extensively about military history. Among his publications are the bestselling *Sniper One-on-One*; *Germany's Lightning War: From Poland to El Alamein*; *POW: Allied Prisoners in Europe 1939–1945*; and *The Imperial War Musem Book of the Desert War*, the latter volume a co-winner of the Duke of Westminster's Medal for Military Literature.

TIM COOKE

Tim Cooke is a specialist history writer. He has written extensively about wars and warfare, including the American Revolution, the American Civil War, both world wars, the Vietnam and Korean Wars, and a wide range of smaller conflicts around the world.

DR. JACOB F. FIELD

Dr. Jacob F. Field is a teacher, writer, and historian. His PhD is on the impact of the Great Fire of London, and he has also been a lecturer of military history at the University of Waikato. He has written books on a range of subjects, including the D-Day Landings, great speeches in military history, and the life of Winston Churchill.

MARK COLLINS JENKINS

Mark Collins Jenkins, a former historian with the National Geographic Society in Washington, DC, is the principal author of *Yardarm to Yardarm: The War of 1812 and the Rise of the U.S. Navy*, the Navy's official history of that pivotal conflict. He is also a major contributor to DK's bestselling *The Civil War: A Visual History* and its successor, *The Revolutionary War: A Visual History*.

MICHAEL KERRIGAN

Michael Kerrigan was born in Liverpool. His many books include *The Ancients in their Own Words* (Amber, 2009), *Cold War Plans that Never Happened* (Amber, 2012), *The War in Afghanistan* (Amber, 2023), and *History of the World: From the Stone Age to the Tech Revolution* (Amber, 2024). He contributed to *1001 Battles that Changed the Course of History* (Cassell, 2011), *The Second World War* (Dorling Kindersley, 2009), and *The World War I Book* in the Big Ideas series (Dorling Kindersley, 2024). He is a regular reviewer for the *Times Literary Supplement* and lives in Edinburgh.

JOEL LEVY

Joel Levy is an author specializing in history and science, who has written extensively on the history of war and weapons. As well as contributing to titles such as DK's *History of the World Map by Map* and *The World War II Book*, he is also the author of works including *History's Worst Battles*; *Fifty Weapons that Changed the Course of History*; *Meltdown: Stories of Nuclear Disaster and the Cost of Going Critical*; and *Reality Ahead of Schedule: How Science Fiction Inspires Science Fact*.

SEUN MATILUKO

Seun Matiluko is a British Nigerian journalist who recently produced and presented a BBC podcast series about British West African life. She holds an MSc, with distinction, in Empires, Colonialism, and Globalization from the London School of Economics where her studies focused on colonial and postcolonial African histories.

CONTENTS

10 INTRODUCTION

ANCIENT WARFARE
3500 BCE–500 CE

18 Destroyer of the enemy land
Mesopotamia and Ancient Egypt

22 I besieged, I captured, and took away their spoil
The Assyrian Empire

23 I am Cyrus, king of the universe
Persia

24 A people of sailors
Classical Greece

28 War is a matter not so much of arms as of money
The Peloponnesian Wars

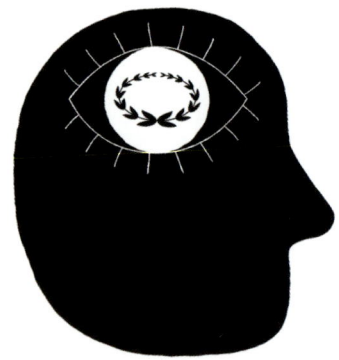

32 Hardship and danger are the price of glory
The conquests of Alexander the Great

40 Three grand new kingdoms … emerged
Alexander's successors

42 The elephants … numbered 9,000
The Mauryan Empire

44 The wise warrior avoids the battle
Origins of the Chinese Empire

48 Planning should be secret, attack should be swift
The Han Empire

50 The might of Rome hath risen high as heaven
The rise of Rome

52 This lesson they … learned by experience
The Punic Wars

54 I came, I saw, I conquered
Caesar and his legacy

56 All roads lead to Rome
The Roman Empire at its height

58 Rome shall fall
Barbarian migrations: the empire under threat

WAR IN THE MIDDLE AGES
500–1500

70 The greatest of God's gifts to men … are priesthood and empire
The Byzantine Empire

74 A rain of their blood as an offering
The Maya civilization

76 Fight in the cause of Allah
The rise of Islam

82 This king, the wisest and most high-minded
The Empire of Charlemagne

- **84** They ravage everything that does not oppose them
  Viking raids
- **85** The duke ... spared no opponent
  The Norman conquests
- **86** The Way of the Samurai is found in death
  The rise of the samurai
- **88** God wills it!
  The Crusades
- **94** If God does not avert it ... a schism will occur
  The Holy Roman Empire versus the papacy
- **96** Never stop until your enemy is on his knees
  The Mongol invasions
- **102** Forward, soldiers of Christ!
  The European Crusades
- **104** A vast walled stronghold
  Zimbabwean kingdoms
- **105** Fearing for their lives, they abandoned all else
  Timur's conquests
- **106** Once more unto the breach, dear friends
  The Hundred Years' War
- **110** Peace among Christians and war against the infidel
  The Spanish Reconquista
- **112** A cannon, which no wall ... could resist
  The rise of the Ottoman Turks
- **114** The flowery death by the obsidian knife
  The Aztecs and Incas

EARLY MODERN WARFARE
1500–1775

- **120** Born to battle and the sword
  The Italian Wars
- **122** Murderous and avaricious conquerors
  The European conquest of the Americas
- **126** He has those captured in combat sold
  Warfare in northern Africa
- **128** The germ of great disaster
  Japan in the Sengoku era
- **130** An impassable wall
  The Ottoman Empire
- **134** Christian and universal
  European wars of religion
- **140** Peace with all
  Mughal conquests in India
- **142** An army like a thick forest and flowing water
  The establishment of Manchu China
- **144** Fear, trembling, and dread pervaded
  The Thirty Years' War
- **148** I am the martyr of the people
  The British Civil Wars
- **150** We have nothing but our lives to lose
  Warfare in North America
- **152** Maintain as many troops as possible
  The wars of Louis XIV
- **158** The unprecedented has happened
  The Great Northern War
- **159** Treaties are only oaths of deception
  The war of the Austrian Succession
- **160** If your number be small, march in a single file
  The French and Indian War

162 **An army in possession of a state**
The Seven Years' War

166 **The bow will be soon unstrung, and the war at an end**
The Ten Great Campaigns

REVOLUTIONS AND EMPIRE
1775–1914

172 **Give me liberty, or give me death!**
The American Revolution

178 **A great wind is blowing**
The wars of Catherine the Great

180 **The just defense of a free people**
The wars of the French Revolution

188 **That synthesis of Monster and Superman**
Napoleon triumphant

192 **Horrors were punished by other horrors**
The Peninsular War

194 **The smell from the gunshot wounds**
Napoleon at bay

198 **Free trade and sailors' rights**
The War of 1812

200 **Long live freedom! Long live independence!**
The Spanish American wars of liberation

204 **Not all heroes are virtuous**
The American-Mexican wars

206 **These dying and exhausted men**
The Crimean War

208 **One flag, one dream**
The wars of Italian unification

210 **To lead the Fatherland on to a blessed future**
The rise of Prussia

214 **They … are afraid of our repeating rifles**
The American Civil War

222 **My people wish for peace**
The conquest of North America

224 **The great naval feat of the … ironclads**
The Paraguayan War

225 **India was the pivot of our Empire**
The British conquest of India

226 **The Scramble for Africa**
Imperial wars in Africa

230 **If we must perish, why not fight to the death?**
China in turmoil

232 **Russia would wipe us off the map**
Ottoman decline and Russian expansion

234 **Casualties of nearly 100,000 men**
The Second Boer War

235 **A new force has been born**
The Russo-Japanese War

236 **A war of liberation became … a war of extermination**
Conflict in the Balkans

THE WORLD WARS AND BEYOND
1914–PRESENT

242 **The rush to the abyss**
World War I: outbreak

248 **We cursed through sludge**
Stalemate on the Western Front

252 **One vast battlefield**
An expanding war

256 The biggest menace ... in this war
The war at sea and in the air

258 We are at the end of our resources
The defeat of the Central Powers

262 You will be shot like partridges
The Russian Civil War

264 Atrocious crimes against humanity
The Second Sino-Japanese War

266 The Nazi war machine
World War II in Europe

272 The U-boat ... must be hunted
The war at sea

274 Bombing them ... around the clock
The air war

276 The war in Europe is over
The defeat of Germany

280 Eight corners of the universe under one roof
Japan ascendant

284 We devoutly hoped that the Japanese would heed our warning
Japan defeated

286 An iron curtain has descended
The Cold War

294 The sky cannot have two suns
The Chinese Civil War

295 Our Big General ... must be recalled
The Korean War

296 Raise aloft the banner of insurrection
Independence in Southeast Asia

298 A country free from foreign interference
Revolution and counter-revolution in Latin America

300 We do not want somebody else's nationalism
The African wars of independence

304 Poverty continues to breed conflict
Postcolonial Africa

306 Enough of blood and tears. Enough
The Arab-Israeli conflicts

312 There was a good war ... and a bad war
Conflict in Afghanistan

314 Deep attack and decisive manoeuver
The Gulf Wars

316 This conflagration will spread
Post-communist wars

317 Corruption is more dangerous than terrorism
Conflict in Iraq

318 The first drone war
The Russian invasion of Ukraine

322 DIRECTORY

328 INDEX

335 QUOTE ATTRIBUTIONS

336 ACKNOWLEDGMENTS

INTRODU

CTION

Military history is the study of armed conflict, a constant in human societies for millennia. Prehistoric cave art from around 10,000 BCE depicts small groups of archers in combat, while ancient mass graves suggest larger battles.

Full-blown war as a more organized, collective enterprise occurred from around 2,700 BCE. Mesopotamia is thought to have had the first standing army, with which its ruler Sargon carved out his Akkadian Empire. Emerging as a nation a thousand years later, the Assyrians were equally warlike and notoriously ruthless, but also innovative, pioneering a style of siege warfare that endured for more than 2,000 years. As their empire fell, the Babylonian Empire rose to replace it—a pattern endlessly repeated over hundreds of years. War was always spreading, and its weapons and strategies would be constantly rethought and refined.

Power, land, and wealth were potent incentives for rulers and their closest circle—people who had fought their way to the top. The fruits of victory enriched this elite, who then sought lasting grandeur, building temples, palaces, and tombs that helped define nations and gave them their identity. With identity came patriotism that encouraged warriors to defend their land against foreign aggressors. Rulers also promised their subjects protection in exchange for their service in time of war, and death in battle was celebrated in epic poetry, which elevated heroic warriors to a godlike status, convincing them that valor was the path to glory.

Inspiring armies

Because war is seldom less than bloody and terrifying, the ability to motivate an army is vital. From Alexander the Great to Napoleon Bonaparte, there were certain great leaders who had that gift, who could inspire commanders, know their forces' strengths and weaknesses, and use effective battle strategies. Before the era of more sophisticated propaganda, it was their charisma that galvanized armies to fight to the death. Religious zeal could be equally inspiring, driving Arab warriors of the 7th century CE to spread the word of Islam by force, Christian Crusaders to take back the Holy Land, and individuals such as Joan of Arc to perform remarkable feats of bravery. Rulers also used the cloak of religion as a pretext for expanding their lands.

Other triggers for war were the miseries of oppression, destitution, and exploitation. The enslaved rose up, the impoverished revolted, and subjugated nations and ethnic groups fought for independence. Revolutions have occurred in the Americas, Europe, Africa, and across Asia.

Tactics and weapons

The battlefield has also been an important arena of technological innovation, which in turn produces new strategic thinking. The ancient Greeks, for instance, refined the weapons and tactics of earlier civilizations, grouping their heavily armed infantry (hoplites) in near impregnable blocks (phalanxes), up to 12 men deep, which proved far

> When battle approaches, when war arises, the plans of the gods, beloved by the gods, are destroyed.
> **Sumerian proverb**
> 3rd millennium BCE

more effective than fighting in hand-to-hand combat. More mobile units made hoplites obsolete, just as much later, Muslim light cavalrymen outstripped and outmaneuvered the armored knights of medieval Europe, who also proved vulnerable to the arrows of the English longbow.

From the late Middle Ages, firearms reduced the use of close combat, while cannon fire that could breach city walls put an end to traditional siege warfare. Pitted against the primitive weapons of Indigenous peoples, firearms also gained colonies in the New World and Africa for European imperial powers. The repeating carbines and automatic handguns invented in the 19th century gave rise to semiautomatic rifles and machine guns used in both world wars, where powerful artillery was also employed to devastating effect.

Artillery transformed naval warfare, too. The forces aboard galleys or later sailing ships would attempt to ram, then board, their opponents' vessels. From the 15th century, cannons were placed on sailing ships to bombard enemy vessels from afar. Believing that naval superiority was essential for its national security, Britain built up a fleet of warships with mounted cannons that, from the 18th century, made its Royal Navy the strongest in the world. A century later, when steamships were developed, the US was the first nation to use them militarily—against Britain in the War of 1812. By the early 20th century, steam power for warships was ceding to diesel power, then to integrated fossil-fuel systems, while a number of today's aircraft carriers and submarines are powered by small nuclear reactors.

Aerial warfare arrived in the early 20th century. In World War I, fighter planes skirmished, the first bombs were dropped, and aerial photography aided reconnaissance. Less than 30 years later, two atomic bombs dropped from American planes obliterated the Japanese cities of Hiroshima and Nagasaki, ending World War II. More recently, remote-controlled guided rockets, cruise missiles, and drones have further distanced aggressors from opponents and the deaths and destruction caused.

War rationale

The frightening knowledge that human ingenuity and technical brilliance could produce weapons that would wipe out life on Earth has neither ended wars nor the arms race between nations. In the Cold War era, Western strategy was underpinned by what US President Dwight D. Eisenhower called the "military-industrial complex." The US government justified massive increases in military spending, highlighting the threat posed by the nuclear bombs and missiles of the USSR, whose Communist leaders similarly claimed to be protecting their people from Western warmongers. This continues to be the case today.

As *The Military History Book* recounts, war has evolved in multiple ways over 4,500 years. Its causes and characteristics have proved infinitely varied, its technologies have been remarkable, and little indicates that it will ever end. ∎

Wars invariably serve as classrooms and laboratories where men and techniques and states of mind are prepared for the next war.
Wendell Berry
American novelist (1934–)

ANCIENT WARFARE
3500 BCE—500 CE

T
RE

INTRODUCTION

Uruk, one of the first great cities, takes root close to the Euphrates River in Mesopotamia. Its population will number 80,000 within 700 years.

Victory at **Megiddo**, northern Israel, gives Egypt's Pharaoh **Thutmose III** control over much of the Middle East.

Persia's **expansion is checked** by the victory of the Greeks at Marathon.

Rome **escapes destruction** at the hands of the invading Gauls. This sets in motion military reforms that help make it an **imperial power**.

c. 3500 BCE — **1457 BCE** — **480 BCE** — **390 BCE**

2721 BCE — **612 BCE** — **431 BCE** — **331 BCE**

History's **first recorded war** is fought in Mesopotamia between the cities of **Sumer** and **Elam**.

The kingdom of **Babylon seizes Nineveh, the** capital of Assyria.

The **Peloponnesian Wars begin** between Athens and Sparta and their allies.

Alexander the Great **defeats Darius III of Persia** at Gaugamela.

Around 12,000 years ago, a temperate climate in the so-called Fertile Crescent in the Middle East and Egypt's Nile valley encouraged people to settle in groups and grow crops. In time, they fought over issues such as natural resources and trading routes. In the first recorded conflict, some 4,700 years ago in Mesopotamia, the two sides did battle with sickles, spears, and copper and bronze axes.

Early empires rise and fall
Sargon I, who ruled Akkad, a kingdom in Mesopotamia, from 2334–2279 BCE, assembled an early professional army of archers and infantry deployed in phalanxes (block formations). His forces conquered lands from the Persian Gulf to the eastern Mediterranean, creating the world's first empire.

Wherever a powerful dynasty arose, others were soon poised to take its place. By around 2047 BCE, the city of Ur had conquered its neighbors in southern Mesopotamia, and its dynasty created a new empire. This in turn fell to Assyria, whose rulers built an even greater empire and further refined the tactics and strategy of war. The Assyrians pioneered siege warfare with earth ramps, battering rams, and wheeled towers built by their innovative engineers. They also used terror tactics, decapitating, flaying, and impaling victims, as they forged a huge empire that reached its height in the early 1st millennium BCE.

Meanwhile, the ancient Egyptian civilization was flourishing along the Nile River. The Hyksos, a Middle Eastern people, who seized power in Egypt around 1640 BCE, had introduced lighter two-wheeled chariots and superior weapons. The Egyptians expelled the Hyksos but embraced their innovations to build a force that enabled them to conquer neighbors and establish their own empire.

Weapons and strategies
Assyria was declining as the Persians grew powerful in the early 6th century BCE. As they conquered, they recruited skilled warriors such as Ethiopian archers and Phoenician sailors. Their empire, the greatest the world had yet seen, included parts of the Balkans and North Africa, and stretched as far as India. It was undented until its first defeat by the ancient Greeks at Marathon, northeast of Athens, in the 5th century BCE. The Greek victory was a triumph for the skilled and

ANCIENT WARFARE

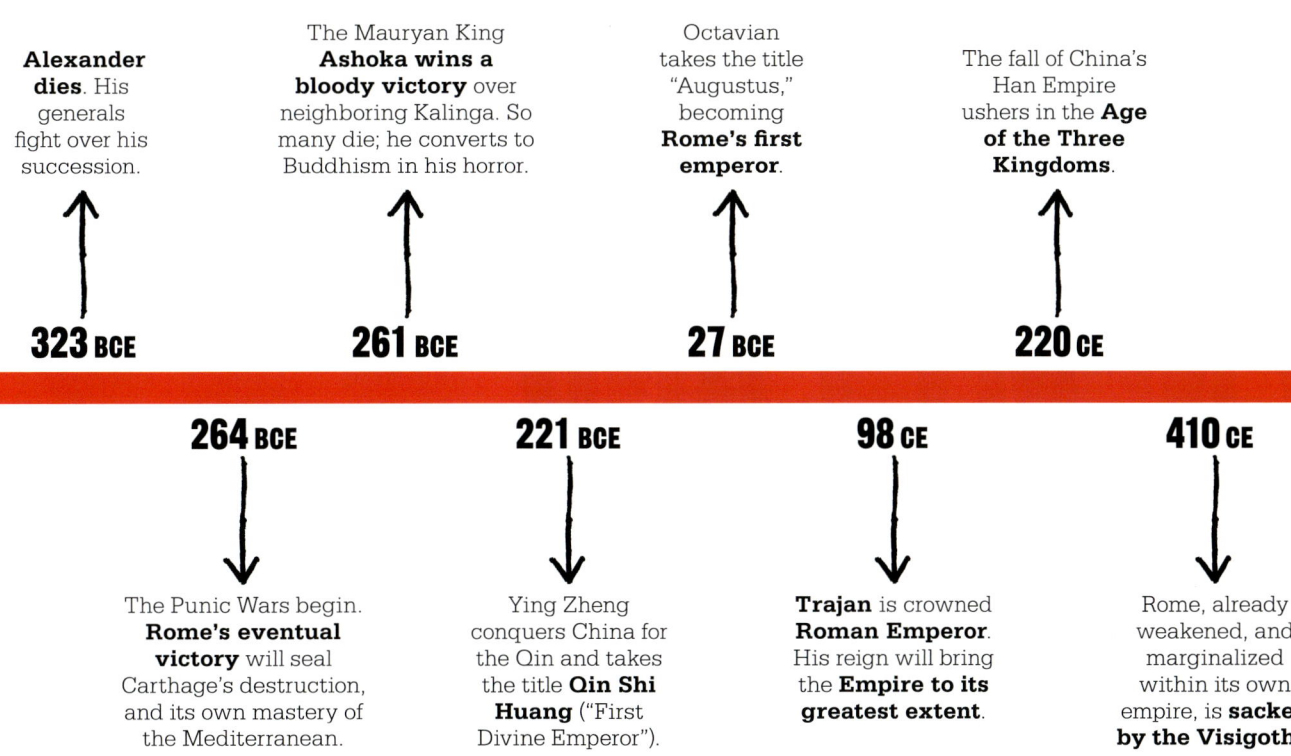

323 BCE — **Alexander dies**. His generals fight over his succession.

261 BCE — The Mauryan King **Ashoka wins a bloody victory** over neighboring Kalinga. So many die; he converts to Buddhism in his horror.

27 BCE — Octavian takes the title "Augustus," becoming **Rome's first emperor**.

220 CE — The fall of China's Han Empire ushers in the **Age of the Three Kingdoms**.

264 BCE — The Punic Wars begin. **Rome's eventual victory** will seal Carthage's destruction, and its own mastery of the Mediterranean.

221 BCE — Ying Zheng conquers China for the Qin and takes the title **Qin Shi Huang** ("First Divine Emperor").

98 CE — **Trajan** is crowned **Roman Emperor**. His reign will bring the **Empire to its greatest extent**.

410 CE — Rome, already weakened, and marginalized within its own empire, is **sacked by the Visigoths**.

disciplined Athenian hoplites (infantry), who overcame a much larger Persian force. Guile, maritime skills, advanced military strategies, and a united front helped the Greeks resist a second Persian invasion, but soon rival alliances of independent city-states tore Greece apart in the Peloponnesian Wars.

In the 4th century BCE, Alexander the Great won a string of victories against the Persians and other nations, traveling huge distances across three continents to create a vast but ephemeral empire that barely survived his death, causing instability across southeast Europe, western Asia and the Aegean.

In India, where Alexander's forces had turned back, a new Mauryan Empire arose. Its armies had a novel attribute—elephants—whose tusks and size terrified the Greek troops, though they would later be used in Greek and Roman armies, and played a key role elsewhere until firearms arrived.

East of India, the vast territory that became China had undergone much the same social evolution as the Middle East and Egypt. Its warlords and individual states vied for supremacy and were, from the 6th century BCE, guided by *The Art of War*, an influential set of essays discussing skills needed for victory in war, including espionage. In the 3rd century BCE, the Qin state emerged as a major power that conquered its neighbors to create an empire. Thousands of ceramic figures, buried with its first emperor, Qin Shi Huang, reveal the structure of his vast army and his court. The Han dynasty, which succeeded the Qin in 206 BCE, produced superior cast-iron weapons and even a form of stainless steel. The Han remained in power for 400 years.

Rome leaves its mark

From the mid-4th century BCE, Rome was in the ascendant. By 275 BCE, it dominated Italy, and 34 years later, after building a navy to reach North Africa, it scored its first victory over Carthage, its rival power in the Mediterranean. Conquests followed in Greece, Africa, and Anatolia. In 50 BCE, Julius Caesar conquered Gaul, and by 77 CE, much of Britain was under Roman rule. New roads and bridges across the empire supplied Roman armies and benefited trade. Yet two centuries later, eroded by barbarian attacks, the Western Roman Empire was collapsing. Rome fell in 476 CE, but its spirit would rise again in Byzantium. ∎

DESTROYER OF THE ENEMY LAND
MESOPOTAMIA AND ANCIENT EGYPT (c. 3500–1200 BCE)

IN CONTEXT

FOCUS
The beginnings of warfare

BEFORE
c. 10,000 BCE The most recent ice age ends, ushering in a milder climate.

c. 9000 BCE The Mesolithic (Middle Stone Age) sees a revolution in human lifestyles. As people settle and cultivate crops, they begin to fight over land and possessions.

c. 7000 BCE Up to 10,000 people live in Çatalhöyük in Anatolia. Recent archaeological findings indicate that violence often erupted in the crowded city. .

AFTER
c. 1077 BCE Egypt's New Kingdom ends with the death of Rameses XI.

332 BCE Alexander the Great invades Egypt.

637 CE Arab forces defeat the army of the Sasanian Empire and control Mesopotamia.

The temperate climate that followed the end of the last ice age, about 12,000 years ago, encouraged people to settle in farming communities where the land was particularly fertile, sparking an agricultural revolution. By the mid-4th millennium BCE, some of these settlements had developed into the first towns and cities, especially in Asia's Fertile Crescent, an arc from what is now Israel through Lebanon, Syria, and southern Türkiye to Iraq.

Managed carefully, agriculture could produce more than was required for a community's survival,

See also: The Assyrian Empire 22 ▪ Persia 23 ▪ Classical Greece 24–27 ▪ The conquests of Alexander the Great 32–39 ▪ Alexander's successors 40–41 ▪ Caesar and his legacy 54–55 ▪ The rise of Islam 76–81 ▪ The Ottoman Empire 130–133

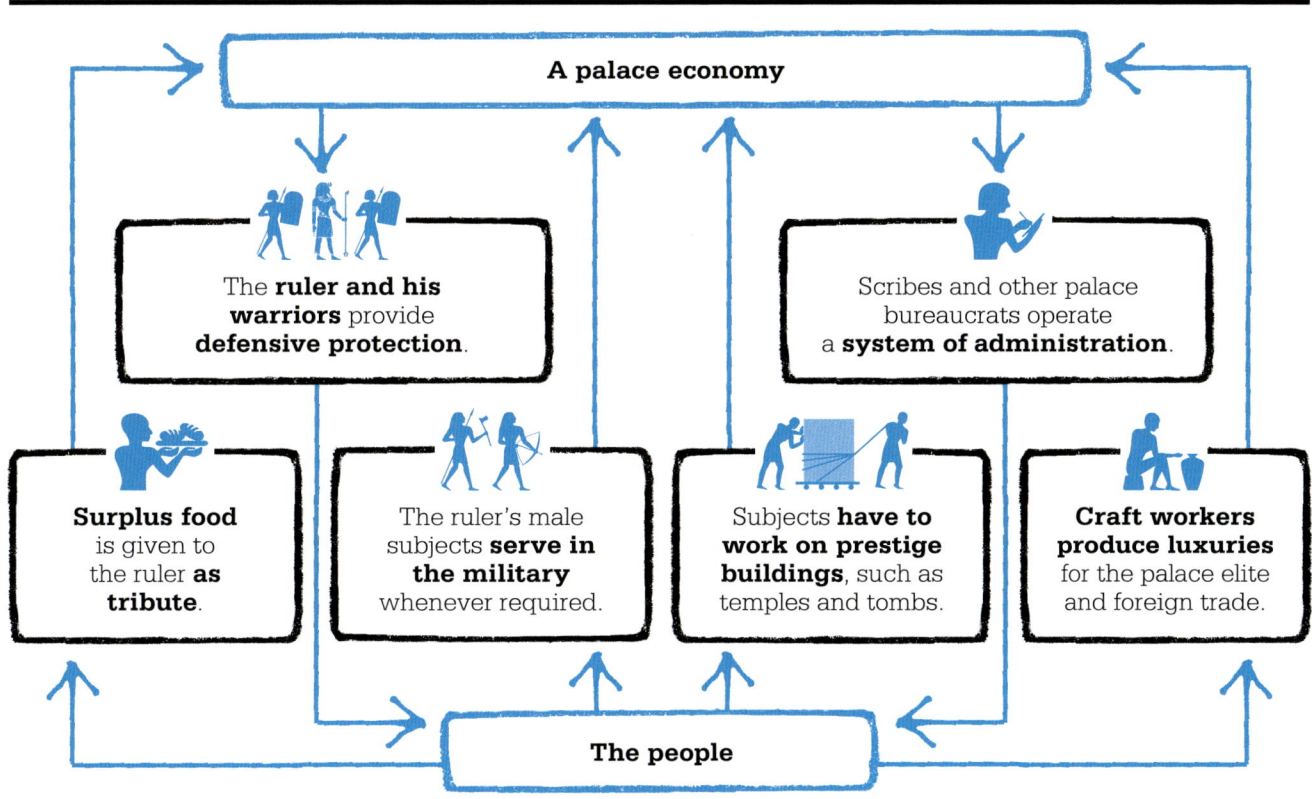

creating surpluses that could be stored, generating wealth. Over time, however, this wealth became increasingly concentrated in the hands of an elite who had the physical strength or personality traits to take charge. They helped themselves to the lion's share of what the people produced, and promised them protection in return.

Known as a "palace economy," the system had sufficient spare capacity to free some people from agricultural labor and create new roles, such as domestic servants and craft workers, to maintain the high status of the rulers. As settlements grew, merchants traded surpluses and crafted goods with the world outside. An administrative class emerged, as did a caste of soldiers to guard their rulers' privilege. War quickly became the business of the elite. Territorial expansion meant greater wealth and access to important water sources or river crossings. Competition was inevitable, and so was conflict.

Civilizations at war

The shift toward competing states occurred on a wider scale in Mesopotamia, a region at the eastern end of the Fertile Crescent. By around 3500 BCE, a substantial city was taking shape at Uruk, in the southern delta marshlands. At its peak, around 2800 BCE, Uruk was probably the world's largest settlement, with a population of up to 80,000. This, and smaller centers nearby, formed the civilization of Sumer. The Sumerian cities jostled for supremacy, but in about 2700 BCE united against the neighboring state of Elam, another agrarian civilization, which had emerged east of Sumer. The war—the first to be recorded—was fought over natural resources and trading routes, between well-trained soldiers armed with spears, sickles, and copper and bronze axes.

Other Sumerian cities followed Uruk's lead, including Umma, which invaded neighboring city-state Lagash around 2400 BCE over disputed water sources. By 2350 BCE, Umma ruler Lugalzagesi had added the cities of Kish and Ur, as well as Uruk, to his list of conquests. Sumer was now »

MESOPOTAMIA AND ANCIENT EGYPT

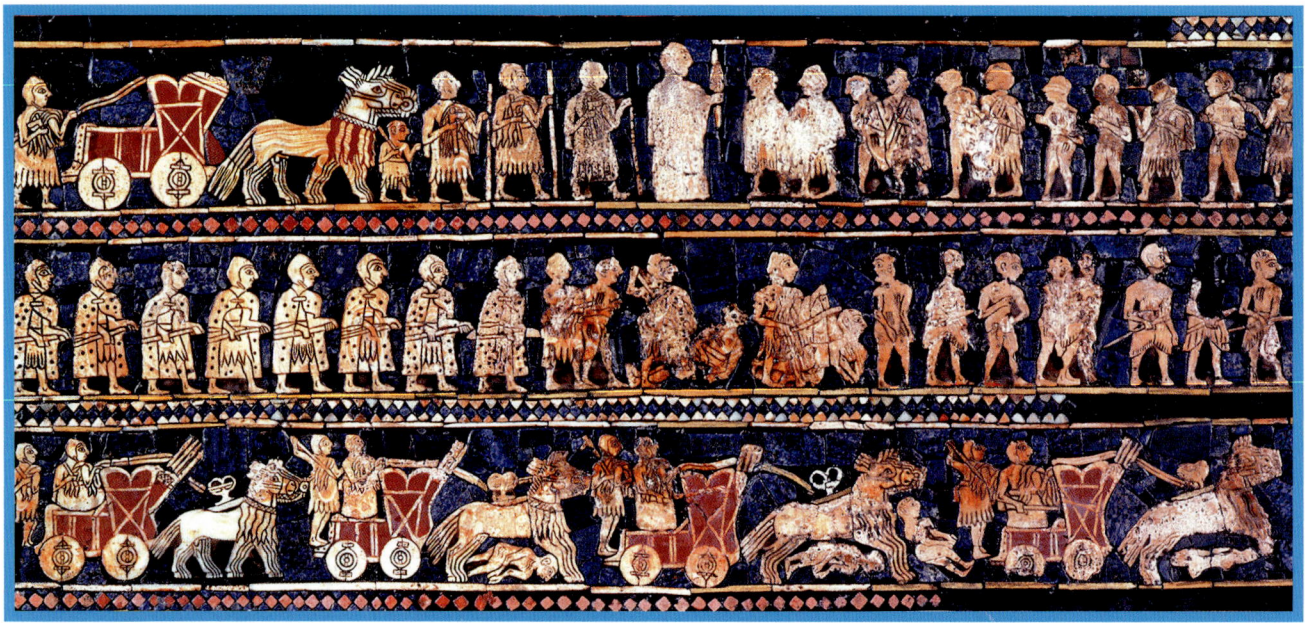

united but threatened by the kingdom of Akkad, whose ruler, Sargon I, had built a professional army. He deployed massed archers and heavily armed infantry in deep formations, known as phalanxes, the front ranks protected by tall shields. Sargon embarked on a program of military expansion, conquering almost the whole of Mesopotamia by 2279 BCE, and creating a multinational empire—the world's first—that stretched from the Persian Gulf to the eastern Mediterranean Sea.

Within 200 years, outside incursions, and possibly severe drought, had fractured the Akkadian Empire. A new dynasty based on Ur filled the Mesopotamian power vacuum until the emergence of a new empire, Assyria, centered on the city of Assur.

Kingdoms of the Nile
While the Tigris and Euphrates rivers nurtured the cities of Mesopotamia, another civilization was taking shape along the Nile River in Egypt. Until the end of the 4th millennium BCE, there were two Egypts—Upper and Lower—each with its own identity and culture. Around 3100 BCE, Menes—a semilegendary king also known as Narmer—is said to have forged a single kingdom from the two states through conquest. A ceremonial slate, or "palette," dated to roughly that time, depicts Narmer striking an enemy—possibly signifying Lower Egypt—with a club, which suggests the violent clashes that may have led to Egyptian unification.

Sargon …took Lugalzagesi… in the course of the battle and led him in a collar to the gate of Enlil.
Inscription of Sargon
Nippur (Nuffar), southeastern Iraq

The Standard of Ur, discovered in a Sumerian tomb of around 2500 BCE, contains one of the earliest depictions of war, including infantrymen killing enemy soldiers with spears and axes.

For 1,000 years from around 2700 BCE, through two periods known as the Old and Middle Kingdoms, Egypt's kings, or pharaohs, ruled the Nile Valley without interruption. War was still a unifying force, bringing plunder to the military elite and glory to the kingdom. As in Mesopotamia, the implicit social contract demanded that the farming subjects of the king should provide the bulk of any campaign army.

Weapons and tactics evolve
The effectiveness of the Egyptian military was thrown into chaos around 1640 BCE when the Hyksos (an immigrant people originally from the eastern Mediterranean Levant region) seized power. Their rule was short—just over a century—but notable. The Hyksos introduced Egypt to the chariot, the horse, superior metal weaponry, and

ANCIENT WARFARE

a strong, flexible composite bow, made from wood reinforced with sinew and horn. By the time the Hyksos were driven out of Egypt in 1532 BCE, their innovations had been adopted by the pharaoh's military. This now developed into a permanent standing army, divided into three to four divisions of 5,000–10,000 soldiers each, with a complex command structure.

The army of the New Kingdom (established around 1570 BCE) enabled a succession of pharaohs to look beyond their own borders and build an empire. Egypt's armies fought campaigns of conquest in Nubia, to the south, and also occupied Gaza, Canaan, and much of Syria. In 1457 BCE, the army of pharaoh Thutmose III crushed an uprising at Megiddo, Canaan, in the rebellious eastern Mediterranean territories, cementing Egypt's hold over the Levant. Thutmose himself led 1,000 chariots into the fray, with mounted archers galloping alongside.

The Hittite threat

Mesopotamia continued to be a source of instability, with its cities rising and falling constantly. The reign of King Hammurabi (c. 1792–1750 BCE) brought Babylon—89 km (55 miles) south of modern

Nubian archers frequently served as mercenaries in Egypt's armies after their homeland was conquered. These are depicted in the mortuary temple of Thutmose II's wife Hatshepsut.

> His majesty went forth in a chariot of electrum, arrayed in his weapons of war, like Horus, the Smiter, lord of power.
> **Annals of Thutmose III**
> on the battle of Megiddo, inscribed at Karnak, Egypt (15th century BCE)

Baghdad—to the fore, but the golden age he established did not outlast him. His kingdom, and Mesopotamia as a whole, were conquered in the 16th century BCE by the Hittites, whose empire had expanded out of northern Syria and Anatolia. They had two great advantages over their opponents—lightweight chariots, used in large numbers as a destructive shock tactic, and tougher, iron weapons.

By around 1300 BCE, the Hittites were also becoming a threat to Egypt. In 1274 BCE, Pharaoh Rameses II engaged the army of Hittite High Prince Muwatalli at Kadesh, near the modern Lebanon–Syria border. Rameses was caught badly off guard, tricked into thinking the enemy was still some way off and allowing the four divisions of his army lose contact with one another. When the Hittite force of up to 40,000 infantry and 3,000 chariots attacked, the similar-sized Egyptian army was unprepared, but it later regrouped and won a major victory.

Within 2,000 years of the first recorded conflicts between the earliest civilizations, the ways of war were well established. ∎

The chariot

By the middle of the 3rd millennium BCE, four-wheeled war wagons, pulled by onagers—Asian wild asses—had appeared on Sumerian battlefields. Although heavy and unwieldy, like ancient tanks, they could carry two or three soldiers armed with spears and axes into the fray.

The invention of the spoked wheel—light but strong and flexible—around 2000 BCE in Central Asia revolutionized chariot technology, and over the next 500 years, it was adopted in Mesopotamia, Anatolia, and Egypt. Two wheels became the norm, as did horses (another Central Asian introduction) in teams of two or four that were chosen for pace rather than for their raw strength. Charging at full gallop, they could reach speeds of 25 mph (40 km/h). The Egyptians innovated further, moving the chariot's axle to the rear of the carrying platform, from where archers, armed with fast-loading and accurate composite bows, could fire streams of arrows at the enemy.

Egyptian Pharaoh Rameses II is shown firing an arrow from a spoke-wheeled chariot at the Battle of Kadesh. This wall carving is on his tomb in the Valley of the Kings.

I BESIEGED, I CAPTURED, AND TOOK AWAY THEIR SPOIL
THE ASSYRIAN EMPIRE (c. 1300–600 BCE)

IN CONTEXT

FOCUS
Siege warfare

BEFORE
c. 2000 BCE A wall painting at Beni Hasan, Egypt, depicts a simple battering ram.

c. 1600 BCE The Hittites start expanding from Anatolia into Mesopotamia, bringing with them new iron weaponry.

1457 BCE The Egyptian army surrounds the city of Megiddo, Canaan, for seven months—the first recorded siege.

AFTER
332 BCE Alexander the Great besieges the Phoenician city of Tyre, building two causeways to reach its walls.

146 BCE After a three-year siege, Carthage is destroyed by a Roman army.

12th–15th centuries CE As castles become the main form of defense, sieges become a common feature of warfare.

The city-state of Assyria—based in Assur in what is now northern Iraq—was in decline by the middle of the 2nd millennium BCE. However, under Tiglath-pileser I (r. 1114–1076 BCE), the kingdom started to reassert itself, and a sustained campaign of imperial expansion followed under Ashurnasirpal II and his son Shalmaneser III. War at first followed a seasonal cycle between spring planting and fall harvest, and then all year round after Tiglath-pileser III created Assyria's first professional standing army in the 8th century BCE.

By the next century, the Assyrian Empire was the world's largest, stretching from the Persian Gulf to the Mediterranean Sea. It collapsed rapidly after the death of King Ashurbanipal c. 631 BCE, and in 612 BCE the Kingdom of Babylon seized Nineveh, Assyria's capital.

Terror and siege tactics
The Assyrians' approach to war was ruthless, striking fear into opponents, who were well aware that they could all be impaled on stakes, decapitated, flayed, or burned alive. First, city walls had to be breached, so beside elite charioteers, archers, and infantry, the Assyrian army fielded siege engineers, who built massive earth ramps, iron-tipped battering rams, and wheeled towers, allowing attackers to engage with defenders from an equal height. Such Assyrian innovations provided the template for siege warfare for the next 2,000 years, until the advent of the cannon in the 14th century CE. ■

I impaled 700 soldiers on stakes before their city gate.
Ashurnasirpal II

See also: Mesopotamia and Ancient Egypt 18–21 ▪ The conquests of Alexander the Great 32–39 ▪ The Roman Empire at its height 56–57

ANCIENT WARFARE

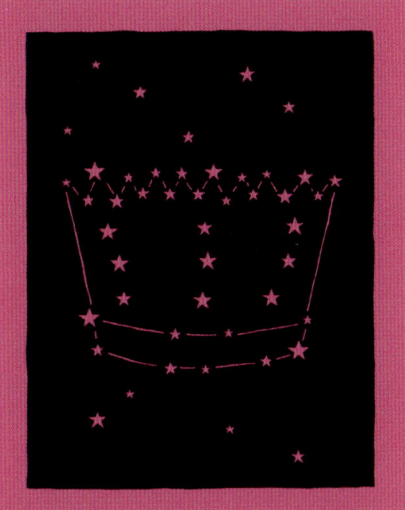

I AM CYRUS, KING OF THE UNIVERSE
PERSIA (c. 600–350 BCE)

IN CONTEXT

FOCUS
An army of many peoples

BEFORE
1457 BCE The king of Kadesh forms a coalition of rebel states in Canaan to fight against Egypt at the Battle of Megiddo.

745–727 BCE Tiglath-pileser III reforms the Assyrian army, recruiting soldiers from regions, including Babylonia, the Zagros Mountains, and Anatolia.

AFTER
331 BCE Alexander the Great vanquishes Darius III at the Battle of Gaugamela and takes control of the Achaemenid Empire.

1914–1918 World War I is fought between two multinational alliances—the Entente, and the Central Powers.

1945 The United Nations is founded; its peacekeeping operations go on to deploy troops from around the world.

In the early 6th century BCE, the Median Empire dominated ancient Iran, including a small Persian kingdom in the southwest, which was ruled by the Achaemenid dynasty. However, when Cyrus II acceded to the Achaemenid throne in 559 BCE, he rebelled against his overlords. Within nine years, he had vanquished the Medes and begun to establish Persia as an imperial power in its own right. He expanded its territories east and west and conquered the Neo-Babylonian Empire in 539 BCE.

The vast Achaemenid—or First Persian—Empire reached its peak under Darius the Great, who ruled from 522 to 486 BCE. It extended from India to the Balkans and North Africa. Darius encouraged recruits to his armies from conquered peoples, such as Ethiopian archers, Egyptian spearmen, Phoenician mariners, and Anatolian cavalrymen. This broader recruitment base enabled him to call on more specialist troops, making his army more resilient and a more effective fighting force. The 10,000 soldiers of the Achaemenid elite heavy infantry unit known as the Immortals were, however, predominantly Persian.

Darius the Great (seated) receives the leader of a subjugated nation. This bas-relief was carved in Apadana Palace in the Achaemenid Empire's capital, Persepolis.

Later Persian attempts to subjugate Greek city-states that challenged its control of Anatolia were thwarted. Despite failed invasions of Greece in 492–490 BCE and 480 BCE, the Achaemenids remained dominant in West Asia until the arrival of Alexander the Great in the 4th century BCE. ∎

See also: Mesopotamia and Ancient Egypt 18–21 ▪ The Assyrian Empire 22 ▪ Classical Greece 24–27 ▪ The conquests of Alexander the Great 32–39

A PEOPLE OF SAILORS
CLASSICAL GREECE (c. 700–479 BCE)

IN CONTEXT

FOCUS
Greek naval ascendancy

BEFORE
c. 7th century BCE Basing their designs on Phoenician craft, the Corinthians develop the first triremes.

7th–6th centuries BCE Seafaring Greeks establish colonies and settlements in Anatolia, Italy, Sicily, France, Spain, and North Africa.

AFTER
449 BCE The Peace of Callias, signed by Persia and Athens, ends the wars between them.

431–404 BCE Athens loses most of its navy when it is defeated by Sparta in the Second Peloponnesian War.

332 BCE Alexander the Great uses quadriremes (galleys with four banks of oars) in his navy in the Siege of Tyre.

After the collapse of the Mycenaean civilization in the 11th century BCE, little is known of developments in Greece until city-states (*poleis*) began to emerge around 800 BCE. Each had its own laws, customs, and patron gods. To avoid being conquered by a more powerful rival, city-states raised armies and made alliances. Many also established navies to fight for maritime supremacy. Two became dominant: Athens and Sparta.

Warfare in Classical Greece was near endemic as city-states vied for regional power, sometimes annexing weaker rivals. While single combat characterized earlier wars, by around 700 BCE, Greek

ANCIENT WARFARE 25

See also: Persia 23 ▪ The Peloponnesian Wars 28–31 ▪ The conquests of Alexander the Great 32–39 ▪ Alexander's successors 40–41 ▪ The rise of Rome 50–51 ▪ The Punic Wars 52–53

Each hoplite was well armed and protected, but his role was not to fight alone. For success in battle, a phalanx of hoplites had to be disciplined and united.

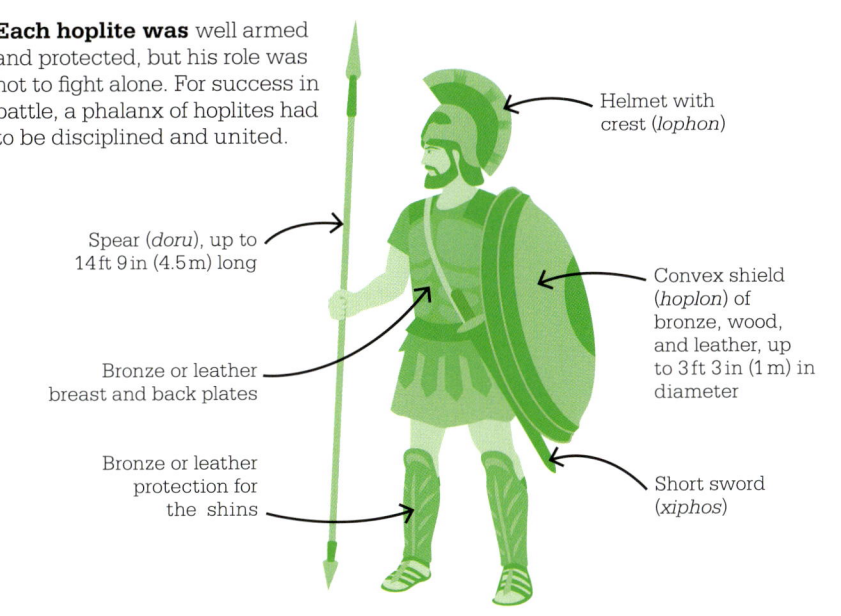

- Spear (*doru*), up to 14 ft 9 in (4.5 m) long
- Bronze or leather breast and back plates
- Bronze or leather protection for the shins
- Helmet with crest (*lophon*)
- Convex shield (*hoplon*) of bronze, wood, and leather, up to 3 ft 3 in (1 m) in diameter
- Short sword (*xiphos*)

forces increasingly employed heavily armored infantrymen, known as hoplites, fighting in a closely packed formation called a phalanx. Most were free men who supplied their own armor, shields, and spears, according to their means. Grouped in a phalanx up to 12 men deep, behind a wall of their heavy, circular shields, they used their spears to repel enemy attacks.

Greek armies of this time also included troops who used long-range weapons, such as javelins, bows, and slings, and sometimes incorporated cavalry. Disciplined infantry phalanxes, however, made victory more likely.

Democracy—or not
By the end of the 6th century BCE, Athens had adopted democratic reforms. Other *poleis* would follow suit. Military service became one obligation of being a citizen of a democracy; in return for the right to vote and hold political office, free men aged between 18 and 60 were expected to serve in the armed forces if necessary.

A notable exception in the trend toward democracy was Sparta—a major power by around 650 BCE. All its citizens were expected to be full-time, professional soldiers; most labor was carried out by Helots, non-Spartan serfs. At age seven, Spartan boys entered the *agoge*, a strict, intensive regime of military training and education. At 20, they officially joined the army but often remained part of the *agoge* for a further 10 years.

Greek warships
From the 8th century BCE, more city-states built up their navies as they began establishing trading colonies across the Mediterranean and, eventually, on the coast of the Black Sea. The city-state with the strongest and largest navy was Athens, which largely financed its shipbuilding with silver from mines to its south in southern Attica.

The foundation of Greek maritime power was the trireme. These vessels were long, slender, highly maneuverable warships, around 120 ft (37 m) in length, with three banks of oars that gave them a top speed of over 8 mph (13 km/h). Although triremes might carry projectile weapons and troops, as well as marines for boarding actions, the main tactic in battle »

The reconstructed Athenian trireme *Olympias* has three banks of oars on each side to accommodate 170 oarsmen, as well as two square sails, and a bronze "beak" for ramming on its bow.

CLASSICAL GREECE

Themistocles

Born around 524 BCE in Phrearrhii, near Athens, Themistocles was the son of an aristocrat and his concubine, who may not have been Greek. He is thought to have grown up in an immigrant district. Thanks to the democratic reforms of his age, however—which ensured that all free men became Athenian citizens—this was no barrier to his rise to power. Aged 31, he became the city's archon (chief magistrate).

One of Themistocles's key policies was to build up Athens's naval strength, its coastal defenses, and its harbors, using the wealth of state-owned silver mines. During the Second Graeco-Persian War, he commanded the Athenian fleet and oversaw their decisive victory at the Battle of Salamis in 480 BCE. However, he fell out with the city-state's council of nobles, was ostracized around 472 BCE, and moved to Argos in the Peloponnese. Some years later, when Sparta accused him of plotting with Persia, Themistocles fled Greece. Granted asylum by the Persian king Artaxerxes, he died in Anatolia in 459 BCE.

Individual **city-states** begin to **emerge** throughout Greece.

↓

As they **fight each other** for power and territory, **combat skills are refined**.

↓

On land, hoplites in tight formations (phalanxes) **prove highly effective**.

At sea, fast, maneuverable triremes outrun and ram enemy vessels.

↓

When city-states, including **Athens and Sparta, unite**, their forces **defeat the mighty imperial Persian invaders**.

---

was to ram ships with the bronze armored beak, fitted at the base of the vessel's bow.

Fighting Persia

As Greek city-states expanded their activities into Anatolia, they came into conflict with the powerful Persian Empire, whose emperor, Darius the Great, planned new incursions into Europe. In 499 BCE, Greek settlers in Ionia on the western coast of Anatolia rebelled against Persia. The Greek city-states of Athens and Eretria sent triremes to support the rebellion, which spread to other Greek-settled areas held by Persia, including Cyprus. However, at the Battle of Lade in 494 BCE, Persian sea power prevailed; the Greek revolt was finally suppressed a year later.

The settlers' rebellions fueled Darius's desire to invade Greece. In 492 BCE, Persian forces advanced west from Anatolia, consolidating their control of Thrace, a region bordering the Aegean and Black seas, and subjugating Macedonia in northern Greece. The following year, Darius sent ambassadors to other Greek city-states demanding their submission to Persia. Fearing reprisals from this powerful foe, they all yielded, except Athens and Sparta, both of which executed the ambassadors sent to them.

The Persians invaded again in 490 BCE, capturing the Cycladic Islands, in the Aegean Sea, before landing on the Greek mainland, where they sacked Eretria and enslaved its citizens. The Persians then sailed south and landed at Marathon in Attica, hoping to advance on Athens, 25 miles (40 km) away. Before the Persians could march out of Marathon, the Athenians, supported by around 1,000 troops from the city-state of Plataea, blocked their path. A runner was sent to the Spartans, asking them to send reinforcements. Aware that the Persian cavalry was elsewhere, the Athenians decided to launch a surprise attack. Despite the numerical superiority of the Persians, the weapons, tactics and discipline of the hoplites secured a Greek victory at Marathon, ending the first Persian invasion.

A second Persian invasion

Darius planned another invasion of Greece but died in 486 BCE, before he could launch it. Xerxes I, his son and successor, gathered a much larger army, possibly 250,000-men strong, and a fleet of more than 800 ships, and took command of the second Persian invasion of Greece in 480 BCE. Although many Greek city-states remained neutral or yielded to the Persians, Athens, Sparta, and 28 others formed an alliance to fight their common enemy.

The Persians marched south from Macedonia into the region of Thessaly. Standing in their way was a force of 7,000 led by Sparta's king, Leonidas I. He made his stand at a narrow mountain pass called Thermopylae, where the Persians could not bring their superior numbers to bear. Leonidas, who died in battle, inspired his men to hold out for three days, giving his allies time to organize. Despite this, the Persians were able to continue their advance south into Attica, sacking Athens and several other cities. Even so, the Greeks would not surrender, consolidating their forces to prevent the Persians from marching into the Peloponnese.

Triumph at Salamis

In September 480 BCE, the Athenian politician and military leader, Themistocles, oversaw the naval Battle of Salamis. As the Persian fleet was made up of more than 1,000 vessels and the Greeks had only 370, Themistocles enticed his opponents into giving battle in a narrow strait to minimize their huge advantage. In the crowded waters, the Greek ships trapped and rammed the congested Persian fleet, which descended into chaos. The Greek fleet triumphed; the Persian ships turned tail for Anatolia, and Xerxes returned to Persia with much of his army.

> The Athenians in the commotion destroyed those [Persian] ships which either resisted or tried to flee.
> **Herodotus**
> Greek historian and geographer (c. 484–c. 425 BCE)

A further Persian force of some 100,000 men, however, again sacked Athens. In response, the Greeks gathered the largest ever hoplite force—some 750,000 men— and won a decisive victory at the Battle of Plataea in August 479 BCE, destroying the remnants of the Persian fleet at the Battle of Mycale the same day. The second Persian invasion was over, but sporadic conflicts between the Greeks and Persians would break out for a further three decades. ∎

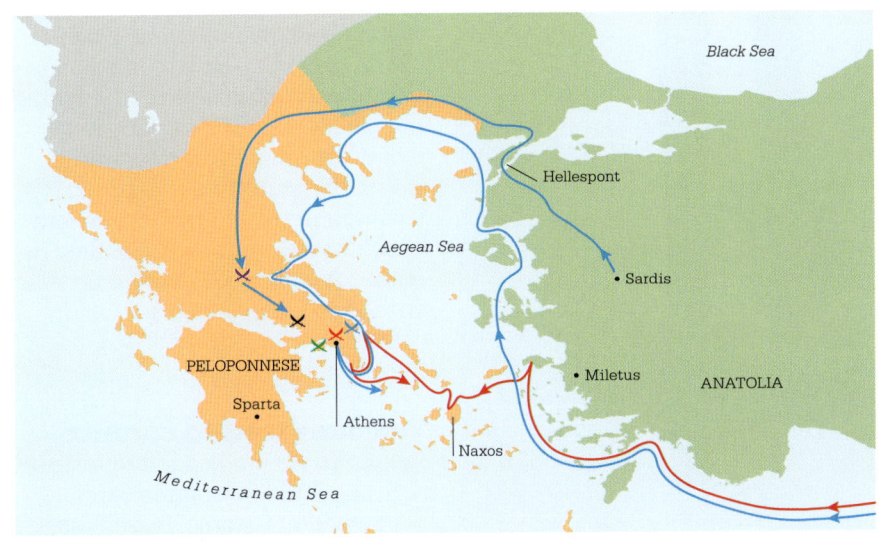

Key:
- Persian Empire
- Greek states
- ← First Persian invasion 492–490 BCE
- ← Second Persian invasion 480–479 BCE
- ✕ Battle of Marathon 490 BCE
- ✕ Battle of Thermopylae 480 BCE
- ✕ Persians sack and burn Athens 480 BCE
- ✕ Battle of Salamis 480 BCE
- ✕ Battle of Plataea 479 BCE

This map shows the routes taken from Persia's vast empire into Greek territory during the Persian invasions, along with the sites of the key battles that changed the course of the conflict.

WAR IS A MATTER NOT SO MUCH OF ARMS AS OF MONEY

THE PELOPONNESIAN WARS (460–404 BCE)

IN CONTEXT

FOCUS
Attritional warfare

BEFORE
c. 550 BCE Sparta founds the Peloponnesian League, an alliance with its neighbors in the southern Greek peninsula.

513 BCE Scythia, a land in central Asia, thwarts an invasion by Darius I, using a strategy of attrition to harry and exhaust his Persian forces.

AFTER
395–387 BCE Sparta fights a coalition of hostile city-states in the Corinthian War and remains dominant but weaker.

1864–1865 CE Union commander Ulysses S. Grant leads a campaign of attrition against Confederate forces during the American Civil War.

1916 The battles of Verdun and the Somme in France are two of the bloodiest battles of attrition in World War I.

In the early 5th century BCE, Athens and Sparta had joined forces against Persia, expelling the invaders in 479 BCE. The historic rivalry between the two powerful Greek city-states resumed, however, resulting in the Peloponnesian Wars, which lasted for decades, sucked in other city-states and foreign powers, and led to thousands of civilian deaths, as each side tried to wear the other down.

Tensions lead to conflict
Ruled by two kings simultaneously, Sparta led the Peloponnesian League of city-states. Its military

ANCIENT WARFARE 29

See also: Persia 23 ▪ Classical Greece 24–27 ▪ The conquests of Alexander the Great 32–39 ▪ Alexander's successors 40–41 ▪ The American Civil War 214–221 ▪ Stalemate on the Western Front 248–251

After their **combined forces** repel the Persian invasion, Greek **city-state rivalries reemerge**.

↓

Athens rebuilds its **defensive walls**, pursues lucrative **maritime commerce**, and **enlarges its navy**.

↓

Sparta's former **military dominance is threatened** and **hostile neighbors** are gaining **Athenian support**.

↓

As both city-states **seek to expand** their influence, **conflict becomes inevitable**.

↓

War ends only when Sparta annihilates the Athenian fleet, terminating its maritime supremacy.

If we go to war … be determined that we are not going to climb down … it is from the greatest dangers that the greatest glories are to be won.
Pericles
Athenian leader and statesman,
431 BCE

strength lay in its formidable army of professional hoplites, supplemented by troops from its allies. The Peloponnesian League had ended its hostilities with Persia, but Athens led the Delian League, a confederacy of city-states that continued fighting Persia in the Aegean Sea and Anatolia until 449 BCE. With its extensive fleet of triremes, Athens became the dominant naval power in Greece. Against Sparta's wishes, Athens also rebuilt its city walls to replace those that Persia had destroyed, extending them to its ports at Piraeus and Phaleron.

Sparta soon began to fear the growing strength and maritime commercial empire of Athens, which could now dictate the policy of its allies, collect tribute from them, and use its wealth to further strengthen its navy.

Tension between the two major powers increased when Sparta called for Athenian help to repress a revolt among its helots (non-Spartan serfs), then rejected Athens's forces for fear that they might support the rebels. This affront, combined with Athens's new alliances with city-states opposed to Sparta and its ally Corinth, triggered the First Peloponnesian War in 460 BCE. Land battles were mostly won by the hoplite armies of Sparta and its allies, while the speed and maneuverability of the Athenian triremes tended to win the naval battles. Fighting would continue periodically until 445 BCE, when the two main opponents and other city-states made a short-lived peace.

War and plague
The fresh clamor for war began in Sparta's powerful ally Corinth, whose leaders accused Athens of breaking the peace by interfering in the economic and political affairs of members of the Peloponnesian League. In 432 BCE, Corinth called on the league to address the Spartan Assembly and persuade it to confront Athens over the allegations. Although an Athenian delegation arrived to warn of the perils of war, and one of the Spartan kings—Archidamus II—also spoke against conflict, the assembly found »

THE PELOPONNESIAN WARS

Thucydides

The second Peloponnesian War inspired one of the earliest, and most influential, works of history. Written by Thucydides (c. 460–400 BCE), an Athenian general who fought in the conflict, *History of the Peloponnesian War* broke new ground. Unlike many of his contemporaries, Thucydides sought to be impartial and to base his account on evidence that he had personally collected. He did much of this after 422 BCE when he was exiled from Athens for his failure to save the city of Amphipolis from capture by Sparta, and spent his time travelling in the Peloponnese, where he gained an understanding of his former enemies.

Divided into eight books, *History of the Peloponnesian War* begins with a summary of Greek history before 431 BCE and the main causes of the conflict. Thucydides then recorded the major events of each year, arranging his work in chronological order.

Thucydides died before he could complete his work. The narrative ends abruptly in 411 BCE, seven years before the war's conclusion.

Athens guilty as charged. This led to a second war in 431 BCE, which proved far more attritional and damaging than the first.

During the opening phase, known as the Archidamian War after Sparta's king, the strength of Sparta and its allies in the Peloponnesian League lay in their formidable armies, while Athens and the Delian League were strongest at sea. As a result, the Spartans could march virtually unchallenged into Attica, the region of the Athens city-state, and ravage its countryside. However, Sparta could never muster enough men to occupy Attica for more than a few weeks at a time, and most of Athens's population had retreated behind the city's defensive walls, now stretching down to its ports. This meant that the city's residents could still receive food supplies by sea.

To counter the threat from Sparta, the inspirational Athenian leader Pericles proposed a naval-based strategy of surprise attacks. These could have succeeded, but in 430 BCE, soon after Pericles had delivered a rallying funeral oration to honor the city's war dead, disaster struck. Plague ravaged the densely packed Athenian population, killing around 30,000 people—more than a third of its residents. Pericles himself succumbed in 429 BCE. His successor, the politician Cleon, favored a more aggressive strategy.

The struggle spreads

Led by the general Demosthenes, Athenian forces now combined naval raids with land advances into the western Peloponnese.

Greek city-state armies increasingly used lightly clad peltasts. These soldiers could throw their javelins up to 82 ft (25 m) and move faster than heavily armored hoplites.

In 425 BCE, they defeated a mighty Spartan phalanx at Sphacteria, an island south of the Peloponnesian harbor of Pylos. Here, Athens had supplemented its hoplites with slingers, archers, and light infantry such as lightly clad peltasts, who fought with javelins and swords. These troops could harass the slower, heavily armored Spartan hoplites with projectile attacks, then flee. Over the course of the war, light infantry became increasingly important and was integrated with hoplites and cavalry.

In response, in 424 BCE, the Spartan general Brasidas led an army north, achieved victories in Macedonia, and encouraged Athenian subject city-states to revolt. In 422 BCE, Brasidas and his army attacked Amphipolis, an Athenian colony in Thrace, hoping to capture silver mines nearby and so deprive Athens of essential income. Sparta, here aided by its own peltasts, won the ensuing battle, but Brasidas was killed, as was the Athenian general Cleon. With both sides exhausted, diplomatic talks began, leading to the Peace of Nicias in 421 BCE.

Despite the temporary peace between Athens and Sparta, tensions in the Peloponnese soon escalated when Argos, a democratic power that was independent of

ANCIENT WARFARE   31

Triremes clash as the Athenian navy seeks to escape a Spartan blockade of Syracuse in 413 BCE. Athens's fleet was destroyed, and its 40,000-strong army was trapped on shore.

Sparta, formed an alliance with neighboring democratic city-states. In 418 BCE, Argos and its allies tried to capture the city of Tegea, close to Sparta. The same year, Sparta defeated the democratic alliance at the Battle of Mantinea and re-established its dominance of the Peloponnese.

War spreads to Sicily

In 415 BCE, Athens launched a more ambitious overseas invasion—an expedition west to the island of Sicily, where Greek colonization had begun in the 8th century BCE. The goal of some—though not all—of Athens's assembly members was to conquer the city of Syracuse and increase Athens's wealth by taking control of eastern Mediterranean trade routes. An Athenian force of around 100 ships and more than 5,000 soldiers set sail. After landing on Sicily, they gathered some local allies but failed to attack before winter set in. This delay gave Sparta time to send reinforcements to Syracuse, allowing the Syracusans and their allies to win a series of victories by sea and land.

With Athens weakened, the Spartans slowly squeezed their enemy's economy. In 413 BCE, they took control of Decelea, blocking land routes into Athens from the north so that all supplies had to be brought in by sea. The city was forced to levy higher tributes from its allies, straining relations with the Delian League. The money was spent mostly on sending a further 5,000 soldiers and 100 ships to Sicily in 413 BCE. By the end of the year, this force had been destroyed in battle. The entire contingent was killed or enslaved and dozens of triremes were lost. Athens found it increasingly difficult to muster enough men and ships, while Persia, which was eager to see Athens destroyed, promised money and ships to Sparta.

Partial recovery

The war dragged on for almost a decade. Athens had retained a reserve fleet of 100 ships, which won a series of victories against the Spartans, stabilizing the city and giving it time to rebuild its strength. Fearing Athens might fully recover, Persia increased its involvement, sending more money and supplies to Sparta.

In 405 BCE, the Spartan king and commander Lysander sailed with his reinforced fleet to the Dardanelles to threaten maritime trade routes into Athens, potentially starving the city. The Athenians were compelled to send their last 180 ships north. At the ensuing Battle of Aegospotami, Lysander oversaw a decisive Spartan victory, in which all but 12 Athenian vessels were destroyed. Surrounded, cut off from troop reinforcements, and faced with starvation, Athens surrendered in 404 BCE, and its allies swiftly followed.

Rather than raze Athens, Sparta destroyed its walls and fleet and imposed a tyrannical oligarchy to rule the city. The Athenian Empire had ended; after three decades of bloodshed, the Spartans were masters of Greece. ■

The Spartans ... exhorted each ... comrade to remember what he had learned before ... aware that the long training of action was of more use for saving lives than any brief verbal exhortation.
Thucydides
History of the Peloponnesian War

HARDSHIP AND DANGER
ARE THE PRICE OF GLORY
THE CONQUESTS OF ALEXANDER THE GREAT (359–323 BCE)

34 THE CONQUESTS OF ALEXANDER THE GREAT

IN CONTEXT

FOCUS
Alexander the Great

BEFORE
c. 808 BCE Caranus becomes king of the Mackednoi tribe of Macedon.

c. 512 BCE Macedon becomes a vassal state of the Achaemenid Persian Empire and is fully subordinate after the Ionian Revolt (499–493 BCE).

479 BCE After the Greeks repel the second Persian invasion of mainland Greece, Macedon regains its independence.

AFTER
322–281 BCE In the Wars of the Diadochi, Alexander's generals and successors fight over his legacy, and the Macedonian Empire fragments.

214–148 BCE The Macedonian Wars are fought by the Romans and their Greek allies against other Greek kingdoms.

In 356 BCE, Greek princess Olympias of Epirus, wife of Philip II of Macedon, gave birth to a son, Alexander. Macedon was, at the time, a small, largely peripheral kingdom in northern Greece that had suffered from a rapid turnover of rulers, succession disputes, and damaging invasions. When Alexander died 32 years later, his vast empire included all of Greece, stretched south into Egypt, and extended east across Asia as far as northwestern India. Building on his father's successful rule, Alexander won battle after battle, establishing himself as one of history's greatest military figures.

Laying the foundations

Philip II had become Macedon's ruler in 359 BCE at the age of 24 and changed his country's fortunes. He had reformed the Macedonian army, improving discipline and training, and increasing the size of its cavalry. His greatest innovation was the introduction of the *sarissa*, a pike or long spear around 20 ft (6 m) in length that became the main weapon of the Macedonian phalanx. Philip oversaw a series of conquests that extended Macedon's borders north into the Balkans and south, further into Greece. By 346 BCE, having capitalized on infighting between other city-states, Macedon had become the leading power in the region. Athens, a possible rival, was roundly defeated at the Battle of Chaeronea (338 BCE), leaving Philip free to face another enemy, the Achaemenids of Persia.

The Achaemenid dynasty ruled the Persian Empire, at that time the largest and most powerful ever to have existed. It included western Anatolia and islands off its coast, which Philip hoped to conquer next. In 336 BCE, he sent an army of 10,000 men into Anatolia and encouraged the many Greeks in the region to rebel against Persian rule. Before he could join his troops, however, Philip was assassinated by a bodyguard during the marriage celebrations for his daughter. Soon Macedon had a new king—Philip's 20-year-old son Alexander.

Carving his path

Alexander's upbringing was instrumental to his future success. From the age of 13, his personal tutor was the philosopher Aristotle, who taught him logic, medicine,

Philip II of Macedon

Born in 382 BCE, Philip II of Macedon was the youngest son of Amyntas III. When his older brother, Alexander II, was assassinated in 368 BCE, Philip was held hostage in Illyria and then sent to Thebes, where the Greek general Epaminondas instructed him in diplomacy and military strategy.

In 364 BCE, Philip returned to Macedon, which was now ruled by his brother Perdiccas III. After Perdiccas was killed in battle, Philip claimed the throne from Amyntas IV, his brother's infant son. Taking on a kingdom that was close to collapse, Philip reformed Macedon's military forces and set about subduing his hostile neighbors. He is credited with creating the *sarissa*-armed phalanx infantry formation, which would prove so important on the battlefield.

By 338 BCE, Philip had dominated all his rivals in Greece, and the next year he founded the League of Corinth, designed to unify the Greek states, with delegates from each of them except Sparta. The motive for Philip's assassination in 336 BCE is not known.

ANCIENT WARFARE 35

See also: Persia 23 ▪ Classical Greece 24–27 ▪ The Peloponnesian Wars 28–31 ▪ Alexander's successors 40–41 ▪ The rise of Rome 50–51 ▪ The Roman Empire at its height 56–57 ▪ The Byzantine Empire 70–73 ▪ The Empire of Charlemagne 82–83

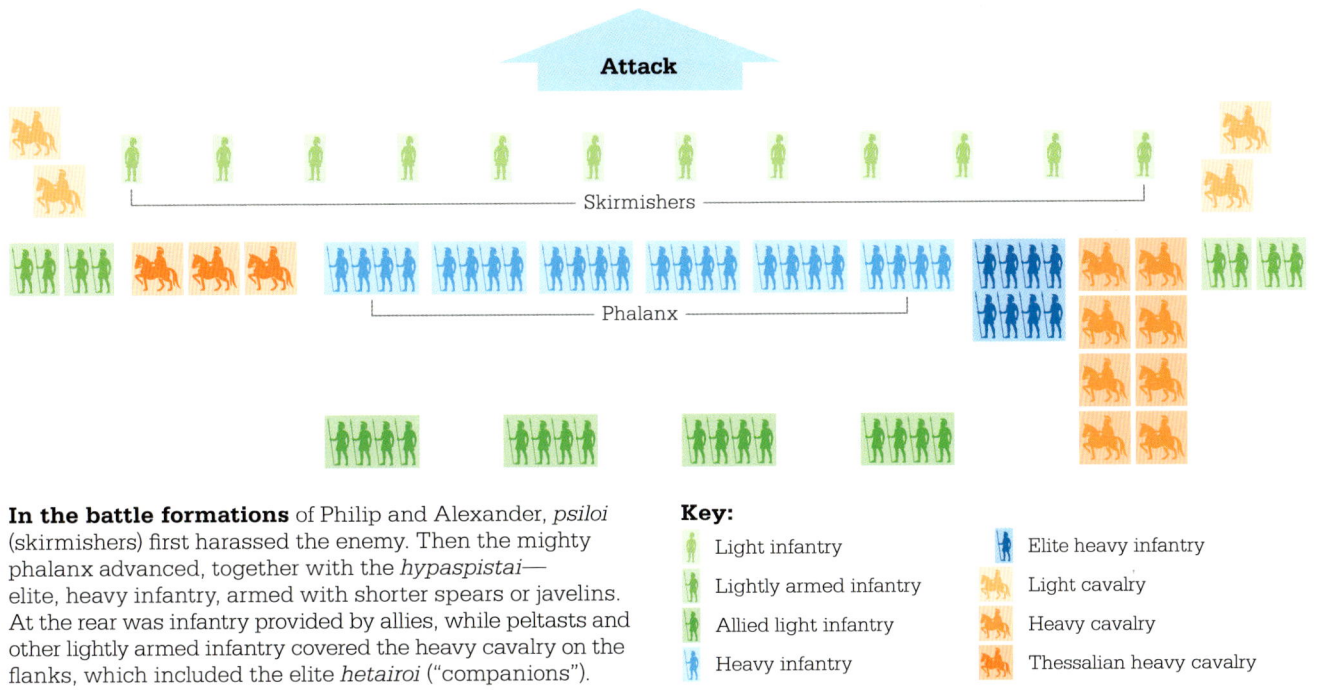

In the battle formations of Philip and Alexander, *psiloi* (skirmishers) first harassed the enemy. Then the mighty phalanx advanced, together with the *hypaspistai*—elite, heavy infantry, armed with shorter spears or javelins. At the rear was infantry provided by allies, while peltasts and other lightly armed infantry covered the heavy cavalry on the flanks, which included the elite *hetairoi* ("companions").

Key:
- Light infantry
- Lightly armed infantry
- Allied light infantry
- Heavy infantry
- Elite heavy infantry
- Light cavalry
- Heavy cavalry
- Thessalian heavy cavalry

religion, and the arts. By the age of 16, Alexander had served as regent while his father was on campaign and had claimed his first victory by suppressing a revolt of the Maedi, a Thracian tribe. At 18, he had commanded the left wing of the Macedonian forces in the Battle of Chaeronea, contributing to his father's victory.

Ruthlessly effective

After acceding to the throne in 336 BCE, Alexander consolidated his position. He ordered the execution of his own cousin (a potential rival), before marching with 3,000 men into southern Greece to put down scattered revolts. He secured his northern borders in 335 BCE, suppressing rebellious factions in Thrace and Illyria. He then laid siege to the rebellious city-state of Thebes, judiciously dividing his force into three. One section attacked the defensive palisade around the city, the second engaged its infantry, and, when Alexander noted an undefended gate, the reserve force attacked and poured into the city, killing some 6,000 fighters. As a warning to other rebels, the city was burned down and the surviving population enslaved. Now, as the unquestioned master of Greece, Alexander pursued his father's unfinished business—the invasion of Anatolia.

Lasting from 334 to 327 BCE, Alexander's Persian campaign was one of the most successful in military history. Despite fighting on enemy territory, having lengthy supply lines, and being frequently outnumbered, he never lost a battle. Alexander was a fearless commander—leading from the front. He typically deployed a central block of infantry in a phalanx formation, flanked by archers and cavalry. While his tactics varied according to enemy numbers, a frequent stratagem was to pin enemy forces with a frontal attack on foot before outflanking and enveloping them with cavalry, forcing a gap in their lines. He could be utterly ruthless with his foes—willing to order the killing and enslavement of civilians to intimidate his enemies.

Conquering Persia

In 334 BCE, Alexander crossed into Anatolia with more than 48,000 soldiers and 6,000 cavalry, transported by 120 Greek naval ships. His first major confrontation with Persian forces occurred in May 334 BCE, at the Battle of the Granicus, a river east of the Dardanelles Strait. Alexander »

THE CONQUESTS OF ALEXANDER THE GREAT

From his father, Philip II of Macedon, **Alexander inherits** a **restructured, disciplined army** and a **conquered Greece**.

Well educated in military matters, Alexander determines to complete his father's mission—**the conquest of Anatolia**.

Alexander wins **victory after victory**, impressing his troops with his **strategies and courageous leadership** from the front.

His **charisma and tactical skills** encourage **high morale and loyalty** from his troops as they do battle across the Middle East and Asia.

Alexander's army proves invincible. In 11 years, he amasses the largest empire in the ancient world.

Our enemies are Medes and Persians, men who for centuries have lived soft and luxurious lives …
Alexander the Great
at the Battle of Issus,
Anabasis of Alexander

Alexander had around 40,000 men, while Darius III commanded more than 60,000 troops, although that numerical superiority was of less benefit to the Persian army as the battleground was a narrow coastal plain.

The Macedonians deployed in their typical formation—a central phalanx of infantry flanked by cavalry. The battle turned when the *hypaspistai* (elite heavy infantry), led by Alexander, pierced the Persian lines. Alexander then led a charge with his elite cavalry, the *hetairoi*, against the position that Darius held. The Persian monarch fled on horseback, his men lost heart, and the conflict quickly became a rout, costing the Persians half of their troops. After the battle, the Macedonians captured Darius's wife, his mother, and two of his daughters (one of whom Alexander would later marry), together with a fortune in treasure.

Instead of advancing east into Mesopotamia, Alexander marched south into Syria. His aim was to dominate the eastern Mediterranean, starting with the independent city-state of Tyre. This major port had

took part in a cavalry charge across the river, but a Persian countercharge almost cost him his life. The Macedonian troops rallied around him, and his heavy cavalry finally broke through the Persian ranks, followed by the phalanx of hoplites, who forced the Persians to flee.

In the aftermath, Alexander captured the provincial capital, Sardis, before advancing south down the Anatolian coast. Persian forces in the region had mustered at Halicarnassus, a major port-city in southwestern Anatolia. Despite facing catapult fire and determined resistance, Alexander's infantry managed to breach the city walls after four months. He now controlled most of western Anatolia.

Leaders face to face

In response to Alexander's early victories in Anatolia, the Persian king, Darius III, took personal command of his forces. In November 333 BCE, the two men faced each other for the first time at the Battle of Issus, in southeastern Anatolia.

a strong fleet and formidable walls and presented a complex military challenge. Hoping to avoid a costly siege, Alexander offered a peaceful alliance, but the Tyrians responded by killing his envoys.

The siege of Tyre

In early 332 BCE, Alexander, whose forces lacked any significant naval strength, began his first attempt to storm Tyre, most of which was on an island. He built a stone causeway 0.6 miles (1 km) long almost to the city walls, then moved his wooden siege towers within range. This extraordinary feat of military engineering proved unsuccessful, as the Tyrians packed an old ship with explosive material, ignited it, and floated it toward the towers, which burned down.

Alexander's earlier victories had brought defections from the Persian ranks; 80 Persian ships joined his forces, and 120 further vessels arrived from Cyprus. With superior naval strength, he could blockade Tyre and prepare to storm it. The Macedonian attack came that July. Using ship-mounted battering rams, Alexander's men breached the walls of the garrison, while the rest of the fleet launched a coordinated bombardment from the sea. Once his men were inside the walls, the garrison was quickly overcome, and the city fell. Enraged by the city's earlier resistance, Alexander had part of it destroyed and sold most of its population into slavery.

Most cities in the region surrendered, hoping to avoid Tyre's fate. The only remaining obstacle to Alexander's advance into Egypt was a strong Persian garrison at Gaza, whose commander refused to surrender, trusting in his hilltop position and strong fortifications. In October 332 BCE, Alexander took Gaza by sheer force of arms, breaching the walls at the fourth attempt, but he suffered a shoulder wound during the action. As the Persian commander refused to submit even in defeat, Alexander had him mutilated and executed by dragging him behind a chariot. Gaza's adult male population was killed, and its women and children were enslaved.

Pharaoh of Egypt

The way to Egypt, ruled by the Persians for more than 200 years, was now clear. Many of its Persian forces had been withdrawn to battle Alexander in earlier conflicts, and knowing the potential cost of defeat, the Egyptians submitted »

Alexander's victorious army at the Battle of Issus relied heavily on 3,000 spear-bearing *hypaspistai* and many heavy cavalry.

38 THE CONQUESTS OF ALEXANDER THE GREAT

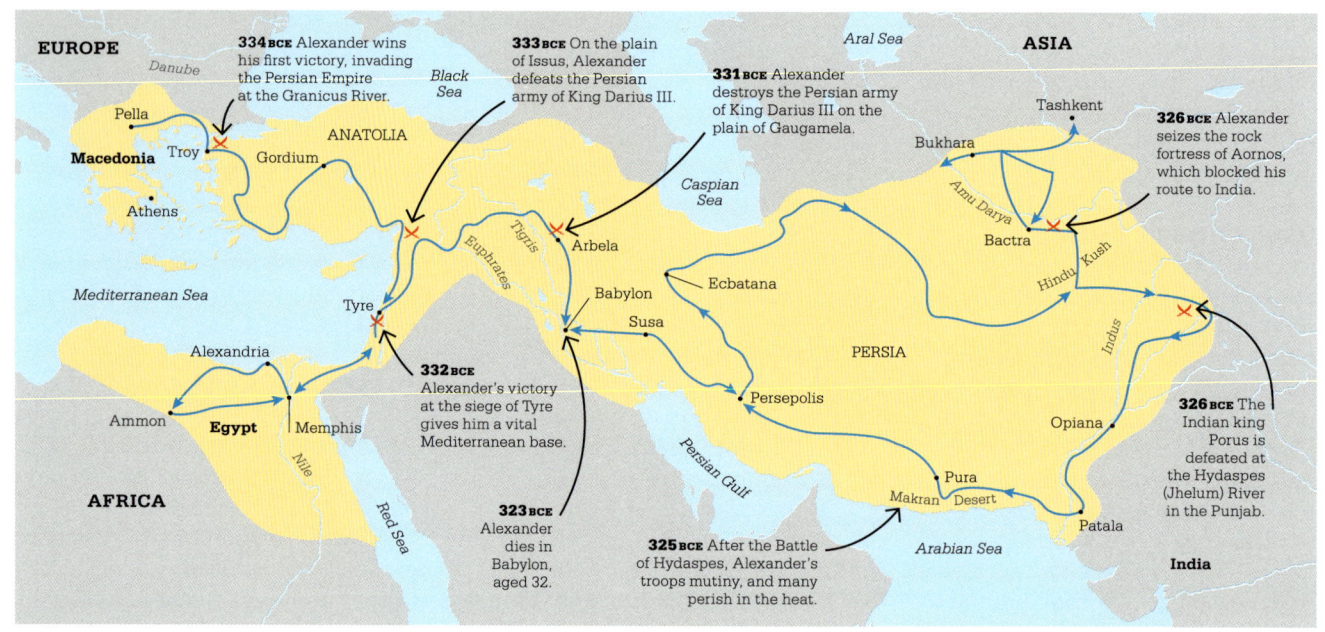

Between 334 BCE and 323 BCE, Alexander built an empire stretching more than 4,000 miles (6,400 km) from Greece through Asia to the Indus River and covering an area of over 2 million sq miles (5 million sq km). He and his troops traveled more than 20,000 miles (32,000 km) across deserts and mountains, in extreme heat and—in India—monsoon rains, while conquering up to 70 cities along the way.

Key:
← Alexander's route
▨ Alexander's empire
✗ Battle

to him, crowning him pharaoh. Together with this title came a steady flow of tax revenue, which helped finance his later conquests.

The Battle of Gaugamela

From Egypt, Alexander and his forces marched largely unopposed into Mesopotamia in the summer of 331 BCE. Darius, who repeatedly offered negotiations—refused by Alexander—had gathered a huge army to confront the Macedonians, who he thought would head directly to Babylon. Alexander, however, wisely took a northern route to avoid extreme heat and to gather more supplies. That October, the two rulers clashed for a second time on the plain of Gaugamela, close to Arbela, a site chosen by Darius as suitable for his vast cavalry and scythed chariots. Alexander was heavily outnumbered, with around 47,000 troops facing a Persian force at least double the size.

Such inequality could have left the Macedonians heavily outflanked, but Alexander came up with an ingenious solution. Darius was at the center of his troops, but Alexander took up a position on the right wing with his elite *hetairoi* (companion) cavalry. Meanwhile, his powerful, pike-wielding phalanx engaged the Persian center. Alexander rode to the far edge of his right flank, drawing the Persian cavalry from Darius's left flank to follow him. This unexpected maneuver eventually created a gap in the Persian lines, leaving their infantry vulnerable.

Although the Persians reportedly breached his ranks once or twice, Alexander had created a reserve line of forces that effectively countered the enemy. After hours of disciplined resistance, Alexander seized his moment. Forming his available cavalry and infantry into a wedge formation, he led a devastating charge against the Persian centre. Isolated and on the verge of being captured, Darius fled the battlefield, and Persian resistance eventually subsided

Persia defeated

The wealth and prestige of the Persian Empire was now open to Alexander. He captured two of its great cities, Babylon and Susa, seizing their treasures to pay his men and send a fortune back to Greece. While Darius was trying to shore up the support of his regional governors and raise an army in western Iran, Alexander advanced on the Persian capital, Persepolis,

ANCIENT WARFARE 39

dividing his forces into two and leading his men on a dangerous route through the Zagros mountains.

In January 330 BCE, Alexander's forces were ambushed by Persian troops in a narrow mountain pass close to Persepolis. They suffered heavy casualties and were forced to leave their dead unburied. Within a month, however, thanks to local intelligence, Alexander outflanked, encircled, and annihilated his opponents. Marching into Persepolis, he seized its treasury and later allowed his men to loot the city and burn down its palaces. He then advanced further east in pursuit of Darius, who had sought refuge with his relative Bessus. Before Alexander could capture Darius, however, Bessus had him killed and declared himself the new Persian ruler. Alexander advanced into Central Asia to defeat Bessus, winning a series of victories over the tribes in the region.

Alexander's end game

Having consolidated his position as new ruler of the Persian Empire, Alexander led his army into the Indian subcontinent in 327 BCE. By May of the following year, he had advanced into the Punjab, where he defeated a local king, Porus, in a battle on the banks of the Hydaspes. It was, however, a bloody struggle. Porus's army included many war elephants, which advanced ahead of the Indian infantry, trampled the Macedonian troops, and terrified their horses. At the battle's conclusion, Alexander's exhausted army mutinied, refusing to march further east. In February 325 BCE, Alexander triumphed again in a siege to the south, at the citadel of the Malli tribe, but was struck by an arrow that almost killed him.

Death and legacy

When he had recovered, Alexander marched his army back to Persia and allowed many of his veterans to return to Greece. He was planning an invasion of Arabia and further campaigns into North Africa and Italy but died suddenly

Porus's war elephants attack the Macedonian phalanx at the Battle of the Hydaspes River. Even here, faced with vastly superior forces, Alexander prevailed by furtively crossing the river to flank them.

in Babylon in June 323 BCE, aged 32. Theories abound as to the cause: a fever, illness, poisoning, or exhaustion following years of campaigning. Unbeaten in battle, he had ruled a mighty empire that stretched across three continents, founding dozens of cities and spreading Greek culture into Asia and North Africa. For the next 40 years, his successors, known as the Diadochi, would fight bitterly over their inheritance. ∎

Bucephalus

One key figure in the legend that grew up around Alexander was his mighty steed Bucephalus, a huge black horse with a white star on its forehead. The name ("ox head") may have related to the horse's stubborn nature, as it was initially thought to be untrainable. The story goes that a young Alexander, noting that Bucephalus seemed afraid of its shadow, turned the horse's head toward the sun before mounting the steed. Once Alexander had tamed it, the horse became his personal mount as he led the elite *hetairoi* cavalry into battle.

Bucephalus accompanied Alexander on every campaign, from Greece to India. After years of loyal service (and even one kidnapping), it finally died in 326 BCE, aged 30. The cause of the horse's demise is unknown. It could have resulted from an injury sustained at the Battle of the Hydaspes River—or simply from old age. Grief-stricken, Alexander gave Bucephalus a state funeral and founded a city in the horse's honor, named Bucephala, on the western banks of the Hydaspes (Jhelum, in modern-day Pakistan).

THREE GRAND NEW KINGDOMS ... EMERGED
ALEXANDER'S SUCCESSORS (323–281 BCE)

IN CONTEXT

FOCUS
The triumph of Hellenism

BEFORE
359–336 BCE Philip II, father of Alexander the Great, transforms Macedon into the dominant power in Greece.

336–323 BCE Alexander the Great establishes an empire that extends from Egypt to northwestern India.

AFTER
168 BCE Roman legions defeat the Macedonian forces at the Battle of Pydna, leading to the fall of the Antigonid dynasty.

129 BCE The Parthian Empire army defeats the Seleucids at the Battle of Ecbatana, ending Hellenistic rule in Iran.

63 BCE Rome ends the Seleucid Empire by annexing its last remaining territory in Syria.

30 BCE Cleopatra, the last of the Ptolemies, dies; Rome annexes the Ptolemaic kingdom.

After the death of Alexander the Great in 323 BCE, his vast empire fragmented as his Macedonian generals, who were known collectively as the Diadochi ("Successors"), vied for dominance. Ultimately, after more than 40 years of war, three major dynasties emerged: the Ptolemies in Egypt, the Seleucids in Asia, and the Antigonids in Macedon and Greece. These dynasties flourished until the mid-2nd century BCE—their colonists integrating Hellenistic (Greek) culture, language, ideas, and warcraft into territories well beyond the Mediterranean.

The road to dynastic rule

Perdiccas, a cavalry commander, was the leading Diadochi at first, until a group of generals, Antipater, Antigonus, and Ptolemy, formed an alliance against him. Fighting broke out in 321 BCE, and Perdiccas was assassinated. By 319 BCE, Antipater controlled Greece and Macedon,

At the Battle of Gaza in 312 BCE, the infantry and cavalry of allies Ptolemy and Seleucus engage the war elephants of Demetrius, son of Antigonus, who suffered a humiliating defeat.

See also: Persia 23 ▪ Classical Greece 24–27 ▪ The Peloponnesian Wars 28–31 ▪ The conquests of Alexander the Great 32–39 ▪ The rise of Rome 50–51

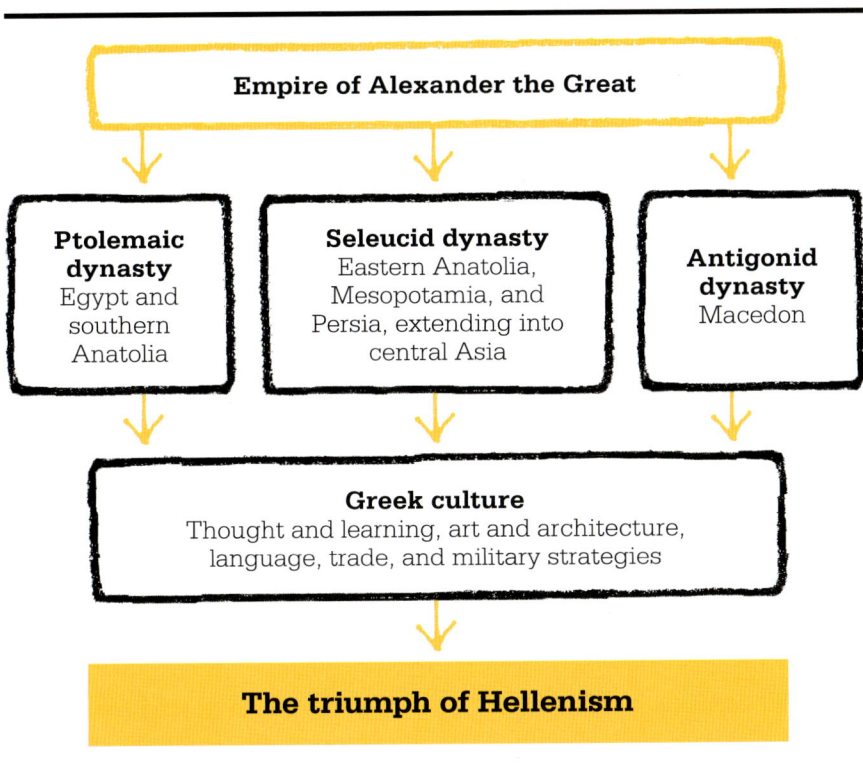

Seleucus I Nicator

Possibly the son of a general in Philip II's army, Seleucus was born around 358 BCE in Europus, Macedon. In 334 BCE, he joined Alexander in his expedition into Asia and, by 327 BCE, had risen through the ranks to command the *hypaspistai*, an elite infantry unit. After Alexander died, Seleucus became the governor of Babylon but was forced out in 316 BCE and fled to Egypt.

Four years later, with the help of Ptolemy, Seleucus retook Babylon, an event that historians usually regard as the beginning of the Seleucid Empire. He extended his rule into Persia, although further expansion eastward was halted by Mauryan Indian forces in 303 BCE. Looking west, he gained Syria in 301 BCE and in 292 BCE turned to his son and heir Antiochus to act as co-ruler in the east of a now vast empire. Seleucus's legacy included establishing the city of Antioch around 300 BCE.

In 281 BCE Seleucus—by then called Nicator ("Victor")—crossed into Europe, hoping to conquer Macedon and Thrace. He was assassinated in the same year by Keraunos, son of his old ally Ptolemy.

Antigonus oversaw Alexander's former territories in Asia, and Ptolemy held Egypt. However, when Antipater died in 319 BCE, he left his territory not to his son Cassander but to his lieutenant Polyperchon. Angered by his father's action, Cassander allied with Antigonus and Ptolemy, and by 315 BCE had won control of Macedon and Greece.

Antigonus's refusal to relinquish territory led to another war that lasted until 311 BCE, during which he lost some of his territories to Seleucus, an ally of Ptolemy who eventually established control over Babylonia and much of Persia. In 301 BCE, Antigonus was killed at the Battle of Ipsus, leaving a victorious alliance of Cassander, Ptolemy, and Seleucus to share his territories. Cassander died in 297 BCE, and three years later, Demetrius—Antigonus's son—seized control of Macedon and Greece, where he established the Antigonid dynasty.

Hellenistic warfare

The new dynasties fought near-constant wars between themselves and against neighbouring states, requiring mercenaries and local recruits to boost troop numbers. The Diadochi generals did little to change Alexander's military tactics. They still relied heavily on the phalanx—a dense rank of infantry armed with *sarissas* (long spears)—its flanks protected by cavalry. There were more mounted archers and cataphracts—heavy cavalry in which both horses and riders were armoured. Some Hellenistic armies also fielded war elephants, fitted with a tower that housed troops armed with pikes. ▪

THE ELEPHANTS... NUMBERED 9,000
THE MAURYAN EMPIRE (321–185 BCE)

IN CONTEXT

FOCUS
War elephants

BEFORE
c. 2600 BCE Elephant images feature on seals and tablets of the Harappa civilization in what is now Pakistan.

543 BCE Bimbisara becomes ruler of Magadha, India. He develops a well-trained elephant corps.

c. 343 BCE Mahapadma Nanda usurps the Magadha throne, founding the Nanda dynasty, whose war elephants later spark fear in Alexander's army.

AFTER
224 BCE Kalinga, conquered by Ashoka the Great, breaks away from the Mauryan Empire in a victory its prized war elephants help him gain.

c. 30 CE The nomadic Kushans of Central Asia invade northern India and adopt war elephants. On later Kushan coinage, their king is depicted riding one.

The empire of Chandragupta Maurya, founded around 321 BCE, united much of South Asia in a single realm that stretched from present-day Afghanistan to Bangladesh, and from the Himalayan foothills to the Deccan Plateau of central India. His son, Bindusara, extended the empire south, and it reached its greatest extent under his grandson Ashoka. Elephants had a symbolic significance within the empire and a practical use as a weapon of war.

After Alexander's retreat

Magadha, the kingdom in northern India where Chandragupta lived, had been thrown into confusion by the triumphant arrival of Alexander the Great in 327 BCE and, two years later, by his departure. Alexander's exhausted troops had refused to continue their campaign when they learned that the army of the neighboring Nanda Empire included several thousand war elephants. Reluctantly, Alexander had turned back toward the west.

With a newly recruited army, Chandragupta had taken control of Magadha by about 325 BCE and all the Punjab region by around 322 BCE. In the following years, he extended its borders west into lands recently vacated by the Greeks, who had earlier controlled Magadha. He then conquered territories to the south.

A ruling philosophy

The polymath Kautilya (Chanakya) who assisted Chandragupta as a counselor, described how a kingdom should be governed and how power could be secured in the *Arthashastra*—a treatise on political, economic, and military strategies. Kautilya acknowledged the ruthlessness necessary to achieve and retain power and advocated a surveillance system of spies and informers, but

A Mauryan war elephant, kneeling for its riders to dismount, is depicted on the Great Stupa, a stone structure in Madhya Pradesh, India, commissioned by Ashoka in the 3rd century BCE.

ANCIENT WARFARE 43

See also: The conquests of Alexander the Great 32–39 ▪ Alexander's successors 40–41 ▪ The Punic Wars 52–53 ▪ Timur's conquests 105 ▪ Mughal conquests in India 140–141 ▪ The British conquest of India 225

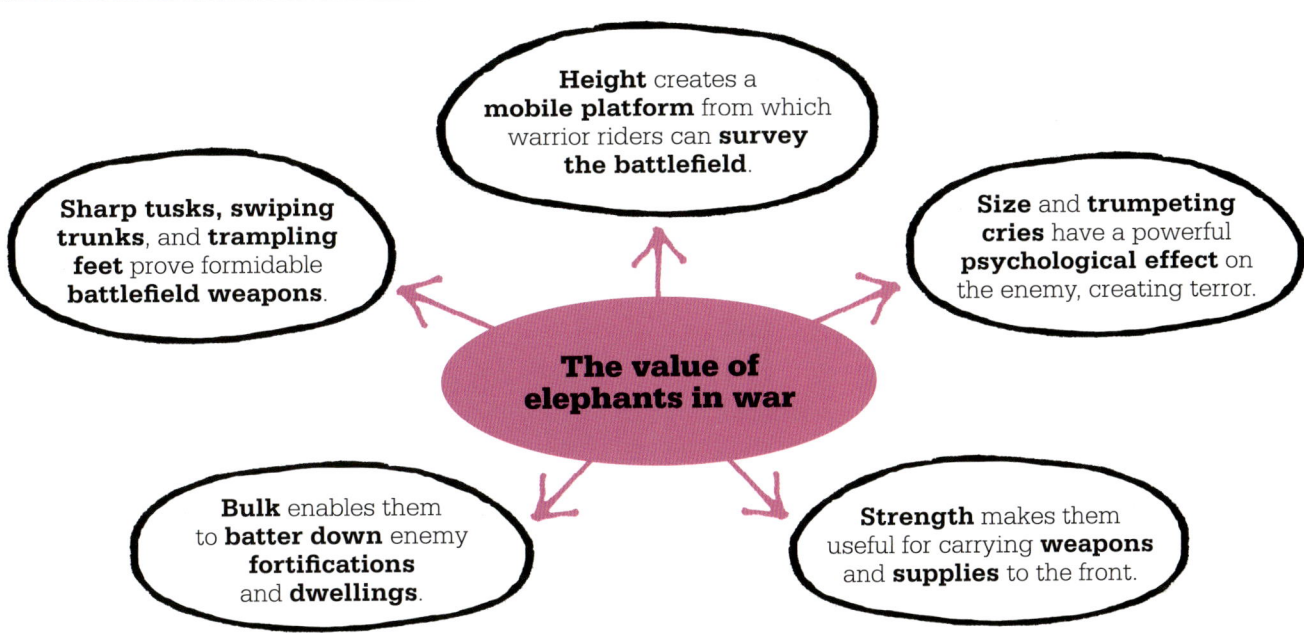

he also maintained that a ruler had ethical responsibilities and set out how a successful government should be organized and function.

Describing how a king should spend his time, the *Arthashastra* divides days into eight periods, each devoted to a specific activity, including supervising elephants, horses, chariots, and infantry. Caught wild, elephants deemed suitable were trained by military experts to perform specific drills for turning, advancing, trampling enemy troops, and attacking hostile elephants and fortifications. In battle, an elephant carried three warriors; a fourth man, the mahout, directed the animal with a goad.

In war and peace

Chandragupta was the first South Asian ruler to maintain a standing army, and elephants were a vital component. His forces included up to 9,000 elephants, as did the armies of Bindusara and those of Ashoka the Great, who reigned from 268 to 232 BCE.

In 261 BCE, Ashoka invaded the eastern state of Kalinga. The conflict cost so many lives that he renounced war in shame and converted to Buddhism. He urged his successors to pursue the path of nonviolence, a principle he publicized in stone inscriptions. After his death, the empire shrank; Brihadratha, its last ruler, was killed in 185 BCE.

The end of elephant power

The use of war elephants had spread west to Greece and Rome by the 1st century BCE, but it had declined. Yet elephants would still play a key role in Persia's Sasanian army in the 7th century CE and in Sri Lanka until the 16th century. Firepower could panic the animals, however. As more powerful cannons and firearms were developed, the war elephant became obsolete. ▪

The sacred elephant

Long before their use as weapons of war, elephants had a profound religious significance in South Asia. In Hinduism and Buddhism, the animals represent fertility, loyalty, power, and wisdom and they are also venerated in the Jain faith.

The *Mahabharata*, one of the great epic poems of ancient India, describes the white king of the elephants, Airavata, who has four tusks and seven trunks, and carries Indra, the king of the gods. The Hindu deities—Ganesha, the Lord of the People, and his feminine form Vinayaki—both have the head of an elephant, while the Ashtadiggajas are eight male elephants who in Hindu cosmology are said to support the Earth.

THE WISE WARRIOR AVOIDS THE BATTLE

ORIGINS OF THE CHINESE EMPIRE (475–221 BCE)

IN CONTEXT

FOCUS
The art of war

BEFORE
597 BCE The Chu state defeats a Jin army at the Battle of Bi. Chu leaders deliberately allow routed Jin troops to escape.

513 BCE Iron is first cast in China. It is soon used in the manufacture of weapons.

521 BCE Border official Hua Bao is killed at Zheqiu, in central China, after missing a shot—then chivalrously pausing to let his opponent return fire.

AFTER
207 BCE Second Qin Emperor Qin Er Shi (Ying Huhai) takes his own life. The Qin dynasty collapses the following year.

3rd century CE Han warlord and poet Cao Cao writes the earliest known commentary on Sunzi's *The Art of War*.

China's agrarian economy flourished from the 1st millennium BCE, and the region made major advances in science and technology, such as improved methods for casting iron and better drainage and irrigation techniques. However, competition and conflict mounted as a handful of more powerful states swallowed up China's small kingdoms and gradually consolidated into what would become the Qin Empire.

As the states battled for supremacy, new military theories emerged, informed by a plethora of philosophical and practical treatises. The most influential of these was a series of essays

ANCIENT WARFARE   45

See also: The Han Empire 48–49 ▪ The Mongol invasions 96–101 ▪ The establishment of Manchu China 142–143 ▪ The Ten Great Campaigns 166–167 ▪ China in turmoil 230–231 ▪ The Second Sino-Japanese War 264–265 ▪ The Chinese Civil War 294

A copy of *The Art of War* found in 1972 was made of bamboo slips, like this reproduction. Many early Chinese texts were written on bamboo, with each slip holding a single column of characters.

attributed to general and military thinker Sunzi (sometimes called Sun Tzu): *The Art of War*.

Shifting allegiances

Sunzi's writing was the product of a complex, violent period in history. Since 1050 BCE, the Zhou dynasty had extended its rule across much of China. Zhou kings had governed through a feudal aristocracy with considerable regional autonomy. This had facilitated expansion, but it had also created rich, rebellious local warlords. A revolt in 771 BCE had forced the Zhou kings to flee their capital, Hao, and establish a new one in Chengzhou.

Over the following centuries—known as the Spring and Autumn Period (771–475 BCE)—the Zhou kings' hold over their territories had gradually eroded. China became a patchwork of small states with shifting alliances to the Zhou dynasty and each other, whose local rulers fought among themselves. There were initially nearly 100 such states, but this number fell very quickly as the smaller kingdoms either banded together for collective safety or were conquered.

By the early 5th century BCE, seven major states remained. Han was at the center of the country, with Wei and Zhao to the north. Chu sat to the southeast, Qi to the east, Yan to the northeast, and Qin to the west. The following century and a half of near-constant warfare between these kingdoms is referred to as the Warring States Period (475–221 BCE).

Theories of war

The leaders of the new powers recruited officials—an early civil service—based on ability, rather than on aristocratic background (as had been traditional under the Zhou). To train these new bureaucrats and instill orderliness and obedience, they established academies teaching science, law, and philosophy. The rise of these academies in the 5th century BCE brought an explosion of scholarly study and philosophical discussion. Warfare was a key area of interest with a wide body of works to debate—from historical texts, including the *Six Secret Teachings* of early Zhou-dynasty general T'ai Kung, to contemporary writings such as the *Wei Liaozi*, a text on military and political affairs attributed to Qin-era theorist Wei Liao. The one that had the most impact, however, was *The Art of War*, for according to tradition it helped the Qin state to achieve dominance over the others.

Sunzi's *The Art of War*

Tradition holds that Sunzi was born in eastern China in around 544 BCE and served as a general and military strategist for the state of Wu in southern China during the Spring and Autumn Period. Very little else is known about his life. *The Art of War* is usually attributed to him, although there is still debate over when it was written, whether Sunzi actually wrote it, and even whether he existed at all. There is no »

In war … let your great object be victory, not lengthy campaigns.
Sunzi
The Art of War

contesting the work's influence, however. Intellectually searching and eloquently expressed, it took a cynical new view of warfare. Sunzi argued that far from being glorious, war is a waste of resources: a swift victory by any means is the best way to achieve peace. This approach reinforced views that had started to emerge during the Spring and Autumn Period.

New tactics

Under the Zhou dynasty, war had been the occupation of a small warrior elite drawn from among the nobility, who were governed by a strict code of conduct. Battles were almost ritualized affairs, in which it was difficult for either side to gain advantage. As conflict between rival states grew more frequent, such stalemates became increasingly problematic. The *Zuo Zhuan*, a commentary written by an unknown Warring-States-era historian about the Spring and Autumn Period, highlights changing attitudes. An old-school general is asked whether he would attack an enemy army in difficulty at a river ford. His response is an indignant negative: "I will not drum to attack when they have not pulled up ranks." His younger comrades react with derisive disbelief.

The demotion of the old nobility during the Warring States era marked the end of such chivalrous ideals. Wars were now fought by vast armies of conscripted infantry. No longer able to claim command as a birthright, their leaders had to be both resourceful and ruthless in order to prove their skill in the field. Sunzi's writings struck a chord. He advised on every aspect of warfare, advocating subtle, flexible strategy based on five major principles: morality, climate, terrain, leadership, and method.

Deception as a tool of war

The Art of War was not universally admired. Its assertion that "All warfare is based on deception" met with disapproval from followers of Kongzi (Confucius)—the renowned philosopher of the Spring and Autumn Period—on the grounds that it did not align with their strong moral code. However, many Warring States generals embraced Sunzi's precepts. At the Battle of Maling in 342 BCE, Sun Bin— allegedly descended from Sunzi, and a student of *The Art of War*— made use of his ancestor's advice.

Outnumbered by his Wei opponents while in command of a Qi army that was defending its ally, the Han state, Sun Bin made a diversionary attack on the Wei capital. Han had been within Wei's grasp, but the Wei general, Pang Juan, had to return home to see off Sun Bin's threat. Aware that his army was still vulnerable, Sun Bin withdrew but made his camp look as though his men had fled in panic. Hoaxed, Pang Juan led his army off in pursuit—and into an ambush from Sun Bin's forces.

Weapons and walls

It was not only new military theories that transformed warfare in China. In the 5th century BCE, annealing— a process that makes cast iron less brittle—was invented, leading to more effective weapons. The vast civil service took on the task of organizing the manufacturing process, thereby equipping the era's huge armies quickly and efficiently.

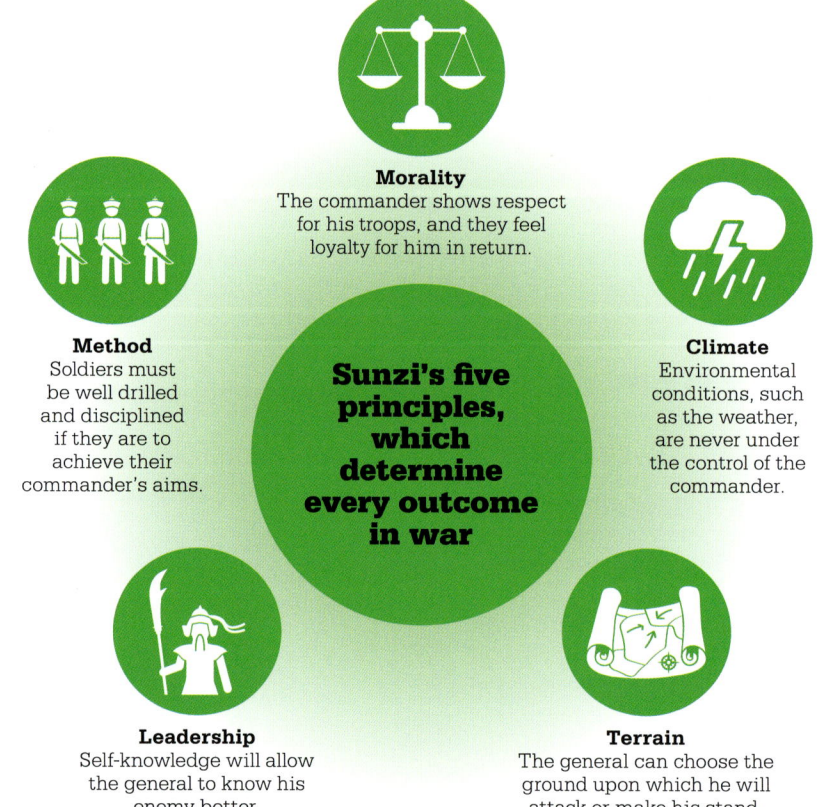

Morality The commander shows respect for his troops, and they feel loyalty for him in return.

Climate Environmental conditions, such as the weather, are never under the control of the commander.

Method Soldiers must be well drilled and disciplined if they are to achieve their commander's aims.

Sunzi's five principles, which determine every outcome in war

Leadership Self-knowledge will allow the general to know his enemy better.

Terrain The general can choose the ground upon which he will attack or make his stand.

ANCIENT WARFARE 47

The Terracotta Army

Qin Shi Huang's model army was buried in pits near his tomb. There are nearly 200 pits in total, of which three contain terracotta soldiers.

In 1974, a group of farmers discovered a huge collection of life-sized terracotta soldiers that had been buried with Qin Shi Huang, the first emperor. Meant to protect him after death, the Terracotta Army includes more than 8,000 infantrymen, crossbowmen, archers, and cavalry. The figures were mass-produced but carefully customized using molded features and paint. The detailed faces, hairstyles, hats, and shoes vary, possibly in order to represent people from the different regions of the empire. Height and poses reveal their specialisms: high-ranking officers are taller than the others; archers kneel as if firing; cavalrymen ride ceramic horses.

Recent digs have uncovered clay officials, musicians, and acrobats in the complex of pits around Qin Shi Huang's tomb. As well as his army, the emperor was buried with an entire pottery court: a microcosm of the system that he had created.

The bureaucrats' skills were also indispensable in marshaling the expertise and labor needed for building fortifications. People sheltered from the conflict in fortified cities. Giant walls of compacted mud, brick, and stone, some of which were more than 500 miles (800 km) long, snaked across vulnerable border areas. As well as protecting the states from each other, the walls were an early attempt to repel nomadic raiders, who periodically attacked from the plains north of China.

Rise of the Qin state
In the 4th century BCE, the Qin state began to gain strength. Its rise was accelerated midcentury by influential statesman Shang Yang. He made a series of successful reforms to the state's legal, taxation, and land allocation systems, which left it both rich and powerful.

In war, Shang Yang, like Sunzi, advocated the pursuit of victory by any means. Over the next century, the Qin state took this approach to heart. Its rulers pressed their advantage over their rivals, gaining victories against the Chu and Zhao states, among others.

When the Qin army invaded Han in 265 BCE, it faced a smaller force from Zhao, which had come to defend its Han ally. The Zhao commander, Lian Po, dug in at Changping to await reinforcements, but Qin forces cut off all support. A stalemate ensued.

Taking advice from *The Art of War*, the Qin sent spies to Zhao to spread rumors that Lian Po was too cowardly to fight. The ploy worked: Lian Po was replaced by a less experienced general who began an unwise offensive. The Qin commanders, anticipating this move, overcame the Zhao troops to win a decisive victory.

Conquering Qin
After the Battle of Changping, Qin's preeminence was clear, but it was still just one of several states. However, by the time Ying Zheng succeeded to the throne in 243 BCE, aged just 13, Qin was unstoppable. Between 230 BCE and 225 BCE, it defeated Han and Wei. The fall of Qi in 221 BCE left its conquest complete.

Ying Zheng adopted the title Qin Shi Huang ("First Divine Emperor"). Embracing Shang Yang's ideas to the full, he forged his collection of conquered states into an empire. He disarmed local warlords, divided his realm into 36 provinces, and set up his own officials in each. He also conscripted hundreds of thousands of soldiers and laborers to connect existing defensive fortifications—the Great Wall—along his empire's entire northern border.

Qin Shi Huang died in 210 BCE. He was buried at Xianyang, his capital in northwest China (now Xi'an) with a vast ceramic army: a memorial to a ruler with military power and bureaucratic guile. ∎

Supreme excellence consists in breaking the enemy's resistance without fighting.
Sunzi
The Art of War

PLANNING SHOULD BE SECRET, ATTACK SHOULD BE SWIFT
THE HAN EMPIRE (206 BCE–220 CE)

IN CONTEXT

FOCUS
The Chinese at war

BEFORE
221 BCE Ying Zheng, ruler of the Qin kingdom, unites China, declaring himself Qin Shi Huang—the first emperor of the Qin dynasty.

214 BCE The completion of the Lingqu Canal linking China's Xiang and Li rivers enables the emperor to supply grain to troops fighting southern tribes.

AFTER
280 CE Sima Yan, a former Wei kingdom general, reunites China as first emperor of the Jin dynasty.

304 Xiongnu general Liu Yuan invades northern China and declares himself ruler of the Northern Han dynasty.

618 As the short-lived Sui dynasty collapses, Li Yuan, Duke of Tang, seizes power and founds the Tang dynasty, ushering in a new golden age.

When Qin Shi Huang, founder of the Qin dynasty, died in 210 BCE, his short-lived empire collapsed. In the battle for succession, one faction supported Xiang Yu, a noble from Chu in southern China, and another Liu Bang, a peasant leader from the Han River region of central China. Although Xiang Yu had a larger army, Liu Bang used superior military and political skills to outmaneuver his opponent, finally defeating him at the Battle of Gaixia in 202 BCE, after a four-year civil war.

Liu Bang—later known as Gaozu ("High Founder")—became first emperor of the Han dynasty that would rule for more than 400 years. As the empire expanded, trade, technology, and the arts flourished, creating a golden age. Initially, however, Xiongnu raiders from the north were a threat.

A section of the Catalan Atlas of 1375 CE depicts a caravan on what was later called the Silk Road. This Eurasian trade route system was active from the Han era to the mid-15th century.

ANCIENT WARFARE 49

See also: Origins of the Chinese Empire 44–47 ▪ The Mongol invasions 96–101 ▪ Timur's conquests 105 ▪ The Ten Great Campaigns 166–167

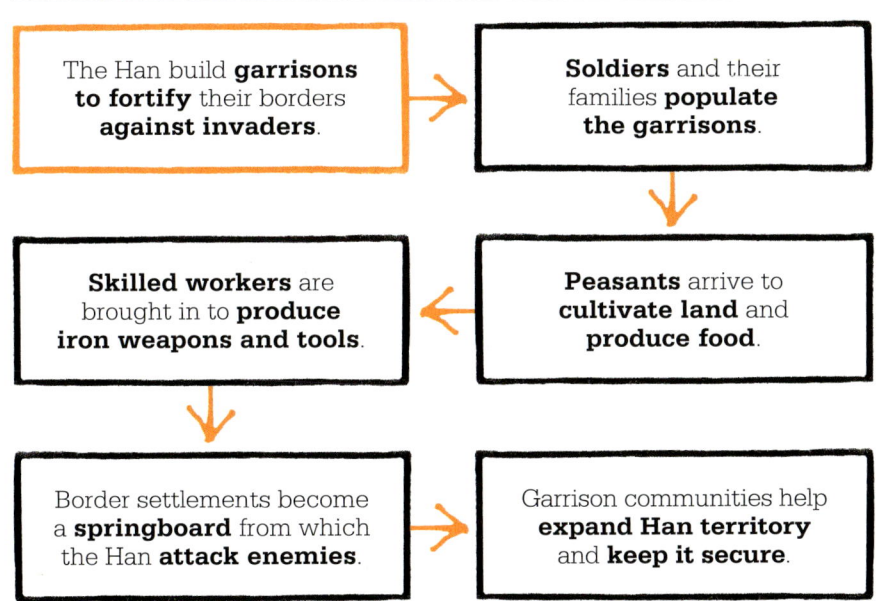

In 200 BCE, Gaozu dispatched a 3,000-strong army to destroy the nomad bands, but the Xiongnu's superior cavalry force crushed the imperial army, forcing Gaozu to conclude a series of peace treaties.

Victory and expansion

Han emperor Wudi, who ruled from 141 BCE to 87 BCE, abandoned the treaties and used huge armies to push the Xiongnu north into the Gobi Desert of present-day Mongolia. To succeed, the Han army had to adapt to the harsh region and learn to fight like the Xiongnu cavalry, most of whom were skilled horseback archers. In 119 BCE, the Han army crushed the Xiongnu, and drove its enemy north beyond the Gobi Desert.

During the long reign of Wudi, the Han empire almost tripled in size, extending east into what is now North Korea and south into Vietnam. The Han capital Chang'an (near present-day Xi'an) became the eastern hub of a vast road network that stimulated trade and carried armies and supplies to the frontiers. Wudi stationed soldiers and their families on the fortified borders and encouraged peasants to live there and grow food and craftsmen to fashion weapons and tools, helping to defend and expand the empire.

Slow decline

In 9 CE, Wang Mang, a former palace official, overthrew the Han and proclaimed the Xin Dynasty. Han power was restored when Wang Mang was killed in 23. In 91, the Han military defeated the Xiongnu again, but by this time the dynasty was in decline. In the 2nd century, drought and famine prompted peasant revolts, which were put down by Han general Cao Cao, whose son Cao Pi seized power in 220. This marked the end of the Han dynasty and its division into the Three Kingdoms of China—Shu-Han, Wei, and Wu. ∎

Chinese military technology

The Han waged war with vast armies, mostly composed of infantry wielding crossbows, swords, and spears. By the 2nd century BCE, they were using blast furnaces to produce cast iron (iron ore strengthened with carbon) for weapons and tools. They had also discovered that reducing the amount of carbon in molten iron creates steel, making swords and spears sharper and even stronger, and that adding chrome to the molten mix prevents rusting, effectively creating an early form of stainless steel.

Like the Romans, their contemporaries in the West, the Han deployed battering rams and mobile towers in siege warfare but rather than use a simple scaling ladder, Han armies wheeled out a hinged "cloud ladder" that quickly unfolded by means of a counterweight. Centuries before its adoption in Europe, they also used the traction trebuchet—a projectile-firing catapult, its tension provided by the weight of a team of men. Further Han siege weapons included large, mounted crossbows, some of which could fire multiple bolts.

The trigger mechanism of a Han crossbow was usually cast in bronze, as here, and engineered to fire bolts more than 820 ft (250 m).

THE MIGHT OF ROME HATH RISEN HIGH AS HEAVEN
THE RISE OF ROME (390–275 BCE)

IN CONTEXT

FOCUS
Development of the legion

BEFORE
578–535 BCE Roman king Servius Tullius ranks citizens by wealth; the poorest group are denied entry to the army, while the wealthiest make up the *equites* (cavalry).

c. 509 BCE Rome's monarchy is overthrown, and the Roman Republic is established.

c. 400 BCE The Roman cavalry, earlier made up of horsemen from the senatorial class, expands to include riders who can pay for their own horse.

AFTER
150–120 BCE Greek historian Polybius describes the Roman maniples' advantages in outmaneuvering the enemy.

107–101 BCE General Gaius Marius replaces the maniple with the cohort and transforms the Roman army into a professional force.

During the 4th and early 3rd centuries BCE, Rome grew from a city-state into a major power. The creation of its highly organized and flexible army played a large part in its ascent.

Around 400 BCE, when Gallic tribes from the north began to invade the Italian peninsula, the Roman Republic had no standing army. It relied instead on free male citizens, called up during wartime. Legions (divisions) of soldiers were organized into phalanxes—the Greek system of heavy infantry fighting in dense ranks of spearmen—supported by some light cavalry recruited from Rome's nobles. In 390 BCE, a Roman army facing the Gauls at the Battle of Allia River, about 10 miles (16 km) from Rome, was overwhelmed and forced to retreat. The Gauls went on to sack the city of Rome.

An engraving of five infantrymen of the early Roman Republic shows how weaponry and protection varied between different types of soldiers.

ANCIENT WARFARE 51

See also: Classical Greece 24–27 ▪ The conquests of Alexander the Great 32–39 ▪ Alexander's successors 40–41 ▪ The Punic Wars 52–53 ▪ Caesar and his legacy 54–55 ▪ The Roman Empire at its height 56–57

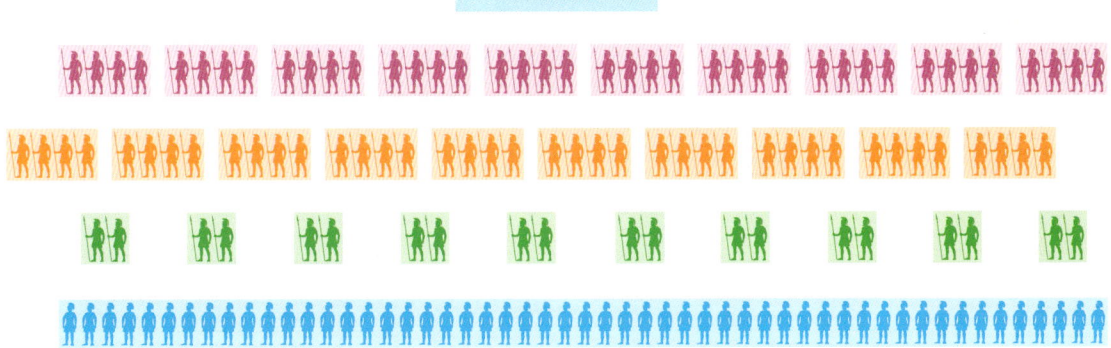

The ranks of the maniple infantry formation were set apart in a checkerboard formation to allow soldiers the space to fight, fall back, or advance. The *hastati*, the most inexperienced soldiers, were first into the fight. The *principes* were more experienced, while the *triarii* were the most seasoned fighters, engaging only if the first two ranks were breached. The *leves* skirmished ahead of an attack before falling back into reserve.

By the mid-4th century BCE, Rome had recovered sufficiently to fight two successful wars against the Samnites, a rival central Italian people, as well as winning battles against the Etruscans, based north of Rome. However, Rome's increasing territorial ambitions persuaded the republic around 315 BCE to reform its army.

New military organization

Seeking a more flexible and agile infantry organization than the phalanx, the Romans created the manipular legion (from the Latin *manipulus*, "handful") of around 4,500 fighting men. The main infantry element was grouped into three ranks of 10 maniples: the *hastati* ("spearmen")—lightly armored, and carrying short, thrusting spears; the *principes* ("first in order")—more heavily armored, with swords and throwing spears; and the *triarii* ("third in order")—the best equipped, held back as a shock force to finish off battles.

Each maniple of 60 to 120 men could act independently, allowing commanders to react quickly in battle. Beyond the maniples were the *leves* ("light")—lightly armed troops recruited from the lowest ranks of citizens—who harassed opponents before the *hastati* engaged. Further support was provided by a few hundred cavalry.

Roman power grows

Victory over the Etruscans and Samnites gave Rome dominance over central Italy but drew it into conflict with the Greek colonies of southern Italy, especially Tarentum, on the coast of Apulia. In 280 BCE, Greek general Pyrrhus of Epirus—in northwest Greece—arrived with an army of around 25,000 to support Tarentum, defeating the Romans in the battles of Heraclea (280 BCE) and Asculum (279 BCE). Cripplingly heavy casualties among Pyrrhus's troops, however, rendered these victories ineffective—the source of the term "Pyrrhic victory." The Romans ground down Pyrrhus, forcing him to return to Greece in 275 BCE and occupied Tarentum in 270 BCE. Rome now dominated southern Italy and was emerging as a Mediterranean power. ■

The Roman greatness is a proof of the excellence of their legions.
Vegetius
Roman military writer, 4th century CE

THIS LESSON THEY ... LEARNED BY EXPERIENCE
THE PUNIC WARS (264–146 BCE)

IN CONTEXT

FOCUS
Learning from mistakes

BEFORE
c. 390 BCE A Gallic tribe sacks Rome, so the Romans extend and rebuild their city walls.

c. 315 BCE Following defeats to the Samnites when using the phalanx, the Romans adopt the maniple formation.

AFTER
105–101 BCE Rome appoints a single general to lead it to victory in the Cimbrian War after two arguing commanders are the cause of defeat at the Battle of Arausio.

9 CE A Germanic army inflicts a devastating defeat on the Romans at Teutoburg Forest; as a result, the Romans decide to fortify their border.

1944 The Allies successfully invade Normandy on D-Day, learning lessons from the disastrous Dieppe Raid of 1942.

By 275 BCE, the Roman Republic dominated Italy and aimed to expand its territory across the Mediterranean, bringing it into conflict with the Carthaginian Empire of North Africa. The Carthaginians, descendants of Phoenicians who had settled in the area of present-day Tunisia, had built an empire extending across North Africa, southern Iberia, Corsica, Sardinia, and western Sicily. Tensions over control of eastern Sicily sparked the First Punic War in 264 BCE.

Rome, until then a land power, first had to build a navy to combat Carthage's supremacy at sea. While its warships used bronze rams to attack enemy vessels, the Roman navy pioneered the *corvus*, a hooked plank that was lowered onto the enemy deck to enable Rome's forces to leap aboard and do battle. It proved spectacularly successful.

On land, apart from a failed Roman invasion of North Africa in 256 BCE, most fighting was in Sicily. Rome steadily gained the island, defeating Carthage's intimidating war elephants by launching volleys of javelins that caused them to panic and flee. In 241 BCE, the First Punic War ended with Carthage accepting Roman control of Sicily. Four years later, Rome annexed Corsica and Sardinia.

Carthage attacks Italy
Soon after its defeat in Sicily, Carthage began to extend its empire in Iberia, with forces led by Hamilcar Barca and then Hannibal, his son. Hannibal's capture in 218 BCE of the city of Saguntum, a Roman ally on the east coast of Iberia, prompted

Carthaginian general Hannibal and his troops—estimated at around 20,000 infantry, 6,000 cavalry, and up to 37 elephants—cross the Alps to Italy, as depicted in this 1866 engraving.

See also: The rise of Rome 50–51 ■ Caesar and his legacy 54–55 ■ The Roman Empire at its height 56–57 ■ The Byzantine Empire 70–73 ■ The rise of Islam 76–81

Rome's expansion plans bring it into **conflict with Carthage**, the dominant Mediterranean power.

To compete at sea, **Rome has to create a navy** to equal that of its rival.

Roman shipbuilders create a **hooked platform** (*corvus*) for boarding ships—it **helps Rome win sea battles**.

Rome's generals use **small armies** and **harassing tactics** to **wear down Carthage's forces**.

Rome learns from its defeats, develops effective military strategies, and builds an army and navy capable of conquering Carthage.

Scipio Africanus

Born into a noble Roman family in 236 BCE, Publius Cornelius Scipio first encountered Hannibal in 218 BCE on the Ticinus River, northern Italy. Carthaginian cavalry had outflanked the Roman forces, but Scipio led a charge that enabled his wounded father to be taken to safety. He survived the Battle of Cannae in 216 BCE, won around would-be deserters after the costly defeat, and in 209 BCE began to turn Rome's fortunes around.

Taking troops to Iberia, Scipio mounted a victorious assault on the Carthaginians' headquarters at Carthago Nova and drove them from the Iberian peninsula within a few years. Elected Roman consul in 205 BCE, Scipio resolved to invade Carthage. His forces landed a year later, stormed their way toward the city, and won a decisive victory at the Battle of Zama in 202 BCE. Dubbed Scipio Africanus for his triumph, he was elected head of the Roman Senate in 199 BCE. When political enmities embittered his later life, Scipio withdrew to the countryside southwest of Rome, dying there in 183 BCE.

Rome to declare the Second Punic War. Rather than sailing from Iberia to northern Italy across Roman-controlled waters, Hannibal took the tough land route over the Pyrenees and the Alps. His initial victories included a lethal ambush of Roman forces at the Battle of Trasimene in 217 BCE and a triumph at Cannae in 216 BCE, when his forces encircled and destroyed a Roman army of around 80,000. As a result, Rome began to use smaller, more agile armies to harass Hannibal's forces, disrupt communications, and block reinforcements to regain lost ground.

A spreading war

In 214 BCE, the independent Greek city-state of Syracuse in southeast Sicily declared war on Rome, after which other Roman-held parts of Sicily rebelled. Carthage sent forces to the island to support Syracuse. The following year, Rome besieged Syracuse by land and sea. At first, its efforts were frustrated by the inventions of Greek mathematician and Syracuse native Archimedes. These supposedly included a giant mirror that directed the sun's rays onto Roman sails to ignite them. However, the Romans persisted, and, in 213 BCE, they broke through the city's defenses. Within three years, they controlled all of Sicily, then won further victories in Iberia.

Carthage is subdued

Roman forces led by general Scipio invaded North Africa in 204 BCE, defeating two Carthaginian armies. In the final battle, at Zama in 202 BCE, even the leadership of Hannibal, recently recalled from Italy, was not enough to resist the Romans. Carthage lost most of its colonies in the peace terms; half a century later, Rome would destroy the city in the Third Punic War (149–146 BCE). ■

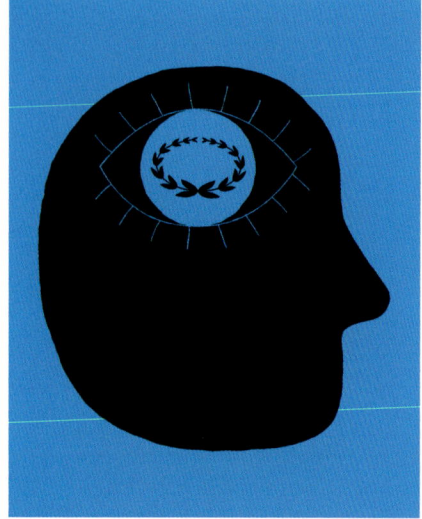

I CAME, I SAW, I CONQUERED
CAESAR AND HIS LEGACY (58–27 BCE)

IN CONTEXT

FOCUS
From republic to empire

BEFORE
73–71 BCE Spartacus, a gladiator, leads a major slave rebellion against the Roman Republic but is defeated.

60 BCE Julius Caesar forms a triumvirate—a political alliance with fellow statesmen Gnaeus Pompeius Magnus (Pompey) and Marcus Licinius Crassus.

59 BCE Caesar is elected consul, the highest official rank in Rome.

AFTER
16 BCE–9 CE The Roman army gains territory beyond Gaul but is beaten back by Germanic tribes.

14 CE Augustus dies and his adopted son Tiberius succeeds him as emperor.

476 Romulus Augustulus, the last emperor of the Western Roman Empire, is deposed.

In the 1st century BCE, the Roman Republic was rocked by political infighting, unrest, and civil war, a situation exploited by skilled general and politician Julius Caesar. His triumphant return to Rome after military successes abroad set in motion the transition from Roman republic to autocratic rule, fully realized by his successor Gaius Octavius (Octavian), the first Roman emperor.

The conquest of Gaul

In 58 BCE, Caesar had embarked on a campaign in Gaul (modern-day France, Luxembourg, and Belgium). Driven by the desire for political acclaim, military glory, and a share in Gaul's natural riches, as well as the need to secure Rome's northern borders, he took advantage of divisions between Gallic and Germanic tribes to win a daring series of victories. Caesar's defining triumph came in 52 BCE at the Battle of Alesia (in present-day Burgundy), where his army of around 60,000

The bridge over the Rhine River built by Caesar's troops in 55 BCE appears in this 1814 painting by British architect Sir John Soane. Finished in 10 days, the bridge was a great feat of engineering.

ANCIENT WARFARE 55

See also: The conquests of Alexander the Great 32–39 ▪ Alexander's successors 40–41 ▪ The rise of Rome 50–51 ▪ The Punic Wars 52–53 ▪ The Roman Empire at its height 56–57 ▪ Barbarian migrations: the empire under threat 58–65

Julius Caesar

Born in Rome in 100 BCE to a patrician (ruling-class) family, Gaius Julius Caesar was 16 when he married Cornelia, daughter of the Roman consul Lucius Cornelius Cinna. When Cinna's enemy Lucius Cornelius Sulla seized power in Rome in 82 BCE, Caesar left to serve as a soldier in Anatolia. On Sulla's death in 78 BCE, he returned to Rome, where he rose rapidly through the political system, from the post of military tribune (a senior infantry commander) to quaestor (a treasury official), aedile (a magistrate supervising public life in Rome), praetor (a senior legal and military figure), governor of Spain, and consul (the highest public office).

Caesar's governorship and conquest of Gaul from 58 to 50 BCE sealed his status as both a brilliant warrior and a consummate politician, paving the way for his return as master of Rome. Despite bringing much-needed reforms, as well as glory, to the city-state, his overweening ambition led to his violent death in 44 BCE at the hands of disaffected senators.

surrounded 80,000 Gauls on a fortified hilltop settlement with siegeworks 10 miles (16 km) long. Despite the arrival of a 250,000-strong Gallic relief force, the Roman siegeworks and army held fast and the Gauls surrendered. Over the next two years, Caesar's forces annexed all of Gaul for Rome.

From general to dictator

Alarmed at Caesar's growing strength, the Senate (the Roman Republic's governing body) ordered him to relinquish his command and return to Rome. Caesar did return—but with his army, crossing the Rubicon River into northeast Italy in 49 BCE.

Most opposition forces fled from Rome to Greece, allowing Caesar to control the Italian peninsula and assume the title "dictator"— a temporary office with sweeping political powers. He defeated his remaining enemies and named himself "dictator for life" in 44 BCE. A month later, a group of senators conspired to assassinate him, claiming that they were liberating Rome from his tyranny. Caesar's main successors were Octavian (his great-nephew and adopted son), and Marcus Antonius (Mark Antony), a politician and general who had been one of his major supporters.

The path to empire

From 43 to 42 BCE, there was civil war as the conspirators who had murdered Caesar fled Italy and took control of Rome's eastern provinces. Antony and Octavian pursued them to northern Greece and defeated them. Octavian returned to Italy, where he restored order and built up popular support. Antony ruled the eastern provinces and began a relationship with Cleopatra, queen of the Ptolemaic kingdom in Egypt.

Over the next decade, relations between Octavian and Antony worsened. In 32 BCE, Octavian encouraged the Senate to declare war on Cleopatra, knowing that Antony—by then her husband— would support her. The following year, Octavian won a decisive naval victory at Actium, in northwest Greece. Cleopatra and Antony, besieged by Octavian in Alexandria, died by suicide in 30 BCE. Octavian annexed Egypt and returned home triumphant. The Senate gave him the name Augustus ("illustrious one") three years later, in effect acknowledging him as emperor.

Octavian had won supreme power, thanks in part to his military victories. The Senate's influence diminished, while the political importance of the Roman army would only grow. ∎

Behold, … a man who was ambitious to be king of the Roman People and master of the whole world.
Marcus Tullius Cicero
Roman politician
44 BCE

ALL ROADS LEAD TO ROME
THE ROMAN EMPIRE AT ITS HEIGHT (30 BCE–180 CE)

Rough tracks exist **before the Romans** but **few paved roads**.

The Romans recognize that a **reliable transportation network** for moving armies and supplies is a **key military asset**.

They use **engineering skills** and **scientific knowledge** from many cultures to build **roads, bridges, and other projects**.

An extensive infrastructure holds the empire together, facilitating military campaigns, diplomacy, trade, and civilian transportation.

IN CONTEXT

FOCUS
Communications and transportation

BEFORE
c. 1000 BCE China's first postal system, established during the Zhou dynasty, uses a network of roads lined with facilities for messengers.

490 BCE A professional courier named Pheidippides reportedly runs 153 miles (246 km) from Athens to Sparta in 36 hours.

312 BCE The first section of the Via Appia (Appian Way) is built to transport troops and supplies for Rome's conquest of southern Italy.

AFTER
476 CE After the fall of Rome, the condition of its roads and viaducts begins to decline.

c. 1096 Early Crusaders from Europe use an old Roman road, the Via Militaris (Military Way), to travel from the Balkans to Constantinople (now Istanbul).

In 27 BCE, Octavian, the adopted son and heir of Julius Caesar, defeated his rivals to win total power and became Augustus, the first Roman emperor. Ending decades of internal strife that had weakened the bonds between Rome and its provinces, Augustus's reign began a period of prosperity and stability for Rome that lasted until 180 CE. During this time—which is known as the Pax Romana ("Roman Peace")—the empire greatly extended its infrastructure.

Roads follow conquest
Rome's long, well-built roads were key to its military success and the management of its expanding territory. Augustus entrusted Gaul,

conquered by Julius Caesar, to his general Marcus Vipsanius Agrippa, who initiated a road network there. Centered on Lugdunum (present-day Lyon) and known as the Via Agrippa, it eventually covered 13,000 miles (21,000 km). From 43 to 84 CE, the Romans conquered most of England and Wales and built paved roads there over more than 10,000 miles (16,000 km).

By 116, Emperor Trajan had expanded the Roman Empire to its greatest extent, annexing territory in eastern Europe and Arabia and conquering the Parthian Empire in Persia. Roads followed: by the end of the Pax Romana period, the empire's total network stretched over 250,000 miles (400,000 km).

Military constructions

Major Roman roads were straight, paved in stone, cambered (raised in the middle) for drainage, and wide enough to allow two wheeled vehicles to pass each other. They were supported by other engineering projects, such as tunnels, viaducts, and bridges. Roman legionaries performed much of the construction work, often building while they campaigned to ensure that supplies and armies could move around more easily. The roads benefited civilians too, but their ultimate aim was to strengthen imperial power. Emperors could quickly send out legions to conquer, put down rebellions, or defend the frontiers.

Business and defense

Improved infrastructure aided both trade and government business. Official letters were sent via the *cursus publicus* (public way)—the government courier and postal service founded by Augustus. Light, horse-drawn vehicles carried regular mail, while a horse and rider would take urgent messages. The same system transported imperial officials around the empire and took tax revenues back to Rome.

Water transportation was also much improved. The Roman navy eliminated piracy, which had been rampant in the Mediterranean Sea and Red Sea. This facilitated trade with regions as far away as India.

Trajan's Bridge across the Tagus River at Alcántara in Spain, built on the orders of Emperor Trajan, has been in almost constant use since it was finished in 106 CE.

Trajan's successors focused more on consolidation than expansion, fortifying vulnerable frontier areas with defenses known as *limes*. The most extensive system, the Germanic Limes, stretched from the North Sea to the Danube. At the peak of Rome's power, its standing army—some 400,000 soldiers— spent more time guarding and building than campaigning. This defensive strategy grew more important over the following century. ∎

Trajan

Born in Italica, in present-day Spain, in 53 CE, Marcus Ulpius Traianus (known as Trajan) was the son of a prominent Roman politician. After a successful military career, he was adopted as Emperor Nerva's successor. On Nerva's death in 98, Trajan became emperor—the first to have been born outside Italy.

Trajan's foreign policy was expansionist. In 106, he annexed territory to create two new Roman provinces: Dacia, in the Balkans, and Nabatea, between the Arabian and Sinai peninsulas. His next campaign in the east, launched in 115 against the Parthians, made conquests in present-day Armenia, Assyria, and Mesopotamia. Trajan commissioned numerous roads and other infrastructure, such as the Via Traiana Nova from Damascus in Syria to Jordan; the Pontes Traiani, a bridge 3,724 ft (1,135 m) long over the Danube River, designed by architect and engineer Apollodorus of Damascus; and the Amnis Traianus, a canal linking the Nile River to the Red Sea. Trajan died in 117 while traveling to Rome.

ROME SHALL FALL

BARBARIAN MIGRATIONS: THE EMPIRE UNDER THREAT (c. 337–476 CE)

BARBARIAN MIGRATIONS: THE EMPIRE UNDER THREAT

IN CONTEXT

FOCUS
Why did Rome decline and fall?

BEFORE
293 CE Diocletian divides the Roman Empire into western and eastern parts, under separate emperors.

306–324 After conflicts between rival emperors, Constantine I triumphs and reunites the empire.

330 Constantine I moves the empire's capital to Byzantium, renaming it Constantinople.

AFTER
527–565 CE Justinian I rules the Eastern Roman Empire and reconquers territory in the former western half.

533–334 Justinian compiles the major points of Roman law into one multivolume work, the *Corpus Iuris Civilis* (*Body of Civil Law*).

Constantine destroyed that security by removing soldiers from … the frontiers, depriving those who were exposed to the barbarians.
Zosimus
***Historia Nova*, early 6th century CE**

The Roman Empire had stretched from Spain east to Assyria and from Britain south to Egypt at its peak during the 2nd century CE. Its rulers had controlled a vast standing army and a highly developed administration. In the 3rd century, however, political infighting, economic difficulties, plague, and barbarian incursions had begun to threaten the empire's cohesion. Diocletian's attempt to stabilize the empire by dividing it into western and eastern areas, under two separate emperors and their named heirs, only created further rivalries and dissensions.

During his reign, Constantine I temporarily reunited and refortified the empire, but after his death in 337 CE, destructive internal disputes recurred, and barbarian attacks on Roman provinces increased. The migration of warrior Huns out of Asia fueled the drift of hostile Germanic tribes into Roman territory.

Military legacy

Constantine had secured Rome's territory in Britain, Gaul, and Spain, rebuilding military bases, and repairing roads. He was an astute political operator and was wary of usurpers. After defeating his rival, Maxentius, in 312, he had replaced the cavalry element of Rome's powerful Praetorian Guard—men hand-picked to protect the emperor and Rome itself—with the Scholae Palatinae, an elite cavalry regiment of 500 men who often accompanied him. It was a strategic move, as the Praetorian Guard had conspired with various emperors' rivals in the past, but the change left Rome less well defended.

Aware that Roman legions often played a key role in plotting, Constantine also restructured his army. He withdrew 100,000 troops from frontier garrisons to create

Constantine commissioned a huge white marble statue—the Colossus of Constantine—which originally stood in the Basilica of Maxentius in Rome. Only its head now remains.

smaller, more mobile field armies (*comitatenses*), stationed within the provinces and at his immediate disposal. He appointed one general to head the infantry (*magister peditum*) and another the cavalry (*magister equitum*). On the empire's borders, he stationed *limitanei* (frontier guards) and *ripenses* (river guards). These were well-trained but lower-paid and lower-status soldiers, grouped in units of around 1,000 men with some cavalry support. Later commentators, such as the Greek historian Zosimus, claimed that this reorganization of the Roman army weakened the empire's defenses.

Succession conflicts

Constantine had named his three sons as his successors, but they fought among themselves for dominance. In 340, Constantine II, who had inherited Britain, Gaul, and Spain, invaded Italy, which together with North Africa and the

ANCIENT WARFARE 61

See also: The rise of Rome 50–51 ▪ The Punic Wars 52–53 ▪ Caesar and his legacy 54–55 ▪ The Roman Empire at its height 56–57 ▪ The Byzantine Empire 70–73 ▪ The Empire of Charlemagne 82–83

Balkans, was ruled by his younger brother Constans I. The invasion came to an abrupt end when Constantine II was killed in an ambush, enabling Constans to claim his territories. However, in 350, Constans was murdered by supporters of Magnentius, a Roman general of Germanic descent, who had claimed the throne in Rome.

Constans' brother Constantius II, who ruled the Eastern Roman Empire, marched west to confront Magnentius. Their armies met in 351 at the Battle of Mursa, in modern-day Croatia. Although his army was outnumbered, Constantius's cavalry routed the right wing of Magnentius's forces, and after a lengthy and bloody battle, the Eastern emperor was victorious.

Although Constantius had won a crucial victory, his army's losses were huge—an estimated 30,000 dead compared to some 24,000 of Magnentius's troops. It was also a short-lived triumph as, rather than pursuing Magnentius, Constantius then did battle with the Sarmatians, a Eurasian tribe that had moved west to areas in the Balkans around the middle Danube. During this period, the Jews of Roman Palaestina also revolted against the harsh rule of Constantius's brother-in-law, Gallus Caesar.

When Constantius and his army finally advanced on northern Italy, garrisons loyal to Magnentius began to defect to the Eastern emperor, and Magnentius withdrew to southern Gaul. In 353, the two armies clashed for the final time at Mons Seleucus, in the Hautes-Alpes. Constantius emerged victorious again, and Magnentius died by suicide rather than face capture.

The rival empire

During his reign, Constantius countered revolts in the provinces and attacks from the Sasanian Empire of Persia to the east—a further cause of Rome's decline. The two powers had fought intermittently for dominance of western Asia since the early 3rd century, draining both sides of men and resources. The long reign of Sasanian ruler Shapur II in the 4th century included two major wars against the Romans (from 337 to 350 and from 358 to 363). In 344, Shapur led his forces against Constantius in Mesopotamia, where the two armies fought the Battle of Singara. Breaking into the Sasanian camp, the Romans killed Shapur's son, Prince Narseh. The Sasanians retaliated and exacted huge Roman losses. With no definite resolution, however, the war dragged on, until Shapur concluded a hasty peace in 350 in order to counter the Huns, a nomadic people who had attacked his empire from the east.

By 358, Shapur was again ready to attack the Romans as Constantius was preoccupied with unrest elsewhere. Sasanian forces marched west to the city of Amida in Mesopotamia and laid siege. They used siege towers and elite Persian archers to gain entry to the city but were repulsed, and they also attacked with their cavalry and war elephants, which the Romans countered with fire. »

Roman scorpions could propel heavy stones or bolts up to 550 yd (500 m). *Ballistae* were larger versions of these weapons.

The fighting forces

First-person accounts by Roman soldier Ammianus Marcellinus describe the battles between Rome and the Sasanian Empire in the 4th century CE in vivid detail. At Amida, both sides employed *ballistae*—military engines with a crossbow-like action for hurling missiles. The Sasanians mounted them on top of iron-fronted siege towers and built earthworks to scale city walls. Their cavalry included armored, lance-wielding horsemen and elite, mounted archers. In response, the Roman *equites sagittarii* (horseback archers) began to play a more prominent role.

Sasanian foot soldiers bore swords and carried large, rectangular shields, while Roman shields of this era were usually, wide and rounded. Instead of the earlier *gladius* (stabbing sword), Roman infantry used a longer *spatha* and a *hasta*, a kind of thrusting spear. Gallic and Gothic recruits to the Roman army often wielded heavy battle-axes.

BARBARIAN MIGRATIONS: THE EMPIRE UNDER THREAT

After the firm rule of Constantine I, the Roman Empire is **riven with political rivalries** and faces **hostile neighbors**.

↓ ↓

Infighting by Roman rulers **divides loyalties and weakens the Empire's defenses**, especially in the west.

Germanic tribes advance west into Roman provinces. The Sasanian Empire also **inflicts huge losses on Roman forces**.

↓ ↓

Roman rulers **make more pacts** with neighboring Germanic tribes and **recruit their warriors**.

↓

Pacts fail, and the tribes turn against Rome. Under increasing attack, the weakened Western Empire collapses.

The Romans used "scorpions," bolt-firing, field artillery pieces, to bring down their opponents' siege towers, but after 73 days, Sasanian forces finally succeeded in scaling the city walls via earth mounds and sacked the city, killing most of the Roman leaders.

Questionable loyalties

Constantius died in 361 and was succeeded in quick succession by Julian, who died in 363, and Jovian, who was found dead in his bed a year later. The empire continued to be weakened from within by mismanagement, plots, and assassinations of political rivals. The rapid succession of rulers after Constantius' death—16 emperors in 100 years, ruling the west, east, or both parts of the empire—created greater instability. Conflicts between leaders divided the loyalties of their troops and, together with battles at its borders, sapped Rome's military strength and emptied its coffers.

In a dual bid to contain external enemies and reinforce their armies, Roman leaders concluded treaties with some Germanic tribes, making them *foederati* of (bound by treaty to support) the Roman Empire and giving them the right to settle in Roman territory in return for their loyalty. In 358, for example, Emperor Julian made such a treaty with the Franks, allowing them to settle in Roman territory in northern Gaul. In exchange, they supplied mercenary warriors and agreed to act as a buffer against hostile forces beyond the province's frontiers. Similar agreements were concluded with other tribes, including the Visigoths.

While barbarian mercenaries were skilled warriors, their loyalty to the empire could occasionally be questionable. As Roman troops, they also acquired inside knowledge that could be used to their advantage when fighting against the empire.

Auxiliaries—noncitizen troops drawn from Rome's provinces—defended the forts along Hadrian's Wall in northern Britain, the barrier between the Roman province and hostile territory beyond. In 367, they rebelled, letting in Picts from the north. Then, in what was known as the Great Conspiracy, other tribes from Ireland and north-central Europe also invaded the province, overwhelming loyal Roman defenders and devastating vast areas of Britain's west and north. Franks and Saxons simultaneously attacked northern Gaul. Roman general Flavius Theodosius, sent by Valentinian I (Jovian's successor), restored order and instituted civil and military reforms the following year. However, raids by hostile tribes continued, and the periodical withdrawal

Then heads were shattered, as masses of stone, hurled from the scorpions [Roman *ballistae*], crushed many of the enemy …
Ammianus Marcellinus
Rerum gestarum libri,
c. 330–395

Picts from Caledonia breach Hadrian's Wall, which the Romans had built to defend Britain. The wall stretched 73 miles (117 km) from the Solway Firth to the North Sea.

of Roman troops to fight unrest elsewhere at times left the province more vulnerable.

Goths move west

Driving much of the unrest around the Roman Empire's European borders were large-scale migrations. During the mid-4th century, the Huns began to migrate out of their homeland in Central Asia. They were skilled warriors, who mostly fought on horseback and excelled at mounted archery. They arrived in eastern Europe around 375, forcing the Germanic peoples living there to flee westward. The following year, thousands of Germanic Visigoths, who had fled settlements north of the Black Sea, crossed the Danube southward into Roman territory.

Initially, the Eastern emperor Valens welcomed the Visigoths, seeing their arrival as an opportunity to recruit more soldiers, and allowed them to settle as *foederati*. They were put under the care of Roman forces, who were supposed to feed and accommodate them. However, since Valens had moved large numbers of troops east to prepare for renewed hostilities against the Sasanians, those left failed to cope with the influx. Facing starvation,

the Visigoths, reinforced by many Ostrogoths whose entry into Roman territory was not sanctioned by Valens, mounted a rebellion, took control along the Danube River, and pillaged the region. Running battles between Romans and Goths ensued.

In 378, Valens led his army against the Goths, and his forces met them close to the city of »

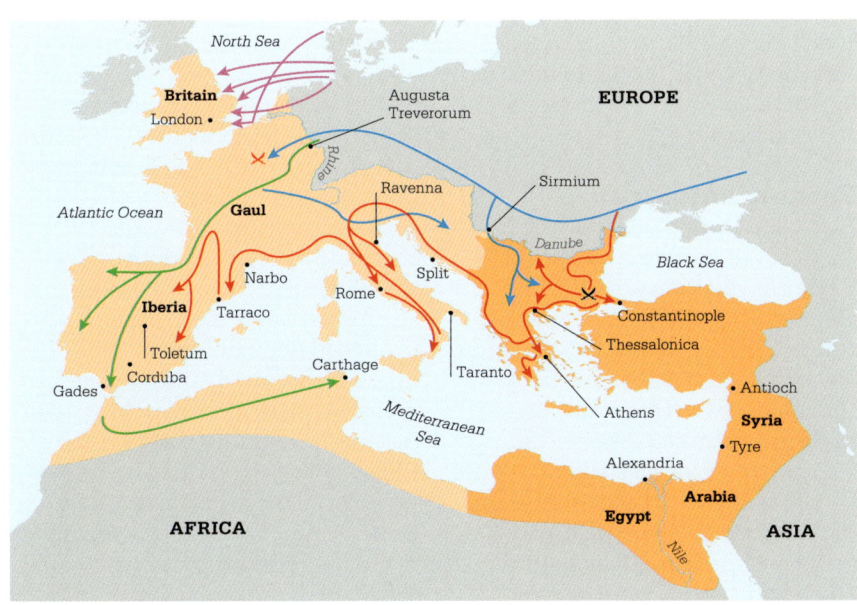

When the Huns stormed westward out of Central Asia in the late 4th century, they drove other peoples before them. By the mid-5th century, hostile tribes encircled much of the Roman Empire and threatened its borders—especially in the west where it was weakest.

BARBARIAN MIGRATIONS: THE EMPIRE UNDER THREAT

The Visigoth king Alaric I (center) is shown here feasting in Athens. During his two-year invasion of Greece, Alaric sacked Athens along with other major cities, including Corinth and Sparta.

Adrianople (modern Edirne in northwest Türkiye). By this time, veterans were being pressed back into service to reinforce an under-strength army, and morale among Valens's soldiers was low. Anxious to secure a victory for himself, the emperor had rejected an offer of reinforcements from the Western emperor Gratian.

According to 4th-century Roman historian and soldier, Ammianus Marcellinus, after the infantry regiments had pounded each other, the Gothic cavalry "descended from the mountain like a thunderbolt," encircling and searing through the Romans. Under this devastating attack, Roman resistance crumbled. Valens was killed in the fighting, as was most of his 20,000-strong army. Valens's successor as Eastern emperor, Theodosius I, was also unable to defeat the Goths. Peace was concluded in 382, with the Goths allowed to settle in the Balkans as Roman allies with a high degree of autonomy.

To Italy and Spain

Alaric I, a Gothic general who had once fought for Rome, became the Visigoths' first king in 395. Like his predecessors, he had rebelled against Rome in a bid to win better pay and conditions for his people. He plundered several cities in the Balkans and raided Greece before making peace and settling with his people in Illyricum, a province on the Adriatic. Between 401 and 403, his forces made incursions into northern Italy but were repelled.

Alaric invaded Italy a second time from 408 to 410. Pushing further south this time, the Visigoths besieged Rome three times and broke through on their third attempt. Although Rome was no longer the capital of the Western empire, its subsequent sack (the first in eight centuries) was a brutal shock to its rulers. Alaric died later that year, but the Visigoths continued to be a powerful force. In 418, they established a kingdom in southwestern Gaul, which grew to eventually cover all of Iberia.

The arrival of the Visigoths displaced another Germanic people that the Huns had forced out earlier —the Vandals, who had devastated parts of Gaul before crossing the Pyrenees into Iberia in 409. Twenty years later, the Vandals set sail for North Africa, where they eventually conquered Roman territory to found their own kingdom in 435.

ANCIENT WARFARE

Having overcome the Germanic tribes and forced many of them west, the Huns established their own empire north of the Danube, ruled from around 430 by King Rua. After his death in 434, his nephews Attila and Bleda succeeded him. At first, relations with the Eastern Roman Empire were mostly positive. The military skills of the Huns were renowned, especially the accuracy of their mounted archers, their ferocious charges, speed, and unpredictable tactics. For half a century, the Romans paid them an annual subsidy in gold in return for their military support.

Conflict with the Huns

Under Attila, the Huns became more antagonistic. After claiming the Romans had breached their territory, they took revenge by sacking several Roman towns in 441. They alleged that their annual subsidies had not been paid and demanded more gold. After a short-lived peace, the Huns returned in 443, raiding as far as Constantinople. In exchange for peace, the Romans tripled their annual payment to 2,100 lb (950 kg) of gold.

In 445, Attila murdered his brother Bleda to become sole ruler of the Huns, then raided the Eastern Roman Empire from 447 to 449 before attacking Gaul in 451. This time, however, the Romans and Visigoths triumphed—Attila's only defeat. In 452, Attila invaded northern Italy. He was poised to launch an attack on Rome itself in 453, but he died suddenly. As his sons quarreled among themselves, the Hunnic Empire fragmented into warring groups.

Rome falls

In 455, the Vandals invaded from North Africa, sacking Rome and later defeating combined Eastern and Western Roman forces. Finally, in 476, Germanic *foederati* broke away from Roman control and declared their general Odoacer as king. He led an invasion of Italy and forced the final emperor, a child named Romulus Augustulus, to abdicate. Odoacer then declared himself King of Italy, bringing an end to imperial Roman rule in the west. However, it would continue in the east, in the form of the Byzantine Empire, for another thousand years. ∎

A Hunnic cavalry unit charges into battle. During the 4th and 5th centuries, the role of cavalry became ever more important in battles between Roman and barbarian forces.

Attila the Hun

Born into a powerful Hunnic family in the early 5th century, Attila grew up north of the Danube River, where his people had settled. Ruling with his brother Bleda from 434, he initially offered the Romans some military support in exchange for gold. In 441, the agreement failed and Attila—a superb military commander—used this as pretext to seize Roman territory south of the Danube. His victorious army then moved south, reaching the walls of Constantinople two years later. Under pressure, the Romans paid more gold to ensure his withdrawal.

After murdering his brother, Attila won fresh victories in the Balkans and Greece, extending his empire. In 450, Honoria, sister of Western Roman Emperor Valentinian III, sought his help to escape an arranged marriage. Attila claimed her for his wife, demanded half the Western Roman Empire as a dowry, then invaded Gaul, where he suffered his only defeat. He died in 453, soon after his marriage to another woman. The cause of death is not known.

WAR IN MIDDLE
500–1500

THE
AGES

INTRODUCTION

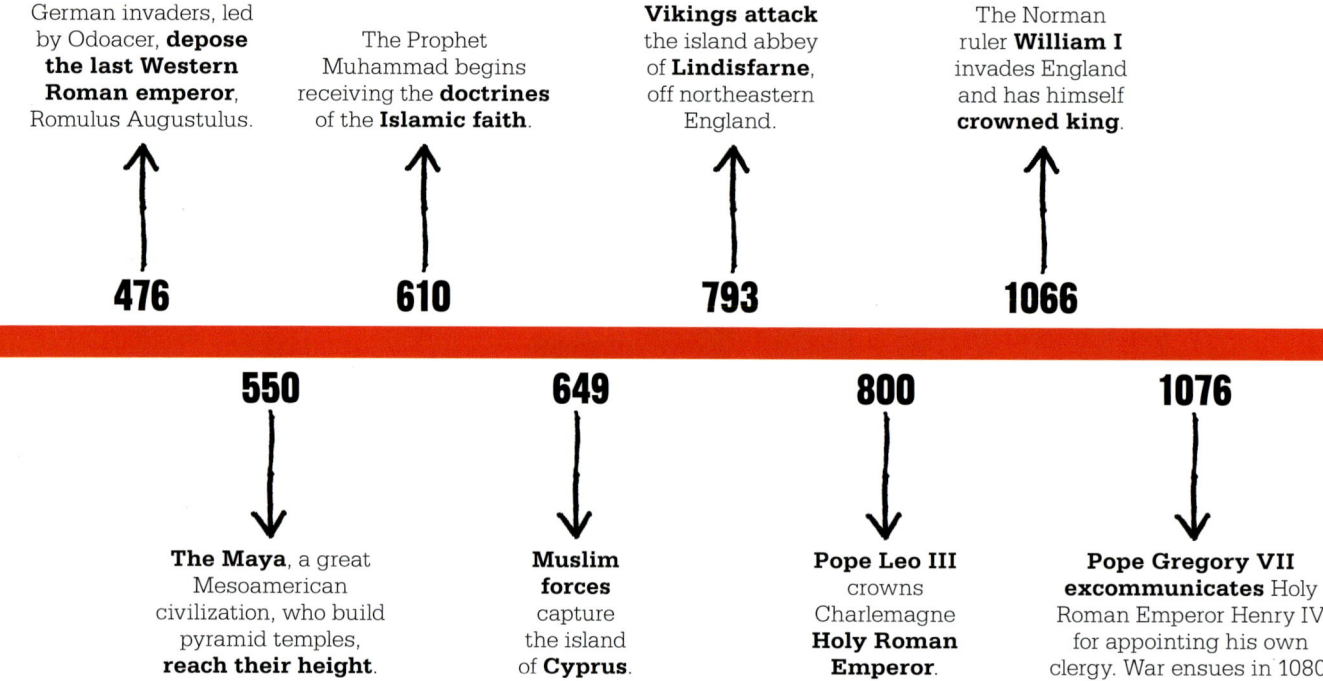

476 — German invaders, led by Odoacer, **depose the last Western Roman emperor**, Romulus Augustulus.

610 — The Prophet Muhammad begins receiving the **doctrines** of the **Islamic faith**.

793 — **Vikings attack** the island abbey of **Lindisfarne**, off northeastern England.

1066 — The Norman ruler **William I** invades England and has himself **crowned king**.

550 — **The Maya**, a great Mesoamerican civilization, who build pyramid temples, **reach their height**.

649 — **Muslim forces** capture the island of **Cyprus**.

800 — Pope Leo III crowns Charlemagne **Holy Roman Emperor**.

1076 — **Pope Gregory VII excommunicates** Holy Roman Emperor Henry IV for appointing his own clergy. War ensues in 1080.

As the Western Roman Empire weakened and fell to the Goths and Vandals, a new Eastern Roman Empire, centered on Byzantium in present-day Türkiye, was in its infancy. Renamed Constantinople, after Constantine I, the Roman emperor who had made it his capital in 330 CE, the city faced new struggles against hostile neighbors but would become the glorious center of a Byzantine culture that endured for more than a thousand years.

While past historians once called the period between the 5th and 10th centuries the Dark Ages for the barbarism afflicting much of Western Europe, in Constantinople arts and architecture thrived—funded by the military conquests of Byzantine emperor Justinian I. In wars against the barbarian Ostrogoths and Vandals, and the neighboring Sasanian Empire of Persia, Justinian extended his empire and regained much of the territory of imperial Rome.

Clash of faiths

The birth of the Prophet Muhammad in 570 CE and the rise of Islam led to a new kind of warfare. His adherents became formidable warriors, driven by religious fervor to spread his message and enforce the Islamic faith by military conquest.

By the early 8th century, Islamic forces had conquered the Middle East, Egypt, and the rest of North Africa. From there, they advanced over the Mediterranean and took most of Spain, pressing up against other areas of Christian Europe. Charlemagne, king of the Franks, a Germanic tribe, would halt their advances in the late 8th century and establish the Holy Roman Empire, marking his conquests in Europe as Christian lands.

Islam's power was directly challenged in the 11th century, when nobles throughout Europe set out on the First Crusade in a bid to drive Muslim forces out of the Middle East and reclaim the so-called Holy Land. It was a cause that Christians continued to fight in further crusades into the 13th century. They ultimately failed, ending the religious quest, but the encounter with Islamic culture and scientific knowledge furthered European scholarship. Meanwhile within Europe itself, Christian rulers had long sought to expel the Muslim Moors—an end finally achieved by Ferdinand II of Aragon and Isabella I of Castile in 1492.

WAR IN THE MIDDLE AGES

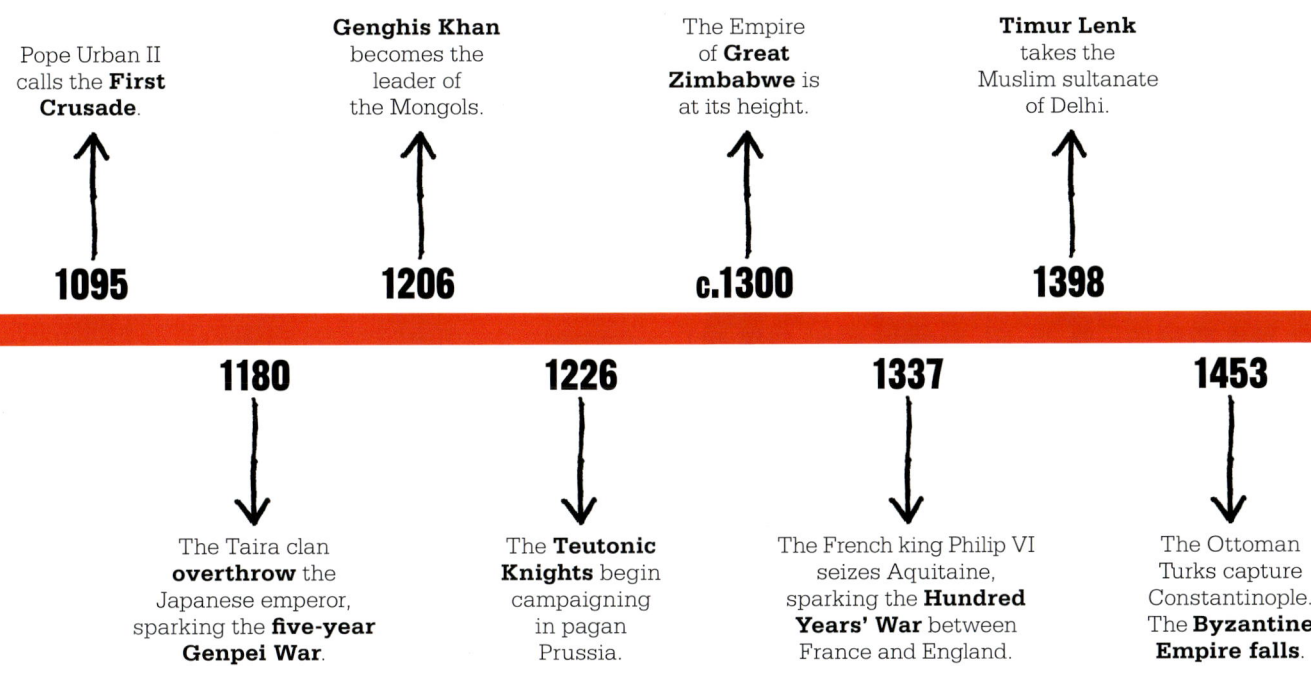

Extreme brutality had marked the crusades, and war was waged with equal ferocity elsewhere. Faith was largely absent as a pretext, although the Mayans, who occupied central America and what is now Mexico from the 4th to the 10th centuries, primarily fought rivals in order to secure sacrificial victims to appease their deities. The Aztecs, their successors in Mexico, also practiced sacrifice and fought bloody wars, armed mainly with spears, and sharp-bladed clubs and knives, while the Incas of South America used clubs, bows, and javelins.

In the 9th century, Scandinavian Vikings set out on longships to ravage Europe's coastline, seizing what they could, and sometimes settling in areas they conquered. Vikings arriving in northern France in the early 10th century converted to Christianity in return for land. A century later, William, duke of Normandy, with an army of elite mounted knights, infantry, and archers, conquered England, too.

Normandy fell to the French in the 13th century, but England still held other areas of France. By the end of the Hundred Years' War—a power struggle between the English and French ruling families that began in 1337—England had lost all its French territories.

Power struggles

Professional soldiers always proved superior fighters. In Japan, the highly skilled samurai were greatly honored, which in time made them powerful. In the 12th century, two samurai clans—the Taira and Minamoto—vied with each other to rule Japan, and the country became locked in civil war. Power struggles also rocked the civilization in Great Zimbabwe, Africa. A lust for power similarly drove the Mongols across Asia. Exceptional horsemanship and archery skills distinguished them in battle, but both Genghis Khan, in the 13th century, and Timur, in the 14th century, fought and ruled by terror, at times piling up skulls of the massacred.

Constantinople falls

In the 15th century, the Ottoman Turks emerged from the Central Asian steppe and closed in on Constantinople. In 1453, a huge cannon, designed by a European engineer, helped them breach the city's supposedly impregnable walls. Making it their capital, the Ottomans again renamed the city—giving it its present name Istanbul. ∎

THE GREATEST OF GOD'S GIFTS TO MEN ... ARE PRIESTHOOD AND EMPIRE

THE BYZANTINE EMPIRE (c. 330–1204)

IN CONTEXT

FOCUS
Byzantium as the new Rome

BEFORE
c. 667 BCE Greek traders from Megara found the colony of Byzantium beside the Bosphorus Strait, where Istanbul, Türkiye, now stands.

513 BCE Persian king Darius I sacks the city of Byzantium before absorbing it into his Achaemenid Empire.

334 BCE Alexander the Great invades the Achaemenid Empire and takes Byzantium.

AFTER
1453 After a lengthy siege Constantinople (Byzantium) is taken by the Ottoman Turks.

1615 Cossacks make the first in a series of raids in Anatolia.

1923 The Republic of Türkiye is established.

In 330 CE, Constantine moved the capital of the Roman Empire from Rome to the city of Byzantium, 875 miles (1,400 km) to the east, in modern-day Türkiye. In military terms, the move might be seen as a strategic withdrawal; it was becoming increasingly difficult to protect the imperial capital from the unrelenting succession of barbarian raids.

Although Rome was still the capital of the Western Roman Empire, it had effectively been downgraded to a province. The contrast with Byzantium could hardly have been starker. While economically Rome was withering, the eastern city was going from

WAR IN THE MIDDLE AGES

See also: The conquests of Alexander the Great 32–39 ▪ The rise of Rome 50–51 ▪ Barbarian migrations: the empire under threat 58–65 ▪ The rise of Islam 76–81 ▪ The Crusades 88–93

Not by numbers of men, nor by measure of body, but by valor of soul is war to be decided.
Flavius Belisarius

strength to strength. Situated on the only maritime passage between the Mediterranean and the Black Sea, Byzantium was a gateway to Asia and all its riches and the center of a flourishing East–West trade. The commerce was cultural, as well as mercantile. It made sense for Constantine to establish his imperial court and government there. He renamed the city Constantinople.

Greek character

The conquests of Alexander the Great had brought much of western Asia into the Greek sphere of influence. Greek was the prevailing language in what had become a hybrid Graeco-Asian cultural zone.

The citizens of Constantinople regarded themselves as Romans—they were governed by Roman laws, and the official language was Latin. "Romanness" was also reflected in the military sphere, as the army

Belisarius leads 5,000 troops into Rome through the Asinarian Gate in December 537, ending 60 years of Ostrogoth occupation. The Goths retreated to Ravenna.

kept the old legionary structures, as well as the traditional values of order and discipline. This logistical efficiency was still much needed, since the barbarian migrations that endangered Rome were also a threat to Constantinople.

Rome remained the capital of the declining Western Roman Empire until 476, when German invaders led by Odoacer deposed the last Western emperor, Romulus Augustulus. Constantinople now stood alone as the center of the "Roman" world.

Rebuilding the empire

Justinian I, who ruled the Eastern empire from 527 to 565, hoped to restore the past glories of the united Roman Empire. He called this goal the *renovatio imperii* ("renewal of the empire") and found in Flavius Belisarius a commander of courage and intelligence who could realize his ambitions.

Belisarius had made his name during the Iberian War (526–32), fought against the Sasanian Empire of Persia for control over Iberia, a kingdom in present-day Georgia. The war spilled into Syria, and in 530 Belisarius defeated the Sasanians at Dara, deploying his *bucellarii* (heavily armored cavalry) with devastating effect.

The following year, the Sasanian and Byzantine troops fought to a stalemate at Callinicum, Syria. An inconclusive peace resulted while Justinian turned his attentions westward to Rome's former province of Africa (roughly corresponding to modern-day Tunisia), now a kingdom of the Germanic Vandal people. Although small, it was a base for Vandal raids across the sea to southern Europe and the Eastern Empire. Justinian resolved to end the irritation.

Belisarius set out by sea in 533, landing east of Carthage and marching toward that city. His army was only 15,000 strong, although a third of it was heavy cavalry. Even so, it outnumbered the Vandal force sent to meet it. The armies clashed at »

Ad Decimum, south of Carthage. Gelimer, the Vandal leader, tried to encircle the attacking force but failed, allowing Belisarius to push through to the city and recover Africa.

Taking back the homeland

Emboldened by this continued military success, in 535 Justinian sent Belisarius to take back the Italian "homeland," by now occupied by Ostrogoths (Goths). The following year, the general recaptured Rome, but winning back the rest of Italy proved tougher. The advantage seesawed back and forth in a succession of hard-fought battles before, in 540, Belisarius occupied the Ostrogoth headquarters of Ravenna. He made it the capital of a reestablished western empire.

The Byzantines' hold on Italy was precarious. Despite their earlier defeats, the Goths were once again a rising force by the 550s. In 568, the Germanic Lombards invaded Italy from the north. Troubles were piling up

A Byzantine army led by Nikephoros lays siege to the fortress of Chandax in this illustration from a chronicle by 11th-century historian John Skylitzes.

> When [Nikephoros] had destroyed everything in his path with fire and the sword, he attacked the fortresses.
>
> **Leo the Deacon**
> Byzantine chronicler,
> on Nikephoros's Syrian campaign

elsewhere as well. In 577, the Slavs and Avars advanced into the Balkans from the north and east.

Prevailing over Persia

Meanwhile, in 572, a new war had broken out between the Byzantine and Sasanian empires. The fighting would rumble on for five decades. Again, heavy cavalry proved crucial. The Sasanian army had thousands of cataphracts—armored horsemen who charged with lances raised and smashed into the opposing Byzantine formations with an irresistible force before whipping out their bows and showering their enemy with arrows.

The Byzantines formed cataphract units of their own, backed by light and heavy infantry. To supplement their own troops, the Byzantines relied on *foederati*, units recruited from barbarian peoples bound by treaty to their cause. They further boosted their numbers—and filled specialized roles—with skilled mercenaries. With the help of these additional forces, the Byzantines kept the Sasanians at bay and, in 627, defeated them at the Battle of Nineveh in present-day Iraq.

The Islamic threat

By now, Islam was on the rise, and the Arab armies converged on the Byzantine Empire with alarming speed. The Byzantines became confined to Constantinople and its immediate environs. In 674, the Arabs of the Umayyad caliphate, who ruled from Syria, laid siege to the city itself, sending out great catapults mounted on galleys to pound the fortifications until a breach was made. The city's walls held firm, however, and the Arabs instead imposed a blockade on shipping, hoping to starve the city into submission. In 678, the Arab troops ended the siege after an attack by a Byzantine fleet armed with Greek fire.

WAR IN THE MIDDLE AGES 73

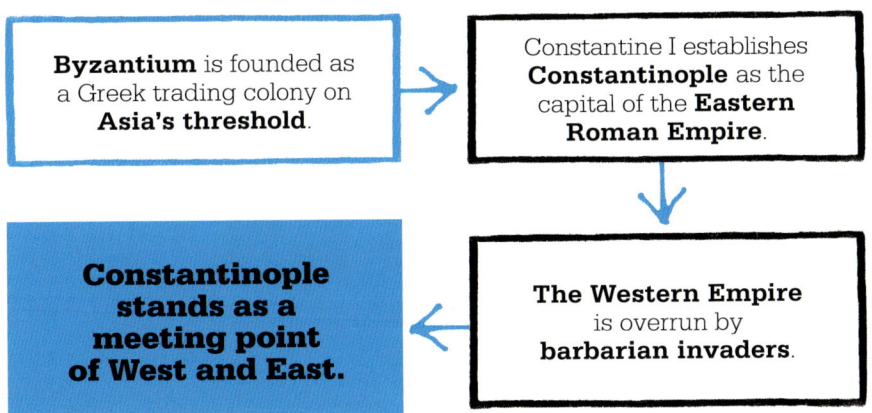

Greek fire

The Byzantines' victory at the Siege of Constantinople in 678 CE was widely attributed to their deployment of "Greek fire." The lethal new weapon, credited to Callinicus of Heliopolis, a Jewish refugee from Syria, is thought to have been a blend of oil and tar, probably with added sulphur or quicklime, although its precise composition is still not known. Thrown from pots or propelled through tubes mounted on the bows of Byzantine ships, it ignited spontaneously, and could not be extinguished by water.

Greek fire played havoc in an age of wooden ships and evidently terrified enemies of the Byzantine Empire when it was first used. Chroniclers of the time describe the panic with which crews reacted to its discharge. Although armies throughout history had used incendiary weapons, such as flaming arrows and burning pitch, Greek fire was far more potent. Its victims were as unprepared for its effects and ill-equipped to counter it as those who would first face gunpowder weapons some centuries later.

Although the Byzantine Empire survived, it was much reduced. The forces of Islam had taken Egypt and Syria. Beyond Constantinople, the Byzantines occupied only Anatolia and various scattered territories around the coasts and islands of the Mediterranean; these were slowly taken away.

In 820, Arab adventurers from al-Andalus (Islamic Spain) seized and occupied Crete; and in 827, the Arabs embarked upon the conquest of Sicily, completing it in 902. Since 681, the Bulgars had been building an empire in the Balkans. Weakened as they were, the Byzantines had to accept the Bulgars' demands to settle in territories south of the Danube.

Rebuilding the empire

In 961, the Byzantine general Nikephoros II quickly reoccupied all of Crete, after taking its main fortress, Chandax (Heraklion). When the sitting emperor Romanos II died, Nikephoros was installed as his successor. He launched an offensive against Islam, taking back the island of Cyprus, and then struck deep into Syria to seize Aleppo in 962.

Nikephoros, who became known as the "Pale Death of the Saracens," died at the hands of his uncle, John I Tzimiskes, another warlike ruler, who defeated the Bulgarians and, in the east, invaded Palestine. In 976, Basil II became emperor after a three-year power struggle, helped by his Varangian Guard of 6,000 Viking mercenaries.

Also in 976, Czar Samuel ascended to the throne of the Bulgar Empire, which extended across the Balkans from the Adriatic to the Black Sea, and threatened to eclipse the Byzantine Empire. Basil was determined to expel Samuel, but first he had to fight off a Muslim invasion of Syria from the south. The Byzantines' position at the meeting of East and West exposed them to danger from both sides. By 1001, however, Basil was taking the fight to the Bulgars. He finally was able to defeat them at Kleidion, Bulgaria, in 1014.

Half a millennium after the fall of the city of Rome, its eastern, Byzantine manifestation remained a major power, but threats continued to come. In 1204, bribed by Alexius, a claimant to Constantinople's imperial throne, the forces of the Fourth Crusade were diverted to Constantinople. In a three-day spree of violence, they sacked the city. Despite this, the empire survived until 1453, when it was destroyed by Ottoman Turks. ∎

Crewmen direct Greek fire at an enemy ship. Panicked sailors often opted to dive overboard into the sea as flames spread up the bows of their wooden vessels.

A RAIN OF THEIR BLOOD AS AN OFFERING
THE MAYA CIVILIZATION (c. 300–900)

IN CONTEXT

FOCUS
Human sacrifice

BEFORE
1200 BCE Mesoamerica's first known major civilization, the Olmecs practice human sacrifice in southern Mexico.

400 BCE The Olmecs, Central America's first known major civilization, practice human sacrifice in southern Mexico.

AFTER
1725 On the death of Tattooed Serpent, chief of the Natchez people based in what is now Mississippi, up to 10 of his attendants choose to be sacrificed and buried with him.

1847 Mayan villagers rise up in the Caste War of Yucatán, objecting to oppression by Hispanic settlers.

2009 Police in Kampala, Uganda, investigate 29 alleged ritual murders of children.

The Maya people settled in the warm, wet forests of southeastern Mexico, Belize, and Guatemala from around the 2nd millennium BCE. Although no clear historical narrative can be pieced together, it is possible to discern distinct phases in the development of the Maya civilization. These stages are linked to the growing size of their settlements, the ever-more ambitious scale of their monuments, and the increasing sophistication of a culture that ranged from a writing system similar to Egyptian hieroglyphs, to mathematics and astronomy—the Maya developed a calendar with accurate recordings of lunar cycles and planetary movements.

Agriculture and sacrifices

By 300 CE, when the Classic Period began, the Maya civilization began to reach its peak with more than 40 cities and up to 10 million people spread over an area about the size of Poland. There was no

A Mayan stele portrays a priest making a ritual offering. He holds a human head in one hand and a sacrificial knife in the other.

WAR IN THE MIDDLE AGES   75

See also: The Aztecs and Incas 114–115 ▪ The European conquest of the Americas 122–125 ▪ Warfare in North America 150–151

Maya warriors battle each other with spears in a fresco dating from 800 CE, in the Painted Temple at Bonampak, Chiapas, Mexico.

winter in this tropical and fertile zone, which allowed for a continual cycle of planting and harvesting crops such as corn, squash, beans, manioc, and peppers.

The Maya attributed their success to the generosity of the gods, whom they appeased with regular tributes and blood offerings. Every major event in the calendar—key points in the agricultural year, the inauguration of a reign, or the construction of a temple—demanded a sacrifice.

Animals were often killed, but human blood was preferable; a man's was considered better than a woman's, and that of a rival king was best of all. In many cases, death was the culmination of a long and elaborate ritual of torture: human victims might be shot with arrows, set on fire, decapitated, or have their hearts ripped out.

After the battle, they cut out the jawbones of the warriors they had killed, cleaned off the flesh, and hung them from their arms as trophies.
Friar Diego de Landa
Relacíon de las cosas de Yucatán, section 52

It was primarily to secure sacrificial victims that Mayan villages went to war with neighboring settlements. They had other motivations, too—domination, vengeance, or enslavement—but sacrifice was what drove them into battle on a regular basis.

Simple weapons

The Maya were well armed, but their weapons were simple. The heads of spears and arrows were made from flint or obsidian, a type of tough volcanic glass that could be sharpened into blades or spikes. Also embedded in clubs called *macuahuitls*, obsidian was highly prized in what was still a Stone Age culture despite all its attainments.

Eventually, the Maya culture seems to have fought itself to a standstill, exhausted by the never-ending rounds of warfare. By the 10th century, its political structures were starting to collapse, its kings' authority failing, and its people gradually moved toward a simpler, village life. ▪

The first sacrifice

The text *Popol Vuh*, which recounts Maya's mythology and history, centers on a story of sacrifice. In this creation myth, twins Hun and Vucub Hunahpu are summoned down to the Underworld and challenged to a ball game by the two Lords of Death. The losers will die, the Lords declare, and the youngsters are no more able to reject these terms than they are to compete against the gods. When they lose, the twins are killed in sacrifice. Hun's head is hung in the branches of a barren tree, which promptly breaks out in flowers and fruit. An array of animal and spirit helpers bring the Hero Twins back to life—and ultimately enable them to overthrow the Lords of Death. Given fresh forms themselves as the sun and moon, they preside over a new, more hopeful order in which humanity is born out of a head of corn.

The Maya myth of the Hero Twins and the Lords of Death is depicted on a painted ceramic vessel from around 600–900.

FIGHT IN THE CAUSE OF ALLAH

THE RISE OF ISLAM (622–756)

THE RISE OF ISLAM

IN CONTEXT

FOCUS
The role of religion in warfare

BEFORE
595 BCE The first of a series of five Sacred Wars is fought by the Greek city of Delphi against neighboring states said to have defiled Apollo's shrine.

492 CE The Frankish king Clovis I goes to war with the Visigoths, who follow what he sees as a "heretical" form of Christianity.

AFTER
945 CE The Buyids—Iranian Shi'ites—conquer the Abbasid heartland of Iraq.

1562 The French Wars of Religion begin, pitting the country's Catholics against its Protestant Huguenots.

1618 The Thirty Years' War starts in central Europe.

Muhammad gave the Arabs first a spiritual mission and then a military one. Until the 7th century CE, to outsiders Arabia had seemed a place apart—an "uncivilized," mysterious land populated by horsemen and camel-drivers.

The reality was that Arabia had its own culture and economic life. Most of its people were nomadic pastoralists, who moved their livestock from oasis to oasis. The desert communities traded with one another, and there were even a few small cities, such as Mecca. It was there that Muhammad (also referred to as "the Prophet"), a middle-aged merchant, began to have visions in 610 CE. Over several years, the angel Gabriel appeared to him, dictating the word of Allah—God. The name for the new religion, Islam, meant "submission to the divine will".

Muhammad was forced to adopt a warlike attitude from the start: Mecca's elite saw his message as destabilizing, forcing him and his followers to leave the city. After their flight to Medina in 622— known as the Hijrah—they struggled to survive, but at the Battle of Badr two years later, they triumphed over their Arab enemies. Defeated and almost destroyed at Uhud in 625, Muhammad's forces recovered to win the Battle of the Trench (627). Three years later, they captured Mecca.

I will be harsh and stern against the aggressor, but I will be a pillar of strength for the weak.
Umar ibn al-Khattab

A war of faith

By the time Muhammad died in 632, his followers were convinced that they had to fight for their faith. The Prophet's successor—or caliph, a title conferring both religious and political authority—was his father-in-law, Abu Bakr, who dedicated his reign to bringing all the Arab tribes under Islamic rule.

The Arabs had been raiders for generations, but Muhammad's injunction that Muslim communities should not prey upon each other forced them to turn their attentions to the wider world. It fell to Umar ibn al-Khattab, Abu Bakr's successor from 634, to carry the new creed further afield. Driven by a sense of duty to spread Muhammad's message, Umar's armies poured out

The Battle of Badr was the first major engagement between Mecca's ruling Quraysh tribe and the followers of Muhammad, who won a decisive victory despite being outnumbered.

WAR IN THE MIDDLE AGES 79

See also: The Byzantine Empire 70–73 ▪ The Crusades 88–93 ▪ The European Crusades 102–103 ▪ The Spanish Reconquista 110–111 ▪ The rise of the Ottoman Turks 112–113 ▪ European wars of religion 134–139 ▪ The Thirty Years' War 144–147

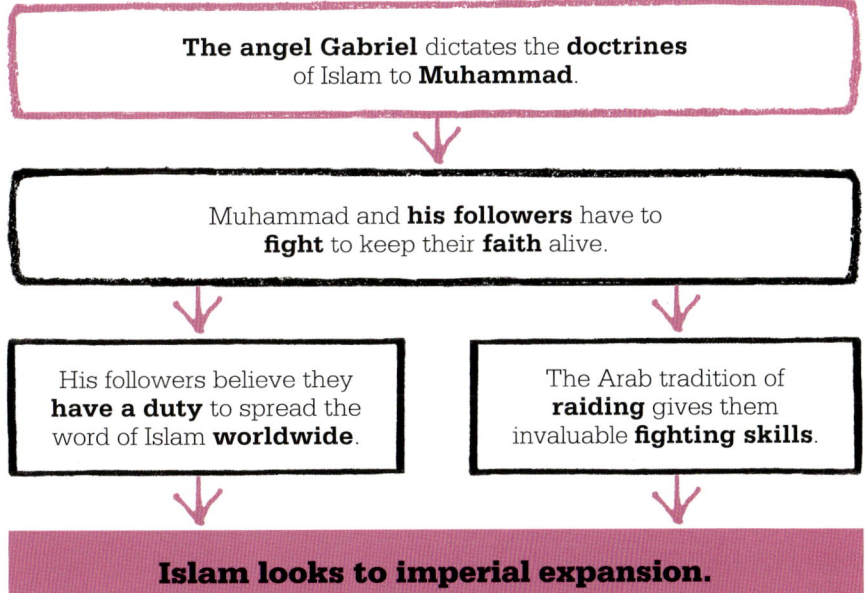

Abu Bakr and Umar ibn al-Khattab are shown conversing in this 1842 engraving. Abu Bakr was Muhammad's successor, but Umar took the message of Islam beyond western Arabia.

of the Arabian Peninsula. Before long, they were attacking the southern borders of the Byzantine Empire, defeating a major force by the Yarmuk River, near the frontier of present-day Syria, Jordan, and Israel, in August 636.

In these early years of Islam, the concept of *jihad* began to be applied to warfare. From the Arabic word for "struggle", *jihad* relates to a determined effort to carry out God's will, including intensely personal strivings for spiritual or moral improvement. Although the Qur'an, the Islamic holy book, insists "there is no compulsion in religion", *jihad* came to justify attempts to enforce Allah's rule by military conquest.

Military strengths
The Arabs were in some ways ill equipped for warfare. As a consequence of their poverty, they had no heavy weaponry or armor; many carried spears, bows, and arrows, but they relied chiefly on swords. These were straight (curved scimitars came later) and carried in wooden scabbards worn on leather straps around the shoulder. Their chief strengths were speed, surprise, and a passionate commitment.

Arab fighters had also been hardened for battle by their way of life. As herdsmen and raiders, they had grown up physically strong, with superlative riding skills. They had the finest horses in the world—fast and smart but also easily trained. The single-humped dromedary camel was used only as a beast of burden, but it was faster and more versatile than any cart. »

An Arab warrior-woman
First written down sometime between the 10th and 12th centuries, the Arabic epic the *Delhemma* offers a romanticized view of the Arab–Byzantine Wars. Its title is believed to be a shortened form of the phrase *Dhat al-Himma* (meaning "woman of noble purpose"), a description of its heroine. Abducted by the warlike Arab Tayy tribe, the delicately nurtured Princess Fatima turns into a formidable warrior-woman. She plays a leading role in the war against the "Romans" during an improbably protracted period between the end of the Umayyad and the early Abbasid era. Brave and resourceful, the princess fights fiercely and escapes whenever she is captured. The tale is more concerned with evoking the excitement of the wars than promoting the supremacy of Islam, with the military advantage swinging wildly back and forth between the Byzantines and the Arabs.

THE RISE OF ISLAM

The Arabs were a formidable fighting force. Three months after their triumph over the Byzantines by the Yarmuk River, they had secured a significant victory over the Sasanians at al-Qadisiya; farther west, they took Jerusalem in 638, after a two-year siege. The holy city of the Jews and Christians was every bit as important for the Muslims. From its Temple Mount, Muhammad was said to have been borne up to heaven by angels in his visionary *Lailat al Mi'raj* ("night flight"). By 641, the Arabs had conquered Palestine, Syria, and Egypt and scored significant victories over the Sasanians, although the complete conquest of Persia would be achieved only under the third caliph, Uthman ibn Affan, who reigned from 644 until he was assassinated in 656. The Arab armies were relatively small, and their expanding empire was already too vast for them to control, but converts flocked to the new religion, and they grew in strength.

Building up resources

Over time, the Arabs' campaigns took them further afield and pitted them against more substantial foes. To meet these challenges, the lightly armed Muslim warriors traded looted treasure for armored breastplates, better swords, more substantial helmets, and other equipment. Meanwhile, their leaders invested in siege engines and other military apparatus, including towers that could be dismantled and powerful catapults, so they could mount successful attacks against the strongly built fortifications or city walls of their enemies. As the Arabs swept on, they also recruited thousands of infantrymen and the heavier cavalry in which the Sasanian and Byzantine armies specialized.

With some difficulty, the military commander Mu'awiya—later to be caliph himself, the first of the Umayyad dynasty—persuaded Uthman to let him build Islam's first fleet. Arab traders had been sailing along the Red Sea coast for generations; Mu'awiya sought their advice and made them his captains. With their assistance, he captured the island of Cyprus in 649. His victory over the Byzantines at the Battle of the Masts, off the south coast of modern-day Türkiye, in 655 confirmed the Arabs' arrival as a naval power. Even so, the Arabs still saw their mobility on land as vital, and whatever the demands of their wars of expansion, they remained reluctant to carry kit that could not be quickly loaded on to a camel.

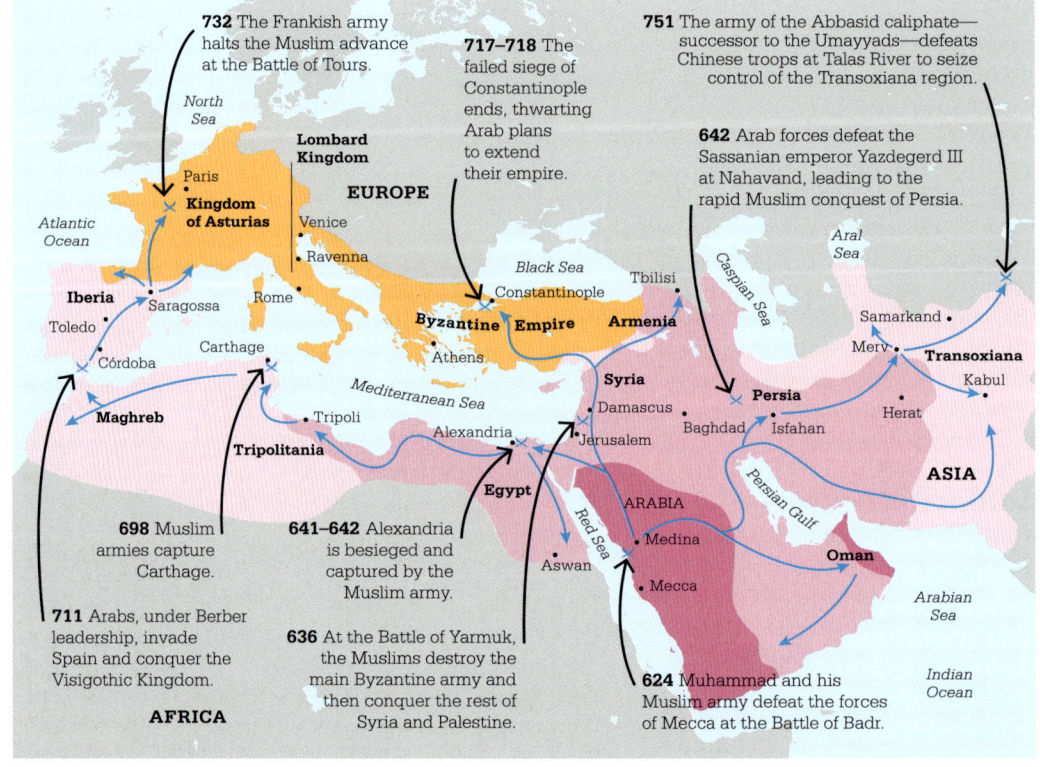

Islam spread rapidly through the 7th and 8th centuries. From Medina, its followers took its message through the Arabian Peninsula, west along the coastal plain of North Africa and into Iberia, north into the Byzantine Empire, and east into South Asia.

Key:
- Conquests under Muhammad 622–632
- Territory gained 632–661
- Territory gained 661–751
- Non-Islamic kingdoms
- → Military campaigns
- × Key battles

732 The Frankish army halts the Muslim advance at the Battle of Tours.

717–718 The failed siege of Constantinople ends, thwarting Arab plans to extend their empire.

751 The army of the Abbasid caliphate—successor to the Umayyads—defeats Chinese troops at Talas River to seize control of the Transoxiana region.

642 Arab forces defeat the Sasanian emperor Yazdegerd III at Nahavand, leading to the rapid Muslim conquest of Persia.

698 Muslim armies capture Carthage.

711 Arabs, under Berber leadership, invade Spain and conquer the Visigothic Kingdom.

641–642 Alexandria is besieged and captured by the Muslim army.

636 At the Battle of Yarmuk, the Muslims destroy the main Byzantine army and then conquer the rest of Syria and Palestine.

624 Muhammad and his Muslim army defeat the forces of Mecca at the Battle of Badr.

Riding a white horse, Abbas strikes a soldier of Yazid's army in retribution for the slaying of his half brother Husayn at the Battle of Karbala. This propagandist painting shows Husayn's enemies suffering in hell (bottom right).

Early seeds of division within Islam had been sown after the death of Muhammad in 632, when Islam's elders chose Abu Bakr to succeed him as caliph. In so doing, they had passed over the Prophet's cousin and son-in-law Ali, apparently unsettled by his moral rigidity and religious fervor. In Islam's First Fitna, or civil war, Ali and his supporters rebelled in 656. The war ended in 661, with Ali's murder and Mu'awiya's recognition as caliph. Despite an early defeat, when Mu'awiya's fleet failed to take Constantinople after a three-year siege that ended in 669, he and his descendants would hold sway throughout the Islamic world for the next 90 years.

Ruled from Damascus, Syria, the new Umayyad dynasty brought a degree of unity and order to the Muslim world. Beneath the surface, however, there were still divisions. Doctrinal differences deepened between those who gave their allegiance to Abu Bakr and the Rashidun, or "rightly guided caliphs," who succeeded him, and those who supported Ali's line. The first group called themselves Sunni, because they followed the Sunnah, or customs laid down by the Prophet. The Shia ("party of Ali") argued that this succession had been corrupted from the outset and that Islamic tradition should have flowed directly through Ali and those imams, or teachers, who followed him.

In 680, Ali's son Husayn tried to overthrow Mu'awiya's heir Yazid. He and his supporters were massacred at the Battle of Karbala, Iraq, giving Shi'ite Islam its first martyrs and a new impetus. Yazid died in 683.

Conflict and change

Despite the ongoing dissension, the Arabs' war of conquest continued. In the second half of the 7th century, Arab armies pushed west from Libya across North Africa. By the beginning of the 8th century, they had taken western North Africa. In 711, the first raiding party of Arabs and Islamized Berbers crossed the Straits of Gibraltar into Spain. Tariq ibn-Ziyad's warriors crushed the defenders sent against them.

The Muslims smote their enemies … and laid waste to the country and took captives without number.
Anonymous Arab chronicler
on the advance through France, 732

By 718, virtually the whole of Iberia was in Muslim hands, though the Frankish force of Charles Martel turned back the invaders at Tours, France, in 732.

Resentment against the Umayyads was mounting. Members of Islam's religious ruling council complained that they had been corrupted by wealth and power. Meanwhile, the northern Qays and the Yamani from southern Arabia were at odds, the Yamani angered by the Ummayad caliph Marwan II's loyal support for their enemy. In 747, a coalition of Arab fighters in the Persian province of Khorasan rose up against the caliphate. Order was restored, but the Umayyads' legitimacy was now questioned.

In 750, a descendant of Ali, Muhammad ibn Ali ibn al-Abbas, led a successful uprising. He established his Abbasid dynasty in western Asia and the Maghreb, ruling from a new capital in Baghdad. In 756, Abd al-Rahman, a member of the ruling Umayyad family, fled from Damascus to Spain and established the kingdom of al-Andalus—a centre for Umayyad rule for centuries. By then, despite the dynastic changes and internal quarrels, Islam was a major spiritual and military force in the world. ∎

THIS KING, THE WISEST AND MOST HIGH-MINDED
THE EMPIRE OF CHARLEMAGNE (768–814)

IN CONTEXT

FOCUS
Restoring order in Europe

BEFORE
476 CE German barbarian warrior Odoacer successfully deposes Rome's last emperor, Romulus Augustulus.

481 Clovis I becomes the first king of the Franks, uniting a collection of Germanic tribes.

732 Charles Martel leads the Franks to victory over the invading Muslims at Tours.

AFTER
814 Charlemagne is succeeded by his son, Louis the Pious.

843 The Treaty of Verdun divides the Frankish realm into eastern and western kingdoms, possibly the origins of Germany and France.

887 The Carolingian dynasty ends when Emperor Charles III is deposed.

At the end of the 8th century, Charlemagne (or *Carolus magnus*, "Charles the great"), king of the Franks, set out to create a super-state capable of resisting Islam's advance into western Europe. Just as ancient Roman order had kept the barbarian hordes at bay, he reasoned, his imperial order would save Christian civilization.

Fighting for peace
Charlemagne aimed to achieve this by diplomatic rather than military means, but the price of peace would prove to be years of war. He began with Saxony, eastern Germany in 772. The territory had not yet converted to Christianity, and its cross-border raids were a constant irritation.

Charlemagne fought the Saxons, on and off, for three decades. Over time, he made piecemeal progress, conquering territory, destroying pagan shrines, and converting local chiefs to Christianity with a combination of threats and inducements. The Saxons were gradually absorbed into the Frankish kingdom, but the task was not completed until 804.

A strategy for victory
In 774, Charlemagne conquered the Lombards, a Germanic tribe in northern Italy, and also brought them under the authority of his Frankish state. The Franks' battle tactics were simple. Armored knights, with their lances leveled, charged the enemy at a gallop. Up close, they fought with long, heavy swords. In their wake, well-drilled infantrymen, holding up spears for thrusting or throwing as required, pressed forwards behind the protective cover of their tightly packed shield walls

No war ever undertaken by the Franks was waged with such persistence and bitterness ... because the Saxons ... were a ferocious folk ... hostile to our faith.
Einhard
The Wars of Charlemagne, c.770–814

WAR IN THE MIDDLE AGES   83

See also: The Roman Empire at its height 56–57 ▪ The Crusades 88–93 ▪ The Holy Roman Empire versus the papacy 94–95 ▪ The European Crusades 102–103 ▪ The Spanish Reconquista 110–111 ▪ European wars of religion 134–139

A 13th-century panel in Aachen Cathedral, western Germany, shows Charlemagne (top right) with an army of knights, lances held high and swords drawn, laying siege to a city.

Their greatest strengths were strategic vision and administrative skill. Charlemagne recruited armies for seasonal campaigns, controlling overall operations centrally but devolving detailed organizational matters to a local level. Nobles and priests sent their own fighting men, weaponry, and rations. This gave Charlemagne great flexibility as commander in chief.

Charlemagne's wars in western Europe were mostly about stopping the spread of Islam. Ever present in Iberia on his southern borders, Muslim forces threatened the whole concept of the Christian monarchy. The king's sole attempt to attack them directly came in 778, when he invaded Spain. This initiative was prompted by Sulayman al-Arabi, the Abbasid-leaning governor of Barcelona and Girona, who suggested they should join forces to defeat Umayyad al-Andalus. In the event, the alliance broke down, and Charlemagne headed home. In the 790s, he returned to take Catalonia as the "Spanish March"—a territorial buffer against Islam.

Rome restored?

On Christmas Day in the year 800, Pope Leo III made Charlemagne the Holy Roman emperor, in the hope that his new state would have the strength and stability of the Roman Empire at its height. A treaty with the Byzantine Emperor Nikephoros I followed in 807.

By the time of his death in 814, Charlemagne had built a powerful and peaceful state. The Carolingian Empire seemed set to recapture some of the glory of ancient Rome. ■

The Battle of Roncesvalles

Charlemagne had many successes, but it was one of his failures that captured the imagination of later times. For the bravery of his troops, the Battle of Roncesvalles would acquire a significance out of all proportion to its scale.

On his southward journey into Spain in the spring of 778 CE, Charlemagne had razed the walls of the Basques' Navarran capital Pamplona. As he made his return, the Basques saw an opportunity to retaliate and ambush a small section of his army that became isolated from the rest as it struggled through a narrow pass high in the Pyrenees mountains. They attacked the Frankish rearguard from every side. Outnumbered and on unfamiliar terrain, the Franks were quickly beaten, but they fought valiantly to the death. Little is known of their leader, but the 11th-century *Song of Roland* eulogizes him as the model of a chivalric, self-sacrificing, knight.

The Franks' defeat at Roncesvalles, depicted here in a French manuscript from 1467, was a minor setback later elevated to a legend of great valor.

THEY RAVAGE EVERYTHING THAT DOES NOT OPPOSE THEM
VIKING RAIDS (793–c. 1100)

IN CONTEXT

FOCUS
Oceangoing boats

BEFORE
1200 BCE The mysterious "Sea Peoples" attack ancient Egypt and Bronze Age Greece.

1085 BCE The semimythical War of Troy is said to begin. This Greek raid turned into a 10-year siege.

800 BCE Piracy rears its head as a problem for Greece's trading cities.

AFTER
1153 CE Descended from Vikings, Somerled, "Lord of the Isles," rises up against the 12-year-old king of Scotland, Malcolm IV, sacking Glasgow.

1631 Barbary pirates from North Africa sack the village of Baltimore, southwest Ireland.

April 2009 Somali pirates board the *Maersk Alabama* and take the vessel's captain, Richard Phillips, hostage.

From the 8th century CE, small groups of young Scandinavian men set out to prey on Europe's coastlines in search of new land, wealth, and adventure. Tough and schooled in seafaring, they carried heavy broadaxes, swords, and spears, and protected themselves with round shields and padded hide tunics.

The most important part of the Viking armory was the longship. Narrow and streamlined, it was built for speed. Its sides were lined with shields, while the prow was carved in the shape of a dragon's head to intimidate enemies.

Brutal voyagers

Viking attacks followed a familiar pattern. First, one or two longships arrived, seemingly out of nowhere, then their crew rushed ashore on foot, using extreme violence to break any resistance. Larger expeditions and full invasions came later, but the basic pattern stayed the same.

The Vikings ranged widely. Danes crossed the North Sea to England or went down the Frisian coast to attack the Carolingian Empire. Norwegians sailed to Scotland and Ireland and then pushed west to colonize Iceland and Greenland. They even established a settlement in Newfoundland, Canada. Farther south, they raided Moorish Spain, northwestern Italy, and Morocco. Swedish Vikings followed Russia's rivers down to the Black Sea and Constantinople, where they enlisted as mercenaries to form the emperor's Varangian Guard. ∎

The harrowing inroads of heathen men made lamentable havoc in the church of God in Holy-island.
Anglo-Saxon Chronicle
Report of Viking raid on Lindisfarne in 793 CE

See also: Barbarian migrations: the empire under threat 58–65 ▪ The Norman conquests 85 ▪ The Mongol invasions 96–101 ▪ Timur's conquests 105

THE DUKE … SPARED NO OPPONENT
THE NORMAN CONQUESTS (911–c. 1100)

IN CONTEXT

FOCUS
Triumph of cavalry

BEFORE
c. 400 CE Stirrups, brought to Europe by outsiders attacking Rome, give the cavalry soldiers greater balance.

c. 600 Strongly constructed saddles, held in place by a girth around the horse's belly, are introduced in Europe.

AFTER
c. 1100 A high pommel at the front of the saddle and a heavy cantle behind offer additional protection to knights when their lances make contact.

c. 1200 Knights start to wear armor plating across their lower back to protect their vital organs when jolted back against the cantle.

1346 At Crécy, England's archers cut down French knights in swathes, leading to a rethinking of cavalry tactics.

After the Vikings raided Paris in 911, Frankish king Charles the Simple granted them territories in what became known as the Land of the Northmen, or Normandy. Charles wanted to placate them but also to secure an ally in his tussles with his own barons.

As a condition of the agreement, the Normans had to convert to Christianity—and embraced the hierarchical culture that came with it. This hierarchy was reflected in the stone cathedrals and castles that the Normans built, and also in the configuration of their armies. At the top, the knight astride his destrier—a stallion trained for war—charged into battle. He supported his lance between his chest and upper arm and braced his body against a specially strengthened wood-framed saddle. His aim was to strike his opponent with a shattering blow.

The lower-born infantry followed the cavalry charge, wielding their long swords, while the peasant archers fired on the enemy before and after the charges. This was the order of battle at Hastings, England, in 1066, when William, duke of Normandy (William the Conqueror) crushed King Harold Godwinson, and in 1069–1070 during the near-genocidal Harrying of the North, the subjugation of northern England.

Although their Viking past was behind them, Norman knights had been serving as mercenaries in Italy since the start of the 10th century, helping the Byzantine authorities and local rulers combat Arab pirates. By 1088, they had established Norman rule in Sicily. ■

Normans on horseback face Saxon infantrymen in this section of the Bayeux Tapestry, which depicts the 11th-century conquest of England.

See also: Viking raids 84 ■ The rise of the samurai 86–87 ■ The Crusades 88–93 ■ The European Crusades 102–103 ■ The Hundred Years' War 106–109

THE WAY OF THE SAMURAI IS FOUND IN DEATH
THE RISE OF THE SAMURAI (9TH CENTURY–1185)

IN CONTEXT

FOCUS
A caste of warriors

BEFORE
607 CE The first of a series of Japanese missions is sent to China to bring back new ideas.

645 The Taika Reform reorganizes Japan along Chinese lines, centralizing power and concentrating land in the hands of great lords.

702 The Taiho Code deepens the division between the spiritual role of emperor and the practicalities of the state.

AFTER
1333 Several decades of civil war start with the collapse of the Kamakura Shogunate.

1877 In Satsuma, Kyushu, samurai rise up in opposition to the modernizing reforms of the Meiji dynasty.

1882 Recruits to the armed forces are compelled to take an oath of loyalty to the emperor.

More than just a group of soldiers, the samurai of medieval Japan comprised a distinct class that was a cornerstone of the entire social order. Within the rigid Japanese class system, samurai warriors occupied the rung above craftspeople and artisans. They acted as bodyguards to the *daimyo*, or great feudal lords, who in turn answered to a shogun ("supreme commander") or military leader. Above them all was the emperor, a figure so rarefied that he seemed almost a living myth. Since the 7th century, however, his status had been only spiritual, and any real political power rested with the shogun.

A military elite
Japan's armies in the 9th century were mostly made up of lightly armed infantrymen, conscripted peasants. The samurai were full-time warriors. Skilled in swordsmanship, they were expert riders and archers, typically firing off shots on horseback from 8 ft (2.5 m) long wooden bows. A distinctive style of cavalry

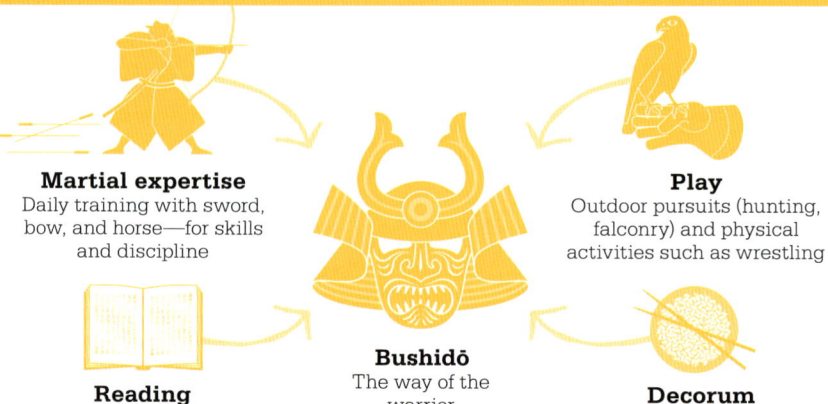

A samurai code for life

Martial expertise
Daily training with sword, bow, and horse—for skills and discipline

Reading
Books on military and moral matters, including poetry; fiction is reserved for women

Bushidō
The way of the warrior

Play
Outdoor pursuits (hunting, falconry) and physical activities such as wrestling

Decorum
Plain food and unadorned clothing only; dancing is a dishonor demanding seppuku

WAR IN THE MIDDLE AGES 87

See also: The Empire of Charlemagne 82–83 ▪ The Norman conquests 85 ▪ The Crusades 88–93 ▪ The Mongol invasions 96–101 ▪ The Hundred Years' War 106–109 ▪ Japan in the Sengoku era 128–129

combat developed, with opponents sidling around one another at close quarters, seeking openings for shots that might penetrate each other's heavy, padded armor.

Samurai were admired as heroes; their code of *bushidō* ("the way of the warrior") summed up the values by which most Japanese would have wished to live. In times of peace, they took on a law-enforcement role.

Struggle for supremacy

The 12th century saw the rise to power of two noble clans—the Taira and the Minamoto, both from Honshu, the main Japanese island—who became locked in a civil war for overall control of Japan. In 1180, the Taira overthrew Emperor Takakura to place his infant son on the throne, bypassing Takakura's half brother, Prince Mochihito, who supported the Minamoto clan. This coup sparked the bitter five-year Genpei War.

Mochihito, on whose behalf the war was waged, and the Minamoto commander Yorimasa both fell in the first battle, at Uji in June 1180.

Taira and Minamoto forces clash during the Hōgen Rebellion of 1156 in this 16th-century image. The rebellion marked the start of the clan rivalry.

The victorious Taira next destroyed the strategic city of Nara, north of Kyoto, before triumphing at Ishibashiyama that September. In 1183, Minamoto no Yoshinaka cleverly encircled the Taira under cover of darkness at Kurikara Pass in western Honshu. Yoshinaka was then defeated by his cousin Yoritomo in a family feud, before the Genpei War resumed.

In March 1184, Yoritomo's Minamoto took the Taira fortress of Ichi-no-Tani, on Honshu's southern coast and wiped out its fleeing garrison at Kojima. A year later, they captured the Taira headquarters at Yashima, although most of the Taira forces escaped along the coast to Dan-no-ura. There, the climactic battle took place in April 1185. Despite technically being a naval engagement, this was really a land battle fought at sea, the warriors showering one another with arrows as their ships approached, then boarding to engage in hand-to-hand fighting. The Minamoto won, and the Genpei War was over.

Supporting the shogun

In 1192, Emperor Go-Toba recognized Yoritomo's position as shogun—once again, the second-ranking man was actually the one in charge. The Kamakura Shogunate would reign as a hereditary dictatorship for 150 years. Throughout, it was backed by the samurai, whose own position had been strengthened as their country's revered military elite. ■

Minamoto no Yorimasa

Born in 1106, Minamoto no Yorimasa was in his 70s and had just entered the Buddhist priesthood when the Genpei War broke out. He joined the fighting at the head of a force of monks. Entrusted with the protection of Prince Mochihito, he was caught by a Taira army on the banks of the Uji River in what became the first engagement of the war. The prince was killed, and Yorimasa was wounded. To escape the shame of capture, Yorimasa disemboweled himself in the first recorded act of seppuku. By tradition, he wrote a poem before he ended his life: "Like an old tree / from which we / gather no flowers, / sad has been my life / fated no fruit to produce." Yorimasa did have children; the "fruit" he had failed to produce were the glory and honor he had hoped to bequeath. Ironically, Yorimasa won renown with that ritual suicide; it showed he had followed the way of the warrior to the very end.

GOD WILLS IT!
THE CRUSADES (1095–1270)

THE CRUSADES

IN CONTEXT

FOCUS
A clash of cultures

BEFORE
985 CE The Seljuk Turks embrace Islam.

1071 At Manzikert, in what is now eastern Türkiye, the Seljuks defeat the Byzantines.

1073 The Seljuks take Jerusalem from its Egyptian Fatimid rulers and close the city to Christian pilgrims.

AFTER
1529 Vienna sees off a siege by the Ottoman Turks.

1571 At the Battle of Lepanto, the fleet of the Holy League (a coalition of Catholic states) defeats that of the Ottoman Empire off the coast of Greece.

1853 The Crimean War is sparked ostensibly by French and Russian concern for the rights of Christian pilgrims in the Ottoman-held Holy Land.

In November 1095, Pope Urban II stirred up the Council of Clermont, a Church assembly, with his call for Christian Europe to arm against a diabolic foe. The forces of Islam, he warned, were occupying Christian land and destroying churches, so believers had a duty to go and defend their faith in a crusade. Thousands were inspired to do their sacred duty, and the mass mobilization that followed brought out not only knights but also tradesmen and peasants.

Organizing such an ambitious venture proved more challenging. Europe's rulers were not united in their support. The German emperor Henry IV, at odds with Urban, refused to take part, but the nobilities of other countries—especially France— rallied around the cause.

The object of the First Crusade was the recovery of the Holy Land (Biblical Palestine). Jerusalem was sacred for Christians as the scene of Jesus's crucifixion, and Muslims also prized it because they believed Muhammad had made a flight to heaven from the city's Temple Mount. The Crusades, also known as the wars for the "Holy Places,"

> Meanwhile, the Turks were howling like wolves and furiously shooting a cloud of arrows.
> **Fulcher of Chartres**
> on the Battle of Dorylaeum, Anatolia, July 1, 1097

pitted Western Christians against Asian Muslims. Although bitter and bloody, they brought contact between peoples with different cultures. Both camps were exposed to new ideas, and the impact on both Muslim and Christian countries would be enduring.

Heading eastwards

By August 1096, the First Crusade was only just setting out from France. There were four main armies, numbering up to 60,000 in all, with a further 40,000 wives, children, and camp followers. The main army was led by Godfrey of Bouillon and set off from Lorraine, France. There were also forces from southern Italy, southern France, Normandy, and the Flemish region. Some marched to the Adriatic then proceeded by sea to Constantinople, the Byzantine capital; others, such as Godfrey's force, traveled overland. They reached Constantinople in the early part of 1097.

Pope Urban II whips a crowd into a frenzy in 1095, preaching about the threat of Islam. This speech led to the launch of the First Crusade.

WAR IN THE MIDDLE AGES   91

See also: The Byzantine Empire 70–73 ▪ The rise of Islam 76–81 ▪ The Holy Roman Empire versus the papacy 94–95 ▪ The European Crusades 102–103

Krak des Chevaliers

A spectacular castle standing near the city of Homs in Syria, Krak des Chevaliers was built between 1142 and 1170 by the Knights Hospitaller, a Catholic military order. Priests provided medical care to Crusaders in the field but were also actively involved in the fighting. Nothing as sophisticated as their fortress had yet been built in Europe, although multilayered defenses had been constructed in West Asia since Assyrian times. The castle housed a garrison of up to 2,000 men.

A "concentric castle," Krak des Chevaliers was doubly defended, its outer wall overlooked by a higher inner wall. The outer wall did not just provide an extra layer of protection; it prevented siege engines from being taken to the places where they were most needed. Projecting towers on and between every corner allowed covering fire from just about every angle. King Edward I of England would build concentric castles at Harlech and Beaumaris during his conquest of Wales in the late 13th century.

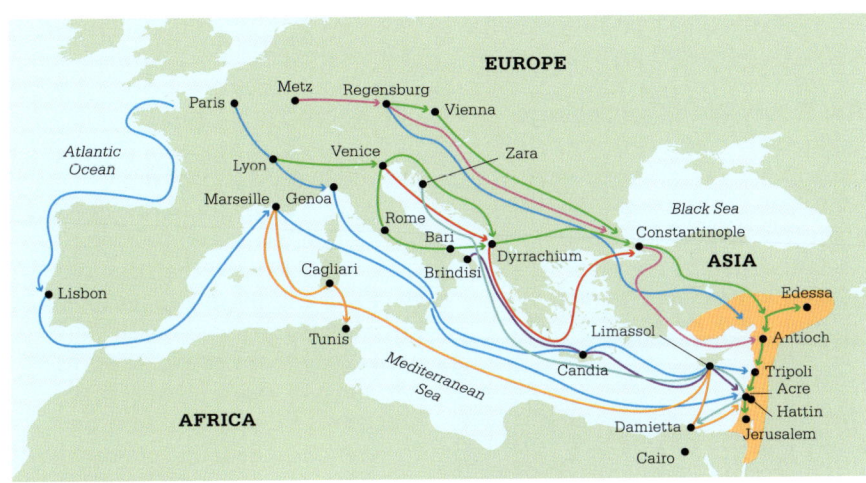

The Crusader armies of the 11th to 13th centuries followed a variety of routes, overland and by sea, to reach their ultimate goal—the holy city of Jerusalem.

Key:
- First Crusade (1096–1099)
- Second Crusade (1147–1149)
- Third Crusade (1189–1192)
- Fourth Crusade (1202–1204)
- Fifth Crusade (1217–1221)
- Sixth Crusade (1228–1229)
- Seventh and Eighth Crusades (1248–1254, 1270)
- Crusader kingdoms

Perched atop a steep-sided hill near the Syria–Lebanon border, Krak des Chevaliers is the largest castle built by European Crusaders.

Ferried across the Bosphorus, the armies pushed southward into Anatolia (modern-day Türkiye). This was the territory of the Sunni Muslim Seljuk Empire. The Crusaders' spirits rose when they captured the city of Nicaea (Iznik) on June 18. Thereafter, they lost cohesion, the column straggling so badly that when, on July 1, a force of Seljuk Turks found the army of Italian prince Bohemond of Taranto outside the city of Dorylaeum, the Turkish forces easily surrounded it. Lightly armed mounted archers galloped into Bohemond's camp, spraying arrows around them. Crusader priest Fulcher of Chartres reported that they spared no one.

The arrival of reinforcements enabled Bohemond's forces to recover. Godfrey brought 50 knights, and further groups also followed. Nonetheless, it was a taste of things to come as the Crusaders continued over Anatolia's mountainous interior, a grueling journey in the searing heat, harried by Seljuk horsemen. Only 40,000 made it as far as Antioch; they settled down to besiege the Seljuk-held city on October 21, 1097, but by December their own supplies of food were running low.

Heavy casualties

Antioch held out until June 1098, by which time thousands of the Crusaders had died of starvation, disease, or in battle. They were winning their war but unable to feed themselves. Taking the town of Ma'arra that December, they fell upon its defenders and—not content with killing them—tore at their bodies for flesh to eat. »

THE CRUSADES

Now only around 13,000 strong, the Crusaders advanced on Jerusalem, arriving at its gates on June 7, 1099. After another siege, a party led by Godfrey breached the walls on July 13. "There was such massacre," the chronicle *Gesta Francorum* (*The Deeds of the Franks*) reports, "that our men were wading up to their ankles in enemy blood." The Crusaders established four states to consolidate their hold upon the region and divide the territorial spoils. These states—the County of Edessa, the Principality of Antioch, the County of Tripoli, and the Kingdom of Jerusalem—prospered as pilgrims flooded in from Europe.

An East–West exchange

If Jerusalem had been recovered more quickly than expected, it was soon under threat again from the resurgent Seljuk Turks. During the Second Crusade, from 1147 to 1149, the Christians were roundly defeated outside Damascus and forced to retreat. In 1187, charismatic Kurdish leader Salah ad-Din (Saladin) recaptured Jerusalem for Islam. King Richard I ("the Lionheart") of England mounted a Third Crusade with other Christian kings in 1189, but this was unsuccessful.

Many Crusaders were surprised to find that Islamic culture was more sophisticated than that of the West—in terms of scientific knowledge, medicine, and astronomy, for example. Muslim nations had also adopted ideas and aesthetic sensibilities from the countries they had conquered—including those of a classical Greco-Roman culture largely lost to medieval Europe. The Crusades gave Europeans an opportunity to benefit from this scholarship. Some of the Crusaders learned Arabic, and Crusader states became centers of commerce and cultural exchange.

Tactics and equipment

Saladin and Richard I's rivalry highlighted the differences between Eastern and Western ways of waging war—setting the agility and skill of the Seljuks against the raw strength and aggression of the Crusaders, reflected in contrasting battle dress and arms. A Crusader knight wore a knee-length hauberk, or coat, of chain mail—each with more than 15,000 rings—over a padded tunic. (The red-cross surcoat that is often depicted in paintings was not featured in representations of the time.) Plates of steel were fixed to an iron frame to make a helmet.

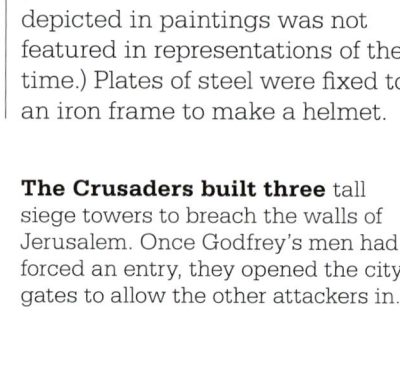

The Crusaders built three tall siege towers to breach the walls of Jerusalem. Once Godfrey's men had forced an entry, they opened the city gates to allow the other attackers in.

Jerusalem is sacred to Judaism, Christianity, and Islam. Under the Muslim Fatimid Caliphate, **all can enter**.

↓

The **less tolerant** Seljuk Turks **bar Christian pilgrims** from the Holy Land.

←

Crusaders come from Christian Europe to **claim the Holy Places** for themselves.

↓

The fighting leads to an exchange of knowledge and ideas between Muslims and the Crusaders.

For fighting on foot, or on horseback at close quarters, the knight had a strong steel sword, its sharp, pointed blade some 30 in (80 cm) long and suitable for cutting, as well as stabbing. His primary weapon was his lance, wedged beneath his arm.

To carry this amount of gear, a Crusader's warhorse had to be strong and heavy, which meant it could manage only brief bursts of speed. Charging at a gallop, knights could smash into the enemy front line with a devastating impact, but their horses tired quickly, after which their lumbering lack of pace and agility showed. The deficit was addressed by the infantry advancing in the cavalry's wake, attacking their opponents to the best of their ability. The infantryman—not professional soldier—had only a skimpy helmet for armor and carried just a spear and perhaps a bow. Few foot soldiers could afford a sword or shield.

Approaching a wall or rampart, Crusader foot soldiers often carried wide wooden panels to protect against the arrows showering down. Towers were constructed for assailing city walls, and traction trebuchets were used for hurling rocks and rubbish. A well-made trebuchet (a type of giant catapult) could hurl a 50 lb (22.5 kg) projectile more than 390 ft (120 m). The tension in these weapons was initially generated by teams of men pulling; later, heavy counterweights were used.

The Muslims did have heavy cavalry, but their prevailing style was that of the Eurasian nomads, the Seljuk Turks having originated from the Kazakh Steppe and its surroundings. Lightly armed, with a short but powerful composite bow, the Seljuk warrior typically carried a curved *kilij*, or scimitar, sharp on just one side for slashing.

A series of failures

The Crusaders' pious desire to redeem Jerusalem had always gone hand in hand with a spirit of adventure—and a lust for loot. However, the Fourth Crusade (1202–1204) saw new levels of brutality and cynicism. Short of funds, the Crusaders diverted to Constantinople and sacked the city amid fearful slaughter. The German army spearheading the Fifth Crusade (1217–1221) tried to approach Jerusalem from the south through Egypt, expecting that route to be less well guarded, but this tactic also failed.

In 1228, Holy Roman Emperor Frederick II negotiated Jerusalem's return. Even so, it later fell into Muslim hands again. Two further crusades were mounted in 1248 and 1270; these catastrophic failures ended the crusading dream. ■

> "What man, however experienced and learned, would dare to write of the skill and prowess and courage of the Turks ... you could not find stronger or braver soldiers."
> **Anonymous Crusader**
> *The Medieval World at War*, 2009

While besieging Nicaea in 1097, Crusaders induced terror into its defenders by using trebuchets to lob heavy projectiles and the heads of dead prisoners over the walls.

IF GOD DOES NOT AVERT IT … A SCHISM WILL OCCUR

THE HOLY ROMAN EMPIRE VERSUS THE PAPACY (1076–1237)

IN CONTEXT

FOCUS
God versus king

BEFORE
c. 420 CE St. Augustine of Hippo publishes *The City of God*, in which he ponders the relationship between earthly power and the spiritual authority of the Church.

c. 460 Pope Leo the Great tells Leo I—the Eastern Roman emperor—that a primary function of the secular state is the defense of the Church.

AFTER
c. 1520 Rejecting Rome's authority, German priest Martin Luther argues that neither Church nor state should have any authority over the other's affairs.

1555 The Peace of Augsburg agrees that Germany's constituent states will follow their rulers in their religious allegiance: *cuius regio, eius religio* ("his realm, his religion").

The Holy Roman Empire was both a territory and a spiritual idea. These two principles often came into conflict and, from the 11th to 13th centuries, frequently resulted in serious dissent and even war. The empire's "Romanness" was largely religious. It did have Italian land, including Rome, but it was geographically focused on Germany.

In 1073, King Henry IV of Germany faced a rebellion in Saxony. After suppressing it, he rewarded his loyal supporters—and hoped to gain allies in important clerical positions—by handing out religious appointments. This act led to the Investiture Controversy, beginning in 1076, over who had the right to appoint bishops: the pope or the king. Pope Gregory VII responded by expelling Henry from the Church and deposing him as king.

Humiliation and recovery

Henry's hope that Germany's nobles would support him proved overly optimistic. Forced to concede defeat, in 1077, he made a penitential walk to Gregory at Canossa, Italy. The pope initially refused to meet Henry but later reversed his excommunication.

Emboldened by the humiliation of Henry, his German enemies rallied around his brother-in-law Rudolf. The result was a second, more serious Saxon revolt. Rudolf's army won the ensuing Battle on the Elster in 1080, but Rudolf died on the battlefield, and the revolt collapsed. With his position now

Henry IV waits, barefoot and fasting, outside Canossa Castle. Sources of the time record that he was there for three days before Gregory would meet him.

WAR IN THE MIDDLE AGES   95

See also: The Empire of Charlemagne 82–83 ▪ The Crusades 88–93 ▪ The European Crusades 102–103 ▪ The Italian Wars 120–121 ▪ European wars of religion 134–139 ▪ The Thirty Years' War 144–147 ▪ The wars of Italian unification 208–209

An emperor is subject to no one but God and Justice.
Frederick I (Barbarossa)

strengthened Henry appointed his own pope, Clement III—installed in March 1084—who then crowned Henry Holy Roman emperor. Pope Gregory appealed to Norman Sicily for support, and the knight Robert de Guiscard marched north with 35,000 men. In May, Guiscard sacked Rome, and Gregory was restored as pope.

Ongoing tensions
In 1105, Henry was forced to abdicate by his son, Henry V, who had the backing of Gregory's successor, Pope Paschal II. In 1122, the Concordat of Worms signed by Henry and Pope Callixtus II seemed to end the Investiture Controversy with a suggested separation of spiritual and secular rights; priests and monarchs would keep to their own spheres of influence.

Underlying tensions remained, however, and in 1154, German king Frederick I (Barbarossa) invaded Italy to force Pope Adrian IV to crown him Holy Roman emperor, which he did the following year. He invaded again in 1158 to quell unrest in Italy's independent-minded northern cities. In 1167, those cities formed a defensive alliance, the Lombard League.

In 1176, Frederick I was back in northern Italy to assert the power of the Holy Roman Empire. At the

The Battle of Legnano was Emperor Frederick I's fifth attempt to quell opposition in the cities of northern Italy by military means. After his defeat, he adopted a more diplomatic approach.

Battle of Legnano, near Milan, his army fought that of the Lombard League. The emperor's army had 4,000 knights armed with lances, maces, and swords. The knights of the Lombard League were quickly dispersed, but their infantry dug in behind earthworks and formed a phalanx around a *carroccio*, or large cart. The cart bore the standards of the Lombard League's constituent cities and became a rallying point for the Lombards. Presenting their long spears like pikes, they held the German force at bay, while archers and crossbowmen picked off the attackers. The Lombard knights, then regrouped, charged back into action and secured victory over the emperor's knights.

Hostilities were renewed again in the 1230s. The new emperor Frederick II was victorious over the Lombard League at the Battle of Cortenuova in 1237, but he failed to crush it. His death in 1250 marked the end of German domination over the Italian city-states. ■

German states jostle for advantage among themselves but (mostly) **defer to the emperor**.

While **the emperor** is supposedly the **overall ruler**, he derives his **divine authority** from the pope.

Heir to St. Peter, **the pope** is spiritually all-important; however, he is **weak** in **worldly power**.

Northern Italian cities, prosperous and independent-minded, are united in preferring the power of a pope over that of a (foreign) emperor.

NEVER STOP UNTIL YOUR ENEMY IS ON HIS KNEES

THE MONGOL INVASIONS (1206–1368)

THE MONGOL INVASIONS

IN CONTEXT

FOCUS
The Mongol way of war

BEFORE
220 BCE Touman becomes the first known leader of the Xiongnu, nomadic steppe people who regularly raid northern China.

916 CE Nomads from the steppes of Siberia and Mongolia, the Khitan people invade northern China and establish the Liao dynasty, which lasts until 1125.

1038 The Sino-Tibetan Tangut people create Xi Xia state in China's northwest.

AFTER
1368 Zhu Yuanzhang brings China back under Chinese rule and establishes the long-lived Ming dynasty.

1571 The Tatars—descendants of the Mongols now settled in Crimea—invade Russia and sack Moscow.

Before the appearance of Genghis Khan, [the Mongols] had no chief or ruler. Each tribe or two tribes lived separately … and there was constant fighting.
Ata-Malik Juwayni
13th-century Persian historian

At its greatest extent, in the late 13th century, the Mongol Empire had a population of about 110 million people and covered 9 million sq miles (23 million sq km). It declined and finally collapsed in the late 14th century.

Key:
■ The Mongol Empire c. 1260

Genghis Khan rose from a poor childhood, first to forge a Mongol nation then to build one of the largest land empires in history. Stretching from the Pacific Ocean to the plains of eastern Europe, it was founded in violence but went on to foster almost two centuries of peaceful trade. It did so partly at the expense of Central and West Asian Islamic dynasties that never fully recovered from the devastation wrought upon them by the Mongol invasions.

Ready for battle
Nomads from the Mongolian steppes possessed a specialized set of skills, chief of which was the ability to ride fast and with great agility. Children learned from an early age and practiced with bows and other weapons. They were also taught strength and endurance, riding for days, sleeping in the saddle, and hunting in subzero temperatures.

Until the end of the 11th century, Mongol tribes fought mainly among themselves. No one knows for sure what prompted them to set out to make war on populations to their south, east, and west. Environmental factors may have played a part; a serious drought had dried up their land, putting pressure on grazing.

Managing the Mongols
Known by his title, rather than a name, Genghis Khan ("Mightiest of Kings") was born around 1162 and called Temüjin. His father, Yesugei, a minor chieftain, died when the boy was young. Without paternal protection, Temüjin surrounded himself with a group of young fighters captivated by his charisma.

Genghis Khan showed strong political instincts. As he rose within his own tribe, then set out to recruit other Mongol tribes, he gave positions of responsibility to trusted friends and promising newcomers from the ranks, sidelining the old tribal leaders.

WAR IN THE MIDDLE AGES   99

See also: Barbarian migrations: the empire under threat 58–65 ▪ The rise of Islam 76–81 ▪ The Crusades 88–93 ▪ Timur's conquests 105 ▪ The rise of the Ottoman Turks 112–113 ▪ The Ottoman Empire 130–133 ▪ Mughal conquests in India 140–141

Likewise, he made himself popular with the people by abolishing taxes for the poorest. By the time he was 44, in 1206, he had won his title as khan of all the Mongols, creating a single people out of multiple fractious tribes.

Skills and discipline

Genghis Khan imposed a strict discipline on his army. His warriors' skills in archery and close-quarters fighting were excellent, but he always saw room for improvement and drilled his men and horses tirelessly. For the most part, Mongol troops traveled light, armored only with layers of seasoned leather. For protection, they relied on their agility in the saddle, and their skill with daggers, handaxes, and occasionally short swords. Enemies were kept at a distance with powerful composite bows made from bamboo, horn, and animal sinew. To increase his options in the field, Genghis Khan had some troops trained to fight as armoured lancers, their leather tunics stiffened with plates of iron or bone.

Even so, lightness and speed predominated. The Mongols swept through eastern Asia, taking the Tangut kingdom of Xi Xia in 1207 and sacking Beijing in 1215, before heading south into the Chinese heartland. Veering westward next, they sacked the cities of the Khwarazmian Empire, a Muslim state in the west of Central Asia occupying much of modern Iran. By 1222, they were looping back into northern India. The following year, they ventured farther north for their first foray in the southern Russian steppe. By the time Genghis Khan died in 1227, his empire extended from the Pacific Ocean to the Caspian Sea and threatened the Arab countries of the Middle East.

The Mongols' most potent weapon was terror. When Samarkand, Uzbekistan, fell to a siege in 1220, Genghis Khan ordered the wholesale slaughter of its people and had their skulls arranged into a giant pyramid. However, there was more to the Mongols' rapid advance than savagery. Genghis Khan took pains to develop his fighting force at every stage. Along with material treasures—gold, jewels, and fine fabrics—the Mongols plundered conquered territories for talent: metalsmiths, weapon makers, armorers, and engineers. The Mongol army, so renowned for its agility, was by now without equal

When [Genghis Khan] was born, he emerged clutching a clot of blood in his right hand the size of a knucklebone.
The Secret History of the Mongols
Anonymous historian, 13th century

in the most static form of warfare: siegecraft. The Mongols could fill deep moats with sandbags in minutes; they had trebuchets that could launch large rocks, barrels of flaming naphtha, or even putrefying carcasses over city walls. When the Mongols besieged Aleppo, Syria, in 1260, they brought 20 traction trebuchets to attack a »

Mongol mounted archers could shoot accurately while riding quickly. Mounted archery was a defining characteristic of steppe warfare throughout Central Asia.

single gate. These torsion-powered weapons, developed by engineers recruited in Persia and Iraq, were capable of shooting dozens of fire-arrows at a time.

Further expansion

Genghis Khan's son Ögedei continued to expand the empire, invading Russia in 1237. Three years later, he besieged and then sacked Kyiv in present-day Ukraine. As punishment for the city's resistance, he burned it and slaughtered most of the population, sparing only 2,000 of the 50,000 inhabitants. He pushed westward, dividing his army in two to mount simultaneous invasions of Poland and Hungary. On April 9, 1241, a small subsidiary force led by the Mongol general Sübedei defeated Duke Henry II's Silesian army at Legnica, Poland. Two days later, Sübedei's main force defeated Bela IV, the king of Hungary, at Mohi.

With Western Europe at the Mongols' mercy, its cities were saved by the news that Ögedei Khan had died. Every Mongol chief was called back to the homeland to elect his successor—Güyük Khan—at a general council. In northern Africa, Cairo was similarly spared in 1259. As Mongol general Hülegü's army advanced on the city, he heard that his eldest brother Möngke Khan had died—and the Mongol leaders were once more summoned to a conclave.

Islamic catastrophe

Baghdad, in Iraq, had not been so fortunate when it was besieged and sacked in 1258. Hülegü's army, which numbered more than 100,000, began its assault of the city—the capital of the Muslim Abbasid dynasty—at the end of January. The city surrendered on February 10, and Mongol forces then looted and destroyed much of it. The casualty figures are not known for certain, but modern historians estimate that at least 200,000 were slaughtered. The fall of Baghdad marked the end of the Abbasid dynasty.

The mere threat of Mongol invasion had traumatized Western Europe, but the Muslim cities of Central Asia, Mesopotamia, and Persia had faced near extinction.. On top of the massacres, palaces,

Genghis Khan's armies fought on horseback, with small but powerful bows. A required "pull" of 110–220 lb (50–100 kg) gave the fired arrows considerable penetrating power.

mosques, hospitals, and public libraries were razed to the ground. While the Islamic world had come through the Crusades and emerged largely unscathed, this invasion was much harder to endure.

A Chinese empire

In 1260, Kublai Khan won a succession struggle to replace Möngke Khan. He had long had an interest in China—occupying much of the north on behalf of his predecessor and mounting raids into Yunnan and Sichuan— and also admired Chinese culture. China's bureaucratic traditions appealed to him, as he seems to have inherited the administrative flair of Genghis, his grandfather. Rather than being a mere raider, Kublai Khan wanted to reign over a settled state.

In 1268, as if to prove that his love of Chinese civilization had not weakened him, Kublai laid siege to Xiangyang, a city on the Han River. Xiangyang was strategically important as the gateway to the heartland of the powerful Song dynasty. In an overwhelming show of force, Kublai brought up to 100,000 men and 120 trebuchets—20 of which were capable of sending 660lb (300 kg) missiles 550 yd (500 m) across the river— and blockaded the city with about 5,000 boats. Despite this immense firepower, his troops did not take Xiangyang for another five years, and both sides suffered heavy casualties. As befitted a ruler with a long-term commitment to the country, however, Kublai spared its citizens.

In 1271, Kublai Khan proclaimed himself Huangdi, or emperor, of China, establishing a capital at Beijing and a new dynasty, the Yuan. His declaration was one of intent rather than a factual statement. Most of China was still under the control of the Song dynasty, as it had been since the mid-10th century. In the years that followed, though, he fought to make his new dynasty a reality. Kublai's last victory against the Song was at sea: the Battle of Yamen (1279). His fleet cornered the Song ships, and his marines boarded and destroyed them. This was the Song dynasty's final stand.

With Kublai Khan's triumph, his Yuan dynasty became one of four khanates making up the Mongol Empire, the others being the Golden Horde, the Chagatai, and the Ilkhanate. Nominally, Kublai was khagan—emperor—of the entire empire, but in practice, each khanate pursued its own interests. After Kublai's death in 1294, the Yuan dynasty was weakened by a series of famines, devastating floods of the Yellow River, disease epidemics, peasant risings against a crippling tax burden, and political intrigues. Widespread peasant unrest eventually brought down the dynasty in 1368. ∎

> If you had not committed great sins, God would not have sent a punishment like me upon you.
> **Genghis Khan**
> to the conquered people of Bukhara, February 1220

Divine winds

The Japanese word *kamikaze*— usually associated with World War II suicide pilots—literally means "divine wind." It references two great typhoons that thwarted Kublai Khan's attempts to invade Japan in the late 13th century.

In November 1274, a large Yuan fleet landed an advance force of mostly Chinese and Korean fighters at Hakata Bay on the Japanese island of Kyushu. Its defenders, caught off guard, were quickly routed, but before the bulk of Kublai's army could be brought ashore, a typhoon hit, and his fleet was all but wiped out. History repeated itself in August 1281, when an even larger invading fleet—consisting of 4,400 ships carrying up to 70,000 soldiers and sailors—was wrecked by another typhoon. Half of the invaders drowned, and most of the rest were hunted down by samurai in the days that followed, then either killed or enslaved. This was one of the most disastrous attempts at a naval invasion in history.

The Mongol Empire lost most of its naval power in the disastrous second invasion of Japan and never tried to conquer the country again.

FORWARD, SOLDIERS OF CHRIST!
THE EUROPEAN CRUSADES (1209–1434)

IN CONTEXT

FOCUS
The rise of infantry

BEFORE
1149 The collapse of the Second Crusade underscores the limitations of Europe's mounted knights against the horseback archers in the Middle East.

1187 European knights suffer shattering defeats at Cresson and Hattin, in the Holy Land.

1202 German knights in the Fourth Crusade dismount to fight on foot with heavy swords.

AFTER
1476 Swiss pikemen and halberdiers in deep formation (at least 20 ranks deep) defeat the army of Charles the Bold, Duke of Burgundy, at the Battle of Morat.

1480 The Knights Hospitaller rely on foot soldiers to crush Mehmed II's Ottoman army at the Siege of Rhodes.

Islam was not the only enemy Christian Europe faced in the late medieval period. There were "pagans" on its northeast border and "heretics" at home. Although condemned for rejecting the Church's religious doctrine, the heretics' real offense was their condemnation of the Church for its wealth and close ties to European rulers. The authorities—secular and religious—knew that such criticism was destabilizing. The idea of launching a crusade against them, as they had against Islam in the Holy Land, began to take shape.

We therefore grant to those who fight with might and courage against the aforesaid pagans, one year's remission of the sins they confess.
Pope Alexander III
on the crusade against the Estonians and Finns, 1171

Among these heretical sects were the Cathars, who despised not just worldly institutions and material wealth but the human body, too, spurning all its feelings and desires as vile. Spreading westward from the Balkans, by the 13th century, the Cathars had found adherents all across Europe, but especially in the Languedoc region of southern France.

Call to arms
In 1209, Pope Innocent III called for a crusade against the French town of Albi, where Catharism flourished. His summons was answered by knights from northern France, drawn by the prospect of securing salvation—and plunder. The knights equipped themselves as though they were fighting in the Holy Land, with a steed, chain mail and armor, a lance, and a heavy sword. Rather than the swift horses, swords, and arrows of the Turks, however, they found themselves facing disorganized peasants, who were armed at best with scythes and pitchforks. The crusading knights threw themselves into their task with genocidal energy, killing 20,000 people in the town of Béziers alone.

WAR IN THE MIDDLE AGES

See also: The rise of Islam 76–81 ▪ The Empire of Charlemagne 82–83 ▪ The Crusades 88–93 ▪ European wars of religion 134–139

In the Battle of the Ice, depicted here in a medieval manuscript, the Teutonic Knights were overrun by Novgorod infantry and archers after their horses lost their footing on frozen Lake Peipus.

In 1226, Holy Roman Emperor Frederick II granted the Teutonic Knights (an armed religious order) a fiefdom in exchange for their help in conquering the people of Prussia. Four years later, Pope Gregory IX licensed the knights to convert the Prussians "on Christ's behalf". Continuing their Prussian Crusade, the Teutonic Knights spearheaded an attack on the pagan peoples of the Baltic area.

Next, on their own initiative, the Knights launched a crusade against followers of the Orthodox Church in Russia—fellow Christians. They took the port city of Novgorod in 1240 but were halted two years later by Prince Alexander Nevsky's infantry in the Battle on the Ice, on the border between Russia and Estonia.

When this campaign—known as the Albigensian Crusade after the people of Albi—ended in 1229, the knights had slaughtered more than 200,000 men, women, and children.

Pacifying the pagans

In Europe's northeast, much of the Baltic region and eastern Prussia had yet to convert to Christianity or accept the authority of adjacent Christian states. In 1147, the Holy Roman Empire mounted its first Northern Crusade against the Wends (Polabian Slavs), around modern Mecklenburg, in Germany. The expedition met with limited success, but forced some defeated Slavs to embrace Catholicism. It also prompted further campaigns against the Wends and pagans in other Baltic countries.

Hussite rebellion

In 1415, the Catholic Council of Constance sentenced Bohemian religious reformer Jan Hus to be burned at the stake as a heretic. Hus had clearly departed from Catholic orthodoxy, but his main offence was exposing Church corruption. His execution enraged his followers, who rebelled against the Bohemian Crown and the Holy Roman Empire. From 1419 onward, Pope Martin V ordered a series of crusades against the Hussites. The wars ended in 1434, the Church finally had to compromise, and in 1436 the Council of Basel agreed that Bohemian priests would be allowed to introduce limited reforms. ▪

Combating cavalry

The Hussites could be considered forerunners of the Protestant Reformation. Following the execution of Jan Hus in 1415, they rebelled against the Holy Roman Empire and the papacy.

During the ensuing Hussite Wars (1419–1434), the rebels fought almost exclusively on foot, and they would have had no chance against the German knights—on horseback and in heavy armor—had they not had handheld firearms: pipe guns, or *Pfeifenbüchsen*, and small cannon. They often fired these from the shelter of the *Wagenburgen* ("wagon forts"), created by arranging farm carts into an impromptu fortress, which broke the force of the enemy's cavalry charge.

Firearms and wagon forts proved indispensable in 1421, at the Battle of Kutná Hora (in modern-day Czechia). Here the Hussites used both to break out of an encirclement by the cavalry of the Holy Roman Empire army, led by Sigismund, king of Bohemia.

Martin Luther, the later German religious reformer, cries, "Ich bin ein Hussite" ("I am a Hussite") during a debate in Leipzig, Germany, in 1519.

A VAST WALLED STRONGHOLD
ZIMBABWEAN KINGDOMS (c. 1220–1450)

IN CONTEXT

FOCUS
Trade in Great Zimbabwe

BEFORE
c. 600 CE Arab and Persian merchants trade gold, ivory, leopard skin, and enslaved people from the Swahili coast of East Africa.

c. 650 Iron is produced at the Leopard's Kopje settlement in southwestern Zimbabwe.

c. 1075 The kingdom of Mapungubwe emerges at the confluence of the rivers Shashe and Limpopo, south of Bulawayo.

AFTER
c. 1575 Portuguese settlers encroach on the trading territory of the Mutapa people, leading to the decline of their civilization.

c. 1600 The Torwa dynasty of Butua has some success in pushing back against Portuguese settlers.

The imposing stone ruins of Great Zimbabwe—the only stone construction of this time in southern Africa—testify to the splendor of the Shona civilization that emerged during the 13th century. Built on mining and farming, the city, west of Lake Mutirikwi, was the hub of a vast network of routes along which gold and ivory were traded.

As many as 20,000 people lived in Great Zimbabwe in the 14th and 15th centuries. Mud-brick homes have not survived, but excavations have unearthed glass beads from Persia (Iran), porcelain from China, and Arab coins, the small change from transactions with merchants from the Red Sea and Persian Gulf.

The bronze spearheads and iron arrowheads found among the ruins suggest the need for protecting this wealth. Wars between neighboring states were frequent, and civil strife and coups within ruling families even more so. It was after one such dispute about supremacy that, around 1430, one of the princes of Great Zimbabwe, Nyatsimba Mutota, advanced north to found his own civilization, Mutapa.

Power shifted as cities and ruling dynasties rose and fell, and these transitions appear to have been marked by war. Decades later, visiting Portuguese merchants noted the area's political volatility. Competition from European traders put additional pressure on these states. In time, it probably led to their downfall. ∎

The Great Enclosure at Great Zimbabwe dates from the 14th century and may have been a royal palace. Its stone walls are 33 ft (10 m) high in places.

See also: Warfare in northern Africa 126–127 ▪ The British conquest of India 225 ▪ Imperial wars in Africa 226–229 ▪ An expanding war 252–255

FEARING FOR THEIR LIVES, THEY ABANDONED ALL ELSE
TIMUR'S CONQUESTS (1381–1400)

IN CONTEXT

FOCUS
Terror as a weapon of war

BEFORE
55 BCE Julius Caesar claims to have killed 430,000 people in a rebellious Celtic community during the Gallic Wars. Modern historians believe this figure is much exaggerated.

1221 CE Genghis Khan massacres the population of Nishapur, Iran—as many as 1.75 million people—to avenge the killing of his son-in-law.

AFTER
c. 1450 Vlad III ("Vlad the Impaler") of Wallachia, in the Carpathian Mountains, sets his slaughtered enemies on sharpened wooden stakes.

1510 The Safavid conquest of Herat brings the Timurid Empire to an end. Shah Ismail has the Uzbek Khan's body dismembered for display around his realms.

Born in 1336, Timur was a member of the Barlas clan, a nomadic Turkic group from Transoxiana, in modern-day Uzbekistan. A disabling injury sustained in 1363 left him with the nickname "Timur the Lame," but it did not prevent him from acting on his genocidal tendencies and implementing his terror tactics.

On his first campaign, heading west toward Persia in 1381, Timur destroyed the city of Herat (in northeastern Afghanistan), and massacred its inhabitants. In 1387, the city of Isfahan (in present-day Iran) rebelled against Timur's tax policies. Chronicles of the time record that Timur ordered every one of his soldiers to bring him a head. They collected 70,000, which they piled up in pyramids before the city walls.

Relentless atrocities

By 1398, Timur was advancing on Delhi—then a Muslim sultanate. The night before he took the city, he had 100,000 Hindu prisoners executed, fearing they might take advantage of the coming confusion to rise up against him. In 1400, he took Sivas, in eastern Anatolia (now Türkiye), after a short siege. He spared the city's Muslim defenders but showed no mercy to 3,000 Armenian Christians, who were cruelly buried alive.

Timur died while on campaign in 1405. Despite his reputation for cruelty, he was a brilliant military commander and a great patron of the arts and architecture. ■

Tall towers were built out of their skulls and their bodies became food for birds and wild animals.
Sharaf al-din Ali Yazdi
Persian historian, on the Sack of Delhi

See also: The rise of Islam 76–81 ■ The rise of the Ottoman Turks 112–113 ■ The Ottoman Empire 130–133 ■ Mughal conquests in India 140–141

ONCE MORE UNTO THE BREACH, DEAR FRIENDS
THE HUNDRED YEARS' WAR (1337–1453)

IN CONTEXT

FOCUS
Bows and cannon

BEFORE
c. 3350 BCE "Ötzi," a man preserved in a glacier in the Italian Alps and discovered in 1991, carries a longbow.

c. 800 CE Japanese samurai horsemen shoot arrows from 8 ft (2.5 m) long *yumi* (wooden bows).

1139 In England, the Church's Lateran Council outlaws the "murderous art of crossbowmen and archers."

AFTER
1508 Scotland's King James IV popularizes the hand culverin, a smaller, portable variant of the cannon.

c. 1515 *L'art d'archerie* (*The Art of Archery*), a treatise on the use of the longbow, is published in France.

Really a series of separate wars between the kings of England and France over territorial rights, the Hundred Years' War went on for rather more than a century. While the quarrel remained substantially the same, the technological and tactical developments the conflict brought were to change the face of warfare. By the war's end, the longbow, England's most effective weapon in a succession of important victories, had been superseded by hand-cannon and heavier artillery.

People held medieval monarchs in higher honor than the lands over which they reigned. The idea of the nation state was not yet fully

WAR IN THE MIDDLE AGES 107

See also: The Crusades 88–93 ▪ The European Crusades 102–103 ▪ The rise of the Ottoman Turks 112–113 ▪ The Italian Wars 120–121 ▪ Japan in the Sengoku era 128–129

The Battle of Sluys proved disastrous for the French, who lost 190 of their 230 ships, 166 of them captured by the English. As a result, the English had complete mastery over the Channel.

formed, so people thought there was nothing absurd about an English king claiming the crown of France. This was the case when Edward III asserted his right to Philip VI's French throne, arguing it was his just inheritance from his grandfather Philip IV. His sense of entitlement flared into rage when, in 1337, Philip confiscated the Duchy of Aquitaine, to which Edward's mother, Isabella of France, still held title.

A land battle at sea
In 1340, Edward promised the people of Flanders—a territory claimed by Philip—that he would defend them against encroachments by the French. That summer, he crossed the North Sea to fulfill this pledge. His fleet met that of France off Sluys (now Sluis, in Dutch Zeeland). Neither side's commanders being comfortable with the art of naval warfare, they fought what amounted to a land battle at sea. The French sailors chained their ships together, making their decks a wooden battlefield. Weakening French resolve with a continuous rain of arrows as they approached, the English then boarded the vessels and engaged in hand-to-hand fighting. By the time the French surrendered, they had lost 18,000 men; the English, by contrast, lost only a few hundred.

Edward's extraordinary victory was tempered by the realities of his financial situation. It took him until 1346 to marshal the men and raise the funding to mount a full-scale invasion of France. Another obstacle presented itself when he landed near Calais with an army of mounted knights, supported by spear-carrying infantry and archers—a force ill equipped to besiege and take a walled city. For the moment, this seemed not to matter. Skirting the city, he led his army inland. They then carried out a *chevauchée* ("horse charge"), careering through the country, burning, looting, and laying waste to the land. Though negligible in its effects on the economy or Philip's military capacities, the attack increased the popular pressure on the French king for action.

A potent weapon
Between 5 and 6 ft (1.5–1.8 m) long, the English longbow was a simple strip of yew or other hardwood, not a composite bow (made from wood, horn, and sinew) of the type traditionally used by nomads from the Eurasian steppes. It could shoot an arrow well over 328 yds (300 m), and while it was hardly accurate at this distance, bowmen could carpet an advancing enemy in lethal fire. Although the highest-quality steel armor withstood their tips at longer ranges, arrows could pierce mail or cheaper cast-iron plate. Young men in English and »

Then the English archers stept forth one pace and let fly their arrows so wholly and so thick that it seemed snow.
Jean Froissart
Chronicles, 14th century

THE HUNDRED YEARS' WAR

Welsh villages were for generations required to turn out for regular archery practice so that this skill could be maintained.

Courage at Crécy

The longbow was to be the decisive weapon in Edward's victory at Crécy, 62 miles (100 km) south of Calais, in 1346. The French army vastly outnumbered the English, but many of Philip's 40,000 foot soldiers were untrained, his 2,000–6,000 crossbowmen were experienced but uncommitted Genoese mercenaries, and his 8,000 knights were divided by factional indiscipline. Edward lined up his forces along a ridge, thus gaining the advantage of height over the advancing French. He reinforced his forward line of 7,000 longbowmen with spearmen, men-at-arms, and knights. Edward commanded the reserve in the center of the English position, while the left was assigned to the Earl of Northampton and the right to his son, Edward the "Black Prince." The English also had a few cannon—their first known appearance on a European battlefield, though they were not to make much of an impression at Crécy.

> Of the love or hatred God has for the English I know nothing, but I do know that they will all be thrown out of France, except those who die there.
>
> **Joan of Arc**
> at her trial, 1431

Seeing that the English had halted, ready to do battle, the French troops pressed forward so eagerly that their formations quickly fell apart. Both contingents of bowmen unleashed extended salvos, each seeking to demoralize the other's army. The English archers could shoot much farther than France's crossbowmen, and also three times faster. A crossbowman had to crank each bolt up to perfect tightness before he could shoot, while a longbowman just had to slip another arrow on to his string. Unable to take this onslaught, the crossbowmen fled, alarming the French infantry, whose progress faltered. Many were then trampled underfoot by mounted French knights, who charged forward in exasperation, only to be mowed down by the English archers before being set upon by English infantry at close quarters. By the time the fight was over, the French had lost 1,500 knights and several thousand infantrymen, while the English had lost just two knights and fewer than 300 foot soldiers.

Siege struggles

Only now did Edward turn his attention back to Calais, which he subjected to a nine-month siege. As the warring sides in the Crusades (1095–1270) had found, a highly capable force of infantry and cavalry did not guarantee success against a well-fortified, staunchly defended city. It took almost a year for Edward's force to starve Calais into submission. Finally taking the town in August 1347, he brought in settlers to make it an English outpost on French soil.

The arrival of the Black Death in October 1347 now compelled a break in the hostilities. Over the

Joan of Arc

Born around 1412, in Domrémy, northeast France, to propertied farmers Jacques d'Arc and Isabelle Romée, Jeanne d'Arc (Joan of Arc) was to become the heroine of the Siege of Orléans. She claimed to have seen her first visions of saints when she was 13 years old and three years later heard a "voice" telling her to go to Orléans and lift the English siege.

Joan of Arc believed God had promised to lead her countrymen to victory over the English. She was taken before King Charles VII, who was impressed by her conviction. Even so, a committee of priests interrogated her to ascertain her Catholic orthodoxy. That test passed, she could fight for France and for her faith. She was wounded at Orléans but inspired the French to victory.

After her success at Orléans, Joan of Arc was captured by Burgundian troops who sold her to their English allies. In 1431, she was tried for witchcraft and burned at the stake. Pope Pius X beatified her in 1909.

next few years, the bubonic plague killed up to a third of Europe's population. By the mid-1350s, however, fighting had resumed, the Black Prince blazing a trail of destruction through northern France in another *chevauchée*.

Another archery victory
In 1356, under King John II, the French confronted the English at Poitiers, in west-central France. As at Crécy, the French army massively outnumbered England's, yet the English longbow won the day. This time, France lost 4,500 knights to England's 40, though infantry losses were high for both.

A few brief flare-ups aside, a lengthy lull in the fighting followed. Not until the accession of Henry V to the English throne, in 1413, was war renewed in earnest. Henry's plan on landing in August 1415 depended on him capturing the port of Harfleur, but once again the English were ill equipped to mount a siege. This one lasted only six weeks, but it took them too close to the end of the usual fighting season. Henry decided to head north to the English outpost at Calais to sit out the winter.

> **Longbows** have a long range and can be **quickly loaded and discharged**.
>
>
>
> While **crossbows offer greater accuracy**, they have a **slightly reduced range**. They are also **slower to load**.
>
>
>
> The **introduction of the cannon** makes it possible to cause **more destruction with less effort** than a bow requires.

The French marched out to engage with the English army and headed it off along the Somme River, forcing a confrontation near Azincourt on October 25. But the Battle of Agincourt (as the English called it) was to be another demonstration of prowess on the part of England's longbowmen and another bloody rout for the French.

Most of France's casualties (6,000 out of 7,000) were knights. Their armor had not protected them, nor had they got close enough to the enemy to test their fighting skills. The days of the knight-at-arms were clearly numbered. It was also obvious to Henry that his troops had to develop a new set of skills if they were to take walled cities.

Artillery takes over
The English used artillery at the Siege of Orléans, in central France, in 1428–1429. However, technology was trumped there by the charisma of Joan of Arc, who led the city's defenders to victory.

By now, it was evident that firearms were the future. It was also clear that longbowmen were no more suited to siege warfare than knights—and both were vulnerable to the cannon, which was constantly improving. England's archers could make no headway against French artillery at Castillon, near Bordeaux, in July 1453. Cutting a swathe through the English forces, French cannon fire ended England's hopes of recovering territories in France and, finally, brought the Hundred Years' War to a conclusion. ∎

English and French archers clash at Agincourt, as depicted in a 15th-century painting. The English were, in fact, some distance from the French when they inflicted the decisive damage.

PEACE AMONG CHRISTIANS AND WAR AGAINST THE INFIDEL
THE SPANISH RECONQUISTA (c. 1100–1492)

IN CONTEXT

FOCUS
Forging a Spanish national identity

BEFORE
711 CE An expeditionary force from Morocco lands in Gibraltar, beginning the Muslim conquest of the Iberian peninsula.

c. 720 Pelagius, king of Asturias, defeats the Moors in northern Spain. It is the first step toward the Reconquista.

AFTER
1492 Christopher Columbus reaches the Americas. The Spanish colonization of the New World—and the Christian conversion of its peoples—is considered a continuation of the Reconquista.

1936 General Franco's military uprising and the subsequent adoption of a national Catholic identity in Spain are promoted as a renewal of Reconquista ideals.

It took about two decades for the Muslim Moorish invaders from North Africa to occupy the Iberian peninsula, but more than 700 years to drive them out again. The war to expel them was long and tortuous, and its politics complex, but the Reconquista ("reconquest") became a foundation myth for modern Spain.

An abstract idea as much as a war, the Reconquista was initially a piecemeal struggle, with local Christian rulers fighting for their own territories. When a wider perspective emerged, the war came to be regarded as a crusade, an idea rooted in comparable religious conflicts in the Holy Land and northern Europe.

Fighting a common enemy

In the Middle Ages, there was no such state as Spain. However, the quarrelsome collection of Christian kingdoms gradually extending their territories south from the Pyrenees found common cause in their fight against the occupying Moors.

In 739, Alfonso I was crowned king of Asturias, a tiny realm in the northernmost part of the peninsula, which the Moors had never taken. His successors extended the kingdom westward into Galicia and southward into León. By 1085, the ruler of what was now the separate kingdom of León and Castile had taken the city of Toledo back from the Moors, and in 1118 the king of Aragon took Zaragoza. The 1236 capture of Córdoba was another breakthrough, since this city had long been one of the jewels of Islamic Spain.

The expulsion of the Moors was a continuous, if slow, process, with armies mobilizing on both sides every spring before disbanding in time for the summer harvest.

The churches and towers where they used to praise God, now in the same places they called upon Mahomet.
13th-century chronicle of Spain

WAR IN THE MIDDLE AGES

See also: The rise of Islam 76–81 ▪ The Crusades 88–93 ▪ The European Crusades 102–103 ▪ The European conquest of the Americas 122–125 ▪ European wars of religion 134–139 ▪ The Thirty Years' War 144–147

Rather than a single all-out war, it played out in a series of local skirmishes, raids, and sieges that saw Christian Spain gradually expand over the centuries. Great castles were built to pin down recaptured territories; walled cities sprang up along new frontiers.

However, the Reconquista was by no means a linear process. Strategic cities were hotly disputed and frequently changed hands. Valencia, recovered by Rodrigo Díaz de Vivar ("El Cid") in 1094, fell to the Moors again in 1102, only to be taken back by James I of Aragon in 1238. The Christian kings spent as much time fighting one another as they did the Muslims, at times even forging strategic alliances with local Muslim governors.

A national cause

Ferdinand II of Aragon and Isabella I of Castile combined their kingdoms when they married in 1469, thereby uniting most of the country for the first time. Fired up with Catholic zeal, they pushed on to complete the expulsion of the Moors, recapturing their final outpost, Granada, in 1492. By this time, they had extended their campaign against non-Christian influences and initiated the wholesale persecution of the country's Jews.

By uniting to expel the various "foreigners" and suppress their religions, Spain had found its guiding principle and identity. It had also embraced what was to be a long-standing paranoia about enemies within—hence the fanaticism with which the Spanish Inquisition rooted out heresy from 1478 onward. ∎

The siege of Granada by Christian forces in 1491 ended with the city's surrender and the Treaty of Granada, signed by Boabdil (left), its last sultan, and Ferdinand and Isabella (right).

El Cid

Born near Burgos around 1043, El Cid ("The Chief") served both Ferdinand I of Castile and his son Sancho II, whose territory he helped expand at the expense of Sancho's brother Alfonso VI. In 1072, when Alfonso became king, he forced El Cid into exile. Working as a mercenary for the Muslim Banu Hud dynasty, which ruled Zaragoza, El Cid took up arms against Christian Aragon.

In the epic poem *El Cantar de Mio Cid* (*The Song of My Cid*), El Cid cuts a heroic, glamorous figure, fighting valiantly for his honor and his comrades and for the restoration of Christian rule in Spain. The real-life leader was a more complex character, embodying not just the heroism of the Reconquista but also its contradictions.

It is true that El Cid struck a serious blow against Moorish rule by taking Valencia in 1094, after a 20-month siege, but he had switched sides several times before that. El Cid died in Valencia in 1099.

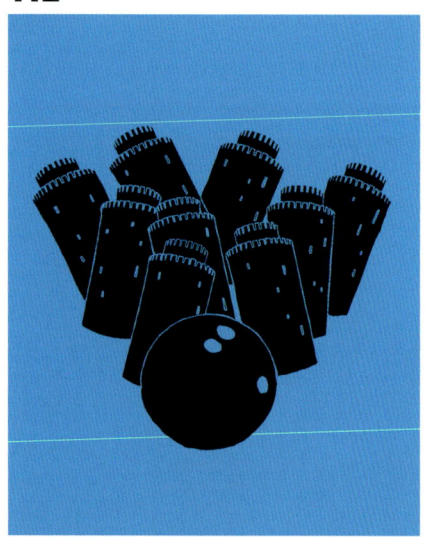

A CANNON, WHICH NO WALL ... COULD RESIST
THE RISE OF THE OTTOMAN TURKS
(c. 1396–c. 1455)

IN CONTEXT

FOCUS
Changing Ottoman fortunes

BEFORE
c. 900 CE Instability in Central Asia sends waves of migration to the west.

c. 950 The Oghuz Turks move into what is now western Kazakhstan, where they embrace Islam.

1071 A victory for the Seljuk Turks at Manzikert, Anatolia, throws the eastern Byzantine Empire into confusion.

AFTER
1459 Under Mehmed II, the Ottomans complete their conquest of Serbia.

1463 Mehmed II brings Bosnia into his growing Ottoman Empire.

1479 The Republic of Venice loses Albania to the Ottomans after a 14-year war but later takes Cyprus from them.

The 15th century saw the Ottoman Turks steadily encroaching on Byzantine territory. They were the latest in a succession of steppe nomad peoples advancing into Eurasia. Since their mounted archers did not have suitable weaponry to attack walled cities, they were forced to master siege artillery techniques. Their new firepower proved highly effective.

1280s: The Ottomans emerge as a **peripheral power** to the east of the **Byzantine Empire**.

↓

1300s: Constantinople is more or less **surrounded by Ottoman forces**.

↓

1360s: Ottoman conquest of Thrace and the Balkans leaves **Constantinople isolated** in Turkish territory.

↓

1453: Mehmed II finally closes in on Constantinople and the city falls.

Strengths and weaknesses
The Ottoman Turks arose as a power in 1281, when Osman I came to prominence in Bursa, Anatolia. Skilled horsemen with a warring heritage, they launched a series of attacks into Bithynia, along Anatolia's Black Sea coast. Contemporary Byzantine writer Georgios Pachymeres describes how "500 of the enemy" captured one fortress at night, having escaped detection. Their ruthless treatment of civilians created widespread fear. Pachymeres adds that the Ottomans cut down "an innumerable crowd" of women and children.

While devastating for the settled population, the Ottomans' strategy of using speed and surprise to take towns and forts had its limitations. They could quickly take control in rural areas, but they lacked the necessary weapons for success in regions that were properly fortified.

See also: The Byzantine Empire 70–73 ■ Timur's conquests 105 ■ The Ottoman Empire 130–133 ■ Ottoman decline and Russian expansion 232–233

Either I shall take this city or the city will take me, dead or alive … The city is all I want, even if it is empty.
Mehmed II
Letter to Emperor Constantine XI, 1453

In 1302, Osman overpowered a Byzantine army at Bapheus, southeast of Constantinople; the road to the Byzantine capital now lay clear. However, while the Byzantines could not match the Ottomans' ferocity and fighting skills in open battle, their garrisons and urban populations were still largely safe, holed up in strongly fortified cities. In 1329, Osman's son Orhan I beat the Byzantines at Pelekanon, near what is now Istanbul, but the essential difficulty remained.

Taking advantage of an earthquake in 1354, Orhan's son Murad I mounted an expedition across the Bosphorus to Gallipoli, seizing its fortress. The Turks now held an important link from Asia Minor into Europe. By the 1360s, Murad had occupied Thrace and the Balkans. Constantinople now stood isolated—but still safe. In 1394, Bayezid I, Murad's successor as Ottoman sultan, brought war engines, including trebuchets, to bear on the Byzantine capital but was thwarted.

The Turks transformed

Ottoman power waned for a while due to internal divisions, but in 1452, Mehmed II built the Rumelihisarı fortress on the west shore of the Bosphorus, specifically to bar Constantinople's access to the sea.

Tightening the blockade still further, Mehmed began his final attack the following year, with 60,000–80,000 men and more than 300 ships. His men dragged 70 of the ships on rollers to the city's inner harbor overnight to provide a platform on that side of the city for some of his heavy guns. The Byzantines held out bravely: it took the Ottomans 55 days to wear them down, but finally, on May 29, 1453, Mehmed's Turks broke through the walls and took the city. From this new capital—renamed Istanbul—they continued to build their empire, a dominant force in the region for several centuries. ■

Constantinople's walls were the most formidable of any European city, but after a long Ottoman siege, a combined artillery, infantry, and naval assault breached the fortifications.

From Osman's dream to Orban's vision

The Ottomans' founder, Osman I, is said to have had a dream in which the moon rose from the sash of a holy sage, flew across the heavens, and set itself on his own chest; a tall tree then sprang from his navel, shading mountains and streams. Although almost certainly concocted in the 14th century, this dream is said to suggest the Ottomans' ruling destiny: the moon symbolizes Osman's dynasty; the trees, his empire. In fact, the secret to their success was a readiness to learn and adapt.

The Ottomans' triumph was arguably down to Orban. An expert-for-hire, this Hungarian engineer had offered his services to the Byzantines, but they had refused his wage demands. Orban's giant cannon, which was used at Constantinople, had a muzzle diameter of 30 in (76 cm) and could fire 1,200 lb (540 kg) cannonballs as far as 1 mile (1.6 km). It needed 60 oxen to move it.

THE FLOWERY DEATH BY THE OBSIDIAN KNIFE
THE AZTECS AND INCAS (c. 1400s–1520s)

IN CONTEXT

FOCUS
Mesoamerican empires

BEFORE
500 BCE An early civilization centered on Chavín de Huántar, in the Peruvian Andes, breaks down in violent disorder.

c. 400 CE Armies from Teotihuacán, in the Valley of Mexico, make conquests—and take prisoners for sacrifice—to the north and south.

900 The Toltec Empire becomes the dominant military power throughout the Valley of Mexico.

AFTER
1572 The "Last Inca," Túpac Amaru, is executed after his rebellion against the Spanish fails.

1967 Inspired by Túpac Amaru, left-wing guerrillas in Uruguay adopt the name Tupamaros for their fight against an oppressive state.

The Aztec civilization came into existence in the Valley of Mexico in 1428, after the rival city-states of Tetzcoco and Tlacopan allied with Tenochtitlán. Expansionist from the outset, the new state became the preeminent power in the region. It was highly militaristic and brought up its males as warriors from a young age.

Battle tactics
Advancing into battle at a rush, the Aztecs banged drums and yelled loudly to intimidate their enemy. They showered them with stones and darts to weaken their defenses as they approached. Warriors used *atlatls*, or spear-throwing tools, to project javelins over considerable distances; these devices had been used by hunters in the Americas since the earliest times.

Often, sheer terror put the opposing force to flight, but the Aztecs were capable of fighting at close quarters as well. For this, they used heavier spears and stone-bladed knives for stabbing and, like the earlier Maya, wielded wooden *macuahuitl* clubs, with projecting razor-sharp obsidian blades. For armor, they relied on quilted cotton tunics and carried shields of wood or woven reeds.

When they were going to war … they wore strings of human teeth that were from the enemies that they themselves or their ancestors had slain.
Father Bernabé Cobo
Inca Religion and Customs (1653)

Imperialism in the Andes
Emerging in the early 13th century, the Inca civilization centered on the Altiplano—a high Andes plateau spanning parts of Bolivia, Chile, and Peru. It was not until 1438, however, when Pachacuti became Sapa Inca ("Unique King"), claiming divine status as Intip Churin ("Son of the Sun"), that the Inca state took shape. At its peak, it extended over 770,000 sq miles (2 million sq km) across Peru, Bolivia, Ecuador, and Chile.

WAR IN THE MIDDLE AGES 115

See also: The Maya civilization 74–75 ▪ The European conquest of the Americas 122–125 ▪ The conquest of North America 222–223

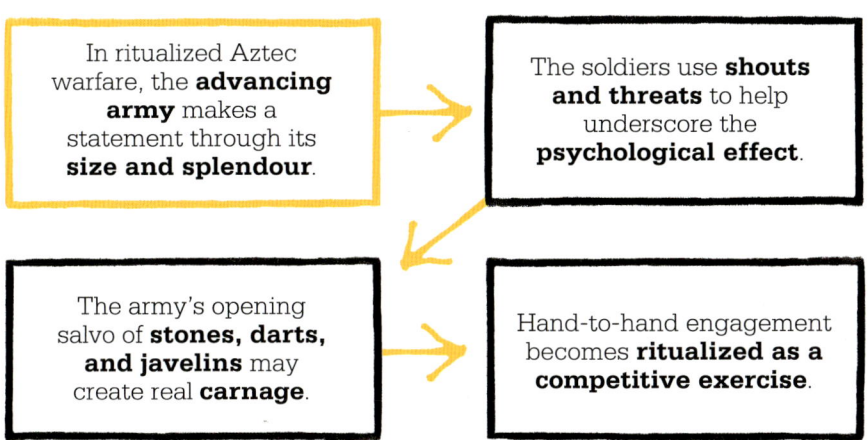

- In ritualized Aztec warfare, the **advancing army** makes a statement through its **size and splendour**.
- The soldiers use **shouts and threats** to help underscore the **psychological effect**.
- The army's opening salvo of **stones, darts, and javelins** may create real **carnage**.
- Hand-to-hand engagement becomes **ritualized as a competitive exercise**.

Inca expansion was partly peaceful, partly military—though the two were not easily distinguished, so ritualistic was their way of waging war. The arrival of an army in the field was primarily a show of strength and a display of wealth. Wearing their finest jewelery over ponchos or tunics, warriors carried their emperor into battle on a litter. Confronted with their enemy, they danced, chanted, and shouted.

Fighting for real

Inca warfare was by no means all posturing. Close up, Andean soldiers fought with heavy clubs of bronze or stone, their handles made of wood, about 3 ft (1 m) long. They carried leather shields and wore plates of gold, silver, or copper over their chests and backs, though the cotton padding of their clothing probably did more to cushion blows. Cane helmets provided some protection for the head, but it was more important to be able to dodge the hail of stones, thrown by hand or hurled by slingshot, or the boulders rolled down mountainsides.

Inca warriors used bows to shoot arrows and, like the Aztecs, they also threw wooden javelins. Inca battle tactics were relatively sophisticated, including ambushes, flanking maneuvers, feints, and counterattacks. Soldiers were called up from the general male population on a rotational basis. Generally, armies probably numbered no more than a few thousand, though on occasion as many as 100,000 might have been put into the field. ■

Long-serving Aztec warriors went into battle wearing a feathered suit or a jaguar skin, as shown in this drawing from the 16th-century *Florentine Codex*.

The "flower war"

Aztec warfare often stopped short of deadly violence, with warriors content to stage a show of strength and advertise their individual prowess in a ritual battle known as a "flower war." During these ceremonial clashes, which were always prearranged, each warring party would field the same number of soldiers. They were usually noblemen and elite warriors who would fight each other at close quarters with a *macuahuitl*. Outwitted opponents were typically taken prisoner rather than killed in battle.

However, the bloodshed here was just deferred. Like the Maya, the Aztecs believed that divine destruction might be kept at bay by the regular offering of human sacrifices. The need to maintain supplies was a major driver of the war machine. Blood sacrifice was especially important in inaugurating a new reign. The waging of a "coronation war" allowed the ruler to demonstrate his dominance and gather slaves for sacrifice.

Aztec priests remove the hearts of defeated enemies to offer them to the gods in this image from the 16th-century *Codex Magliabechiano*.

EARLY M
WARFAR
1500–1775

ODERN
E

INTRODUCTION

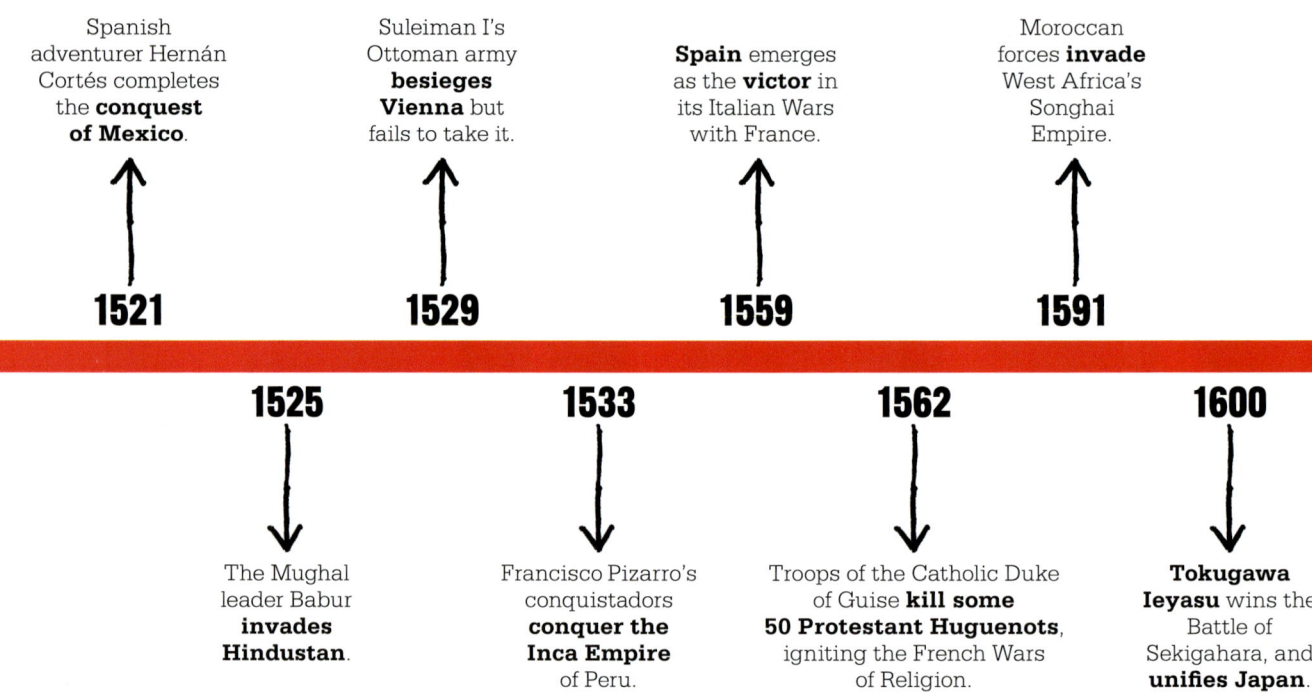

From the early 16th century, firearms began to play a key role in many wars. Factors fueling conflict included religion, the internal politics of nations, fluctuating relations between countries, and territorial expansion in the New World and Africa.

The power of the gun
In the Italian Wars (1494–1459), for control of Italy, Spain prevailed over rival Italian states and France. This was largely due to the skills of its *terciers*—elite infantrymen, who advanced into battle ahead of other troops and fired harquebuses (long-barreled guns) into the ranks of their opponents. Spanish troops had an even greater advantage in Latin America, whose Indigenous peoples had no firearms. Tiny bands of conquistadors, armed with guns, defeated armies of Aztecs in Mexico and Incas in Peru. Europeans also unwittingly brought diseases such as smallpox, which devastated the Indigenous populations of the New World. In North America, tribes had traded with early settlers but were soon fighting for their lives as their land was seized and culture erased.

The import of European firearms helped Oda Nobunaga, a feudal lord in Japan, to capture Kyoto in 1560, setting the course for Japanese unification 40 years later. The guns of Morocco's army were also key to its victory over the West African Songhai Empire, which had none.

Religious rivalries
Opposing faiths continued to be a cause and pretext for conflict, fueled by the spread of firearms. Islam, a driver for military conquests, was still expanding. Since taking Constantinople in 1453, the Ottoman Turks had extended Islamic rule over the Byzantine Empire's European territories. Ottoman craftsmen produced the most accurate muskets and cannons of the era; and their janissaries—an elite military unit of initially non-Turkish Christians—were especially skilled in their use. Firearms helped the Ottomans defeat the forces of Safavid Iran (which did not yet have them), and those of Egypt and Arabia. In 1529, the Ottomans' siege of Vienna failed, but they suffered no further major defeats until 1571, when they lost the Battle of Lepanto to a Christian fleet.

With gunpowder weapons supplementing the traditional bows of steppe warfare, Muslim Mughals

EARLY MODERN WARFARE

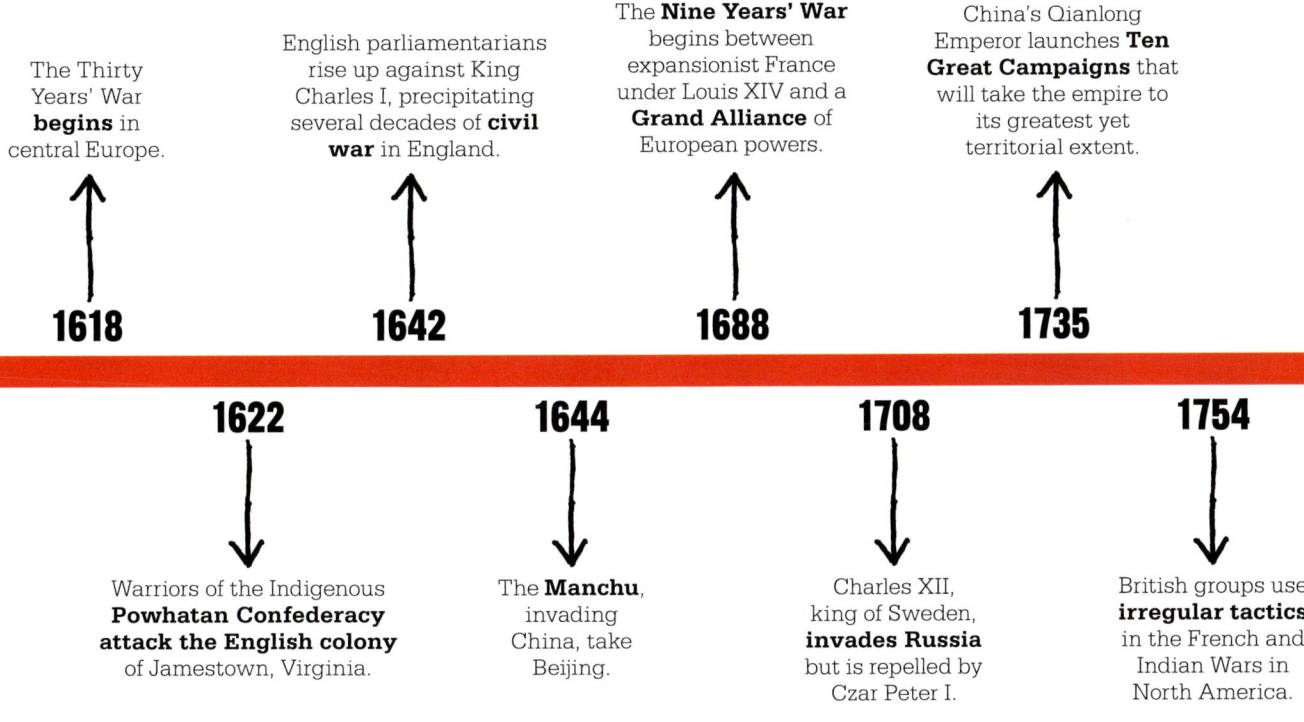

- **1618** — The Thirty Years' War **begins** in central Europe.
- **1622** — Warriors of the Indigenous **Powhatan Confederacy attack the English colony** of Jamestown, Virginia.
- **1642** — English parliamentarians rise up against King Charles I, precipitating several decades of **civil war** in England.
- **1644** — The **Manchu**, invading China, take Beijing.
- **1688** — The **Nine Years' War** begins between expansionist France under Louis XIV and a **Grand Alliance** of European powers.
- **1708** — Charles XII, king of Sweden, **invades Russia** but is repelled by Czar Peter I.
- **1735** — China's Qianlong Emperor launches **Ten Great Campaigns** that will take the empire to its greatest yet territorial extent.
- **1754** — British groups use **irregular tactics** in the French and Indian Wars in North America.

from Central Asia conquered northern India in the 1520s. They extended their land via alliances with Hindu princes, as well as by force, founding the Mughal Empire, known for its religious tolerance. Aurangzeb (r. 1658–1707) imposed a stricter interpretation of Islam.

Christendom suffered internal tensions after the Reformation, the rise of churches that challenged the spiritual monopoly of the Roman Catholic Church and gave rise to new, sectarian enmities. In France, thousands of Protestant Huguenots were killed on St. Bartholomew's Day in 1572. The Protestant Dutch revolted against their Catholic Spanish ruler. Spain was also drawn into conflict against the Protestant English, who scored a resounding naval victory against the Spanish Armada in 1588.

In 1618, Protestant nobles threw representatives of the Catholic Habsburg dynasty from a window of Prague Castle, Bohemia, sparking the bitter Thirty Years' War that left more than four million people dead. Both Protestant and Catholic forces claimed that God was on their side.

Charles I triggered the English Civil Wars from 1639 with his claim of a "divine" right to absolute rule. The monarch was a High Church Protestant, close to Catholicism; the Parliamentarians opposing him and his Cavalier army were severely puritanical in their faith.

Eastern imperialism

While the fight for parliamentary democracy was starting in England, across the world the Manchu were gradually taking over China by force, massacring 300,000 people in one eastern city in 1645. The Qing dynasty they established lasted almost 300 years. By the 18th century, a series of military campaigns had extended its territory, making it the largest empire in China's history.

European rivalries expand

Back in Europe, France's powerful monarch, Louis XIV, challenged Spain's earlier supremacy. After his vast standing army, equipped with new flintlock muskets, won a series of expansionist wars in Europe, rival states—England, Spain, Austria, and the Dutch Republic—allied against him, eventually with some success. By 1756, however, new alliances had formed and the territorial disputes of European powers had spilled over into Africa, Asia, and the Americas. ∎

BORN TO BATTLE AND THE SWORD
THE ITALIAN WARS (1494–1559)

IN CONTEXT

FOCUS
The arrival of mercenaries

BEFORE
1339 The first major mercenary company, the Compagnia di San Giorgio, is founded in Italy.

1423–1454 Alliances of Italian city-states fight a series of conflicts called the Wars in Lombardy, relying heavily on the use of mercenaries.

1458 King Matthias Corvinus of Hungary founds the Black Army, a multinational standing force of mercenaries that fight across Europe.

AFTER
1618–1648 Mercenary armies play a major role in the Thirty Years' War.

1848 Switzerland forbids its citizens to undertake military service for other countries, the only exception being the papal Swiss Guard.

During the Renaissance, Italy became a major cultural and economic hub. However, it was split into many rival states, and this lack of a strong central power led to France and Spain fighting for control of the land.

The main powers in northern Italy were the wealthy city-states of Venice, Milan, Genoa, and Florence. Dominating central Italy were the Papal States, where the pope combined his religious duties with the role of a territorial ruler. The Kingdom of Naples presided over southern Italy.

Success in War depends in a great measure … on Reputation, and when this declines the Valor of the Soldiers declines with it.
Francesco Guicciardini
Florentine statesman and historian
(1483–1540)

Most of these states did not have their own military, so they hired local mercenary companies led by captains known as *condottieri* (from the Italian for "contractors") to fight on their behalf. These were generally heavy cavalry, although larger companies also included infantry. It is likely that most mercenaries had their own weapons or were provided with arms by their captains.

Mercenaries were recruited from further afield, too. The most sought-after fighters were the highly disciplined Swiss infantry, who fought mainly with long pikes, as well as German mercenaries known as *Landsknechts*, who usually fought with the pike and harquebus (an early firearm largely replaced by the musket from the early 16th century). Mercenaries were often highly effective, albeit with the potential to mutiny—or even defect to the enemy—if they were not paid.

Expanding theater of war
The Italian Wars erupted in 1494, when France invaded Italy in an attempt to conquer Naples. Over the next few years, it captured Milan and Genoa. France had a

EARLY MODERN WARFARE

See also: The Spanish Reconquista 110–111 ▪ The European conquest of the Americas 122–125 ▪ European wars of religion 134–139 ▪ The Thirty Years' War 144–147 ▪ The wars of the French Revolution 180–187 ▪ The wars of Italian unification 208–209

The Battle of Pavia of February 1525 was a key moment in the Italian Wars. It resulted in victory for the Habsburgs, led by Charles III, and the capture of King Francis I of France.

small standing force of cavalry and archers, supplemented by part-time militia infantry, as well as contracted Italian fighters who had abandoned their *condottieri*.

The French invasion prompted Spain, which also ruled Sicily and Sardinia, to intervene. During the course of the war, both Spain and France formed frequently shifting alliances with Italian states in an attempt to gain dominance. In 1496, England joined the war on Spain's side (briefly fighting against them from 1526 to 1528). The fighting eventually spilled out of Italy into the Low Countries, Germany, France, and the Mediterranean Sea.

Spanish advantage

Eventually, Spain gained the upper hand over the French, seizing Naples in 1504 and Milan in 1535. Spain's success relied on its infantry using firearms, but the harquebus and musket were often inaccurate and slow to reload, making the soldiers who used them vulnerable to attack. Spain resolved this by protecting its firearms soldiers with pikemen.

The "pike and shot" formation was effective in both defensive and offensive warfare and could hold its own even when outnumbered and facing cavalry. The gunmen moved in advance of the pikemen but could retreat inside the pike square to escape cavalry charges.

Although Spain contracted mercenaries and used some less experienced part-time soldiers, its elite units were professional infantry formations called *tercios*. These men were highly trained and recruited not just in Spain but also in Italy, Germany, and the Low Countries. Their organization and spirit made them the finest fighting force in 16th-century Europe. The mercenary, although still used, declined in popularity as European states began to develop their own national armies. ▪

Charles III

Born in 1490 into one of France's leading noble families—second only to the royal family—Charles III became Duke of Bourbon through marriage at the age of 15. As a result, he inherited the lands and titles of the Bourbons. In 1515, King Francis I named him Constable of France and made him commander in chief of his army.

Charles was joint commander of the French army that won a great victory at the Battle of Marignano (1515), giving the French control of Milan. However, his relationship with Francis I soon soured; the king refused to repay debts to him and withheld important commands. This led an embittered Charles to betray Francis and switch allegiance. In 1523, he fought for the Habsburgs, helping to lead their forces at the Battle of Pavia two years later.

Charles remained in Italy to command the Habsburg forces there, but without the money to pay them, he allowed them to pillage and loot instead. In 1527, Charles led his troops on Rome but was fatally shot outside of its walls. After his death, his men brutally sacked the city.

MURDEROUS AND AVARICIOUS CONQUERORS
THE EUROPEAN CONQUEST OF THE AMERICAS (1519–1536)

IN CONTEXT

FOCUS
The collapse of the Aztec and Inca civilizations

BEFORE
1494 Spain and Portugal sign the Treaty of Tordesillas, which divides the recently discovered territories of the New World between them.

1502 Moctezuma II becomes ruler of the Aztec Empire. He will still be in power when the Spanish arrive.

AFTER
1538 The Spanish begin their conquest of northern South America. They call these lands the New Kingdom of Granada.

1541 Pedro de Valdivia begins his conquest of Chile in the name of the Spanish crown.

1572 Spain captures the last Inca stronghold in Peru and kills its ruler, Túpac Amaru.

During the early 16th century, in less than 20 years, Spain conquered vast swathes of the Americas, destroying the Aztec and Inca empires in the process. In October 1492, an expedition financed by Spain and led by Italian navigator Christopher Columbus landed in what is now the Bahamas.

Columbus made three more voyages to the Americas, each time claiming more territory for Spain, including the islands of Puerto Rico and Cuba. Thousands of settlers followed, colonizing Caribbean islands and coastal areas of Central America. These lands were not empty. The

EARLY MODERN WARFARE 123

See also: The Spanish Reconquista 110–111 ▪ The Aztecs and Incas 114–115 ▪ The Italian Wars 120–121 ▪ Warfare in North America 150–151 ▪ The Spanish American wars of liberation 200–203 ▪ The American-Mexican wars 204–205

Indigenous inhabitants fought back, but the Spanish had superior weapons: firearms, cannons, steel swords, and crossbows—not to mention cavalry. The Indigenous peoples had never seen a horse before, and the cavalry proved a key factor in the conquest.

The Spanish also brought influenza, measles, and smallpox. The impact of these European diseases on the Indigenous peoples, who had no natural resistance to them, was catastrophic, wiping out a large percentage of the population.

Motivated by the prospect of gold and the idea of spreading Christianity, Spain then set its sights on the American mainland, home to the Aztecs and Incas.

The Aztec army
Based in modern-day Mexico, the Aztec Empire originated in 1428, when three city-states—Texcoco, Tenochtitlan, and Tlacopan—formed an alliance to become the leading power in the region. Tenochtitlan (in modern-day Mexico City) emerged as the dominant force and became the empire's capital.

The military played a central role in Aztec society. Boys began military training at around 15; after turning 20, they were called up for military service when needed.

The Aztecs also had a small number of professional, full-time soldiers, many of whom came from the nobility. They usually joined "warrior societies," elite corps that were the first to enter the fray in battle. Only those who captured at least four enemies in battle were allowed to join these societies. Taking prisoners, who

Our cavalry ... charged with such great effect that, next to God, it was to them we owed the victory.
Bernal Díaz del Castillo
on the battle between Hernán Cortés and Tlaxcalan troops, 1519

Aztec fighters went into battle wearing elaborate headdresses related to their warrior societies, as shown in this stone relief in Mexico City's National Museum of Anthropology.

would then be used as sacrificial victims in religious rituals, was considered a superior skill to dispatching an enemy in battle.

Inca warfare
From around 1438, the Incas started to expand from their Andean capital Cusco (in modern-day Peru); within a century, their territories stretched from modern-day Ecuador to Chile. It was a formidable empire, with an advanced bureaucracy, an efficient transportation network, including a coastal road that ran for 2,250 miles (3,620 km), and the strongest military in the New World.

The Incas practiced *mit'a*, a mandatory system of public service for males aged between 15 and 50. Most people labored on farms or construction projects, but one in 50 were drafted into the military, producing a standing army of up to 100,000. »

THE EUROPEAN CONQUEST OF THE AMERICAS

Hernán Cortés

Born in the Extremadura region of Spain in 1485, Hernán Cortés left his native country for the New World in 1504. He initially settled on the Caribbean island of Hispaniola.

In 1511, Cortés moved to Cuba, where he quickly rose through the ranks, holding several important positions in the colonial government. His career progression was partly linked to his friendship with Diego Velázquez de Cuéllar, governor of Cuba. The relationship between the two Spaniards turned sour when Cortés started courting Velázquez's sister-in-law, whom he later married.

After the fall of the Aztec Empire, which became the Spanish colony of New Spain, King Charles V appointed Cortés as its first governor. The conquistador continued to lead largely self-financed expeditions to lands such as Honduras (1524–1526) and Baja California (1535). In 1526, after clashing with other colonists, Cortés was relieved of his duties as governor.

Cortés lived in Mexico until 1541, when he returned to Spain. He died of pleurisy near Seville six years later.

Officers were career professionals chosen in an annual festival called Warachikuy, where they performed tests of skill and bravery.

In battles with local rivals, the Incas usually triumphed as a result of their superior numbers, discipline, and organization. Unlike the Aztecs, the Incas tended to kill their enemies as a warning to rivals.

Cortés and the Aztecs

Rumors about the Aztecs' wealth led Spanish colonists to launch two exploratory expeditions to Mexico, in 1517 and 1518. When Juan de Grijalva, leader of the 1518 voyage, returned to Spain with gold artifacts acquired from the Indigenous people, the governor of Cuba, Diego Velázquez de Cuéllar, approved a third expedition. This was to be led by one of his officials, Hernán Cortés. Later, doubting his subordinate's loyalty, Velázquez revoked his permission, but Cortés departed from Cuba regardless, in February 1519.

Cortés landed in Mexico in March 1519 with just 11 ships, 600 soldiers, and 16 horses. He led his men inland, clashing with some Indigenous tribes and allying with others, such as the Tlaxcalans, long-standing enemies of the Aztecs.

Cortés entered Tenochtitlan in November. Emperor Moctezuma II received him peacefully, but the Spaniard exploited this welcome by imprisoning the emperor.

In April 1520, Cortés heard that Velázquez had sent an army to kill or capture him. He left Tenochtitlan to meet these troops and persuaded them to join him, promising great wealth. Meanwhile, the Aztecs in Tenochtitlan had risen up against the small garrison he had left behind. Cortés was forced to retreat to Tlaxcala, only narrowly escaping death; in the confusion, Moctezuma was killed.

The following spring, Cortés cut off Tenochtitlan from supplies of food and fresh water. To add to the terrible conditions, smallpox swept through the city, killing thousands of people, including the new emperor, Cuitláhuac.

Tenochtitlan fell on August 13, 1521; the last Aztec emperor, Cuauhtémoc, was killed trying

Factors in Spain's successful colonization

- Spanish **iron and steel**, which makes for **stronger weapons** and armor
- The Spanish **cavalry**
- The use of **gunpowder weapons**, such as **muskets and cannons**
- **The importation of diseases** to which Indigenous peoples had no resistance
- **Civil war** in the Inca Empire
- **Divisions between rival groups** in Peru and Mexico

Atahualpa's unarmed retinue did not stand a chance against Pizarro's troops at the Battle of Cajamarca. This engraving shows the Inca emperor held aloft at the center of the action.

Pizarro was assassinated in 1541 during a power struggle between rival colonists. Three years later, the Spanish killed Manco Inca, but his sons led an insurrection that was not fully defeated until 1572. By then, Spain was firmly in control of most of the former Inca territories.

Spain's American colonies
This territorial expansion into the Americas contributed to making Spain the leading power of 16th-century Europe.

The Spaniards' weapons killed thousands, but the diseases they brought caused even more destruction; it is estimated that as many as 20 million people—about 95 percent of the population—died as a result. The Spanish settlers forced most of the Indigenous people who survived warfare and pestilence to labor for them as part of a system of enslavement called *encomienda*. The Spanish Empire in the New World would last for more than three centuries, permanently changing its society and culture. ■

to flee. The city, already damaged by fires and cannon, was mostly destroyed by Cortés's men. On its ruins, the Spaniards built Mexico City, the capital of New Spain, which eventually covered present-day Mexico, parts of what is now the US, Central America, northern South America, and the Caribbean.

Pizarro and the Incas
In January 1531, conquistador Francisco Pizarro, having previously led two expeditions into western South America, landed in Ecuador, hoping to advance into Peru and conquer it. Pizarro's timing was convenient. The Inca Empire was ravaged by epidemics and in the midst of a civil war between half brothers Huáscar and Atahualpa, the sons of Emperor Huayna Capac, who had died of a European disease (possibly smallpox) in 1527.

By April 1532, Atahualpa had defeated and captured his half brother—and ordered his execution. He then encamped near the town of Cajamarca, northwestern Peru, with an army of 30,000 warriors. Strengthened by some Spanish reinforcements and local allies, Pizarro exploited this opportunity. He traveled to Cajamarca and invited Atahualpa to meet him.

On November 16, 1532, Atahualpa progressed into the city with an escort of about 4,000 men, thinking that Pizarro's smaller force, which numbered just 168, posed no threat. His confidence was misplaced: Pizarro launched a devastating surprise attack of cavalry and infantry. The Spaniards shot hundreds of Inca warriors or cut them down in cavalry charges, while there was not a single Spanish death. Atahualpa was taken prisoner; although he paid a huge ransom for his release, the Spanish had him executed in August 1533.

Pizarro then marched on Cusco. He captured it that November and installed Huáscar's younger brother, Manco Inca, as a puppet emperor. In 1536, Manco Inca rebelled and laid siege to Cusco for 10 months, but he was unable to break through the Spanish defenses. After lifting the siege, he retreated to Vilcabamba, northwest of Cusco, where he established the Neo-Inca State, an attempt to continue Inca civilization away from the Spanish.

So great was the terror of the Indians … that they thought more of flying to save their lives than of fighting.
Francisco de Xeres
on the Battle of Cajamarca, 1532

HE HAS THOSE CAPTURED IN COMBAT SOLD
WARFARE IN NORTHERN AFRICA (15TH–16TH CENTURIES)

IN CONTEXT

FOCUS
The "slave wars"

BEFORE
992 CE The Ghana Empire secures the oasis town of Aoudaghost (in modern Mauritania) as a northern terminus for its trans-Saharan trade—much of which is in enslaved people.

c. 1077 Almoravid Berbers from Morocco conquer Ghana. Their empire relies heavily on slavery.

c. 1235 Sundiata Keita, king of Mali, abolishes slavery. It is reintroduced after his death.

AFTER
1518 A Spanish ship carries enslaved Africans directly to the West Indies, starting the Atlantic Triangular Trade.

1610 The African kingdom of Dahomey emerges, chiefly as a center for the slave trade.

Since the 8th century, the consolidation of the Muslim faith in the North African coastal region of the Maghreb had been largely peaceful. However, when it began to expand across the sub-Saharan area, conflict arose, much of it rooted in a growing trade in enslaved people.

A succession of states had risen in the Sahel, the semiarid land between the Sahara Desert and the tropical rainforests to the south. Centered north of its modern-day namesake, the Ghana Empire was preeminent until around 1150. Iron, gold, and agriculture formed the basis of its prosperity, and the enslaved people Ghana gained in wars with neighboring states were set to work in these industries. They also proved a valuable commodity in themselves, to be traded for other goods with Berber

---

As **military powers emerge**, they gain wealth and power through **wars for enslaved people**.

The successive **Ghana, Mali, and Songhai empires** of West Africa **enslave opponents** during their wars.

Moroccan armies, **advancing south for slaves**, dominate West Africa.

European powers encourage enslavement in the region to feed the Atlantic slave trade.

EARLY MODERN WARFARE 127

See also: The rise of Islam 76–81 ▪ The rise of the Ottoman Turks 112–113 ▪ The Ottoman Empire 130–133 ▪ The American Civil War 214–221 ▪ Imperial wars in Africa 226–229

The Great Mosque of Djenné, Mali, dates from the late 13th century. Legend has it that local ruler Kunburu had his palace torn down and rebuilt as a place of worship after converting to Islam.

societies to the north. A cultural exchange accompanied this trade, and people in the Sahel increasingly adopted Islam as their religion.

Enslaved people quickly became a recognized currency in the region. The competition to procure them became not just the cause of constant war but the reason for the rise and fall of empires. The Ghana Empire declined in the 12th and 13th centuries, eclipsed by the Mali Empire, which reached its peak in the 14th century when it extended beyond the borders of present-day Mali. In turn, the Mali Empire collapsed in the mid-15th century, replaced by the Songhai Empire.

Regional conflicts

In East Africa, Ethiopia, a Christian country since the 4th century, became a major power under Amda Seyon I (1314–1330). Like Ghana and Mali, it had built its wealth and power around the trade in enslaved people. In 1529, the Muslim Adal sultanate mounted an invasion from its heartland in the Horn of Africa, but Ethiopia fought back, prevailing at the Battle of Wayna Daga (1543).

A key engagement in the wars for supremacy in the Sahel took place in 1591, at Tondibi in modern-day Mali, and witnessed the arrival of Morocco into the affairs of the region. Led by Judar Pasha, the army of Morocco's Saadian dynasty included 1,500 harquebusiers, infantry who fired primitive muskets using lighted fuses, as well as 1,500 light cavalry and 500 regular infantrymen with bows, lances, and swords. It also had eight cannon. The Saadian army challenged the Songhai king, Askia Ishaq II, whose 40,000-strong army drove a herd of 1,000 cattle before it; he believed that the dust thrown up by their hooves would confuse the enemy. Instead, the cattle were startled by the gunfire and stampeded back into the Songhai ranks. The sultan's harquebusiers then attacked, cutting down the king's troops.

Changing realities

The Moroccan sultan had justified the invasion of another Muslim state by claiming he was saving it from European exploitation. This was a cynical argument but reflected the growing importance of Morocco in the western Sahara.

In 1578, Morocco decisively defeated Portuguese forces at the battle of Alcácer Quibir. In the period that followed, however, it would be European powers that increased their involvement in the region, exploiting the continent as a source of enslaved people for plantation work in the Americas. ∎

Islamic slavery

Slavery had been common in North Africa since at least the time of ancient Carthage (c. 814–146 BCE), well before the rise of Islam. The practice continued under Islam, though only non-Muslims could be enslaved. As many as 5 million Africans were transported across the Sahara to be sold over the centuries, mainly by Muslim traders.

Enslaved people, including those from territories conquered by Islamic armies in the Balkans and western Asia, did domestic work or labored on the land. Girls and young women might be kept as concubines, while men were sometimes trained and deployed as soldiers. The army could at least offer a chance for advancement. Some slave-soldiers rose to positions of command, and there were even reigning dynasties of slave-soldiers—like the Mamluks, who ruled Egypt from 1250 to 1517—mostly of European and western Asian origin.

THE GERM OF GREAT DISASTER
JAPAN IN THE SENGOKU ERA (1467–1615)

IN CONTEXT

FOCUS
Civil wars

BEFORE
1331 The two-year Genkō War starts in Japan.

1336 Japan's Ashikaga shogunate is established.

1350 Factional feuding in the Ashikaga shogunate sparks civil war known as the Kannō disturbance.

AFTER
1635 The Sakoku Edict formalizes Japan's isolation from the world. Japanese subjects are banned from leaving the country, European traders are not allowed to land, and Catholicism is outlawed.

1638 A rebellion by Catholic peasants in western Kyushu is brutally put down by local *daimyo* samurai.

1853 US warships arrive in Edo Bay, Honshu, demanding a trade treaty.

For a century and a half, from the middle of the 15th century, Japan was plunged into almost ceaseless civil conflict. Engrossed in its internal struggles, it shut out the outside world except for the import of foreign firearms.

Japan's *daimyos*—feudal lords—had been a powerful force for centuries, but under the Ashikaga shogunate in the 15th century their significance grew, as did their unruliness. In 1464, the shogun Ashikaga Yoshimasa adopted his younger brother as his son so that he would not die without an heir.

Every day when one's body and mind are at peace, one should meditate upon being ripped apart by arrows, muskets, spears, and swords.
Yamamoto Tsunetomo
Hagakure, late 17th century

Within months, however, his wife gave birth to a son, and the stage was set for a succession struggle. The opposing factions did not wait for Yoshimasa to die. The *daimyo* took sides, and in 1467, the 10-year Onin War began. Even after it was over, trouble simmered. The shogunate's weakness invited ambitious *daimyos* to take their chance at seizing power. In turn, this encouraged rural populations to rebel.

The disorder deepens
When firearms arrived from China and Portugal early in the 16th century, this only added to the already toxic mix. The 1560s saw the rise of warrior Oda Nobunaga in Owari, Honshu. In 1560, against opposition from the Yoshimoto and Matsudaira clans, he marched on Kyoto with 1,800 men—many of them armed with matchlock harquebuses—and defeated a defending army of 20,000. Hundreds of *daimyos* flocked to Nobunaga's banner, including Matsudaira Motoyasu (Tokugawa Ieyasu) and Toyotomi Hideyoshi. This trio would eventually be known as Japan's Great Unifiers. First, though, there would be

EARLY MODERN WARFARE

See also: The rise of the samurai 86–87 ▪ The British Civil Wars 148–149 ▪ The American Civil War 214–221 ▪ The Russo-Japanese War 235 ▪ The Russian Civil War 262–263 ▪ The Second Sino-Japanese War 264–265 ▪ The Chinese Civil War 294

The gun factor

Guns were long assumed to have reached Japan with the first Europeans in 1543, when a storm forced a China-bound ship to land on the southern island of Tanegashima. (Early matchlock guns were called *tanegashimas*.) In fact, the first firearm was probably shipped in from China in 1510. Not much more than an iron tube on a wooden stock, a matchlock musket would have been held tightly beneath the left arm then lit with a match cord and used to blast at advancing cavalry. Gunpowder and firearms were widely available by the mid-16th century, with Portuguese merchants bringing in the best that Europe could provide.

At the Battle of Nagashino, warriors Nobunaga and Ieyasu deployed 3,000 harquebusiers against Takeda's troops, and they were the key to an unlikely victory. Nobunaga placed them behind a palisade of wood, from which they fired rolling volleys at the enemy cavalry, cutting them down in what should have been their triumphant charge.

much fighting, chiefly with Takeda Shingen, a *daimyo* from Kai in central Honshu.

Takeda's samurai inflicted a serious defeat on Ieyasu at the Battle of Mikatagahara in January 1573, but at Nagashino, two years later, his forces were decisively beaten by an alliance of Nobunaga and Ieyasu. When Nobunaga died in 1582, Hideyoshi and Iesayu were left fighting for the succession with Nobunaga's son. Hideyoshi was ultimately victorious.

Ieyasu had to accept defeat, but when Hideyoshi died in 1598, he did not extend the same respect to his son. Again, the *daimyos* took sides, and a civil war broke out, but Ieyasu triumphed at the Battle of Sekigahara in 1600. Although the last of the opposition was not wiped out until 1615, the Sengoku period was effectively over, and the Tokugawa shogunate began.

Peace did nothing to foster a less insular state. After many decades of disruption, Ieyasu and his Tokugawa successors controlled every aspect of Japanese life. They cracked down on Christianity and barred foreign vessels from Japan's harbors. This isolationist attitude toward the rest of the world prevailed until the 19th century. ▪

Nobunaga's use of firearms was decisive in crushing Takeda's army at Nagashino, Japan's first "modern" battle, in 1575. Victory paved the way for the country's unification.

AN IMPASSABLE WALL

THE OTTOMAN EMPIRE (1512–1697)

IN CONTEXT

FOCUS
The janissaries

BEFORE
1363 Murad I, the third Ottoman sultan, creates the Janissary Corps.

1453 Mehmed II conquers Constantinople; renamed Istanbul, it becomes the Ottoman capital.

1499–1503 Ottoman victory over Venice gives the empire control of Venetian territory in Greece.

AFTER
1716–1718 Türkiye cedes territory in the Balkans to the Habsburgs after defeat in the Austro-Turkish War.

1735–1739 The Russo-Turkish War ends with the Ottomans ceding territory to Russia.

1826 Sultan Mahmud II abolishes the Janissary Corps.

By the early 16th century, the Ottomans already ruled most of Anatolia, in modern-day Türkiye, as well as territory in Greece and the Balkans. In Europe, following the defeat of the Byzantine Empire in 1453, their main rival had been the Venetian Republic, while in Anatolia they had defeated a rival Turkish dynasty, the Karamanids. At its height in the second half of the 16th century, the Ottoman Empire spread out to rule territory in Arabia, southeastern Europe, North Africa, the Caucasus, and Central Asia.

The Ottoman military had started using gunpowder weapons instead of mounted archers in the

EARLY MODERN WARFARE

See also: The rise of the Ottoman Turks 112–113 ▪ Warfare in northern Africa 126–127 ▪ The Crimean War 206–207 ▪ Ottoman decline and Russian expansion 232–233

> The janissaries do handle the harquebus very well … They will fight resolutely for honor.
> **Lazaro Soranzo**
> *The Ottoman of Lazaro Soranzo*, 1603

14th century. Under the sultans Selim I and Suleiman I, the elite of the empire's formidable military were its janissaries (from the Turkish word for "new soldiers"), a standing force that pioneered the mass use of firearms. The empire's highly skilled craftsmen forged the steel used in muskets and cannon, which were more accurate and had longer ranges than those of their rivals.

A new force

As well as having superior military technology, the Ottomans could call upon a professional army, which included the janissaries. To ensure the loyalty of the janissaries, they were recruited as children from non-Turkish Christian families (until around 1570, when Muslim-born boys were allowed to join) and ordered to cut all ties with their families. This meant they would be wholly dependent on the sultan.

Elite Ottoman infantrymen, the janissaries fought with muskets and other firearms by the 16th century, as well as with a short Turkish sabre called a *yatagan*.

The process of recruiting the children was known as *devshirme* ("collecting"). In a system that lasted until the mid-17th century, collectors took boys from their families in Ottoman-controlled areas of Europe, enslaved them, and transported them to Istanbul, where they were forcibly converted to Islam. The boys were subjected to a strict regime of training and examination. The more scholarly served as administrators, and a few would be castrated to serve as eunuchs in the imperial harem, but most were recruited into the Janissary Corps.

Life as a janissary was tough, and recruits were subjected to strict discipline. They were not allowed to marry, though this ban was overturned in 1566. Some janissaries were given specialized training as engineers or artillerymen, but mostly they fought as infantry, renowned for their skill with muskets, pistols, and grenades. They were particularly valuable in sieges, where their engineering and artillery skills came to the fore. »

Suleiman I ("the Magnificent")

Born in Trabzon (present-day Türkiye) in 1494, Suleiman was the son of Ottoman Sultan Selim I, whom he succeeded in 1520. As a boy, he studied history, science, theology, and military strategy at the Topkapı Palace in Istanbul. While best known for expanding the empire, he also enacted major judicial reforms, was a great patron of the arts and learning, and oversaw the building of many public works.

In its first decade alone, Suleiman's reign saw the Ottomans capture Belgrade (Serbia) and Rhodes (Greece), and achieve a crushing victory over Hungary. However, there was also a notable defeat—the failure to capture Vienna.

Toward the end of his reign, Suleiman was troubled by rebellion and succession disputes. He ordered the execution of two of his sons, Mustafa in 1553 and Bayezid in 1561. Suleiman died in 1566 while campaigning in Hungary, leaving his only surviving son, Selim III, as his successor. Suleiman's reign was the longest of any Ottoman sultan.

THE OTTOMAN EMPIRE

The original basis of Ottoman military strength was the empire's cavalry. The *akinji* were irregular light cavalry who acted as scouts, often striking the enemy as an advanced guard. The Ottomans' professional mounted troops were the *sipahi*, most of whom were timariots, men who were given land to farm in return for fighting when needed. They were expected to pay for their own equipment and training. In battles, they generally fought with bows, maces, axes, lances, and *kilij* (single-edged scimitars) and were stationed on the flanks.

The sultan's elite household cavalry, the Kapikulu Sipahis, maintained a fierce professional rivalry with the janissaries, whom they viewed as their social inferiors. By the 16th century, however, firearms had become more valuable than cavalry in open battle and siege warfare. This is where the janissaries came into their own.

Gunpowder prevails

Selim I became sultan in 1512, succeeding his father, Bayezid II. By the time Selim died in 1520, a series of conquests had doubled the size of the Ottoman Empire. In 1514,

he launched a campaign against Safavid Persia, which threatened the Ottoman Empire's eastern border. His army inflicted a crushing defeat on the Persians at the Battle of Chaldiran, enabling the Ottomans to conquer eastern Anatolia and northern Iraq. Unlike the Safavids, the Ottoman forces had gunpowder weapons, and the janissaries were able to inflict significant damage with their muskets and cannon.

Selim then turned his attention to the Mamluk Sultanate that ruled Egypt, the Levant, and western Arabia. Like the Safavids, the Mamluks had little experience with firearms. In 1516, Selim won a series of battles, which gave him control of the Levant. The following year, he advanced into Egypt, leading to the fall of the Mamluk Sultanate. This allowed Selim to extend his empire over much of Arabia, making him guardian of the holy cities of Mecca and Medina.

Many units of *sipahi*, along with thousands of janissaries, formed the backbone of Suleiman's army at the failed Siege of Vienna in 1529.

Peak Ottoman power

The empire continued to grow under Selim's son Suleiman I, who ruled from 1520 to 1566. Initially, he set his sights on southeastern Europe, then in 1526 invaded Hungary, winning a major victory at the Battle of Mohács. The Ottoman cavalry encircled the Hungarians while the janissaries in the center fired coordinated volleys with their muskets. The victory allowed Suleiman to annex some Hungarian territory. Three years later, though, he suffered his first major setback when he failed to capture Vienna, the capital of his main European

---

Major 16th-century Ottoman victories involving the Janissary Corps

Battle of Chaldiran (1514) over the Safavid Empire; leads to Ottoman conquest of eastern Anatolia and northern Iraq

Siege of Belgrade (1521) over the Kingdom of Hungary; leads to Ottoman capture of the city

Battle of Mohács (1526) over Hungary and its allies; allows Ottomans to control much of Hungary

Siege of Buda (1541) over Hungary; allows Ottomans to capture the city

Siege of Famagusta (1570–1571) over Venice; leads to Ottoman control of all of Cyprus

Battle of Marj Dabiq (1516) over the Mamluk Sultanate; allows Ottoman annexation of Syria

Capture of Cairo (1517) over the Mamluk Sultanate; helps win Egypt for the Ottomans

Siege of Rhodes (1522) over the Knights Hospitaller and Venice; enables Ottoman conquest of the island

Siege of Tripoli (1551) over the Order of St. John; allows Ottomans to capture the city

Battle of Çıldır (1578) over the Safavid Empire; enables Ottoman capture of Georgia

enemies, the Habsburgs. The city's defenders fought off a 19-day siege imposed by Suleiman's army.

Undaunted, Suleiman turned his attention to other fronts. In Asia, he resumed war against the Safavids, conquering the rest of Iraq in 1534, while in North Africa, the Ottomans extended their rule west to Libya, and made Algeria a client state. Suleiman's successors, son Selim II and grandson Murad III, generally favored consolidation over expansion, although the empire made gains in the Caucasus and conquered Cyprus. There were signs of weakness, however, notably in the Mediterranean, where the Ottomans were frustrated in their attempt to capture Malta in 1565 and were dealt a major defeat by a Christian fleet at the Battle of Lepanto in 1571. From this time on, the strength of Ottoman naval power steadily waned.

Stagnation and decline

The sultans of the 17th century struggled to match the feats of the previous century. The Ottomans' old enemies, the Habsburgs and the Safavids, remained strong, and Poland and Russia emerged as new rivals. The Ottoman economy declined, and disorder increased. The janissaries, once a pillar of strength, began to become a problem. Rather than devote themselves to military service, many grew rich as landowners and merchants. Their sons were allowed to follow them into the Janissary Corps, creating an entrenched hereditary elite that was resistant to change.

Two huge fleets of galleys clash at the Battle of Lepanto in the Ionian Sea, off the Greek coast, in 1571. The Holy League captured or destroyed more than half of the Ottomans' vessels.

> Finally, after a Vigorous Defense and a Resistance without parallel, Heaven … retorted the Terror on a powerful Enemy, and drove him from the Walls of Vienna.
>
> **English eyewitness**
> Siege of Vienna, 1683

In 1589, the janissaries rebelled in demand of higher salaries. Worse was to follow in 1622, when they launched a coup against the teenage sultan Osman II. The sultan had blamed them for his failure to win a war against Poland and planned to replace them with an army recruited in Anatolia. The janissaries had Osman II captured and killed, and then they replaced him with his more compliant uncle, Mustafa I.

In 1683, the Ottomans launched their final attempt to take Vienna. That year, 150,000 Ottoman troops laid siege to the city. The janissary engineers captured the outer defenses, but as Ottoman soldiers advanced on the inner city, a relief force of 80,000 arrived, led by Polish King Jan Sobieski, an ally of the Habsburgs. In a 15-hour battle, the Ottomans were driven from the city. After the battle, the Austrian Habsburgs, Poland-Lithuania, Russia, Spain, and Venice formed an alliance that won several victories over the Ottomans.

By the early 18th century, the Ottomans were on the defensive in Europe and in their wars with the Safavids. Where the Ottoman army—with the janissaries at its heart—had once represented the cutting edge of military power, it was now outmatched by the growing strength of its rivals. ■

CHRISTIAN AND UNIVERSAL
EUROPEAN WARS OF RELIGION (1522–1648)

136 EUROPEAN WARS OF RELIGION

IN CONTEXT

FOCUS
Confessional war

BEFORE
1419–1434 Supporters of Catholicism and followers of Czech theologian and reformer Jan Hus clash during the Hussite Wars.

1517 During his tenure at the university of Wittenberg, Germany, Martin Luther challenges Catholicism in his *Ninety-five Theses*, beginning the Protestant Reformation.

AFTER
1655 Charles Emmanuel II, Duke of Savoy, massacres thousands of Waldensians, a religious group seen as heretical, in Piedmont, in the northwest of Italy.

1685 King Louis XIV of France issues the Edict of Fontainebleau, which removes the Huguenots' right to freedom of worship.

Martin Luther shall hereafter be held and esteemed … as a limb cut off from the Church of God, an obstinate schismatic and manifest heretic.
Extract from the Edict of Worms, 1521

During the first half of the 16th century, religious reformers such as German priest Martin Luther and French theologian John Calvin challenged traditional Catholic teachings. Their ideas coalesced into a movement known as the Reformation, giving rise to a new branch of Christianity: Protestantism. Although there were differences between the various Protestant churches, they all rejected the pope's authority.

Confessional (or theological) differences—both between and within countries—led to a series of long, destructive wars and to the religious division of western Europe.

State versus Church
Many European rulers—displeased with the influence of the Catholic Church—welcomed reformist ideas that gave them more power. England, Denmark–Norway, and Sweden all established their own national Protestant churches. This created conflicts with states that continued to support Catholicism.

The reformed faith found many early adopters in Germany, which was then part of the Holy Roman Empire, a patchwork of hundreds of states that covered much of central Europe. Its ruler was the Holy Roman Emperor, a position held by members of the Habsburg dynasty since 1452.

The Habsburgs tried to extend their jurisdiction, raising tensions with local rulers, many of whom welcomed the chance to create their own state churches. Standing in their way was Holy Roman Emperor and king of Spain Charles V. A committed Catholic, Charles was determined to meet any challenges to his faith or authority.

A lone knight is surrounded and about to be slain by an angry crowd wielding farming tools during the German Peasants' War in this woodcut printed in 1539.

Wars in Germany
The European wars of religion began with the Knights' War (1522–1523), a small-scale conflict that was quickly subdued. It started when a group of knights who supported religious reform tried to confiscate the lands of the archbishop of Trier (Germany).

The German Peasants' War (1524–1525) was a larger uprising. Angry at their socioeconomic conditions, hundreds of thousands

EARLY MODERN WARFARE

See also: The Spanish Reconquista 110–111 ■ The Italian Wars 120–121 ■ The Thirty Years' War 144–147 ■ The British Civil Wars 148–149 ■ The wars of Louis XIV 152–157

of peasants—some inspired by the challenge to authority represented by the Reformation—rose up. They were poorly organized and lacked military experience and artillery, which made it easy for German nobles and cities to defeat them.

In 1531, Lutheran princes in the Holy Roman Empire formed a mutual-defense alliance, the Schmalkaldic League. Charles V, occupied with fighting the Ottomans and French, granted its members religious concessions. In 1546, believing that the emperor's tolerant attitude was temporary, the league occupied several Catholic-controlled towns, including Füssen, in Bavaria. This preemptive strike lit the spark for the First Schmalkaldic War, which ended the following year when Charles V defeated the league army at the Battle of Mühlberg.

The Second Schmalkaldic War broke out in 1552. This time, the Protestant princes could count on the support of French king Henry II, who despite being a Catholic was hoping to acquire territories in the Lorraine region. Unable to defeat the league, Charles V was forced to sign the Peace of Augsburg in 1555. It allowed local rulers in the Holy Roman Empire to choose either Catholicism or Protestantism as their state religion.

Confessional wars in France

By the mid-16th century, about one-tenth of the population in France had embraced the new, reformed faith. Protestants there were known as Huguenots.

After the premature death of Henry II in a jousting accident in 1559, his sons—Francis II (r. 1559–1560), Charles IX (r. 1560–1574), and Henry III (r. 1574–1589)—proved to be ineffective rulers, incapable of mediating between Catholics and Huguenots.

The French Wars of Religion began on March 1, 1562, when the Duke of Guise, a powerful Catholic noble, ordered the massacre of a group of Huguenots at Wassy, in northeastern France. This ignited a series of nine conflicts that »

> **Protestantism** rejects the pope's authority and **challenges Catholic teachings**.

> The growing divide between **Protestants and Catholics** ignites fierce passions and **leads to conflict**.

> Exhausted by **years of fighting**, the various factions agree to **accept each other's faith**.

> **Religious wars are often marked by brutal episodes of intolerance.**

Charles V

Born into the Habsburg dynasty in 1500, Charles V inherited a realm that covered Spain, much of Italy, Austria, the Low Countries, and territories in the Americas.

Charles became king of Spain in 1516 and Holy Roman Emperor three years later. Seeing himself as the guardian of the Catholic faith against reformers such as Martin Luther, he spent much of his reign waging war against his enemies. He fought France for control of Italy and western Europe, clashed with the German Lutheran states of the Schmalkaldic League, and battled the Ottoman Empire in the Mediterranean, North Africa, and eastern Europe.

In 1555, exhausted after decades of warfare, Charles signed the Peace of Augsburg, which allowed rulers in the Holy Roman Empire to choose between Catholicism and Protestantism. The following year, he abdicated, dividing his lands between his son Philip II of Spain and his brother Emperor Ferdinand I. Charles died in a monastery in 1558.

lasted until 1598 and caused large numbers of deaths. Atrocities were widespread; the most infamous, the massacre of St. Bartholomew's Day of August 24, 1572, resulted in the slaughter of thousands of Huguenots across the country.

In 1589, a fanatical Catholic monk assassinated the childless Henry III, who was succeeded by his distant cousin Henry IV, a Huguenot. Many Catholics refused to accept him as king, even after he converted to Catholicism in 1593. It took until 1598 for Henry to finally subdue his opponents, before passing the Edict of Nantes, which granted the Huguenots religious rights. Although Henry restored peace and order to France, many Catholics still despised him. The king was assassinated by one such zealot in 1610.

Revolt in the Low Countries

The most protracted of the wars of religion was the Dutch Revolt, also known as the Eighty Years' War (1568–1648). Although many in the Low Countries had adopted Protestant beliefs, they had been ruled since 1555 by Philip II of Spain, son of Charles V and a staunch Catholic. He was widely disliked for his hostility to the Protestant faith and his tax policies, and in August 1566 these resentments erupted. Protesters rioted, destroying Catholic images and statues in churches across the land.

The leaders of the revolt were called to appear before the Catholic authorities. Among them was William of Orange, a Protestant Dutch noble, who refused and fled the country. In 1568, he raised an army to fight the Spanish rulers but was defeated. A second attempt in 1572 was more successful, with Leiden, Rotterdam, and other Dutch cities joining William's fight.

To make matters worse for Spain, the Crown was unable to pay its soldiers. This led to a series of violent mutinies, such as the 1576 Sack of Antwerp, during which more than 10,000 civilians were killed. Incensed by this brutal event, Catholics and Protestants in the Low Countries united in rebellion against Spain, demanding the withdrawal of all foreign troops.

The man who stopped the Low Countries from completely breaking away from Spain was Italian military leader Alexander Farnese, Duke of Parma. From 1578, he recaptured the southern

St. Bartholomew's Day marked the start of a killing frenzy by French Catholics. This work by contemporary Huguenot artist François Dubois depicts the mayhem in Paris.

EARLY MODERN WARFARE   139

> [W]e shall shortly have a famous victory over these enemies of my God, of my kingdom, and of my people.
>
> **Elizabeth I**
> Speech at Tilbury, 1585

Low Countries (roughly modern-day Belgium) for Spain, though he could not quash the rebellion in the northern Low Countries (most of modern-day Netherlands), which declared independence in 1581. The Dutch continued in their defiance of Spain even after the 1584 assassination of William, by a Catholic seeking the Spanish bounty on his head, and Farnese's capture of Antwerp in 1585.

The Spanish Armada

Spain also found itself drawn into conflict with England, which had become Europe's most powerful Protestant state under Elizabeth I. English privateers had been attacking Spanish ships in the Atlantic and the New World since the 1560s, but open war broke out in 1585, when Elizabeth I sent troops to support the Dutch rebels.

The English intervention in the Netherlands was largely unsuccessful, but Philip II was determined to overthrow the English monarch. In 1588, he sent a great fleet of 150 ships, the Spanish Armada, to invade England. They never got the opportunity to do so. When the Armada anchored off Calais, a night attack by English fire ships (vessels packed with flammable material that were set alight and floated toward the enemy) scattered the Spanish ships. Over the following days, bad weather and constant harrying by the more maneuverable English ships, whose cannon were more accurate and powerful, destroyed Philip II's careful plans.

Subsequent armadas sent between 1596 and 1601 also failed due to bad weather and effective English resistance. The two countries made peace in 1604.

The Dutch Republic

Having declared independence in 1581, and become a republic in 1588, the Dutch provinces continued to fight Spain under the leadership of William of Orange's son, Maurice of Nassau. Inspired by the ancient Roman military, he turned the Dutch army into a well-drilled and cohesive force capable of defeating the Spanish in open battle.

Maurice, who was also skilled in siege warfare, won a series of victories that extended the Dutch Republic's territory. At the same time, the Dutch were building up a highly effective navy that often defeated the Spanish and helped establish and protect their lucrative trading empire in Asia.

In 1609, both sides, struggling to finance the war, signed a truce. This was a great humiliation for Spain and a tacit acceptance of the Dutch Republic as an independent state. Warfare between the Spanish and Dutch resumed in 1621, but neither side made a decisive breakthrough. With the 1648 Peace of Münster, Spain formally recognized Dutch independence.

After the late 17th century, religious differences between Catholics and Protestants continued to cause tensions and disagreements, but they no longer had the power to be the main cause of warfare between states. By then, though, religious wars had already shaped the course of the continent's history. ∎

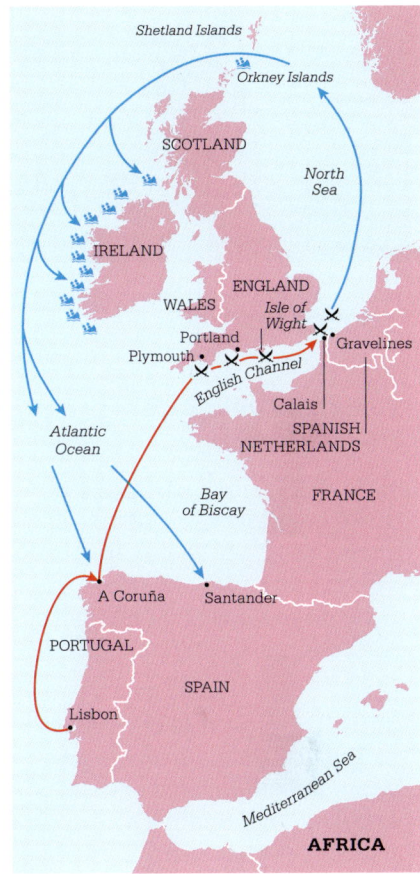

Key:
→ Outward route
→ Return route
✕ Main battle
⚓ Area of shipwrecks

The Spanish Armada left Lisbon, Portugal, in July 1588. It was sighted off the British coast, and battles at Calais and Gravelines in France greatly weakened it. Blown off course, the Armada then had to circumnavigate the British Isles. Many Armada vessels were shipwrecked, and fewer than half of the 150 ships returned to Spain.

PEACE WITH ALL
MUGHAL CONQUESTS IN INDIA (1525–1707)

IN CONTEXT

FOCUS
Religious tolerance as state policy

BEFORE

1264 Bolesław the Pious issues the Statute of Kalisz, which grants Jewish people in Poland religious and financial liberties, as well as protection from discrimination.

1492 The Ottoman Empire of Sultan Beyazid II opens its doors to the Muslims and Jews expelled from Spain by King Ferdinand and Queen Isabella.

AFTER

1773 Catherine the Great of Russia issues the Toleration of All Faiths edict, which allows Muslims to build mosques, go on pilgrimage to Mecca, and practice their faith freely.

1948 Article 18 of the United Nations' Universal Declaration of Human Rights states that everyone has the freedom to practice their religion or belief.

In 1525, Babur, leader of the steppe-based Mughals and emir of Kabul, launched a full-scale invasion of Punjab after local nobles asked for his help to overthrow their Afghan ruler, sultan of Delhi Ibrahim Khan Lodi.

This colorful Mughal miniature portrays the chaos of the 1526 Battle of Panipat and the death of Sultan Ibrahim, who was abandoned by his generals on the battlefield.

Babur had already revolutionized warfare in South Asia, arming his men with new gunpowder weapons to supplement the traditional skills of archery-based steppe warfare.

In April 1526, on an open plain near the village of Panipat, north of Delhi, Babur divided his troops into units made up of smaller divisions, making it easy to change formation as tactics demanded. He also lashed together 700 carts to protect his artillery behind defenses of earthen ramparts and trenches.

As Ibrahim's Afghan warriors advanced, Babur's men bombarded them with cannon fire. The loud sound of the artillery terrified the Afghans' elephants, which trampled many of Ibrahim's soldiers. It is thought that about 20,000 Afghans were killed in the battle. Babur was now ruler of northern India.

Empire building

A Sunni Muslim himself, Babur promoted religious tolerance that allowed his Hindu, Shia, and Christian subjects to practice their own faith. When Babur's grandson Akbar the Great came to the throne in 1556, he took religious pluralism further. He would hold debates with representatives from different

See also: The rise of Islam 76–81 ▪ The Mongol invasions 96–101 ▪ Timur's conquests 105 ▪ The rise of the Ottoman Turks 112–113 ▪ The British conquest of India 225

faiths, and introduced a policy of interfaith tolerance known as *sulh-e-kul* ("peace with all").

Conquests over the Rajputs, Hindu princes of the northwest, and subsequent political bartering resulted in Akbar expanding his northern territories. By the time he died in 1605, Akbar had extended the Mughal Empire eastward to Bengal and Orissa (modern-day Odisha) and set the southern border along the Godavari River.

Expansion and fall

Subsequent rulers Jahangir and Shah Jahan consolidated the territory, but it was under Aurangzeb (r. 1658–1707) that the Mughal Empire reached its peak. However, his reign was dogged by unrest and continual warfare.

Unlike the previous Mughal rulers, Aurangzeb was a strict Muslim. He abandoned religious tolerance, placing higher taxes on non-Muslims and destroying Hindu temples. His death left the empire severely weakened. In 1739, at the Battle of Karnal, Nader Shah of Iran defeated the Mughal army. He ordered that the Mughal capital city of Delhi be sacked in a final act of humiliation. ■

> A monarch should be ever intent on conquest, lest his neighbors rise in arms against him.
> **Akbar the Great**

Babur

The founder of the Mughal dynasty and the first Muslim emperor of India, Babur was born in Andijan (in modern-day Uzbekistan) in 1483. His ancestors included both Genghis Khan, the first Mongol conqueror, and the Turkic warrior Timur.

Babur was just 14 years of age when he first seized Samarkand, the former Mongol capital founded by Timur. He captured it again in 1501 but lost it to Uzbek leader Muhammad Shaybani in 1503.

After conquering Kabul in 1504, Babur launched a series of raids into India. His campaign ended with the defeat of Delhi sultan Ibrahim Lodi in 1526.

Babur's military acumen was complemented by his gift for poetry and his love of nature. He constructed gardens wherever he went.

In 1530, Babur's son Humayun—who would prove to be a weak ruler—was deathly ill. Babur is said to have prayed for Humayun's life, offering his own in return. His son recovered, but Babur died later that year.

Babur allows the construction of **Hindu temples** with permission.

↓

Akbar marries both Hindu and Muslim women. He finds **spiritual truths** in **Islam, Hinduism, Christianity, and Buddhism**.

↓

Jahangir restores orthodox Islam as the state religion but continues to promote religious tolerance.

↓

Aurangzeb ends religious tolerance. He **reimposes Sharia law** on the whole empire, as well as **taxes for non-Muslims**. He **tears down Hindu shrines**.

AN ARMY LIKE A THICK FOREST AND FLOWING WATER
THE ESTABLISHMENT OF MANCHU CHINA (1616–1685)

IN CONTEXT

FOCUS
China's northern frontier

BEFORE
1115 Wanyan Aguda, leader of northeastern China's Jurchen tribes, establishes the Great Jin dynasty. He soon rules a large swathe of northern China.

1234 The Jin dynasty is overthrown by Genghis Khan's Mongols.

1583 A Ming army sent to put down unrest kills more than 2,000 people in a Jurchen village.

AFTER
1696 Under Kangxi Emperor Sun Sike, Qing dynasty forces win the Battle of Jao Modo, effectively completing the conquest of Mongolia.

1912 The Qing emperor abdicates in the wake of the Chinese Revolution.

The Ming dynasty, rulers of China since 1368, had been plagued by raids on its northern border for centuries. Waves of nomadic horsemen regularly descended from the north, pillaging the countryside. The Manchu of Manchuria posed a more serious threat. They had no nomadic heritage—their ancestors, the Jurchen tribes, were sedentary farmers and hunter-gatherers—but they had trained themselves to fight as mounted archers like the Mongols. A series of raids and relatively small inroads slipped imperceptibly into an invasion.

Nurhaci's nation
The Manchu began to pose problems for the Ming under the leadership of Nurhaci, who forged

EARLY MODERN WARFARE

See also: Origins of the Chinese Empire 44–47 ▪ The Han Empire 48–49 ▪ Barbarian migrations: the empire under threat 58–65 ▪ The Mongol invasions 96–101 ▪ China in turmoil 230–231 ▪ The Second Sino-Japanese War 264–265

Nurhaci established a Manchu state, then moved to conquer China, in a project that was not completed until many years after his death.

a loose grouping of peoples into a nation. He united them behind the Eight Banners—military and administrative divisions into which all Manchu households were placed. Nurhaci subjugated the neighboring Yehe and Hada tribes in the 1590s and declared himself emperor of a new Jin dynasty in 1616. Two years later, he proclaimed his "Seven Grievances" against Ming China, which included accusations that the latter had killed his father and grandfather and violated several territorial agreements.

Birth of the Qing
Nurhaci's son Hong Taiji, who succeeded his father in 1626, pronounced himself first emperor of the Qing dynasty in 1636. He had already led an army against Korea, in retaliation for the latter's support for the Ming, in 1627, and he also set about reinforcing his army's artillery. However, Ming China was vast and powerful; it did not view the Manchu as a major threat, and even thought that they could be allies.

In 1644, when peasant rebels in northwestern China's famine-hit Shaanxi province overthrew the Ming emperor, desperate members of the ousted dynasty called on the Manchu to come and restore order. Troops of the new Shun dynasty—created by the peasant rebels and freshly installed in Beijing—tried to hold them at northeast China's Shanhai Pass, where there was a gap in the Great Wall. The Manchu—led since Hong Taiji's death the previous year by Dorgon, another of Nurhaci's sons—forced their way through and went on to take Beijing from the Shun.

Vengeful rulers
When the Manchu occupied the eastern city of Yangzhou in 1645, they massacred 300,000 people. In a single region of Shandong province, they beheaded more than 16,000 people in a month. Such atrocities were a warning against resistance. The regime also imposed Manchu customs on the general population. Chinese men and boys, for example, were required to wear their hair in the traditional Manchu style, shaved short above the brow but with a long braid at the back.

By 1685, when they completed their conquest, the Manchu had killed an estimated 25 million people. However, despite its violent birth, the Qing dynasty would go on to rule China until 1912. ▪

The Great Wall

Nomadic raids on the northern frontier were a fact of life, as old as China itself, as were attempts to exclude them with earthen fortifications. China's first emperor, Qin Shi Huang, had built a "great wall" of sorts as early as 214 BCE. This had been restored and strengthened intermittently ever since.

Between the 14th and 17th centuries, the Ming dynasty had rebuilt some 3,880 miles (6,250 km) of wall—in carefully constructed masonry and brick rather than packed earth and rubble—and added more than 25,000 rectangular watchtowers. (The most famous sections of the Great Wall date from this time.) Where the nature of the terrain prevented such construction, workmen dug defensive ditches—more than 186 miles (300 km) in all. The slow rate of advance of the Manchu invasion over the first few years was a clear demonstration of the Great Wall's effectiveness.

The best-preserved sections of the wall are 23–26 ft (7–8 m) high and 21 ft (6.5 m) wide at the base, with signal towers at regular intervals.

FEAR, TREMBLING, AND DREAD PERVADED
THE THIRTY YEARS' WAR (1618–1648)

IN CONTEXT

FOCUS
Just wars?

BEFORE
4th century BCE Aristotle argues that war should only be used as a last resort.

5th century CE Roman Berber theologian St. Augustine outlines the Christian theory of the "just war."

Late 13th century Italian priest Thomas Aquinas attempts to define a just war.

AFTER
1864–1949 Four Geneva Conventions are signed, defining rules of warfare under international law.

1899, 1907 The Hague Conventions set out formal definitions of war crimes.

1998 The Rome Statute establishes the International Criminal Court.

One of the longest and bloodiest conflicts in European history, the Thirty Years' War resulted in the deaths of up to 8 million people, mostly civilians. The scale of destruction led to debates over how war could be justified and what could be done to regulate it. The carnage also brought into question the concept of the "just war."

In the early 17th century, the Holy Roman Empire was a collection of hundreds of states, mostly in modern-day Germany. Theoretically, its overlord was the Holy Roman Emperor, but in practice the component states, particularly larger ones, enjoyed a high degree

EARLY MODERN WARFARE

See also: The Italian Wars 120–121 ▪ European wars of religion 134–139 ▪ The British Civil Wars 148–149 ▪ The wars of Louis XIV 152–157 ▪ The Great Northern War 158 ▪ The war of the Austrian Succession 159 ▪ The Seven Years' War 162–165

> The clouds gather thick in the German sky; jealousies and discontents arise between the Catholics and the ... Lutherans.
>
> **Account of the situation in Germany,** c. 1618

of independence. Since 1555, local rulers had been allowed to choose between Lutheranism and Catholicism as their state religion.

Outbreak of war

Distrust between states remained, leading to the creation of rival Protestant and Catholic alliances. The Austrian branch of the Catholic Habsburg dynasty ruled the Holy Roman Empire, which included Austria and Bohemia (modern-day Czechia). However, many of the empire's constituent states had significant Protestant populations. In addition to tensions between Habsburg rulers and Protestant populations, there were underlying territorial and commercial rivalries between states.

On May 23, 1618, Protestant Bohemian nobles—who wanted guarantees of religious freedom—

Imperial regents William Slavata and Jaroslav Martinic, along with their secretary, survived being thrown from a Prague Castle window, but the event sparked the war.

threw representatives of the Habsburgs from a window of Prague Castle. This so-called Defenestration of Prague began the Bohemian Revolt (1618–1620), the first episode in what would become an ever-expanding war.

The rebels offered the Bohemian crown to Frederick V, a Protestant who already ruled much territory in western Germany. Seeing this as a threat to his authority, Habsburg emperor Ferdinand II sent the Imperial Army to crush Frederick, which it did at the Battle of the White Mountain, near Prague, in 1620. Frederick fled, the battle resolved nothing, and the rebellion developed into a civil war within the empire. As the war spread, its protagonists, whether Catholic or Protestant, argued that it was a just one because they had God on their side.

Battles in the Thirty Years' War were fought mostly between infantry forces bearing pikes and muskets, supported by cavalry and artillery. Another common feature was the employment of mercenaries. Although mercenary troops were skilled professionals, their loyalty went only as far as their next payment. If they were unpaid, they frequently mutinied, abandoning the army they were contracted to. Since they then had to secure their own food and shelter, they plundered the local civilian population.

Armies were joined by thousands of "camp followers," family members, servants, and support personnel. Their presence frequently stretched supply logistics beyond breaking point. Again, when supplies ran low, generals often turned their men loose on the local population. It became expected that soldiers would extort civilians in the territory they occupied. Anyone who resisted was usually killed; even those who did not resist were often raped or driven out of their homes.

A wider conflict

The Bohemian Revolt triggered a broader conflict as Protestants in other states within the empire—including Silesia and Moravia—took up arms for the right to practice their faith. Ferdinand responded by suppressing them, »

THE THIRTY YEARS' WAR

Important battles of the Thirty Years' War

November 1620: Spanish–Imperial Army defeats Bohemian rebels at the Battle of the White Mountain.

August 1623: Imperial forces defeat the Electoral Palatinate at the Battle of Stadtlohn, Münster.

September 1628: Imperial forces defeat the Danes at the Battle of Wolgast, Pomerania, ending their war involvement.

September 1631: Gustavus Adolphus defeats the Imperial Army at the First Battle of Breitenfeld, Saxony.

November 1632: Gustavus Adolphus dies leading Sweden to victory at the Battle of Lützen, Saxony.

November 1642: Sweden wins victory over Imperial forces at the Second Battle of Breitenfeld.

May 1643: France is victorious over Spain at the Battle of Rocroi, France.

August 1645: France defeats the Bavarian–Imperial Army at the Second Battle of Nördlingen, Bavaria.

---

winning a string of victories with support from Spain. He also contracted mercenary general Albrecht von Wallenstein. Fear of regional Habsburg ascendancy led Protestant Denmark to join the war in 1625, invading northern Germany; it withdrew four years later, after a series of defeats. Nevertheless, Protestant states continued to resist the Habsburgs and soon welcomed a new, more powerful ally, Sweden's King Gustavus Adolphus, who went on to invade Germany in June 1630.

Swedish intervention

For many Protestants, Gustavus Adolphus appeared to be a savior, but his real motive was to extend his influence in the Baltic. He had built up Swedish military power by introducing nationwide conscription, creating a well-drilled standing army. He invested in mobile, lightweight artillery and boosted his firepower by increasing the ratio of musketeers to pikemen in his infantry. In 1631, he signed a treaty with France, which agreed to provide financial support for him. Even though France was a Catholic state, it wanted to prevent the Habsburgs from growing too powerful.

In May 1631, another event galvanized the Protestant cause. After a five-day siege, the Imperial Army of the Holy Roman Empire sacked the largely Protestant city of Magdeburg, Germany, burning it to the ground. Protestant leaders vowed to take revenge, leading to an ever more destructive spiral of violence. In the years that followed, even soldiers who surrendered were killed, and cities were regularly plundered. After Magdeburg, combatants felt they could justify violence against anyone of another faith as acts of righteous vengeance.

The destruction of Magdeburg was the single worst event of the Thirty Years' War. Rampaging Imperial soldiers killed at least 20,000 of its inhabitants in a day.

EARLY MODERN WARFARE

Hugo Grotius

Born in Delft in 1583, Hugo Grotius was a Dutch lawyer and philosopher who was a major figure in the development of international law. In 1609, he published *The Freedom of the Seas*, in which he argued that all states should have the liberty to use the oceans for trade.

In 1625, Grotius wrote *On the Law of War and Peace*. In it, he suggested that war was justified under certain circumstances. However, he also proposed that nations should agree to a common set of laws governing their behavior during conflicts; these would apply to all people, regardless of their religion. He also argued that wars should only be fought in defense of states rather than simply for conquest—and even then, any military reaction should be proportional to the initial attack.

Grotius lived in Paris for many years and in 1634 became Sweden's ambassador to France. He died in 1645, after being shipwrecked following a visit to the Swedish capital, Stockholm.

With the support of powerful German Protestant states such as Saxony and Brandenburg, Gustavus Adolphus went on the offensive. In September 1631, he won the Battle of Breitenfeld, the first major Protestant victory of the war. Although Gustavus Adolphus was killed the following year, while leading another victory at the Battle of Lützen, Sweden continued its attack, pushing into southern Germany.

Meanwhile, Wallenstein began to make peace overtures. This angered Ferdinand, who had him assassinated in 1634. Ironically, this deprived the emperor of perhaps his strongest general and made him even more dependent on Spanish support. Initially, though, combined Imperial–Spanish forces drove the Swedish back to northern Germany.

There was a new twist in 1635, when France declared war on Spain and invaded western Germany. Under pressure, Ferdinand agreed to the Peace of Prague with Saxony, which left its alliance with Sweden and formed a united Protestant–Catholic Imperial army in return for religious concessions. Other Protestant states followed, but Swedish forces remained in Germany. The war spilled over into Flanders and northern France, although neither side was able to land a decisive blow.

The Peace of Westphalia

In 1637, Ferdinand died and was replaced by his son, Ferdinand III. Perhaps realizing that there was little to be gained from continuing the war, he initiated peace talks in 1644. Finally, in 1648, 109 states signed the Peace of Westphalia, bringing the war to an end. Under the terms of the treaty, states within the Holy Roman Empire were given internal autonomy and

I have already gone through many dangers and seen much shedding of blood and have come through it all so far.
King Gustavus Adolphus
Speech on leaving Sweden, 1630

their peoples the right to choose between Catholicism, Lutheranism, and Calvinism. France and Sweden were granted additional territory. Although the empire was at peace, France and Spain continued fighting until 1659.

Rules for warfare?

Great swathes of central Europe had been devastated by the Thirty Years' War. Thousands of villages and towns lay in ruins. The movement of soldiers and refugees had spread diseases such as typhus and plague, which killed more people than the fighting. With harvests disrupted and farms plundered, many people starved.

The sheer scale of death and destruction caused some people to question the concept of the just war. Scholars and lawyers such as Hugo Grotius proposed that war should be better regulated to mitigate its effects on noncombatants. On paper, the rules laid down by the Geneva and Hague conventions of the 19th and 20th centuries went a long way to regulating conflict to protect civilians. Even so, noncombatants still make up most of the casualties of war. ∎

I AM THE MARTYR OF THE PEOPLE
THE BRITISH CIVIL WARS (1639–1653)

IN CONTEXT

FOCUS
King versus Parliament

BEFORE
1625 Charles I becomes king of England, Wales, Ireland, and Scotland.

1628 Parliament passes the Petition of Right, which challenges the Crown's right to tax without its consent, imprison without due process, quarter soldiers, and impose martial law during peacetime.

1629 Charles I's "personal rule" begins, as he attempts to govern without Parliament.

AFTER
1658 Oliver Cromwell dies, and his son Richard succeeds him as Lord Protector.

1660 The monarchy restored, Charles II becomes king.

1689 Parliament passes the Bill of Rights, which limits the powers of the monarchy.

In the mid-17th century, a series of civil wars devastated Britain and Ireland. They culminated in the abolition of the monarchy and its replacement with a republic.

The British Civil Wars arose out of King Charles I's ambition to be an absolute monarch, which he claimed by divine right. The spark for conflict was his imposition of religious reforms on Scotland. In 1639, his opponents there—the Covenanters—rebelled. After some minor skirmishes, Charles made peace with them, agreeing not to interfere in Scottish religious affairs. Then, in 1641, Catholics in Ireland rebelled and formed the Irish Catholic Confederation, which fought London's Protestant-dominated government for control of Ireland.

War and execution

Without the funds to fight such rebellions, Charles had been forced to summon Parliament in 1640 for the first time in 11 years. Parliament was unwilling to grant him any new taxes until he addressed its grievances. Tensions increased, and in August 1642, the king raised an army—seemingly to fight an Irish uprising—against the wishes of Parliament, who feared it would be turned against it. This triggered the First English Civil War.

Parliament formed an alliance with the Covenanters, and in February 1645, it gained the upper hand after forming the New Model Army (NMA). Professional and meritocratic, it turned out highly motivated and well-drilled soldiers.

In 1646, with defeat imminent, Charles surrendered to Covenanter forces, who handed him over to Parliament. Most Parliamentarians hoped that the king would accept some form of constitutional monarchy. However, in December 1647, Charles made a treaty with some Covenanters, promising to

God hath put the sword in the Parliament's hands— for the terror of evil-doers.
Oliver Cromwell
Letter to Parliament, 1645

EARLY MODERN WARFARE

See also: European wars of religion 134–139 ▪ The Thirty Years' War 144–147 ▪ Warfare in North America 150–151 ▪ The American Revolution 172–177 ▪ The American Civil War 214–221

An aide turns Charles I's horse, confusing his troops, at the final battle of the First English Civil War at Naseby in 1645. The New Model Army's victory owed much to its superior discipline.

support their religious reforms if they invaded England to restore him as king. This alliance triggered the Second English Civil War from February to August 1648, at which point the NMA defeated the Scots and dispersed Royalist uprisings.

The devastation of the two wars and Charles's duplicity led many—including the NMA's commander of cavalry, Oliver Cromwell—to demand radical change. In December 1648, Parliament tried Charles I for treason; the following January, he was found guilty and executed. England was declared a republic, the Commonwealth.

Cromwell triumphant

The execution of Charles prompted Scotland and Ireland to unite against England's Parliament and recognize Charles's son, Charles II, as their king. Cromwell was tasked with defeating them. His army landed in Ireland in August 1649, and over the next four years, it defeated the Irish Confederates and their Royalist allies. The conquest was brutal and bloody: including disease and famine, it led to more than 200,000 civilian deaths. In 1650, Cromwell returned to England to defeat his remaining enemies.

In December 1653, Cromwell took political control, dismissing the English Parliament and imposing a new constitution. This created a unified Parliament for England, Wales, Scotland, and Ireland and installed him as the Lord Protector. Cromwell's sweeping executive powers surpassed even those of Charles I. ■

Oliver Cromwell

Born in Huntingdon, England, in 1599 and educated at Cambridge University, Cromwell became a Member of Parliament in 1628. An opponent of Charles I's policies, he lived in obscurity until the First English Civil War.

Despite his limited military experience, Cromwell found success as a cavalry leader. When the New Model Army was formed in 1645, he was made the commander of cavalry and took part in the defeat of the Royalists. He also played a key role in the trial of Charles and the establishment of a republican Commonwealth.

From 1649 to 1650, Cromwell led the Parliamentary invasion of Ireland; he then went on to defeat the Scottish Royalists in 1650–1651. In 1653, he was declared Lord Protector of the Commonwealth, giving him great powers for life. Then, having negotiated an end to the First Anglo-Dutch War, he entered into war with Spain, a conflict that led to England acquiring several Caribbean colonies. In 1657, Parliament suggested Cromwell crown himself king, but he declined. He died the following year.

WE HAVE NOTHING BUT OUR LIVES TO LOSE
WARFARE IN NORTH AMERICA (c. 1610–1680s)

IN CONTEXT

FOCUS
Indigenous peoples and European settlers

BEFORE
1565 The Spanish establish the first enduring European settlement in North America at St. Augustine, Florida.

1598 A Spanish settlement is founded at Santa Fe, in what is now New Mexico.

1607 English settlers establish the Jamestown settlement, in the Colony of Virginia.

AFTER
1696 Indigenous people rebel against their Spanish colonizers. In the Second Pueblo Revolt, at least 21 settlers and five missionaries are killed.

1837 The Chimayó Rebellion sees Pueblo peoples and poor settlers working together to depose Albino Pérez, the centrally appointed governor of New Mexico.

In North America, the 17th century was marked by a succession of small-scale conflicts between Indigenous communities and European settlers. Indigenous peoples lacked firearms at first, but they made up for that disadvantage with their well-crafted hand weapons and their understanding of guerrilla tactics.

Both sides inflicted serious damage, but the settlers had the upper hand. Acts of resistance by Indigenous peoples were used to justify cruel retaliations and the imposition of disadvantageous treaties.

Expansion and reaction

At first, the Powhatan people of coastal Virginia had enjoyed good trading relations with their new English neighbors. However, dealings became strained as settlers demanded more land.

In 1609, Chief Powhatan placed the Jamestown settlement under siege. The English survived this period, known as "Starving Time," and retaliated by burning down villages and killing women and children—terror tactics originally used to suppress colonial unrest in Ireland. They also took Powhatan's daughter Pocahontas hostage.

During her captivity, Pocahontas converted to Christianity and married an English farmer. Their union led to a period of peace

The werowance, or chief, in this 16th-century drawing wears the attire for a solemn gathering. The chief has feathers in his hair, a beaded necklace, and body paint.

between settlers and Indigenous people, but this only encouraged the growth of the English colony. New immigrants arrived, seeking fresh lands for the intensive cultivation of tobacco; this exhausted the soil, prompting the settlers to seize yet more Powhatan lands.

In 1622, Powhatan's brother Opechancanough launched surprise attacks on outlying settlements. Carrying meat and fruit as though to trade, the raiders were welcomed into the settlers' homes, where they attacked their hosts. As many as 347 men, women, and children were killed. In retaliation, the outnumbered colonists invited Powhatan leaders to a meeting, where they plied them with poisoned wine before opening fire, killing up to 200 in all.

Massacres and exploitation

The larger the European settlements grew, the more marginalized the Indigenous communities became, and the harder it was for them to negotiate on equal terms. This pattern soon became the norm.

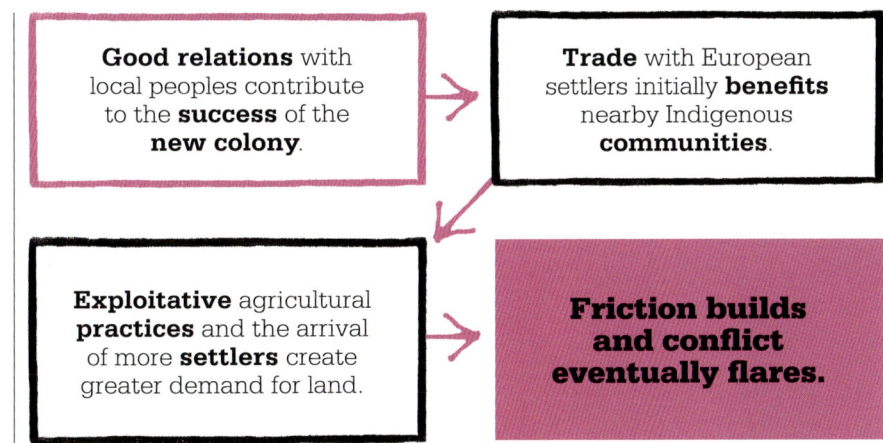

In 1637, an English militia massacred the Pequot people in Mystic, Connecticut; after King Philip's War (1675–1678), New England colonists wiped out the Wampanoag of Massachusetts.

"King Philip" was the nickname given by the English to Wampanoag chief Metacom. He had sought a peaceful coexistence with the settlers, but when that proved impossible, he had led an uprising, alongside other local tribes, such as the Narragansett and Nipmuc.

For almost three years, rebel raids and English reprisals alternated, leading to the deaths of more than 3,000 Indigenous people and up to 2,000 colonists.

In addition to the exploitation they endured, the Indigenous communities felt culturally erased. The imposition of Catholicism and suppression of ancestral rituals and beliefs are thought to have sparked the Pueblo Revolt of 1680, in which Pueblo peoples rose up against their Spanish occupiers at Santa Fe, New Mexico. ■

Brothers, we must be one as the English are, or we shall be destroyed … Stand not in your own light, I ask you, but resolve to act like men.
Miantonomoh
Narragansett chief, 1642

Indigenous ways of war

Many Indigenous peoples were masters of guerrilla warfare. Their style of fighting made them appear a disorganized rabble to European troops, but they were disciplined and fluid in formation. When pressed, they simply melted away and came back from a different direction. They were skilled with the bow and arrow and, at closer quarters, with the tomahawk, which they could use as a hand weapon or hurl with great accuracy.

There are also numerous reports of the practice of scalping, with Indigenous warriors apparently carrying specially sharpened knives exclusively for this purpose. British traveler Jonathan Carver described scalping in his 18th-century journals. The victorious fighter would seize his dead or dying prisoner's head, place one foot on their neck, then grab and twist their hair with one hand, stretching the skin of the scalp, which was then removed "with a few dexterous strokes."

MAINTAIN AS MANY TROOPS AS POSSIBLE

THE WARS OF LOUIS XIV (1661–1714)

THE WARS OF LOUIS XIV

IN CONTEXT

FOCUS
The standing army

BEFORE
c. 359–336 BCE Philip II of Macedon reforms his army to make it a full-time, professional, and well-trained force.

c. 221 BCE Having a standing army helps the Qin dynasty to install imperial rule over China.

1447 CE Charles VII establishes the *compagnies d'ordonnance*, which combine into France's first standing army.

AFTER
1804 Napoleon creates the Grande Armée, which numbers more than 600,000 soldiers.

1914 At the start of World War I, the size of the French military reaches 1.3 million troops.

1927 China founds the Red Army. Renamed the People's Liberation Army 20 years later, today it is the largest standing army in the world.

During his 72-year reign, Louis XIV transformed France into the greatest power in Europe. He built up a vast standing army for his expansionist wars, often fighting several major states simultaneously.

Louis became king in 1643, at the age of four. His mother, Anne of Austria, acted as regent until he came of age, appointing powerful clergyman Cardinal Jules Mazarin as chief minister. Mazarin was determined to extend central royal authority, which angered many, particularly members of the nobility. This led to the 1648 outbreak of the Fronde, a series of uprisings that was not fully quashed until 1653.

The Fronde left a young Louis determined never to have his authority challenged again. After Mazarin's death in 1661, he personally took over France's government, doing without a chief minister. His plan was to rule as an absolute monarch.

Upgrading the army

When he began his personal rule, Louis could raise an army of about 70,000—a fairly large force by contemporary standards but not

A king need never be ashamed of seeking fame, for it is a good that must be ceaselessly and avidly desired.
Louis XIV

enough to match his territorial ambitions. There were other issues, too. The army had only a small core of permanent troops, the rest being part-time militia and mercenaries. Officers and generals were largely selected on the basis of ancestry rather than skills.

The king had inherited from Mazarin a highly efficient secretary of war, Michel Le Tellier, who was instrumental in reforming the army. In 1666, Le Tellier was succeeded by his son, the Marquis of Louvois, who continued to improve the quality and discipline of the troops.

Sébastien Le Prestre, Marquis of Vauban

The great military engineer Sébastien Le Prestre de Vauban was born into France's minor nobility in 1633. His service to the crown began in 1655, when he was appointed royal engineer.

After the Franco-Spanish War (1635–1659), Vauban planned and oversaw the construction of fortifications in France's new territories. These eventually grew into the *Ceinture de fer* ("Iron Belt"), a formidable system of fortresses, citadels, and batteries.

During the Franco-Dutch War (1672–1678), Vauban directed the French capture of Maastricht.

On this occasion, he pioneered the use of three lines of trenches dug parallel to the city's fortifications. Communication trenches ran perpendicular to these lines, connecting them and allowing the besieging French troops to safely approach the city. This tactic remained in use until the 20th century.

In the Nine Years' War (1688–1697), Vauban directed the French seizure of Namur, Valenciennes, and Ath. He withdrew from active military service in 1703 and died in Paris four years later.

EARLY MODERN WARFARE 155

See also: The Hundred Years' War 106–109 ▪ The Italian Wars 120–121 ▪ European wars of religion 134–139 ▪ The Thirty Years' War 144–147 ▪ The war of the Austrian Succession 159 ▪ The Seven Years' War 162–165 ▪ The wars of the French Revolution 180–187

Louvois ensured that officers would be chosen based on ability, and he insisted that recruits should be under the age of 40, physically fit, and willing to sign up for at least four years. This reformed army was epitomized by the grenadiers, elite infantry soldiers trained to carry and use hand grenades.

Louis could also rely on the Marquis of Vauban, the finest military engineer of his day, who designed France's system of border defenses. All these army reforms were made possible by a strong bureaucratic state led by Louis's finance minister, Jean-Baptiste Colbert, who worked to improve the economy, ensuring a steady stream of taxation revenue.

Military reforms in Europe

Other European countries were also reforming their armies. By the mid-17th century, Sweden had already developed a standing army, albeit a fraction of the size of France's; Spain could field around 300,000 men, although it often struggled to pay and supply them.

The English were also working toward an effective bureaucracy and more robust fiscal system, but this was largely used to fund the Royal Navy, while the army remained comparatively small. Austria, Prussia, and Russia began modernizing their militaries from the mid-17th century, but the fruits of these reforms would not be fully evident until the early 1700s.

Early wars

Louis XIV was eager to expand French territory, particularly on his kingdom's eastern and northern borders, and to test the mettle of his army. He soon got his chance.

When he married his first wife, Maria Theresa of Spain, she had given up her rights to inherit any Spanish territories in return for a large cash dowry. However, the »

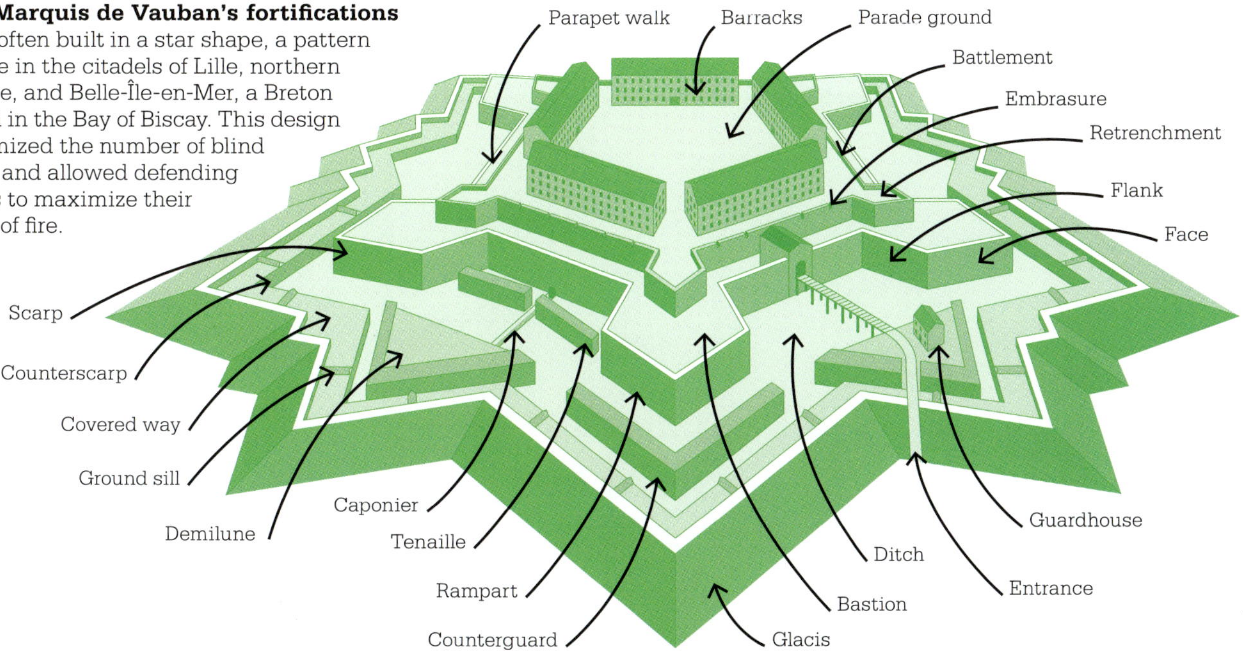

Louis XIV appears in full armor, combined with lace and plumes, in this 1754 portrait by an unknown artist, hinting at the French king's conquering ambitions and refined tastes.

The Marquis de Vauban's fortifications were often built in a star shape, a pattern visible in the citadels of Lille, northern France, and Belle-Île-en-Mer, a Breton island in the Bay of Biscay. This design minimized the number of blind spots and allowed defending forces to maximize their fields of fire.

dowry was never paid, which allowed Louis to claim that some of Spain's territories had "devolved" to him. He targeted the Spanish Netherlands (modern-day Belgium and Luxembourg) and the region of Franche-Comté (now in eastern France), invading and occupying both in 1667.

The War of Devolution came to a negotiated end within a year. Under the peace terms, Louis withdrew his troops in exchange for territory in modern-day northern France. Although it was a success, Louis was not satisfied.

Wars in the Low Countries

Louis XIV's next target was the Dutch Republic. He prepared for war, raising about 180,000 troops and amassing supplies to feed all of these soldiers for more than six months.

The French army invaded the Dutch Republic in May 1672, and within weeks it had occupied most of the country. The Dutch began peace talks, but Louis's terms were so harsh that they resolved to continue the war. They allied with Austria, Spain, Prussia, and Denmark–Norway, all of which were alarmed by the speed of French gains in the region. Louis's only reliable ally among the major powers was the Swedish Empire.

The Dutch turned the leadership of their state and military over to their hereditary prince, William of Orange. He slowed the French advance by breaking open the North Sea dykes, flooding the countryside.

The conflict descended into an attritional series of sieges, and Louvois was forced to increase the size of the army to about 280,000.

Peace talks began in 1676 and concluded two years later. Louis was awarded Franche-Comté and more territory from the Spanish Netherlands to bolster his northern border. Despite facing an alliance of powerful enemies, Louis had triumphed, leveraging France's size, wealth, and military power to achieve his strategic aims.

A monarch at his peak

In 1682, Louis XIV moved his court to Versailles, west of Paris, where he had transformed a former hunting lodge into a vast royal residence. With its gilded halls featuring multiple representations of the king as a victorious warrior, the Palace of Versailles was a reflection of Louis's self-glorification as an absolute monarch.

Meanwhile, the French king's territorial campaigns progressed. In the War of the Reunions (1683–1684), France acquired Luxembourg from Spain and the city of Strasbourg from the Holy Roman Empire. To support his expansionist policy,

---

Louis XIV rules as an **absolute monarch**, focusing all **authority on himself**.

→ **His expansionist policy requires military reforms, including the creation of a standing army.**

↓

Military successes and **territorial acquisitions** bolster France's **political power**.

← Fearing **Louis XIV's ever-growing influence**, other European countries join in the **Grand Alliance**.

The Palace of Versailles became Europe's most elegant and glittering royal court under Louis XIV. This detailed 17th-century etching shows the entrance to the palace in 1682.

Louis continued to strengthen the French military. The infantry transitioned from matchlock to flintlock muskets, which could be fired more quickly and reliably, and introduced the socket bayonet, which could be fixed to the muzzle of a musket. This period also saw the establishment of the Mounted Carabiniers, heavy cavalry units.

These changes proved timely in the Nine Years' War (1688–1697), which France fought alone against a Grand Alliance of England, Scotland, Spain, Austria, the Dutch Republic, and the Duchy of Savoy. Louis could now field an army of 395,000, its peak size during his reign. However, William of Orange, who had become King of England and Scotland through his marriage to Mary II, frustrated Louis's ambitions to further extend his influence. After the Nine Years' War, France was forced to return Luxembourg to Spain.

Succession issues

On November 1, 1700, Charles II, Spain's final Habsburg ruler, died without children. In his will, he had nominated as successor his great-nephew Philip, Duke of Anjou, who was also Louis XIV's grandson. This arrangement would increase French influence in Europe in addition to delivering Spain's empire in the Americas and Asia to France. For Louis's enemies, this was unacceptable.

England, Spain, Austria, and the Dutch Republic renewed the Grand Alliance, nominating Archduke Charles of Austria, who also descended from Spanish royalty, as their candidate for the Spanish throne. Once again, Louis XIV faced an array of great powers, with Bavaria and his grandson's supporters in Spain as his only reliable allies.

The War of the Spanish Succession began in 1701. There were clashes in Italy, Iberia, and the Americas, but the majority of the fighting took place in the Low Countries and Germany.

Grand Alliance victories

A significant turning point in the conflict came in August 1704, when a Grand Alliance army defeated Franco-Bavarian forces at the Battle of Blenheim, in southern Germany. This prevented Louis's planned capture of Vienna, which would have fatally weakened the Grand Alliance.

Two years later, Grand Alliance victories at Ramillies (in modern-day Belgium) and Turin drove the French out of the Spanish Netherlands and northern Italy. Peace talks began in 1709, but the war dragged on until 1714. Louis secured the Spanish throne for his grandson, who had to renounce his claims on the French crown. However, Louis was forced to give up territory to Austria, which also gained the Spanish Netherlands. The war left Britain as Europe's dominant maritime power.

Louis XIV died in 1715, aged 76. Although France was mired in debt and no longer Europe's greatest power, he still left his successor, his great-grandson Louis XV, in a strong position. France had the largest standing army in Europe, providing an example that the rest of the continent strove to emulate. ∎

The Battle of Blenheim proved disastrous for the French army. This painting by English artist John Wootton shows the Duke of Marlborough (bottom right) directing the final charge.

Fortification, or Military Architecture … teaches men to fortify themselves … to the end the Enemy may not be able to attack such a part without great loss of his men.
Vauban
A New Treatise of Fortification, 1691

THE UNPRECEDENTED HAS HAPPENED
THE GREAT NORTHERN WAR (1700–1721)

IN CONTEXT

FOCUS
The rise of Russia

BEFORE
1547 Ivan IV ("the Terrible") imposes military discipline and centralizes administration.

1613 The Romanov dynasty comes to power. It will rule until the 1917 Revolution.

1699 After becoming Czar of All Russia in 1682, Peter I establishes a program of military conscription.

AFTER
1721 Russia acquires Estonia and Livonia (modern-day Latvia) and establishes a naval presence in the Baltic Sea.

1772–1814 Russia conquers a vast region, including Crimea, Ukraine, Georgia, Belarus, Moldova, and parts of Poland.

1918 The Russian capital moves back to Moscow. It had been relocated to St. Petersburg in 1713.

Charles XII was only 15 years old in 1697, when he became king of Sweden, then northern Europe's dominant military power. Hoping to take advantage of his youth, Sweden's neighbors Denmark–Norway, Saxony, Poland–Lithuania, and Russia formed an alliance in 1700 in an attempt to limit Swedish influence. Instead, a series of tactically outstanding victories against the alliance left Sweden unchallenged in the region.

Sweden overreached itself in 1708, when Charles invaded Russia, then ruled by Peter I. Seeing an opportunity to gain territory on the Baltic Sea, Peter ordered his troops to retreat and regroup, adopting scorched-earth tactics to destroy anything the invaders might be able to use. Peter's army defeated the Swedes at the Battle of Poltava, in modern-day Ukraine, in 1709.

Sweden continued to fight the alliance, defeating the German states of Prussia and Hanover, as well as Denmark and Norway. In 1718, Charles invaded Norway again, but he was shot and killed while mounting a siege against the fortress of Fredriksten.

The war finally ended in 1721, after Sweden signed separate peace treaties with its former enemies. That same year, Peter I adopted the moniker "the Great." He continued his program of modernization in Russia, while Prussia established itself as a significant military power in the region. ■

Under Peter I, who brought the Swedish Empire to an end at Poltava, Russia emerged as an undisputed power in the Baltic region.

See also: The Thirty Years' War 144–147 ▪ The Seven Years' War 162–165 ▪ The wars of Catherine the Great 178–179 ▪ The Crimean War 206–207

TREATIES ARE ONLY OATHS OF DECEPTION
THE WAR OF THE AUSTRIAN SUCCESSION (1740–1748)

IN CONTEXT

FOCUS
Europe in turmoil

BEFORE
1713 The Pragmatic Sanction states that a female could inherit all the territories of the Habsburg monarchy. Maria Theresa of Austria is born four years later.

1715 A Jacobite rising attempts to restore the former James II to the thrones of England, Ireland, and Scotland. It is defeated.

1731 Britain and Austria sign the Treaty of Vienna, forming an alliance.

AFTER
1756 With the "Diplomatic Revolution", Europe's major powers switch long-standing alliances: Austria allies with France, Britain with Prussia.

1763 The Anglo-Prussian-led alliance wins the Seven Years' War.

In 1740, Maria Theresa acceded to the Habsburg throne, ruling over Austria and territories in Eastern and Central Europe, the Low Countries, and Italy. However, the idea of a female ruler of these lands led to a series of conflicts known as the War of the Austrian Succession.

Among the challengers to Maria Theresa were France, Prussia, and Spain, while Britain, Russia, and the Dutch Republic supported Austria. Fighting began when Prussia invaded the Habsburg province of Silesia. Although Prussia used the era's standard weapons and tactics—massed volleys of muskets supplemented by artillery, with cavalry deployed to protect flanks and for shock attacks—its superior logistics gave it the upper hand over Austria, which also faced a French-Bavarian invasion.

Changes across Europe
The long-term Anglo-French rivalry was also a factor in the conflict. France supported the Jacobites, who wanted to replace the Protestant Hanoverians on the British and Irish thrones with a Catholic Stuart monarch. In 1744, France advanced into Habsburg territory in the Low Countries; as a result, when the Jacobites launched an uprising in Scotland in 1745, it was without the support of French troops.

Peace was made in 1748. Europe's great powers recognized Maria Theresa's legitimacy, but Austria had to cede territory in Italy and hand Silesia over to Prussia. Tensions remained, and Europe was soon plunged into war again. ∎

I am undertaking a war in which I have no allies but your valor and your good will.
Frederick II of Prussia
addressing his generals before the invasion of Silesia, 1740

See also: The wars of Louis XIV 152–157 ▪ The Great Northern War 158 ▪ The Seven Years' War 162–165 ▪ The wars of Catherine the Great 178–179

IF YOUR NUMBER BE SMALL, MARCH IN A SINGLE FILE
THE FRENCH AND INDIAN WAR (1754–1763)

Before and during the **Seven Years' War** in Europe, **Britain and France** fight in **North America**.

The two countries clash over the **borders of their colonies**, and often skirmish in **remote areas**.

Both powers rely on small armies of volunteers and Indigenous peoples.

The **conflict develops** into **a series of raids** in wild countryside.

IN CONTEXT

FOCUS
Irregular warfare

BEFORE
1689 King William's War begins between the French and English colonies in North America. France adopts the hit-and-run tactics of its Indigenous allies to prevail over the larger English army.

1722 Dummer's War breaks out between the New England colonies and the Indigenous Wabanaki Confederacy. Captain John Lovewell's tactics anticipate those of later "ranger" forces.

AFTER
1777 During the American Revolution, George Rogers Clark leads his Kentucky County militia in ranger-style actions against the British.

1812 The US enlists new companies of rangers to support its regular troops in their war with the British.

Even before Britain and France faced each other in the Seven Years' War (1756–1763), fighting between the two had flared up in their North American colonies. The conflict featured a series of skirmishes and raids by small forces, a type of combat that became known as irregular warfare.

Building forts

In 1749, French Canadian patrols laid claim to the Ohio Valley, stating that the 17th-century explorations of Frenchman Robert La Salle gave them rights to this region, which the English had claimed since 1609. Tensions mounted, and in January 1754, volunteers from Virginia began building a fort at the confluence of the Ohio and Monongahela rivers, in what is now Pittsburgh, Pennsylvania. In April, a larger French force drove the volunteers off the site and established their own outpost, Fort Duquesne.

On his way to help protect the British fort, a young George Washington met the retreating British. He pushed on with his party, which included Virginia volunteers and members of the Mingo tribe. When he learned that a French detachment was encamped near Uniontown, Washington launched a surprise attack. In the Battle of Jumonville Glen (May 28), his troops killed most of the French and their Indigenous allies, igniting a bitter and protracted war.

EARLY MODERN WARFARE 161

See also: Warfare in North America 150–151 ▪ The Seven Years' War 162–165 ▪ The American Revolution 172–177 ▪ The wars of the French Revolution 180–187 ▪ The War of 1812 198–199

The death of General Wolfe, who was killed by two bullets in the chest at the Battle of Quebec, is portrayed in this 1770 painting by British American artist Benjamin West.

Expecting a reaction, Washington built a defensive stockade nearby, at Fort Necessity. On July 3, 1754, an 800-strong French army encircled him, forcing him to surrender.

French victories

In July 1755, when General Edward Braddock set out with an army of 2,200 men to take Fort Duquesne, he was foiled at the Monongahela River by a French and Indigenous force less than half of that size. The British blamed this defeat on the panic and disorientation caused by the Indigenous fighters' tactics, including their whooping war cries.

Building on their success so far, the French sent a strong contingent of professional soldiers under the experienced leadership of General Louis-Joseph de Montcalm. With their Indigenous allies, they captured Fort Oswego, beside Lake Ontario (August 1756), and Fort William Henry, at New York Province's northern frontier (August 1757). The war was going France's way, not least because it had the support of local tribes, many of them part of the Iroquois Confederation.

The battle for Quebec

Britain stepped up its commitment. In May 1758, General James Wolfe set off on an expedition to Cape Breton Island, where he set up an artillery battery, besieging France's Fortress of Louisbourg. The fort's fall at the end of July secured British access to the St. Lawrence River, opening the way to Wolfe's subsequent capture of Quebec.

With his men outnumbered by Montcalm's, Wolfe chose to attack by an unexpected route, from the river, scaling the clifflike Plains of Abraham to take the city on September 13, 1759. The French had been forced out of North America. ∎

Rogers's Rangers

Small, informal groups of volunteers had always helped to defend the British colonies. In the rugged northeastern woodlands, this called for special skills. Forest rangers learned about tracking and reconnaissance by hunting and trapping, often under the direction of Indigenous guides.

One group, led by Major Robert Rogers, came to the fore in 1757 and 1758 in two skirmishes, both known as the Battle on Snowshoes. This winter footwear, adopted from the Algonquin peoples, gave them the mobility to beat the French. In 1758, Rogers's Rangers helped blunt the edge of the French attack at Louisbourg, patrolling the nearby woods to head off raids.

Rogers's Rangers were well equipped to carry out raids themselves, as at St. Francis, Quebec (1759) and Ste-Thérèse (1760). They also played a key role in preparing the ground for more conventional attacks, as in the Quebec (1759) and Montreal (1760) campaigns.

AN ARMY IN POSSESSION OF A STATE

THE SEVEN YEARS' WAR (1756–1763)

IN CONTEXT

FOCUS
Rise of militaristic Prussia

BEFORE
1713–1740 Frederick William I transforms Prussia into a centralized, bureaucratic, and militarized state. He is succeeded by his son Frederick II.

1740–1748 The War of the Austrian Succession ends with Prussia in control of Silesia but does not resolve tensions across Europe.

AFTER
1768–1774 Russia is victorious in the Russo–Turkish War, winning territory at the expense of the Ottomans.

1778–1779 Austria and Prussia resume conflict in the War of the Bavarian Succession.

1786 Frederick II dies at his palace in Potsdam.

The Seven Years' War, caused by territorial disputes and rivalries between European powers, led to the first truly global conflict, with fighting in Europe, Asia, Africa, and the Americas. Before the war, the "Diplomatic Revolution" of 1756 saw the realignment of alliances in Europe. France and Austria, previously rivals, became allies, joining Russia and Sweden. Their main opponents were Britain and Prussia.

Emerging power
Prussia, declared a kingdom in 1701, originated as a duchy in modern-day eastern Germany and Poland. The architect of its military

EARLY MODERN WARFARE 163

See also: The wars of Louis XIV 152–157 ▪ The war of the Austrian Succession 159 ▪ The French and Indian War 160–161 ▪ The wars of Catherine the Great 178–179

Pray every day that God does not allow this enemy to get too mighty and conquer us.
Prussian soldier
Letter of 1758 about the threat of the Russians

power was Frederick William I, "the Soldier King," who came to the throne in 1713. He introduced military conscription and created a professional standing army that was organized by an efficient bureaucracy based in Berlin.

When Frederick died in 1740, his son and successor, Frederick II (later known as Frederick the Great), inherited an army of 80,000, the fourth-largest in Europe. He expanded his forces and introduced annual fall maneuvers. He put this military power to use in the War of the Austrian Succession (1740–1748), in which Prussia forcibly annexed the wealthy region of Silesia from Austria.

Increased firepower

The armies fighting the Seven Years' War relied heavily on flintlock muskets. Highly inaccurate at long ranges, they were nonetheless very effective when used by large groups of infantry who would march within range of the enemy, deliver a massed volley, and then reload and fire again. Infantry formations were drawn out into longer lines so that they could deliver more firepower, usually supplemented by artillery. This meant large armies could be slow to maneuver and highly vulnerable to cavalry attacks from the flanks and rear. Battles were typically won by those armies that could march quickest and remain the most disciplined under fire.

As armies grew larger, another key factor for success was having the finance and logistical expertise to deliver sufficient supplies and »

Frederick the Great

Born in Berlin, Prussia, in 1712, Frederick had a keen interest in the arts and often clashed with his authoritarian father. He even attempted to flee to Britain in 1730, leading to the arrest and execution of his best friend. Frederick ascended the throne in 1740. That year, he invaded and occupied the Austrian province of Silesia.

Despite having no experience as a general, Frederick secured numerous victories in the subsequent War of the Austrian Succession, which ended in 1748 with Prussian control of Silesia. Frederick resumed conflict with Austria eight years later.

During the subsequent Seven Years' War, Frederick and Prussia survived, despite being outnumbered and facing enemies on all sides. As well as being a skilled, original, and inspirational general, often personally leading his armies into battle, Frederick was a superb administrator and patron of the arts and sciences. He died near Berlin in 1786, having transformed Prussia into one of the great powers of the continent.

Anatomy of a flintlock musket

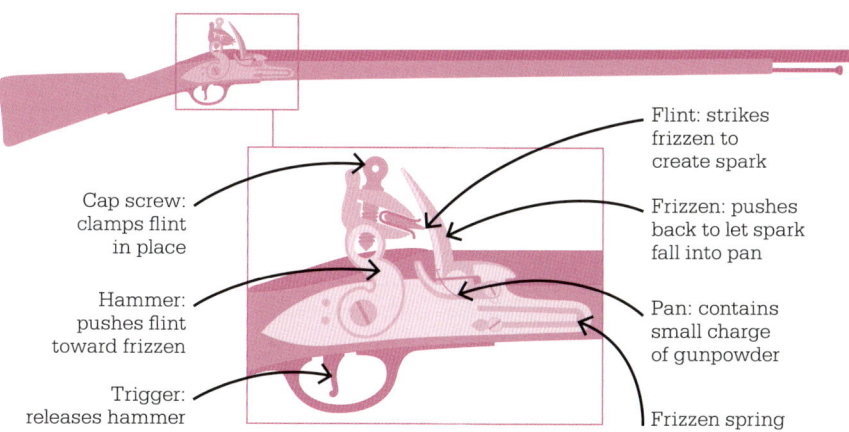

Cap screw: clamps flint in place

Hammer: pushes flint toward frizzen

Trigger: releases hammer

Flint: strikes frizzen to create spark

Frizzen: pushes back to let spark fall into pan

Pan: contains small charge of gunpowder

Frizzen spring

164 THE SEVEN YEARS' WAR

munitions to the front. Armies were forced to retreat to winter quarters when cold weather made maneuvers and fighting impossible, only to emerge again when conditions improved during spring. In naval battles, the side that delivered more firepower typically won the day. Navies, especially the powerful British Royal Navy, could also enforce blockades, disrupt shipping, and bombard enemy ports.

British involvement

Most of the fighting in the Seven Years' War occurred in modern-day Germany and Poland. This posed a challenge for Britain, which was primarily a maritime power. Since Britain's King George II also ruled the German state of Hanover, he wanted to protect it from France and Austria, but most British politicians were eager to avoid entanglements in Europe while expanding their empire. In the end, Britain opted to pursue naval dominance and focus its armies on colonial warfare in India and North America, sending only limited forces into Europe. Britain would also use its financial power—most of which came from its burgeoning colonial empire—to bankroll its allies, principally Prussia.

French and British colonists had been fighting in North America since 1754, but Britain formally declared war on France in May 1756. Three months later, Frederick entered the war by invading Saxony, an Austrian ally. He hoped this would protect Silesia and act as a launchpad for attacking Austrian territory in Bohemia and Moravia. Prussian forces occupied Saxony and forced the surrender of its army. In April 1757, Frederick invaded Bohemia but was later forced to withdraw when Austria, Russia, and Sweden attacked Prussian territory. He became more isolated when France's successful invasion of Hanover made it easier to send troops to fight Prussia.

Decisive battles

The course of the war turned in Prussia's favor, thanks to two victories in late 1757. At Rossbach, in Saxony, Frederick defeated a French–Austrian army of 41,000, despite commanding only 22,000. At the start of the 90-minute battle, Frederick tricked opposing generals into believing he was retreating. When they pursued, Frederick unleashed a devastating cavalry charge. The Prussian infantry then wheeled around to attack, supported by a second cavalry charge. All the while, Prussian artillery, mobile enough to be repositioned rapidly, bombarded the enemy. After this defeat, France never again sent armies against Prussia.

Seeking to maintain momentum, Frederick marched his army 170 miles (270 km) northeast into Silesia to fight the Austrians at Leuthen. His forces were again outnumbered, this time by 65,000 to 35,000. Frederick deployed one of his signature tactics, the "oblique order." This involved strengthening one flank to encourage the enemy to attack the weaker one, which would pin them in place. The stronger flank would then circle

> The peace is a jack-o'-lantern that dances before one's eyes … ready to lead some folks into a woeful quagmire.
>
> **Horace Walpole**
> British politician, 1762

The massed ranks of Frederick's Prussian infantry, carrying flintlock muskets with bayonets attached, advance on Austrian troops at Leuthen on December 5, 1757.

The one-day Battle of Kunersdorf was the only time the Prussian army lost the upper hand during the Seven Years' War. Even the victors suffered losses of more than a quarter of their troops.

around and attack the enemy from the rear, surrounding them. The tactic was risky, since it relied on high levels of cohesion and required officers to maintain control of their men. The Austrians fell into the trap and were defeated. Frederick recaptured all of Silesia, and the Austrians retreated into Bohemia. The following year, 1758, saw a series of inconclusive battles, in which neither side was able to gain the initiative.

War outside Europe

The war was not confined to Europe. While fighting in Germany, France was less able to defend its colonies and trade routes from Britain. In North America, British forces had taken control of all French colonies on the continent by 1760.

France and Britain were also rivals in India, where both sought to be the dominant colonial power. The British East India Company vied for influence with the French, who were themselves allied with the local powers of the Mughal Empire and the Nawab of Bengal. In 1757, British forces led by Robert Clive won a major victory at the Battle of Plassey, allowing the East India Company to annex swathes of territory in Bengal, laying the groundwork for the company to eventually go on to rule most of India. Subsequently, British forces captured France's settlements in southern India.

Prussia threatened again

In August 1759, Prussia was once again on the precipice, following a crushing reversal at the hands of an Austro-Russian army at the Battle of Kunersdorf. This was Frederick's worst defeat, but disagreements between the Austrian and Russian forces prevented the two from consolidating their success.

France, meanwhile, was faced with determined resistance from Hanoverian forces, a damaging blockade at the hands of the British Royal Navy, and setbacks in North America, leaving it less able to support its allies. Nevertheless, the war continued to go badly for Prussia, which faced an occupation of its capital Berlin by Austrian and Russian forces, and dwindling recruits. Then, on January 5, 1762, Frederick received a stroke of good fortune when Empress Elizabeth of Russia died. Her nephew and successor, Peter III, who greatly admired Frederick, changed sides and arranged a truce between Sweden and Prussia. This allowed Prussia to force Austria out of its territory and once more gain control of Silesia.

A new world order

By 1763, the combatants were exhausted. Britain had stopped sending aid to Prussia, while in Russia, Catherine the Great had overthrown Peter III and withdrawn her empire from the war. Neither France nor Austria had the resources or energy to take advantage of this.

A series of peace treaties ended the Seven Years' War. Britain gained territory in North America at the expense of France and Spain and had its status confirmed as the leading colonial power in India. Meanwhile, Prussian control of Silesia was consolidated. Prussia now challenged Austria for regional dominance and was unquestionably one of Europe's great powers. ∎

> I shall not survive this cruel misfortune … I have no resources left, and to speak quite frankly, I believe everything is lost.
> **Frederick II**
> after the Battle of Kunersdorf (1759)

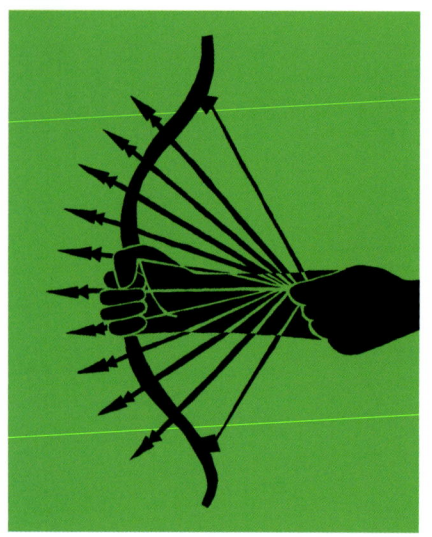

THE BOW WILL BE SOON UNSTRUNG, AND THE WAR AT AN END
THE TEN GREAT CAMPAIGNS (1755–1792)

IN CONTEXT

FOCUS
Hongli's campaigns: success or failure?

BEFORE
1678 In northwest China, Dzungar nomads expand into the Tarim Basin of Xinjiang.

1720 A Chinese expedition to Tibet expels the Dzungars and brings the country under Manchu rule.

1745 Dzungar khan Galdan Tseren dies, creating a power vacuum in the Tarim Basin.

AFTER
1858 With the Treaty of Aigun, China cedes Manchuria to the Russian Empire.

1862 The mainly Muslim Hui people revolt, sparking massacres and forced migrations in western China.

1949 After the triumph of communism on the mainland, Chinese Nationalists establish a Republic of China in Taiwan.

After coming to power in China in 1735, the Qianlong Emperor, also known as Hongli, took the Qing state to its greatest geographical extent. An accomplished poet, Hongli called his reign that of the Ten Great Campaigns, though he fought more than 10 wars—not all of them successfully—in half a dozen theaters.

Hongli's first three campaigns (in 1755, 1756–1757, and 1758) focused on the Dzungars of Xinjiang, a nomadic population of the steppe. The Qianlong Emperor could rely on 200,000 troops from the Eight Banners army—most of Manchu origins—and 600,000 soldiers from the Green Standard army, consisting largely of Han soldiers.

Following an uprising against Qing authority led by Dzungar ruler Amursana, Hongli ordered the complete extermination of the Dzungars. Having decreed the massacre of all men—up to half a million, according to scribes—he allowed his troops to enslave the women and children.

A civilizing mission
Hongli set about "civilizing" Xinjiang. He brought thousands of Chinese colonists to cultivate the land, build towns, introduce laws, and trade. The results were mixed. There had been good reasons for the nomadic lifestyle adopted by the Dzungars in the grasslands of the steppe. Water was scant, and the soils were poor; agricultural production rose only very slowly.

It proved difficult to organize labor, too. In newly conquered areas, Hongli instructed his soldiers to work the land, but they did not adapt easily to a peasant life. It also took time to establish

Show no mercy at all to these rebels. Only the old and weak should be saved. Our previous military campaigns were too lenient.
Qianlong Emperor, 1757

EARLY MODERN WARFARE 167

See also: Origins of the Chinese Empire 44–47 ▪ The Han Empire 48–49 ▪ The European conquest of the Americas 122–125 ▪ The establishment of Manchu China 142–143 ▪ Ottoman decline and Russian expansion 232–233

A portrait of a bodyguard armed with a sword and bow and arrow is one of 100 artworks commissioned by Hongli to memorialize his most loyal warriors and public servants.

civilian families in what could be an arduous existence; many became disillusioned and fled. As a result, convicts were brought in and forced to follow the strict work regime.

Despite these difficulties, Hongli took the conquest and colonization of Xinjiang as a template for subsequent ventures against the hill peoples of Jinchuan, in the north of Sichuan, central China. It took the Qianlong Emperor two hard-fought and extraordinarily costly campaigns, in 1747–1749 and 1771–1776, to impose his rule there.

Paying the price

Turning south, Hongli declared war on Burma (Myanmar) four times in quick succession—in 1765, 1766, 1767–1768, and 1769. Burma resisted all these attacks. China was hit hard, both financially and in terms of military strength: over five years, the conflicts cost the Qing army about 70,000 lives. Hongli's army had more luck in Taiwan, where, in the campaign of 1786–1788, it suppressed a rebellion by groups loyal to the Ming dynasty, which had collapsed in 1644.

However, success was not to last. In 1788, the emperor sent his troops into Tibet to repel an invasion of Gurkhas from Nepal. The invaders withdrew without a fight, but returned three years later. The Qing army prevailed, but it had been stretched to its limit, and in 1792 Hongli and the Gurkhas signed a peace treaty. A campaign in Vietnam, in 1788, did not achieve even this qualified success. Hongli's generals overplayed their hand, and the army of the Tay Son dynasty won a decisive victory at Ngoc Hoi Dong Da.

The financial and military costs of Hongli's Ten Campaigns were vast. Eventually, they would trigger the decline of the Qing dynasty. ∎

Hongli's **policy of expansion** results in **punitive expeditions** against neighboring peoples.

Colonizing the new territories proves **more challenging** than expected.

Continuing **campaigns stretch** the Qing army to its **limit**.

The Ten Great Campaigns yield only modest results.

Boundary issues

The Qianlong Emperor did not see himself as an empire builder—more as one entrusted with helping his kingdom to realize its historic role. It seemed clear to Hongli that the wild steppe should be tamed and that the mountain peoples should be subjected to civilizing rule. He also believed that Taiwan—which was not just geographically but politically isolated—should be brought back into the Qing fold, where he believed it belonged.

In the 20th and 21st centuries, Western critics have highlighted the more imperialistic aspects of Chinese politics, such as the annexation of Tibet (1950–1951), threats toward the island of Taiwan, and the persecution of the Uyghur people of Xinjiang. China views things differently, and these differences have important historic precedents. China sees Tibet as part of its territory—going back to Tibet's conquest by the Mongol Empire in 1240—as it does Xinjiang, annexed even longer ago, by the Han dynasty around 130 BCE.

REVOLU
AND EM
1775–1914

TIONS
PIRE

INTRODUCTION

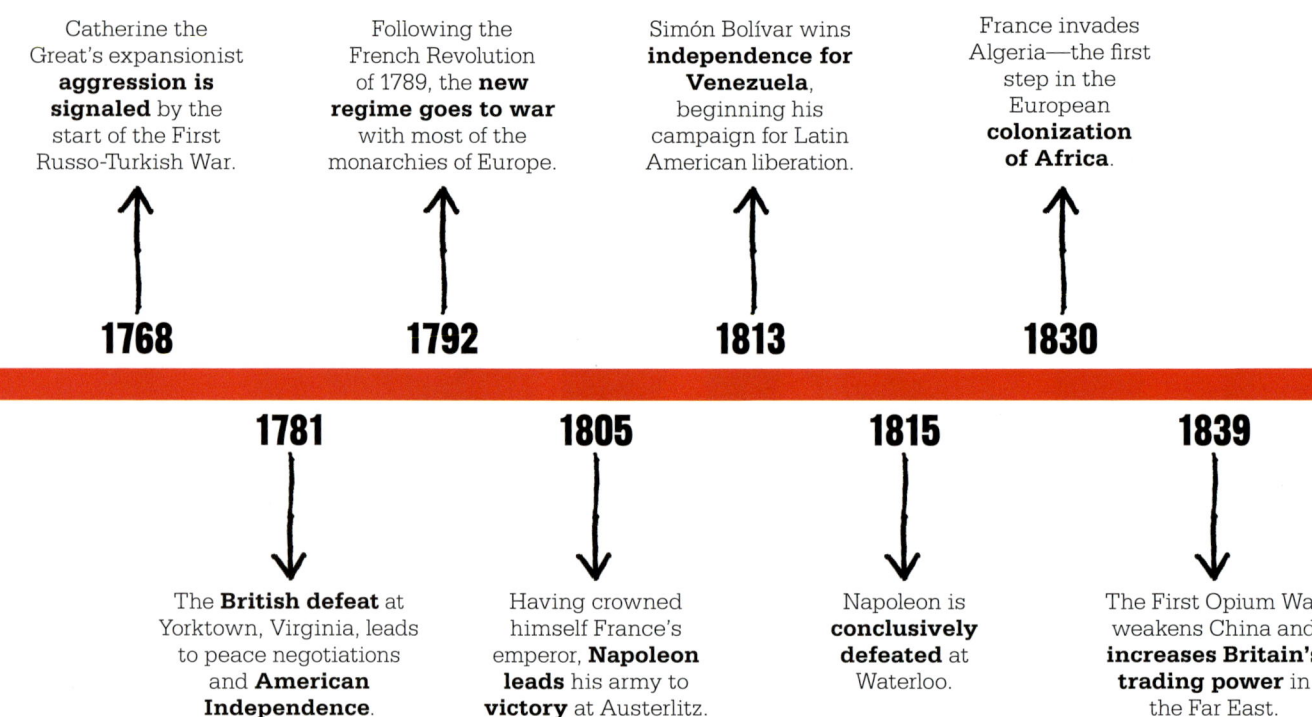

The late 18th and 19th centuries were marked by the making and breaking of empires in wars fought with ever more sophisticated weapons and strategies. In the 1760s, Empress of Russia, Catherine the Great, set out to extend her nation's territory at the expense of the Ottoman Turks, whose empire was beginning to decline. Britain's empire in North America shrank after its 13 colonies rebelled and, with French military and naval support, fought their way to independence as the nascent United States.

Inspirational leaders
France faced chaos at home when its people overthrew the French monarchy in 1789. Its revolution took on an international dimension as European neighbors rallied against the new regime, fearing its anarchy and class hatred could spread. Their desire to crush the spirit of revolution only served to fire the zeal of France's new leaders, who introduced mass conscription and appointed a dynamic but ruthless military commander—Napoleon Bonaparte. His audacious victories across Europe enabled him to seize control of France, declaring himself First Consul and then Emperor of the French.

Yet Napoleon's forces were not invincible. They faced defeat on the sea at the Battle of Trafalgar in 1805, and during the Peninsular War (1808–1814) British forces aiding Spain and Portugal against the French invaders gained significant victories. In 1813, Napoleon's ill-conceived campaign in Russia ended in a humiliating retreat, and the French emperor was finally crushed by a coalition of European forces at Waterloo in 1815.

Like all great leaders, Napoleon had the ability to inspire the men he led. In South America, Simón Bolívar of Venezuela ignited a spirit of revolt against oppressive Spanish rule. His relentless campaigns eventually led to the fall of Spain's New World empire, the emergence of a new republic, and finally, separate independent states.

To the north, the US was set on expansion. Texas, a state within the Mexican Republic in the 1820s, fought for and won independence in 1836. Nine years later, US president James K. Polk annexed Texas, sent his troops south, and declared war on Mexico, which—within two years—lost almost half of its land. In the course of the war, the US had

REVOLUTIONS AND EMPIRE 171

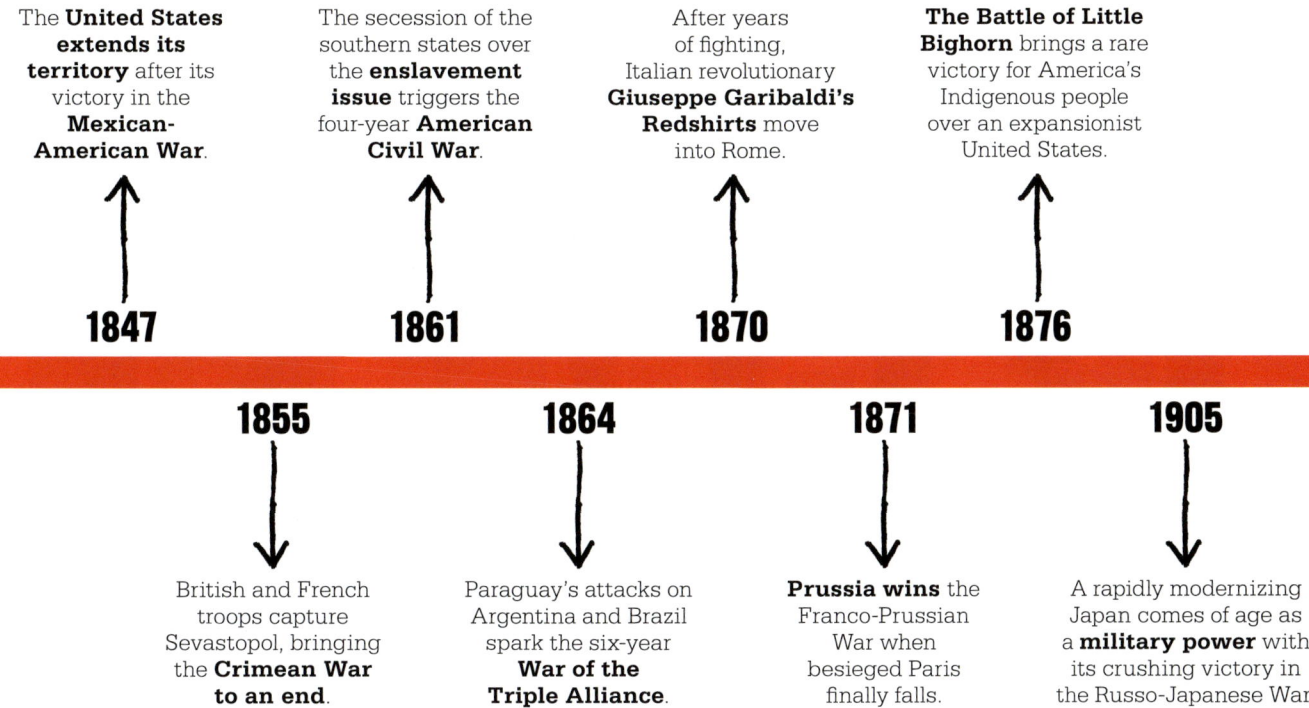

A century of change

In the 1800s, care for the wounded improved. Napoleon's chief military surgeon, Dominique-Jean Larrey, introduced wagons to transport wounded men from the battlefield and triage to prioritize casualties. In the Crimean War (1853–1856), fought between Russia and an alliance of the Ottoman Empire, Britain, and France, Florence Nightingale and Mary Seacole highlighted the need for good hygiene and effective nursing care. Swiss businessman Henry Dunant, who helped tend the wounded at Solferino during Italy's wars of unification, later founded the International Red Cross. Troops also gained a new weapon—the Colt revolver, which revolutionized handguns and became known as "the gun that won the West."

As technology advanced, deadlier weapons were deployed. Britain, which completed its conquest of India in 1857, had carved out a great empire, but Imperial Germany, with its backbone of Prussian military might, was emerging as a rival. Equipped with powerful, accurate guns, Prussia had led the German forces that defeated France in 1871. From the 1880s, Germany, Britain, and other European nations fought for land in Africa using superior weapons, such as the Maxim gun, the first automatic machine gun, to subdue Indigenous Africans.

Advances in America made its own bitter civil conflict—between the northern United States and the 11 southern Confederate States—the first modern war. It featured repeating rifles, ironclad warships, reconnaissance balloons, railroads for transporting troops, and telegraph communication. At the war's end, in 1865, the Union was restored but the brutal suppression of its Indigenous people continued; by 1890, survivors were left with just 2 percent of North American land.

Global losses and gains

The world order was changing. By 1900, the US was becoming an industrial giant. In the Far East, Japan was on the rise after victory in its first war against China, which had been weakened by the earlier Opium Wars and its own internal conflicts. A militarily strong Russia had driven the Turks out of areas of the Balkans in 1878, but in 1905, Japan would impose a humiliating defeat on Russia and destroy its fleet. In Europe, too, tensions were steadily reaching boiling point. ∎

GIVE ME LIBERTY, OR GIVE ME DEATH!

THE AMERICAN REVOLUTION (1775–1781)

174 THE AMERICAN REVOLUTION

IN CONTEXT

FOCUS
Colonial discontent

BEFORE
1765 A group of British colonists in North America issues a Declaration of Rights and Grievances in response to taxation policies.

1770 Nervous British troops fire on protesters in Boston, killing five.

1773 Settlers protesting over taxation throw crates of tea from a British ship into the harbor—an event later known as the Boston Tea Party.

AFTER
1783 The Treaty of Paris brings the American Revolution to its official end. Britain still has territories in Canada.

1803 President Thomas Jefferson completes the Louisiana Purchase, buying French territory in the Midwest and Mississippi Valley.

While Britain was occupied in Canada with the French and Indian War (1754–1763), its Thirteen Colonies along the Atlantic Seaboard fended for themselves. They prospered, prompting a beleaguered Britain to raise revenue by increasing taxes.

The wealthiest colonists were already struggling under restrictions that Britain had placed on their expansion into Native American territories beyond the Appalachians. They had hoped to establish—and make huge profits from—plantations that would be worked by enslaved people. The colonists, claiming that taxation without representation within the British Parliament was unconstitutional, aired their grievances at the First Continental Congress in Philadelphia in 1774. Britain responded by restricting the colonists' freedoms even further.

The militias mobilize

The colonists had long had their own militias to defend against Native American attacks. These now formed the basis of a rebel army, soldiers of which would later be known as Patriots. By April 1775, the situation in Massachusetts was

British Redcoats attacked militiamen at Lexington on April 19, 1775, though it is unknown who fired the first shot. This wood engraving of the battle dates from c. 1840.

so volatile that the British attempted to preempt worse trouble by seizing all the military supplies in the settlers' arsenal at Concord, northwest of Boston. Instead, they triggered all-out war.

At Lexington, while en route to Concord, a 700-strong army of British "Redcoats" clashed with a group of militiamen, killing eight. The Redcoats pressed on to Concord, where more militiamen fired upon them, forcing them to retreat. The American Revolution had begun—with a victory for irregular troops over a conventional army.

The Marquis de Lafayette, Gilbert du Motier, was a French aristocrat and military officer. He is considered a hero in both France and the US.

The French connection

It was a spirit of anti-Britishness rather than democratic fervor that prompted French king Louis XVI to embrace the Patriots' cause. He may also have been swayed by the Committee of Secret Correspondence, a lobbying group that the Thirteen Colonies had founded in 1775 to raise support for American independence.

Some French noblemen—such as the Marquis de Lafayette—would play an important part in the fighting against the British in America and then go home and spread the revolutionary message there. Mostly, though, the Patriots drew France's staunch conservatives to their cause by demonstrating how the Revolution was damaging British interests in North America. Throughout the 18th century—from the Spanish War of Succession, to the French Revolutionary Wars—Britain and France would remain enemies.

However mixed their motives, the French played a vital role in the American Revolution. They supplied weapons, as well as troops and naval support.

The British withdrew to the supposed safety of Boston. There they were besieged by local militias, who were joined in June by the newly formed Continental Army led by General George Washington.

On June 17, 1775, Britain's General Sir William Howe took Patriot positions on Bunker Hill and Breed's Hill, overlooking the city. However, he lost more than 1,000 men, many of them officers, and failed to break the siege.

Howe withdrew to Halifax, Nova Scotia, in March 1776, and the Americans took back Boston. The revolution was making ground: in Philadelphia, on July 4, the Second Continental Congress issued the Declaration of Independence.

Setbacks and victories

Howe and his forces returned by land and sea in early July. After winning the Battle of Long Island, he took New York, forcing Washington to retreat across New Jersey and west into Pennsylvania.

Despite his army suffering from defections and shrinking supplies, Washington planned a surprise attack. He was outnumbered and outgunned by Britain but more motivated and equipped with local knowledge. On Christmas Night 1776, he crossed the frozen Delaware River with 2,400 men, who surrounded and captured a force of Hessians, German mercenaries fighting for the British, at Trenton, New Jersey. After defeating British Lieutenant

Washington Crossing the Delaware, by 19th-century German American artist Emanuel Leutze, highlights the heroism of the Patriots as they row their general across the icy river.

> Despite the day's misfortune … most of my men are in good spirits and still have the courage to fight the enemy another day.
>
> **George Washington**
> **Report on Brandywine Creek**

General Charles Cornwallis's army at Princeton, north of Trenton, Washington pushed the British northward and out of New Jersey.

In September 1777, determined to take Philadelphia, capital of the Thirteen Colonies, Howe landed at the head of Chesapeake Bay, about 50 miles (80 km) southwest of the city, and sent 5,000 troops on toward Philadelphia. Washington, waiting inland at Brandywine Creek, engaged this group but failed to anticipate the arrival of Howe himself with 6,000 more men. The British took Philadelphia with ease, but the Continental Army was able to retreat, largely intact.

Early the following month, Washington attacked Howe's army, which was encamped at Germantown, north of Philadelphia. British resolve and American miscommunication resulted in the Patriots retreating. Again, though, making the most of his militia-based force's flexibility, Washington got away with only minor casualties.

British surrender

Meanwhile, General John Burgoyne was leading a British army down the Hudson River Valley from Canada. Under General Horatio Gates, the Americans had built fortifications along the Bemis Heights, north of Albany, New York State, and blocked the valley with 7,000 infantrymen. They had also stationed snipers farther upriver and sent out skirmishers to harass the approaching force. »

Gates's effective irregular tactics left the British demoralized before they even reached the main Patriot line. On October 7, Burgoyne launched his attack. His men fought bravely, but they were exhausted and short of supplies. They fell back to the nearby town of Saratoga, where, on October 17, they became the first British army ever known to surrender.

Regrouping at Valley Forge

In December 1777, Washington and his 11,000-strong army established an encampment in Valley Forge, Pennsylvania. The plan was to recover, regroup, and resupply there—within a day's march of Philadelphia. Many of the soldiers did not have any footwear or winter coats, so they set about building wooden huts to protect against the weather. Within weeks, Valley Forge had become the fourth-largest city in the colonies. Malnutrition and disease killed as many as 2,000 men during that harsh winter. Spring came and the weather improved, but Washington prolonged the encampment to June, all the while retraining and restructuring his army.

From early 1778, the Patriots were also being helped by France. King Louis XVI had so enjoyed news of the British surrender at Saratoga that in February he recognized the American Republic. With the Treaty of Alliance, France also agreed to supply ammunitions, troops, and materiel support to the Patriots. However, the Anglo-French (or Bourbon) War (1778–1783) erupted in June, and America became just one theater in a wider conflict.

Despite the symbolic importance of Philadelphia, and the cost of taking the city only months before, the British withdrew to concentrate their forces around New York. Lieutenant General Henry Clinton, who had taken over from Howe, led his army northward to take up this deployment.

Washington set out to cut off the British. On June 28, his new, improved Continental Army caught Clinton's rearguard at Monmouth Court House, in New Jersey, where they fought to a standstill. The Battle of Monmouth was inconclusive, with heavy casualties on both sides, but Clinton had to slip away to the coast to have his men evacuated by the Royal Navy.

The Southern theater

Within a few months, Clinton was striking farther south, where Britain could count on the support of resident loyalists. In December 1778, a seaborne British expedition captured Savannah, Georgia. An attempt in 1779 to take it back failed, so the southern city remained in British hands until the end of the war. In March 1780, Britain's army also besieged Charleston, South Carolina, taking it by May.

The race was now on for the bulk of the British forces to reach New York, where their headquarters was under siege by Patriots backed by Commander Comte

> The general is well, but much worn with fatigue and anxiety. I never knew him to be so anxious as now.
>
> **Martha Washington**
> at Valley Forge

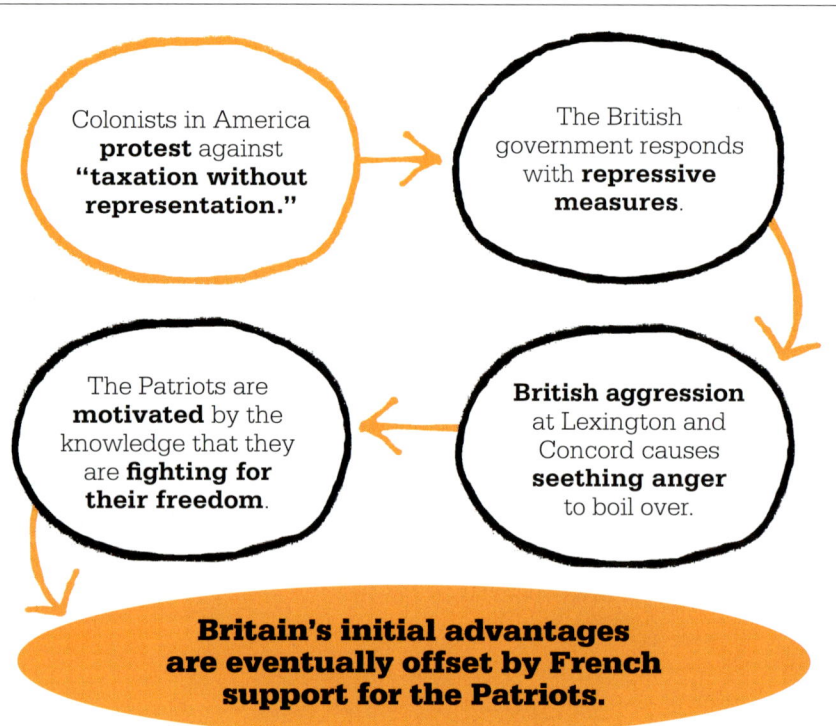

de Rochambeau's French army. Clinton left the South in the hands of Cornwallis, who controlled key outposts and supply depots, such as Camden, South Carolina. In August 1780, the Patriots sent Horatio Gates to recapture Camden, but his largely inexperienced troops suffered one of the Revolution's most devastating defeats at the hands of Cornwallis's army.

Slow attrition

In October 1780, Nathanael Greene was given command of the Continental Army in the South. His administrative background as a quartermaster made him seem an uninspiring choice, as did his strategy of avoiding confrontation with Cornwallis. Instead, Greene split his army and allowed the British to chase him all over the South, making only the occasional small-scale attack. Months went by without any indication of a breakthrough from either side. Meanwhile, Cornwallis's troops were approaching exhaustion, dogged by hunger and disease.

In a bid to break the deadlock, General Clinton started to plan a major expedition to the South and instructed Cornwallis to find and fortify a suitable deep-water port.

The major battles of the American Revolution saw alternating fortunes between the British and the Patriots. Most engagements took place close to the coastal areas of the Thirteen Colonies, between New York State and Georgia.

Key:
✗ British victory
✗ American victory
⚓ British blockade
□ Fort
▇ New England colonies
▇ Middle colonies
▇ Southern colonies

In August 1781, Cornwallis occupied Yorktown, Virginia, with further fortifications added across the York River at Gloucester Point.

While Cornwallis readied his base, Lieutenant General Comte de Grasse's French fleet was sailing up from the Caribbean. British Admiral Thomas Graves's ships arrived in Chesapeake Bay on September 5, to find the French already there. The ensuing Battle of the Chesapeake took a huge toll on the British fleet, which fled to New York, leaving the French in control of the bay. This allowed fresh troops and supplies to be brought to the American forces already arrayed around Yorktown.

The Siege of Yorktown started on September 28. With only 8,000 men against a Franco-American force of 17,000, Cornwallis had to abandon his position. He surrendered on October 19, his defeat marking the collapse of the British war effort.

America's resistance to British rule harnessed the discontent, fighting spirit, and skills of a colonized people, and their desire for liberty. That the people could collectively exert great force was to be the United States' lesson to the modern world. The British learned it at considerable cost. ■

At the Battle of the Chesapeake, the French fleet blocked the entrance to Chesapeake Bay to British ships, which meant that General Cornwallis's army at Yorktown was left without support.

A GREAT WIND IS BLOWING
THE WARS OF CATHERINE THE GREAT (1768–1795)

IN CONTEXT

FOCUS
A Russian empire

BEFORE
1547 Ivan the Terrible, who has been ruling as grand prince of Moscow since 1533, appoints himself Russia's first czar.

1722 Peter the Great launches a war on Safavid Iran over territories in the Caucasus and the Caspian Sea.

1739 In the Treaty of Niš, signed with the Ottoman Empire, Russia agrees to keep its fleet out of the Black Sea.

AFTER
1796 Catherine's son Paul I becomes czar after her death.

1813 Following a nine-year war with Persia, Russia gains Georgia and other territories in the southern Caucasus.

1829 With the Treaty of Adrianople, the Ottomans cede the eastern shore of the Black Sea to Russia.

In 1762, Catherine, empress consort of Russia, overthrew her husband, Peter III, to become the country's ruler. German by birth, she fully embraced her adopted homeland, but her views were inspired by the Enlightenment, a European philosophical movement that valued logic and reason. In a 1767 legal code, Catherine stated that Russia was "a European state." By this, she meant that it was a place of culture but also that it had the right to govern lesser nations.

Russo-Turkish wars
Catherine, who would become known as "the Great," dedicated herself to the expansion of Russia, which shared a border with the Ottoman Empire. The two countries had been fighting on and off since the 16th century. In 1768, a Cossack-led massacre in Balta (then in the Ottoman Empire, now in Ukraine) led to a six-year conflict. That Russo-Turkish war was complicated by the involvement of the Bar Confederation, a group of Polish nobles angered by Russian interference in their country's politics and royal elections.
With no Black Sea fleet to deploy since the 1739 Treaty of Niš, the Russians brought in ships from the Baltic. In July 1770, this force defeated the Ottoman fleet at Chesma, on the Aegean Sea.

Russian victories
In Moldavia, Field Marshal Pyotr Rumyantsev routed the Turks at Larga and Kagul (July and August 1770) before pushing westward into modern-day Romania. By 1771, General Alexander Suvorov had defeated the Bar Confederation too.

Catherine the Great is portrayed as a military leader in this equestrian painting by 18th-century Danish artist Vigilius Eriksen. She is wearing the uniform of the Life Guards Regiment.

REVOLUTIONS AND EMPIRE 179

See also: Classical Greece 24–27 ▪ The rise of the Ottoman Turks 112–113 ▪ The Ottoman Empire 130–133 ▪ The Great Northern War 158 ▪ The Ten Great Campaigns 166–167 ▪ Ottoman decline and Russian expansion 232–233

> Is it not better to finish a war with the death of 7,000 people rather than to drag it on and kill 100,000?
> **Alexander Suvorov**
> Russian general, 1794

In 1772, Russia, Prussia, and Austria each took a tranche of Polish territory in the First Partition of Poland agreement; two years later, the Russians took the Crimean Khanate from the Ottomans, making it their dominion. Catherine's lover, Field Marshal Grigory Potemkin, annexed it in 1783. Russian court poets compared these victories to those of ancient Athens over Persia—a triumph of Western civilization over so-called Eastern barbarity.

In 1787, the Ottomans tried to recover the lands lost to Russia in Crimea. Potemkin, supported by Suvorov, led Russia's brutal response. In an assault on the citadel of Ochakov (in modern-day Ukraine) in December 1788, his troops killed up to 11,000 men in a few hours; two years later, at the Siege of Izmail, they slaughtered 26,000 Ottomans over three days.

Further expansion

Russia had also been extending its empire on other fronts. In 1783, the Nogai people east of the Azov Sea had killed their own women and children, before fighting to the death, rather than submit to Russia. In 1785, an uprising in Chechnya supplied the pretext for a punitive expedition. A pattern emerged of Russia seizing on local resistance to justify wholesale invasions.

A Russian victory in 1795 led to the final Partition of Poland: the country effectively ceased to exist for more than 120 years. Meanwhile, the Russian Empire continued to expand after Catherine's death. ∎

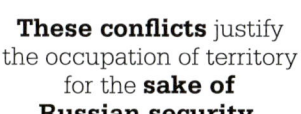

Russia enters into **diplomatic quarrels** with Poland and **border disputes** with Turkey, before **encroaching into the Caucasus**.

↓

These conflicts justify the occupation of territory for the **sake of Russian security**.

↓

Holding these territories requires a **Russian administrative presence**.

↓

Catherine's empire expands inexorably.

The Battle of Kazan, depicted here by 19th-century artist Otto Friedrich Theodor von Möller, was a key moment in Catherine's reign.

The Cossacks

For centuries, the mainly Slavic and Christian Cossacks had led a seminomadic life as herders on the Pontic steppe, a vast expanse of grassland northeast of the Black Sea. They looked upon settled civilization with a degree of disdain and kept themselves detached from wider Russian culture. Ironically, this made them the ideal servants of a czarist state that frequently saw its own people as the enemy. In addition to serving as cavalry, the Cossacks often played a policing role in times of disorder or social stress; they became "enforcers" to successive czars from the time of the first one, Ivan the Terrible (r. 1547–1584), onward.

The Cossack uprising known as Pugachev's Rebellion (1773–1775) was an early test of Catherine's resolve. At the Battle of Kazan in July 1774, her army quelled the insurgents and captured the leader of the rebels, Yemelyan Pugachev, who was publicly executed in Moscow the following year.

THE JUST DEFENSE OF A FREE PEOPLE

THE WARS OF THE FRENCH REVOLUTION (1792–1805)

182 THE WARS OF THE FRENCH REVOLUTION

IN CONTEXT

FOCUS
Mass conscription

BEFORE
1618–1648 The Thirty Years' War ravaging Central Europe is fought largely by mercenary units, who are little better than armed mobs.

1645 Oliver Cromwell's New Model Army is England's first truly national army.

1789 Before the Revolution, France's Royal Army contains numerous mercenary units of foreign origin.

AFTER
1806–1814 The Prussian Army creates an innovative system of male universal conscription on a short-term, rotating basis.

1861–1865 The Union and Confederate governments use compulsory military conscription to maintain their armies in the American Civil War.

Young men will go to the front; married men will forge arms and transport foodstuffs; women will make tents and uniforms and serve in the hospitals …
French Convention decree
ordering the *levée en masse*, 1793

The French Revolution of 1789–1799 convulsed Europe as nothing else had since the Thirty Years' War (1618–1648). Europe's other great powers, all monarchies, formed a series of military coalitions against France's new, radical egalitarianism, usually involving a combination of the Austrian Empire, Prussia, and Britain. Their military and naval forces, initially triumphant, soon faced a massive French army of conscripts who were full of revolutionary zeal. Led, from 1796, by Napoleon Bonaparte—the most talented commander since Alexander the Great—this army threatened to overwhelm Europe.

The *levée en masse*

However ardent, the volunteers of 1792—when the War of the First Coalition (1792–1797) against Austria, Britain, Prussia, Spain, and other nations began—did not mix well with the regulars of the French Army. The revolutionaries wore republican blue, while the regulars were still uniformed in royal white. The revolutionaries did not even receive training. They never lacked courage but

French troops at the Battle of Valmy sang revolutionary songs, such as their new national anthem, "Chant de guerre pour l'Armée du Rhin" ("War Song for the Army of the Rhine").

could hardly execute the simplest bayonet charge. One of the army's few victories in 1792, at Valmy, was won by the French artillery, largely manned by veterans.

As defeat mounted upon defeat, the infamous Reign of Terror—when thousands were executed for opposing the Revolution—saw many of the army's officers guillotined. The military situation became desperate. In 1793, coalition forces threatened to take the French naval base at Toulon.

On August 23, the National Convention (the revolutionary government) in Paris decreed a *levée en masse* (mass conscription) requisitioning the services of all French people for the war effort. This was not mere conscription; the decree essentially mobilized the entire French economy: every blacksmith would hammer out arms, every plowshare would become a sword, and every haywain would now carry provisions. Women were

REVOLUTIONS AND EMPIRE 183

See also: The American Revolution 172–177 ▪ Napoleon triumphant 188–191 ▪ The Peninsular War 192–193 ▪ Napoleon at bay 194–197 ▪ The American Civil War 214–221 ▪ World War II in Europe 266–271

- **France** is **beleaguered** on all sides by enemies intent on **destroying the Revolution**.
- The entire **French nation** must be **mobilized** to counter the threat.
- New **recruits** are interspersed with **trained veterans**, more than doubling the army's size.
- **A mass-conscription program swells the army's ranks.**
- Innovative **tactics overwhelm** smaller, more traditional **enemy armies**.
- **Economic reforms** are introduced to finance the **enlarged army**.

---

included in the *levée*, serving in hospitals or making tents and clothing, and even children would scrape linen into lint to be used for dressing wounds.

The *levée* was not only a summons to prepare for total war; it was also an ideological call, stemming from the same egalitarian motivations as the Revolution's Declaration of the Rights of Man and the Citizen. It was not addressed to foreign mercenaries, the source of reinforcements in all previous 18th-century wars. Rather, it was an appeal to the people of a nation made up of fellow citizens, not serfs or subjects ruled by a tyrannical monarch. Reactionary forces were threatening to crush a citizens' republic, the embodiment of the Revolution's higher values, if not of its actual practices. *Liberté*, *égalité*, and *fraternité* were at stake. The *levée* marked the birth of modern patriotism.

Surge to victory

Lazare Carnot, the new French minister of war, was the main author of the *levée* decree. As the "organizer of victory," he also oversaw the decree's implementation. Within weeks of the decree's enactment, Carnot had overseen the recruitment of 300,000 men and raised an astonishing 14 new armies. The recruits came mainly from rural villages rather than towns, as had previously been the case, thus mirroring the population of France as a whole. They were also integrated into the ranks so that they learned the basics of warfare more quickly.

By 1794, these brothers-in-arms had gone on the offensive, turning a string of defeats into a tide of victories that washed over the Low Countries. In June of that year, at Fleurus in the Austrian Netherlands (modern-day Belgium), the Revolutionary armies defeated both the Austrians and the Dutch, winning the entire left bank of the Rhine River for the French Republic. Holland became a French client state, called the Batavian Republic. By 1795, Spain and Prussia had abandoned the war, leaving only Austria and Britain still fighting the French. »

During the Reign of Terror (1793–1794), France's Committee of Public Safety executed thousands of people thought to be disloyal to the Revolution, including numerous army officers.

184 THE WARS OF THE FRENCH REVOLUTION

French morale soared. The victories not only democratized an army that was once rigidly hierarchical but also helped develop the intangible quality of élan, or spirit, that would dominate the French military mind for decades.

The Italian campaign
In early 1796, France's Army of Italy was scattered in detachments between Nice and Genoa on the Mediterranean coast, where it watched the enemy in Austrian-controlled northern Italy. In March, it received a new commander, a 27-year-old general named Napoleon Bonaparte, who promptly launched its 38,000 men and 60 cannon on a campaign so dazzling that it won not only battlefield victories against larger opponents but also diplomatic benefits. In April, crossing the passes in the Maritime Alps, Napoleon entered the Italian Piedmont region and, using his lines of communication to his advantage, won a series of key engagements.

Within two weeks, Napoleon had forced the King of Sardinia to sign an armistice, surrendering three fortresses and his artillery. Breaking out onto the plains of Lombardy in 1797, Napoleon continued to win battles, including Rivoli, near Lake Garda, and Faenza, near Bologna, where he forced Pope Pius VI to sign an armistice. Altogether, in a campaign lasting a year, Napoleon, a former artillery officer, used his army's guns so effectively that he won 18 major battles and lost only one. He captured hundreds of cannon and thousands of prisoners. His army also looted and extorted— money, paintings, and statues—as they went, the men sharing in the booty in an act that always boosted morale for recruits from the *levée*.

Britain alone?
In April 1797, as Napoleon approached Vienna, the Austrians sued for peace. On May 12, his threat to declare war on Venice unless it democratized compelled its last head of state to abolish the Most Serene Republic of Venice after 1,100 years of independence. As a further insult, Napoleon took the bronze horses from St. Mark's Square. When, in October, France and Austria signed the Treaty of Campo Formio, ending the War of the First Coalition, only Britain was left facing France.

Napoleon returned to Paris as a hero on December 5, 1797. There, he took command of the Army of England, which was being assembled at the Channel ports for a planned invasion of Britain.

British resources
Invading Britain would mean facing a British Army that was a mix of upper-class officers and lower-class foot soldiers, sometimes swelled by volunteers. It was buttressed by a part-time, largely rural militia, which was assembled when war broke out and was the closest thing to a *levée en masse* in Britain. Constitutionally separate from

When Napoleon crossed the Alps en route to Italy in May 1800, he did so on a mule. French artist Jacques-Louis David portrayed a more romantic image of the future emperor.

> None but the Republican phalanxes, the soldiers of liberty, could have endured what you have done.
> **Napoleon**
> Proclamation to the French army, May 1796

the army, the militia was still a dependable source of volunteers, especially when induced to enlist by bounties. Tens of thousands did so, and—facing France alone—the militia grew to 82,000 men in 1799.

Britain primarily relied on its Royal Navy for protection, which in turn depended for recruitment on its notorious press gangs, which roamed the nation's ports coercing men to serve. In 1795, a quota system had been imposed on each county to ensure that the warships were adequately manned. Counting the army and the militia together, the British military was three times the size of that employed during the course of the American Revolution (1775–1781).

The task of tackling Britain seemed so formidable that Napoleon postponed the invasion in favor of another expedition. Egypt, he reasoned, was the key to British India. He decided to seize Egypt for France, ally with anti-British Indian princes, and block access to Britain's richest colony while diverting trade to France.

The Egyptian expedition

For France, Napoleon's 1798–1799 Egyptian expedition was a journey of discovery. As a member of the French Academy of Sciences, Napoleon included 167 scientists and intellectuals in the expedition. They not only discovered the Rosetta Stone, which enabled the translation of Egyptian hieroglyphs, but also published *Description de l'Égypte* (*Description of Egypt*), a series of books that influenced the decorative arts and launched the discipline of Egyptology.

The French won numerous battles with great ease over the ruling Mamluks and the Ottoman Turks, in whose empire Napoleon was trespassing, but the clear enthusiasm of his troops withered in the desert heat, with thousands dying of hunger, thirst, and disease. On August 1, 1798, a British fleet under Vice Admiral Horatio Nelson captured or destroyed all but two of his ships in the Battle of the Nile, effectively marooning Napoleon and his men. The French then had to quell repeated uprisings and committed atrocities in a large raid into Palestine, which ended in defeat at Acre. After slightly more than a year, Napoleon and a small retinue managed to board a ship for France and pass blockading British squadrons. Despite the mixed fortunes of the Egyptian campaign, Napoleon returned to Paris a hero. Before the end of 1799, a coup d'état made him First Consul, effectively the military dictator of France.

The Second Coalition

In the meantime, the War of the Second Coalition (1798–1802) was well under way. In addition to Britain and Austria, France's opponents now included Russia, the Ottoman Empire (because of the Egyptian venture), and Portugal (Spain was now allied with France). France had already lost most of Napoleon's conquests in Italy.

Spring marked the start of the campaign season, and on May 15, 1800, Napoleon and some 40,000 troops began to cross the Alps into Italy. They chose the shortest but most difficult route—the high, windswept, snowbound Great St. Bernard Pass. For five days, »

The French were facing defeat at the Battle of Marengo when General François-Étienne Kellermann launched a devastating surprise cavalry attack on the Austrian troops.

THE WARS OF THE FRENCH REVOLUTION

the army dragged dismounted guns up and down goat paths. Finally emerging onto the Piedmont plains, they resumed maneuvers against the Austrians. On June 14, Austria, with a much larger force, engaged the French near the village of Marengo and, for most of a long day of battle, outdid them. His men on the point of collapse, Napoleon made some hasty adjustments. He sent in his cavalry, outflanked his opponent, and by twilight had wrested victory—one of his most inspired—from near-certain defeat.

Nearing the end?

Austria agreed to an armistice on June 15, 1800, and prepared to evacuate Italy. That truce held until November 13, when hostilities resumed along the Rhine. The First Consul, ensnared in political matters, remained in Paris while his subordinate, General Jean Moreau, decisively defeated Austrian and Bavarian forces in the forests of Hohenlinden, east of Munich, on December 3. Five months later, on April 2, 1801, Britain's Vice Admiral Horatio Nelson sailed a squadron led by 12 ships-of-the-line into Copenhagen's harbor and destroyed the Danish fleet at anchor. The Admiralty in London had feared a looming Franco-Danish alliance and was desperate to keep Napoleon from amassing any naval forces.

Nelson's attack on Copenhagen was the only strategic setback for France before the 1802 Treaty of Amiens ended the War of the Second Coalition. France still held the entire left bank of the Rhine and had established puppet states in Italy. Many historians believe that the treaty should be considered the end of the French Revolutionary Wars, since by the time fighting resumed in 1805, Napoleon had crowned himself Emperor of France (which he did in December 1804).

The Battle of Trafalgar

At least 36 naval campaigns or clashes characterized the French Revolutionary Wars. In addition to Nelson's engagements at the Nile and Copenhagen, the British Royal Navy won victories against French forces at the Fourth Battle of Ushant on June 1, 1794, and the Battle of Cape St. Vincent on February 14, 1797.

Outside of the 1812–1815 war between Britain and the US, only one great sea battle was fought after the close of the Revolutionary Wars, but the Battle of Trafalgar was the most decisive one of all.

By 1805, Napoleon was planning, once more, to invade Britain. He had amassed 2,293 ships in the ports around Boulogne, France, and was preparing to embark 161,215 men and 9,059

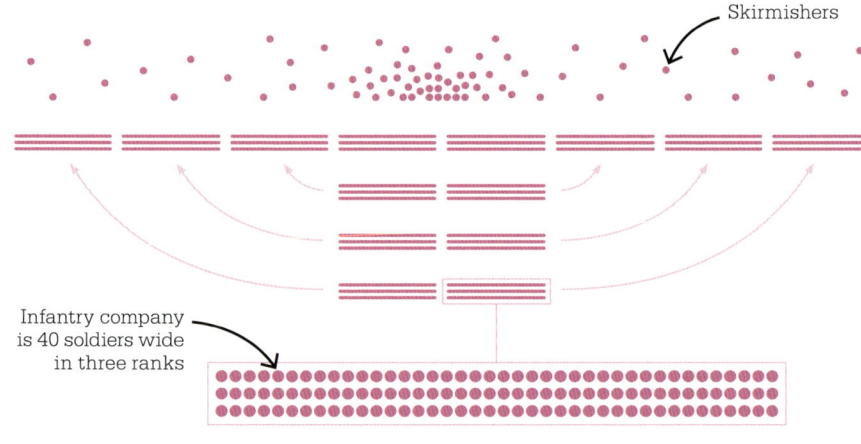

As a Napoleonic battalion advances, the lead companies break rank and skirmish with the enemy. Behind them, the other companies change configuration from column to line.

Skirmishers

Infantry company is 40 soldiers wide in three ranks

The role of skirmishers

French military tactics improved as a result of the *levée en masse*, and the army's stiff battlefield formations became more flexible. Conscripts helped perfect a new formation based on the age-old skirmish line. The command *déployez en tirailleur* ("deploy as skirmishers") triggered a complex frontal maneuver in which soldiers split into a loose, open formation, providing cover for the main battalions while advance scouts looked for the enemy line. Skirmishers were trained to take the initiative, using any available cover and firing either in position or while advancing and even retreating to keep an enemy off-balance. Working in pairs allowed one to reload while the other fired.

These refinements would later be used during the US Civil War, when the use of rifled muskets (with a grooved barrel), which were accurate at a longer range than their smoothbored predecessors, enhanced the value of the skirmish line.

At Trafalgar, the 104-gun British flagship HMS *Victory* (center right) broke the enemy line between *Bucentaure* and *Redoutable*; all three vessels were badly damaged.

horses. Before launching an invasion, he needed to control the English Channel by decisively defeating the dispersed Royal Navy, the famed "wooden walls" of Britain. Having successfully lured the British fleet, commanded by Nelson, far into the Atlantic Ocean, Napoleon's Combined Fleet of French and allied Spanish warships departed Cádiz, Spain, on October 17, bound for the Channel.

Napoleon underestimated Britain, which, between 1800 and 1812, expended nearly a quarter of its annual budget on its navy. Nelson's fleet intercepted the Combined Fleet on October 21, 1805, off Cape Trafalgar, in southwestern Spain. Dividing his smaller force into two columns, Nelson sailed eastward on a 90-degree course and smashed through the northbound enemy line, breaking it into three pieces, two of which he defeated in the battle that followed.

The Combined Fleet lost a third of its warships without capturing or sinking a single British vessel. A French sharpshooter did mortally wound Nelson, who afterward became a British national hero, but the Battle of Trafalgar would always be considered the Royal Navy's most famous victory.

Recruits aplenty

Britain had retained supremacy at sea. Napoleon's upcoming wars would all be fought in continental Europe. In addition, a 1798 law decreeing that every Frenchman was a soldier who "owes himself to the defense of the nation" ensured that the *levée en masse* was continued. Napoleon therefore had a regular and abundant supply of conscripted soldiers to feed into his superb instrument of war, the Grande Armée. ∎

Key
- British fleet
- French fleet
- Spanish fleet

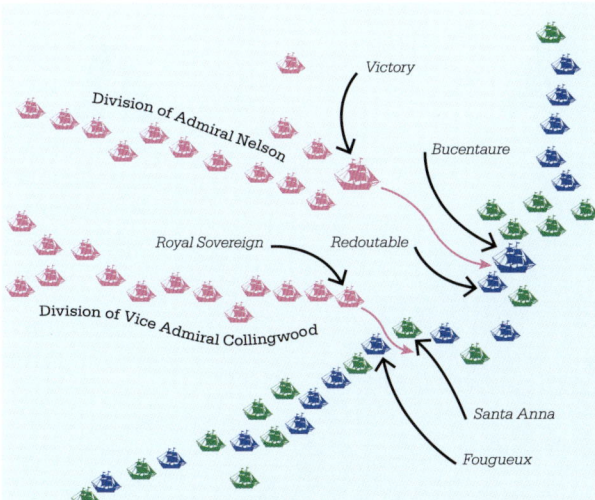

Nelson's winning strategy at Trafalgar relied on two columns of ships to break the Franco-Spanish fleet in three. His vessel was HMS *Victory*, and that of his second in command, Vice Admiral Cuthbert Collingwood, was HMS *Royal Sovereign*.

Never mind maneuvers. Always go at them.
Admiral Horatio Nelson

THAT SYNTHESIS OF MONSTER AND SUPERMAN
NAPOLEON TRIUMPHANT (1804–1809)

IN CONTEXT

FOCUS
The Grande Armée

BEFORE
1792 A decade of French Revolutionary Wars begins, creating a need for a bigger, more powerful army.

1793 The *levée en masse*—conscription of all young, able-bodied men—begins to transform the French army.

1796 Napoleon embarks on his Italian campaign, the start of his military conquests.

AFTER
1812 The Grande Armée reaches a peak strength of around 600,000 men.

1813 More than half a million soldiers fight in the Battle of Leipzig. Napoleon is defeated by an alliance of Austria, Prussia, Russia, and Sweden.

At the start of the 19th century, Europe's five great powers—Britain, France, Austria, Russia, and Prussia—were in competition for territorial and trading dominance. In 1804–1805, Austria, Britain, and Russia formed the Third Coalition, an alliance to oppose the expansionist intent of Napoleon, who had just crowned himself Emperor of France. In August 1805, Napoleon responded by marching nearly 200,000 soldiers from the French coast of the English Channel—from where he planned to invade Britain—eastward to meet a more immediate threat to the French Empire: the armies of Austria and Russia.

REVOLUTIONS AND EMPIRE

See also: The Seven Years' War 162–165 ▪ The American Revolution 172–177 ▪ The wars of the French Revolution 180–187 ▪ The Peninsular War 192–193 ▪ Napoleon at bay 194–197 ▪ The War of 1812 198–199

Philosophers of war

Two military theorists who had fought on opposite sides at the Battle of Jena (1807) made great contributions to the philosophy of war. Carl von Clausewitz (1780–1831) was a Prussian officer wounded and taken prisoner at the battle. His major work, *On War* (1832), contains the declaration, "War therefore is an act of violence intended to compel our opponent to fulfil our will." The book, which draws greatly from his study of the armies of the Napoleonic Era, remains an influential work to this day. Antoine-Henri Jomini (1779–1869), served under Napoleon at Jena. His *Summary of the Art of War* (1838) was widely read in military academies in the 19th century. Jomini put into words what Napoleon accomplished in deed, providing a comprehensive description of what the French emperor saw intuitively with just a glance. Many US Civil War generals were disciples of Jomini.

Napoleon's troops, which he called his Grande Armée (Grand Army), were arguably the best-drilled and trained military force in the world. Its organization was part of a new approach to military strategy, which also covered logistics, tactics, and communications. It was made up of six self-contained corps, each 10,000- to 50,000-strong and encompassing several divisions, themselves incorporating two or three brigades of two regiments each. The six corps, with their own cavalry and artillery, could work as independent armies, although they were ultimately controlled by the emperor. Napoleon also kept an Imperial Guard—a powerful elite reserve of infantry, cavalry, and artillery—at his disposal.

The thorough drilling given to each soldier was as important as the army's reorganization. When, for example, the army crossed bridges over the Rhine River to face Austrian and Russian armies advancing into Bavaria, every infantryman knew how to deploy, either as a battering-ram column or a line spanning the battlefield. Each cavalryman was skilled at riding through enemy fire, and every artillery unit was trained to deploy its guns quickly and bring them into play at the decisive place and time.

The first major land battle of the War of the Third Coalition was against the Austrians around Ulm in the Electorate of Bavaria, in the south of modern-day Germany, fought October 16–19, 1805. Here, Napoleon outmaneuvered the smaller opposition army, 27,000 of whom surrendered.

A series of victories

Napoleon's victory at Ulm opened the road to Vienna, 300 miles (480 km) to the east, which the Imperial Russian Army was approaching. Napoleon got there first, awaiting the arrival of the Russians near the village of Austerlitz (near Brno in modern-day Czechia).

Czar Alexander I's Russian army, now swelled by Austrian forces, numbered almost 90,000 men. Napoleon's Grande Armée amounted to some 75,000 and was 1,000 miles (1,600 km) from its depots around Paris. Winter began to set in, and now Prussia was threatening to enter the war against France. »

Napoleon accepts the surrender of an Austrian army at Ulm after bombarding its troops, under siege in the town. Anticipated Russian support for the Austrians did not arrive in time.

NAPOLEON TRIUMPHANT

Although the situation did not seem favorable for the French, on December 2, Napoleon lured his opponents into a trap. Feigning weakness, he drew their armies into rough terrain and then struck their exposed center with 10 regiments of heavy cavalry that routed the Russian Imperial Guard. The czar's army was forced to retreat, and Austrian emperor Francis I sued for peace. While the Third Coalition had fallen apart, the Grande Armée had won its most famous victory.

Only six weeks separated Britain's overwhelming naval victory against the French at Trafalgar from Napoleon's equally commanding triumph at Austerlitz. While the first confirmed the Royal Navy's maritime control, the second demonstrated the Grande Armée's dominance of continental Europe.

On August 6, 1806, Napoleon dissolved the 800-year-old Holy Roman Empire and replaced it with the Confederation of the Rhine, a collection of German client-states of the French Empire. This move alarmed Prussia, which declared war on October 9. Five days later, France decisively defeated Prussia at the twin battles of Jena and Auerstedt, in what is now Germany. Incredibly, at Auerstedt, a single corps of the Grande Armée defeated the bulk of the Prussian army. On October 27, the victors marched through Berlin.

Enemies to allies
Napoleon kept his army moving eastward through Russian-held Poland in the fall and winter of 1806–1807 because the French were still at war with Russia. On February 7, 1807, the czar's troops caught the Grande Armée at Eylau, 130 miles (208 km) outside the Russian border, before it could properly ready itself for battle. In swirling snow, the Russians deployed twice as many cannon as the French and tore great holes in the Grande Armée's columns, lines, and skirmish formations. Again, Napoleon turned to the heavy cavalry for support. He mustered 80 squadrons of his Imperial Guard's cavalry—10,700 troops—and launched them at the Russian center in one of the great cavalry charges of history.

The battle ended in a qualified victory for Napoleon. Then, four months later, at Friedland, near Kaliningrad, the Grande Armée won a much more decisive victory, forcing the Russian czar to sign the 1807 Peace of Tilsit, which allied his empire with that of Napoleon.

The French emperor returned to Paris in the summer of 1807, once again the conquering hero. The new alliance between the Russian and French empires, together with Napoleon's denial of European ports to British shipping (known as the

> A battle was fought today which did not turn out very well.
>
> **Emperor Francis I**
> to his wife after Austerlitz

Napoleon, on a white horse, surveys the battlefield at Austerlitz, where the Russians and Austrians suffered 16,000 dead or wounded—compared with French losses of fewer than 9,000.

REVOLUTIONS AND EMPIRE 191

Huge French cavalry charges played a key role in Napoleon's victory against the Russians at Friedland. After breaking, the Russians retreated chaotically across the Alle River.

Continental System), looked set finally to force Britain into peace talks. These were abandoned, however, when Portugal continued to trade with Britain, sparking the Peninsular War (1808–1814), in which France was pitted against Portugal, Britain, and then Spain.

Dual priorities

Although its name lingered on informally until 1815, the Grande Armée was officially reorganized into the Army of Spain and the Army of the Rhine in October 1808, while its best troops, and Napoleon himself, were in Spain. With Napoleon entangled in Spain, the Austrian Empire seized the opportunity to reestablish hegemony over Germany at the expense of the French-controlled Confederation of the Rhine.

In January 1809, the Austrian army mobilized. Napoleon hoped that Russia would restrain Austria, but his new ally refused to move, even after Austria declared war in February. Leaving his best troops in Spain and accompanied only by his Imperial Guard, Napoleon returned to France, took command of the Army of the Rhine, stormed through Bavaria, and occupied Vienna again in May.

On May 21, 1809, the French crossed the Danube River to confront the 100,000 troops of a reinvigorated Austrian army. The French established bridgeheads close to the villages of Aspern and Essling, but furious Austrian counterattacks sent them reeling. This was Napoleon's first defeat on land since becoming the French head of state.

The Battle of Wagram

Six weeks after Aspern–Essling, on the evening of July 5, Napoleon successfully crossed the Danube with a massive army of 173,000 French, Saxon, and Bavarian troops—the largest force he had yet fielded. They launched an assault on entrenched Austrian positions along a low ridge of hills topped by the village of Wagram. In the deepening twilight, more than 300,000 men fought each other, the thunder of artillery rattling windows in Vienna, 9 miles (15 km) to the southwest. That night, Napoleon resolved to break the stalemate by a renewed assault along the whole Austrian front, while also turning its left flank, but the Austrian troops hit him first, before dawn. They struck so hard that the French lines were on the verge of breaking when Napoleon assembled a grand battery of more than 100 guns, concentrating its firepower on the Austrian right flank and center. The French guns let off more than 71,000 rounds—a barrage possibly not equaled until World War I. The artillery fire cleared the way for a final charge by the cavalry of the Imperial Guard and gave Napoleon another victory, albeit at a heavy price in terms of casualties.

The Battle of Wagram was the largest to have been fought in Europe to date, with perhaps 70,000 casualties in total, many mangled by artillery rounds. Austria was compelled to make peace, but the career of the world's greatest military leader, Napoleon—and the fortunes of the army that had won his battles—had peaked. ∎

… it will be enough for you to say, 'I was at the Battle of Austerlitz,' for people to reply, 'There goes a brave man.'
Napoleon
to his troops after Austerlitz

HORRORS WERE PUNISHED BY OTHER HORRORS
THE PENINSULAR WAR (1808–1814)

IN CONTEXT

FOCUS
Atrocity in warfare

BEFORE
1209–1229 Pope Innocent III launches the Albigensian Crusade against Cathar "heretics" in southern France. The Crusaders kill tens of thousands of civilians.

1649–1653 During the Irish Confederate Wars, Cromwell's army massacres thousands of priests and civilians.

1755–1758 At least 480,000 die as China's Qing dynasty attempts to wipe out the Mongol Dzungar people.

AFTER
1864 The first Geneva Convention lays down rules on the treatment of wounded and sick prisoners of war.

2007 The International Court of Justice recognizes that the 2005 massacre of Muslims in the Bosnian town of Srebrenica was genocide.

In 1807, Spanish King Ferdinand VII gave the French army permission to march through his country en route to subdue Portugal, an ally of Britain. Trusting his subordinates to manage without him, Napoleon remained in France. Portuguese resistance quickly crumbled, with Queen Maria I and her court withdrawing to Brazil.

The following year, however, it became clear that the French had no intention of leaving Spain, and the country erupted. Angry at the presence of French troops in Madrid, its citizens staged the Dos de Mayo (May 2) uprising. A French military tribunal decreed that anyone caught with arms would be shot. Several hundred faced firing squads the following day, not all of whom had been armed. The brutality with which the rising was suppressed enraged the Spanish further, but Napoleon was undeterred: he ousted Ferdinand and made his own brother King Joseph I of Spain.

Within weeks, Napoleon was forced to review his strategy because of the humiliating

Guerrillas or brigands?

The Peninsular War was the original guerrilla war, with French invaders struggling to contend with small bands of Spanish fighters known as *guerrilleros* or—if female, as they sometimes were—*guerrilleras*. Although no match for a full-strength force, they harassed the invading army on its fringes, preyed upon stragglers, and attacked small encampments and supply convoys. They knew the ground well and were fighting to defend their homes. Among their most notable actions was an attack on a French convoy at Arlabán, Spain, in 1811, which liberated more than 1,000 prisoners of war.

In the years since, Spain has honored the memory of these *guerrilleros*, who played an important part in demoralizing the occupying French. Skeptics argue, however, that the Spanish countryside had long been plagued by brigands and that these "freedom fighters" were, in fact, bandits drawn to a new prize, often even pillaging and robbing their own compatriots.

REVOLUTIONS AND EMPIRE   193

See also: Warfare in North America 150–151 ▪ The Spanish American wars of liberation 200–203 ▪ The Chinese Civil War 294 ▪ Independence in Southeast Asia 296–297 ▪ Revolution and counterrevolution in Latin America 298–299

Francisco Goya's painting *The Third of May 1808* depicts the horror of civilians facing a French firing squad. The work commemorates Spanish resistance to Napoleon.

defeat at the Battle of Bailén, southern Spain, in July 1808. No one would have predicted that Napoleon's first defeat on a European battlefield could be inflicted by a demoralized Spain.

After a Spanish appeal for help, about 14,000 British troops led by Arthur Wellesley (the future Duke of Wellington) landed at Mondego Bay, Portugal, in August 1808. They won a series of victories, and by October the French had been forced out of Portugal. Napoleon responded by sweeping south into Spain at the head of the Grande Armée.

British tactics
Forced into a desperate rearguard action, the British Army retreated in the depths of winter. Although it inflicted a tactical victory over the French at the Battle of Corunna (January 1809), it was still forced to conduct a seaborne evacuation from Spain. The French invaded Portugal again, but after the British won victories at Grijó and Porto on May 11–12, 1809, the French were again forced to retreat.

Wellington trained some 70,000 Portuguese patriots in infantry skills. Although the French had greater numbers overall, Wellington countered this through his superior tactical knowledge. The French favored mass attacks by dense infantry columns, and while this enabled swift movement over the battlefield, it left their soldiers vulnerable to well-directed fire from artillery and infantry. Wellington made a virtue of holding defensive positions with his infantry deployed in line and capable of directing withering fire on the advancing French columns.

A run of victories
Despite being forced to retreat to Portugal, Wellington inflicted a series of defeats on the French, at Talavera in Spain (July 1809), and Bussaco (September 1810).

He had the Lines of Torres Vedras fortifications built north of Lisbon to protect the Portuguese capital before leading successful sieges of Ciudad Rodrigo and Badajoz in Spain, in early 1812. In both cities, British troops ran amok in the captured cities, storming into private homes to loot and rape. In July 1812, in the Spanish city of Salamanca, the British line held firm against French columns at the center, while its heavy cavalry attacked on either flank.

In late 1813, Wellington's army invaded France and, on April 10, 1814, defeated the French at Toulouse. Napoleon abdicated a few days later. The war had been costly, with at least 240,000 Spanish military and civilians dead, as well as 180,000 French and 60,000 British troops. ■

The guerrillas have caused more losses to the French army than all the regular troops … It has been proved that they murdered more than one hundred of our men a day.
Auguste-Julien Bigarré
French general

THE SMELL FROM THE GUNSHOT WOUNDS
NAPOLEON AT BAY (1812–1815)

IN CONTEXT

FOCUS
Medicine at war

BEFORE
1545 French surgeon Ambrose Paré publishes *The Method of Curing Wounds Caused by Arquebus and Firearms*.

1806 British doctors meet in London to discuss ways to improve the treatment of wounded soldiers.

AFTER
1846–1848 In the Mexican-American War, deaths by disease outnumber those in combat by a ratio of 7:1.

1862 Jonathan Letterman organizes a system of military medicine for the Army of the Potomac in the US Civil War.

1870 In the Franco-Prussian War, Prussian deaths from combat wounds exceed those from disease for the first time.

In June 1812, Napoleon invaded Russia with the largest army Europe had ever seen, half a million strong. A generation after its introduction, France's *levée en masse* (conscription program) was producing enormous numbers of soldiers, and battles were becoming scenes of ever-greater slaughter. Critics of Napoleon maintained that he treated his troops as *chair à canon* ("cannon fodder"), but the French did take measures to ease the plight of battlefield casualties, as shown by the appointment of Dominique-Jean Larrey—the most innovative field surgeon of the day—as surgeon-in-chief of the Grande Armée.

REVOLUTIONS AND EMPIRE 195

See also: The wars of the French Revolution 180–187 ▪ Napoleon triumphant 188–191 ▪ The Peninsular War 192–193 ▪ The Crimean War 206–207 ▪ The rise of Prussia 210–213

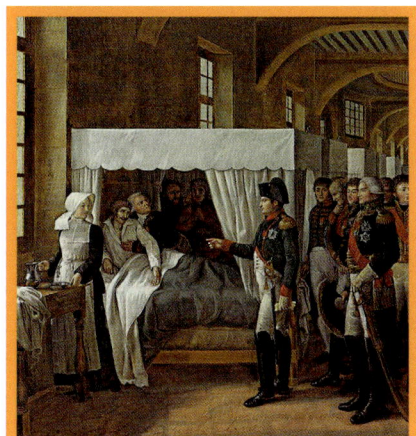

Napoleon's attack on Russia was hugely ambitious—and not only because the armies of the czar were strong. To reach any significant urban center within Russia, an invading force had to march for weeks across open country. In western Europe, the men would have been able to live off the land, pillaging farms and villages for food, but Russia's countryside was utterly impoverished. Napoleon understood the challenges but, supremely confident as ever, still believed he would prevail.

Others were aware of the problem, too, but let themselves be swayed. "It was so sweet to abandon oneself to that star!" recalled French general Philippe Paul about his emperor's persuasiveness.

Advance to Moscow
On June 24, the Grande Armée crossed the Neman River into western Russia (modern-day

Huge fires rage across Moscow in September 1812, coinciding with the French arrival in the city. Russians almost certainly set the fires as part of their scorched-earth strategy.

Napolean visited the Hôtel des Invalides in Paris on several occasions. In 1815, the hospital cared for up to 5,000 wounded soldiers of the Grande Armée at any one time.

Lithuania); they reached Vilnius four days later and Smolensk on August 16. Napoleon had expected Czar Alexander I, faced with such a fearsome invading army, to have sued for peace by then, but he did not. Instead, Russia's forces retreated, burning anything that could help the invaders.

On September 7, what seemed like a climactic confrontation took place at Borodino, 70 miles (110 km) west of Moscow. A quarter of a million men fought for 15 hours, with Napoleon winning the day. The carnage was immense, with 25,000 dead and 55,000 wounded across both sides. The French used horse-drawn wagons (*ambulances volantes*) to ferry the wounded from the battlefield after providing initial treatment where they lay. This was one of Larrey's innovations, along with early amputations to save lives

The wine has been poured; it has to be drunk.
Napoleon
to officers begging him to call off the Moscow Campaign

that otherwise would have been lost to infection; at Borodino, he performed 200 amputations in a day.

Marching into Moscow, the French found that its defenders had melted away and the city was alight. Even now, the czar did not surrender but instead maintained a strategy of passive resistance.

A harrowing retreat
Five weeks passed before Napoleon realized that the surrender was not going to come. With fall »

Dominique-Jean Larrey

Napoleon's chief military surgeon, Dominique-Jean Larrey was born in southern France in 1766, the son of a shoemaker. After serving as a naval surgeon, in 1792, he joined the Army of the Rhine, where he began to make vital improvements to battlefield first aid. Larrey is best known as the originator of modern ambulances. Basing these on artillery gun carriages—designed to be moved around swiftly under battlefield conditions—he created *ambulances volantes* ("flying ambulances"). These could be deployed quickly to take the wounded to safety behind the lines.

Modern healthcare is also indebted to Larrey for the concept of triage (from the French word for "sorting"), prioritizing the most urgent cases over less serious ones. He was innovative, too, in insisting that the seriousness of a wound trumped both social class and military rank. Napoleon once described Larrey as "the soldier's friend." His work laid the basis for modern battlefield healthcare. He died in 1842.

fast approaching, he risked being marooned. Ignoring his generals' advice, he decided to take the same route home, over territory already comprehensively laid to waste. Weighed down with booty—from candlesticks to carriages—the French found it hard going and abandoned much of their loot along the way. As before, the Russians avoided attacking the French directly but harried stragglers and picked off isolated groups sent out in search of supplies.

The French had been defeated long before the Russian winter mounted its offensive, but this made the situation worse. When subzero temperatures bit, soldiers supplemented their inadequate uniforms with furs, silks, and satins stolen as trophies. With their boots in tatters, many were forced to walk barefoot. Hunger and extreme cold took a massive toll, and only about 112,000 of those who participated in the invasion made it out of Russia. About 100,000 of the Grande Armée had been killed in combat, but more than twice that number perished from disease, hunger, and cold.

Cornered by the coalition

Napoleon now faced a broad coalition of enemies, which came together in the early fall of 1813. They cornered him at Leipzig. Over four days (October 16–19), the Battle of Leipzig pitted the Grande Armée against the combined armies of Austria, Prussia, Russia, and several smaller states—the Sixth Coalition. It was the largest battle in European history prior to World War I, involving 560,000 soldiers and frequent shifts in balance as fresh detachments of troops from various armies arrived at different times.

Napoleon's 195,000-strong army was eventually ground down by the sheer size of the opposition—more than 365,000. Those of his troops who survived retreated toward France in good order, but time was running out for Napoleon. Sixth

---

The **sick and wounded** are an **encumbrance and expense** for every army.

Effective care is not just **humane**—it gives an advantage.

With so much at stake in war, **governments** are ready to act with **an urgency they have lacked** in peacetime.

Benefits to the military spill over into society at large.

Defeat for Napoleon at the Battle of Leipzig marked the end of the French Empire east of the River Rhine. The Grande Armée suffered more than 70,000 casualties in the battle.

Coalition armies invaded France, taking Paris in March 1814. They forced Napoleon to abdicate and go into exile on Elba, an island off the coast of Italy. Louis XVIII was installed as French monarch.

The road to Waterloo

In February 1815, Napoleon managed to escape from exile and returned to Paris, where he ended Louis XVIII's brief reign. He immediately set about mobilizing some 250,000 troops for a war against a fresh coalition of Austria, Prussia, Russia, and Britain, each of which had pledged to provide 150,000 troops.

Napoleon did not give the coalition any time to prepare. He acted swiftly to tackle his opponents one by one and so preempt a unified, overwhelming attack. Fearing that British and Prussian armies, under the Duke of Wellington and Gebhard Lebrecht von Blücher respectively, might link up, he sent Marshal Michel Ney to intercept Wellington at Quatre Bras, Belgium, on June 16. While Wellington successfully fought off the French, the delay thwarted his plan to link with Blücher, who on the same day was stopped by Napoleon himself at Ligny, to the south.

Having sent Marshal Emmanuel de Grouchy after Blücher's Prussians with 33,000 men, Napoleon led the rest of his force against the British and their Dutch and German allies. Wellington was at Waterloo, 12 miles (20 km) south of Brussels. He lined up his front ranks along a ridge, the bulk of them concealed behind it. This was a technique he had developed in the long campaigns of

the Peninsular War (1808–1814). The British line was anchored at its right end by the Château de Hougoumont, a walled manor that Wellington had packed with men and guns, and at its center by the house and outbuildings of La Haye Sainte farm.

Fighting to the last

Torrential rain made life difficult for Napoleon's infantry, which had to struggle uphill over muddy ground. The men were also pinned down by furious fire from British troops around Hougoumont. A downhill charge by British cavalry swept away the French infantry attack on the British center, while a series of French cavalry charges failed to have an impact. Even so, Napoleon might have won the Battle of Waterloo by sheer attrition (Wellington's troops were taking heavy casualties) had Blücher and his Prussians not pushed past Marshal Emmanuel de Grouchy's units and rushed to Wellington's assistance. Badly outnumbered now, with the Prussians attacking from their right, Napoleon's Imperial Guard made one last bid to break the British line. However, when they were repelled and fled the battlefield, the rest of the French army followed suit. Casualties were once again heavy, totaling around 48,000. The death toll would have been higher if not for the French fleet of horse-drawn ambulances—each with rear doors to allow a stretcher to slide in—marshaled by Larrey.

With the battle lost, Napoleon was dethroned and exiled to St. Helena in the South Atlantic, and Louis was restored to the throne. In November 1815, France signed the Treaty of Paris, by which the coalition took away territory won by France since 1790 and occupied some parts of the country. The map of Europe would never be the same again. ∎

> Those who are dangerously wounded must be tended first entirely without regard to rank and distinction.
> **Dominique-Jean Larrey**
> *Memoirs of Military Surgery, 1814*

FREE TRADE AND SAILORS' RIGHTS
THE WAR OF 1812 (1812–1815)

IN CONTEXT

FOCUS
Maritime trade

BEFORE
1775 During the American Revolution, the Continental Congress authorizes privateers (independent seafarers) to disrupt the British supply chain in the Atlantic Ocean.

1780 Trade between the Dutch Republic and the American colonies leads to the Fourth Anglo-Dutch War.

1794 The US and Britain sign the Jay Treaty, agreeing rules for maritime trade.

AFTER
1862 The Lyons–Seward Treaty, signed by Britain and the US, effectively ends the Atlantic slave trade.

1914–1918 During World War I, U-boats (submarines) sink up to 5,000 British merchant ships in retaliation for the Royal Navy's blockade of Germany.

On June 18, 1812, the US declared war on Britain. This was in response to a British maritime blockade of Napoleonic Europe, which interrupted US trade, and the Royal Navy's impressment (forced recruitment) of US sailors to serve on British ships fighting Napoleon.

The US was also motivated by a desire for territorial expansion. Many Americans believed that Canada would welcome a US invasion as an opportunity to rid itself of its British rulers. The US was also eager to stop the British in Canada supplying weapons to Indigenous tribes who resisted westward US expansion. More than a dozen tribes, including the Shawnee, Muscogee, and Creek, formed a coalition to oppose the US, and thousands of their warriors fought alongside the British.

Exploitation of Indigenous peoples

The British believed **Indigenous tribes** could be **useful allies** against the Americans.
↓
They relied on **Tecumseh** and his confederation to protect the **Great Lakes area** of Canada.
↓
They **abandoned** their **Indigenous allies** at the end of the war.

Americans felt entitled to **control the entire continent**, including **Indigenous lands**.
↓
They killed **Tecumseh** at the **Battle of the Thames**.
↓
They **expanded** their **settlements, forcibly removing** Indigenous American inhabitants.

After the Battle of Lake Erie, US troops gained control of the lake. The British Army retreated up the Thames River, where they suffered another defeat a month later.

The US stormed Canada in July 1812. However, the invasion failed because of poorly equipped and trained US troops and the incompetence of their leader, General William Hull. The result was the loss of the town of Detroit and Michigan territory to the British.

Against all expectations, the tiny US Navy defeated the Royal Navy in the Atlantic Ocean and on the Great Lakes in the battles of York and Lake Erie (April and September 1813, respectively). In retaliation for these military humiliations, the British launched a counteroffensive along the mid-Atlantic coast. On August 24, 1814, 4,000 Royal Marines marched on Washington, where they set fire to both the White House and the Capitol Building. The British offensive came to a halt outside Baltimore, Maryland, in September, when a small US garrison at Fort McHenry withstood a 27-hour naval bombardment by 19 ships firing Congreve rockets and mortar shells.

Stalemate and betrayal

Britain's failed attempt to take Fort McHenry marked the end of the British offensive. Neither they nor the Americans could afford to continue the conflict, and the war ended in a stalemate. A peace treaty was signed on Christmas Eve 1814 in Ghent (in modern-day Belgium) that restored the prewar borders of the US and Canada.

News of the signing of the Treaty of Ghent came too late for 5,000 British troops outside New Orleans. They attacked the city but were easily defeated on January 8, 1815, in a notable victory for US forces led by future president Andrew Jackson.

Ultimately, the biggest losers of the War of 1812 were Indigenous peoples. Abandoned by the British, they lacked the financial and military backing needed to defend their ancestral lands and faced increasing waves of westward-bound settlers who were determined to remove them. ■

Tecumseh

Born in 1768, Indigenous military commander Tecumseh, who led the Shawnee tribe of the Ohio River Valley, believed in the communal ownership of land, resistance to European expansion, and the power of diplomacy over weapons. He was a formidable orator who united several Indigenous tribes in a confederation to resist US settlement in the valley.

As war approached in 1812, Tecumseh persuaded his followers to support British forces led by General Henry Procter on the Canadian side of the Detroit River at Fort Malden. With Tecumseh's support, the British successfully captured Detroit and invaded Ohio, seizing 2,500 US soldiers.

When US forces triumphed at the Battle of the Thames in October 1813, the British fled, but Tecumseh's warriors continued to fight until their chief was killed. Tecumseh's death marked the end of Indigenous resistance in the Ohio River Valley, lower Midwest, and the South.

LONG LIVE FREEDOM! LONG LIVE INDEPENDENCE!
THE SPANISH AMERICAN WARS OF LIBERATION (1808–1833)

IN CONTEXT

FOCUS
The role of leaders in the liberation of South America

BEFORE
1789 In Brazil, Joaquim José da Silva Xavier leads a failed revolt against Portuguese colonial rule.

1791 Toussaint Louverture leads the first of a series of ultimately successful uprisings against French rule in Haiti.

1795 José Leonardo Chirino mounts a challenge to Spanish rule in Venezuela but is arrested and later executed.

1806 Francisco de Miranda, supported by volunteers from the US, launches an expedition to liberate Venezuela.

AFTER
1903 Panama secedes from Colombia, with which it has long been united.

In the first decades of the 19th century, while Spain struggled to throw out French invaders, Simón Bolívar and his comrades set out to liberate Latin America's Spanish colonies. While they were successful in freeing a huge area, reaching from Panama to Patagonia, political rivalries and local interests forced them to abandon their dream of a federation of all the South American states.

Like many affluent young gentlemen, Simón Bolívar, the son of a wealthy planter from Caracas, Venezuela, did the Grand Tour of Europe to broaden his horizons and learn about European culture. Awestruck amid the ruins of Rome,

See also: The European conquest of the Americas 122–125 ▪ The American Revolution 172–177 ▪ The Peninsular War 192–193 ▪ The American-Mexican wars 204–205 ▪ The Paraguayan War 224 ▪ Revolution and counterrevolution in Latin America 298–299

Simón Bolívar

Born in 1783, Simón Bolívar was 16 when he was sent to Europe to complete his education. There, he was influenced by the French Revolution and the writings of authors such as Voltaire. Upon his return to South America, he threw himself into its fight for independence, working to create a clearly structured, professionally run rebel army.

In 1817, Bolívar established an elite, 450-strong guard of honour to form the core of the army. He also created a general staff, with officers in charge of the army as a whole and of each division—and a clear command structure with disciplinary rules and a system of courts martial.

To prevent the creation of private armies, Bolívar insisted that generals recruit on the basis of merit from beyond their immediate kinship groups. Ironically, his aim was probably to guard against the kind of dictatorial power-grab he was later responsible for. He died of tuberculosis in 1830.

---

he is reputed to have asked himself why, if the great Roman Empire had decayed, could that of Spain not do the same. By 1807, he was back in Venezuela, planning—with revolutionary soldier Francisco de Miranda—the fight for Venezuelan independence. The "patriots," as they were known, drove out the Spanish and declared the first Republic of Venezuela in 1811.

Harsh reality

The Spanish soon returned to Venezuela, and Bolívar had to flee to Cartagena, in New Granada (present-day Colombia). He raised an army of 17,000 and came home to establish a provisional government in Caracas. His army defeated the Spanish and their local royalist supporters and, in 1813, proclaimed a Second Republic. Many called Bolívar—still just 30 years old—*El Libertador* ("The Liberator"), but this republic soon began to founder. The Spanish allied with traditionally conservative *llaneros*—ranchers and cowboys from Venezuela's interior—to bring it down.

Bolívar was forced into exile once more, this time to Jamaica. In 1817, he returned again, this time with a small force of about 300 men. They were mostly officers, and Bolívar believed they would gather fighters in the thousands as they marched toward Caracas. In fact, it took them several attempts even to land in the face of royalist vigilance. When they succeeded, the people failed to respond, doubtless fearful that a third independent republic would also end in failure and be the prelude to cruel reprisals. Fearing arrest, Bolívar returned to exile.

Unexpected assistance

Support for the independence struggle then arrived from an unexpected source: Britain. Although a monarchy and officially Spain's ally, Britain was seeking new markets for its industrially produced goods and looked toward those who might become South America's new rulers. It offered Bolívar money, weapons, and even troops. Support also came from the US, which was full of revolutionary fervor—though it, too, was eager to secure an influential role in South America. With this help, Bolívar started to rebuild an army.

Meanwhile, in territories farther south, the revolution gathered pace. Fighting for their freedom since 1810, the United Provinces of the Río de la Plata succeeded in 1816, forming the basis for modern-day Argentina and Uruguay. The Irish-descended Chilean patriot »

> *I swear by my honor, I swear by my country, that I will not rest body or soul until I have broken the chains with which Spanish power oppresses us.*
> **Simón Bolívar**
> at Monte Sacro, Rome, 1805

202 THE SPANISH AMERICAN WARS OF LIBERATION

Bernardo O'Higgins called on his compatriots to "live with honor or die with glory." His campaign to liberate Chile started disastrously, in October 1814, with the Battle of Rancagua, when the Spanish army badly mauled his 2,000 soldiers.

O'Higgins nearly suffered a similar fate three years later at the Battle of Chacabuco, but the arrival of his friend José San Martín's Army of the Andes saved the day. San Martín, an Argentine soldier, had marched 5,000 men over the mountains with all their horses, pack mules, guns, and munitions—an extraordinary achievement in itself—then led his mounted grenadiers in a charge that cut the Spanish cavalry to pieces.

Alarmed, Spain sent armed reinforcements. At Cancha Rayada, Chile, in March 1818, the army of the Spanish governor of Chile—Mariano Osorio—defeated the Army of the Andes. San Martín had misjudged the situation by ordering a tactical withdrawal, allowing the enemy to spring a surprise attack.

San Martín took back the initiative shortly after, attacking Osorio's army as it crossed open country in the mountains south of Santiago in April 1818. As the Battle of Maipú developed, infantry on both sides exchanged fierce fire, and San Martín's mounted grenadiers attacked the Spanish left flank. Spain's cavalry countered but were put to flight. The Spanish right flank proved more obdurate, with the feared infantry of the Burgos Regiment exacting heavy casualties. San Martín brought up his reserve, backed by a heavy artillery bombardment. The reserve was no match for the Burgos Regiment, but as San Martín had hoped, the regiment's elite troops advanced so quickly that their formation fell apart, allowing the rebels to regain the initiative and win the day.

Bolívar returns

Deployed far to the north, Bolívar's reinforced patriot army retook some of the Venezuelan territories he had lost previously. In 1819, he pushed west into New Granada, a territory encompassing the whole of present-day Colombia and Panama. He led his small army of about 2,500 troops on a difficult route through the mountains to challenge Spanish forces based in Bogotá, Colombia. Brushing aside a succession of small royalist forces sent to intercept it, his army fought and won the two-hour Battle of Boyacá on August 10.

The road to Bogotá now lay open. Bolívar was cheered in every town he passed through. Even the *llaneros* fell into line. By December 1819, he could proclaim the birth of the Republic of Gran Colombia. This federation extended across modern-day Venezuela, Colombia, and Panama, but Bolívar had yet to take his home capital of Caracas, and Ecuador remained a Spanish colony. Then, in April 1821, when Venezuela's Maracaibo province rose up against the Spanish, Bolívar's chief of staff Rafael Urdaneta and his lieutenant José Bermúdez took advantage of the confusion to attack the Spanish garrisons at Caracas and Puerto Cabello.

Bolívar was making for Puerto Cabello with 6,500 troops when he met Miguel de la Torre's Spanish

> The Battle of Chacabuco can be described as the work of the squadrons of mounted grenadiers.
> **José San Martín**

The Army of the Andes secured victory at Chacabuco, but it came at a great cost. San Martín lost 2,000 of his men to the harsh conditions as they crossed the mountains.

Simón Bolívar celebrates after the Battle of Carabobo in 1821, which was a victory for his patriots and a huge step toward liberating the whole of northern South America.

force at Carabobo, west of Caracas. *El Libertador* tried to outflank his enemy by sending some of his troops across country, but Torre sent his own patrols to cancel out this maneuver. Occupying higher ground, his men could now fire down on the patriots.

Bolívar's risky maneuver appeared to have failed, especially when his main column—mounting a frontal attack on Torre's force—met a sudden hail of fire from about 3,000 Spanish muskets. Utterly demoralized, the patriots broke and fled. The volunteers sent by the British proved their worth at this point. They met the enemy fire with volleys of their own before fixing bayonets and charging. The astonished royalists ran in panic. Victory led to the establishment of the Republic of Gran Colombia.

Battles in the Andes

Ecuador remained in Spanish hands, its royalists repelling two invasions from Gran Colombia in 1820 and 1821. In 1822, however, Bolívar's chief lieutenant Antonio José de Sucre tried for the third time. In May of that year, he fought the Battle of Pichincha on the slopes of an active volcano high above Quito. Both sides were slowed by altitude sickness and a steady rain that turned the ash beneath their feet to mush, but Spanish governor Melchior Aymerich's royalist army had the higher ground. Sucre's force looked like being slaughtered. Again, however, British volunteers proved decisive, arriving late but turning the tide in the patriots' favor. Ecuador was freed from colonial rule.

Peru was left as the final bastion of Spanish rule in South America. While Bolívar and Sucre advanced on it from the north, San Martín led an invasion from the south. The decisive battle was fought outside Ayacucho, Peru, in December 1824. Sucre's army, 5,700 strong, met the 9,000 soldiers of Viceroy Antonio José de la Serna high on the *altiplano*, the Andean plateau. It took Sucre only 30 minutes to outmaneuver the Spanish royalists so comprehensively that they fled, despite their superior numbers.

In August 1825, Peru became an independent nation, as did Upper Peru, which was named Bolivia after Bolívar.

Independence was bittersweet, however. Gran Colombia had barely been founded before it began to disintegrate, pulled apart by the personal ambitions and parochial agendas of its rulers. One by one, Bolívar's generals turned away from him. In 1831, Gran Colombia was dissolved, breaking into the successor states of Venezuela, Colombia, and Ecuador.

The Brazilian exception

Brazil—a colony of Portugal rather than Spain—took a very different course to independence. When Napoleon Bonaparte invaded Iberia in 1807, the Portuguese court had fled to Brazil. After peace was restored in Europe, King John VI returned to Lisbon in 1821. He left behind his son, who proclaimed Brazil independent and declared himself Emperor Pedro I. He and his successors faced constant agitation from republicans; even so, the "empire" of Brazil endured for decades before becoming a republic in 1889. ∎

Francisco de Miranda proclaims the short-lived **First Republic** of Venezuela in July 1811.

→ **Simón Bolívar** builds on the success of his **first revolution** to create a **Second Republic** in 1813.

A further republic is **declared, but not delivered**, by Bolívar in 1817. Spain holds out against **rebel forces** from both north and south.

→ **The Republic of Gran Colombia is established in 1819. It extends from Peru to Panama, Ecuador to northeast Brazil.**

NOT ALL HEROES ARE VIRTUOUS
THE AMERICAN-MEXICAN WARS (1835–1848)

IN CONTEXT

FOCUS
Rise of the caudillo

BEFORE
1813 The Venezuelan people acclaim Simón Bolívar as *El Libertador* ("The Liberator"). Much of South America is inspired by his example.

1829 After making a name for himself as a caudillo, Juan Manuel de Rosas becomes governor of Buenos Aires and unofficial dictator of what will become Argentina.

AFTER
1854 Captain General Rafael Carrera protects Guatemala against US interests and homegrown rebels. Many see him as the country's savior.

1876 Caudillo Porfirio Díaz seizes power in Mexico. His dictatorship lasts 35 years.

1959 The left-wing guerrilla leader Fidel Castro seizes power in Cuba.

In the mid-19th century, the US expanded south and westward, largely at the expense of Mexico. While the Texas Revolution of 1835–1836 may have had justification, the Mexican-American War of 1846–1848 was a cynical land grab.

This period saw the rise of the caudillos, Latin American military leaders wielding enormous political power. One such figure was Antonio López de Santa Anna, a hero of the Mexican War of Independence (1810–1821). After seizing a leadership position, he made his strong military background and impatience with the democratic process the basis of his political career.

Texan independence

In the 1820s, Texas was a state of the Mexican Republic. Encouraged by the 1824 Colonization Law, which granted land and tax-free benefits to settlers of all nationalities, ever larger numbers of American colonists began to occupy lands in the region. Cohabitation was not easy, with the outlawing of slavery in Mexico (1829) a particular aggravation for slave-holding Americans.

In 1835, settlers rebelled against the Mexican government and proclaimed themselves the Republic of Texas. Rising to the challenge, Santa Anna sent an army north to take back the territory. About 200 Texan rebels, including Jim Bowie and Davy Crockett, who later became a folk hero, had taken refuge in the Alamo Mission, San Antonio. They held out for 13 days, before being massacred on March 6, 1836.

The Alamo fell after a 90-minute battle in which all its defenders were killed. The Mexican army's brutal suppression acted as a major catalyst for Texan resistance.

>
> War in defence of our rights, our oaths, and our constitutions is inevitable, in Texas!
> **Sam Houston**
> **5 October 1835**
>

A few weeks later, on April 21, Santa Anna clashed with a larger force of settlers on the San Jacinto River. The Mexican caudillo was defeated and captured, regaining his freedom only by personally recognizing the Republic of Texas as an independent state.

All-out war

In December 1845, US President James K. Polk officially annexed Texas. Five months later, he sent a detachment of US soldiers into the Nueces Strip, a disputed territory between the Rio Grande and Nueces rivers. When Mexican troops tried to stop these troops, Polk claimed that Mexico had committed an "act of aggression."

Fought over many thousands of square miles, the Mexican-American War of 1846–1848 was disastrous for Mexico, which was severely outgunned by the US. Even Santa Anna's military experience could not help: in February 1847, he lost one of the war's key battles, at Buena Vista, near Saltillo. That September, six Mexican cadets in Chapultepec Castle, near Mexico City, fought to the death rather than surrender, attaining the same legendary status as the American heroes of Alamo.

Within two years, Mexico was forced to surrender. As a result of the war, it had lost almost half of its total territory: the present-day US states of California, Nevada, and Utah; vast areas of Arizona, Colorado, and New Mexico; and a small section of Wyoming. ∎

Economic problems and **political** divisions lead to a desire for a **strong government**.
The **military** is the only convincing **model of discipline and order** available.
The caudillo seems to offer a solution.
The price of **stability** under a caudillo is **political repression**.

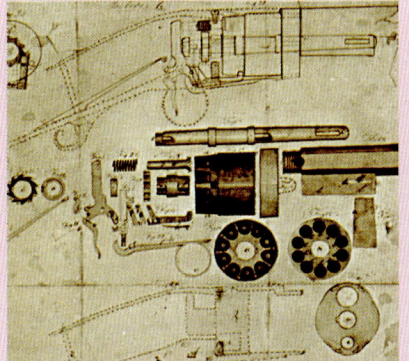

Samuel Colt's patent drawing indicates that he had planned 10 chambers for cartridges. The caliber also changed before production.

The Colt revolver

Originally known as the Colt Walker, because it was made to the specifications of Texas Ranger Captain Samuel Hamilton Walker, the Colt revolver revolutionized firearms. Instead of having to reload it after each shot, the user could fire six times in succession, the revolving cylinder automatically turning to place a fresh round ready for firing.

In 1847, the US government ordered 1,000 Colt revolvers for use in the Mexican-American War. There were teething troubles, though: the cylinder, which was the gun's key feature, tended to rupture from the strain; and the lever that moved it around did not always catch at first. However, after these difficulties were ironed out, the Colt revolver became known as "the gun that won the West." Ironically, co-inventor Hamilton Walker died in the Mexican-American War, at the Battle of Huamantla on October 9, 1847.

THESE DYING AND EXHAUSTED MEN
THE CRIMEAN WAR (1853–1856)

IN CONTEXT

FOCUS
Medical improvement

BEFORE
1517 German surgeon Hans von Gersdorff publishes his *Field Manual for the Treatment of Wounds*.

1718 In France, surgeon Jean-Louis Petit introduces the screw-tightened tourniquet.

1799 British chemist Sir Humphry Davy uses nitrous oxide as an anesthetic.

AFTER
1861 French microbiologist Louis Pasteur publishes a paper on germ theory and its medical applications.

1865 Antiseptics for the prevention of infection are developed by British surgeon Joseph Lister.

1879 Pasteur injects chickens with the first cholera vaccine.

1914 Blood transfusions are commonplace in World War I.

In the early 1850s, a dispute over Russian Orthodox Christians' access to Jerusalem gave Russia the pretext it needed to test the flagging strength of the Ottoman Empire and declare war. Alarmed by the prospect of Russian expansion, Britain and France came to Türkiye's aid. From a military point of view, the Crimean War was one of the first to use modern weaponry, rendering established conventions of warfare obsolete—at terrible cost to combatants. However, important developments in military medicine mitigated the death toll.

The war begins

In the summer of 1853, Russian armies occupied the Ottoman-ruled principalities of Moldavia and Wallachia (modern-day Romania). Fighting erupted on the Danube River and the Black Sea. After destroying the Ottoman fleet at Sinop, in northern Türkiye (on November 30), where their new explosive shells obliterated Sultan Abdülmecid's timber-built warships, the Russians felt emboldened to occupy the Crimean peninsula.

Britain and France had supported the Ottomans from the start, and by March 1854, they were directly involved. That September, the Anglo-French expedition landed and immediately outfought the Russian army sent to cut them off at the Alma River.

Uneven forces

Pitted against Europe's industrial powers, the weaknesses of the Russian army soon became apparent. With no railroads south of Moscow, it took them three months to bring up supplies; France and Britain could do it in three weeks by sea. There was also a disparity in their weapons: the French Minié rifle (and its British Enfield copy) had five times the accurate range of

Death is always terrible—no one need be ashamed to fear it.
Mary Seacole
Wonderful Adventures of Mrs. Seacole in Many Lands, 1853

See also: The Ottoman Empire 130–133 ▪ The wars of Catherine the Great 178–179 ▪ Ottoman decline and Russian expansion 232–233 ▪ Conflict in the Balkans 236–237

The Light Brigade is shown charging Russian forces in this 1855 painting. The bravery of the British troops inspired Alfred, Lord Tennyson's poem, "The Charge of the Light Brigade."

Russia's smoothbore muskets. From a strategic viewpoint, Russia's old tactics, such as the cavalry charges against infantry and artillery, were now doomed to failure.

This development was confirmed by the disastrous charge of the British Light Brigade at the Battle of Balaclava (October 25, 1854), which also highlighted the need for better battlefield communication. When Lieutenant General Lord Cardigan misunderstood an order and attacked the wrong Russian objective, the British brigade rode into a deathtrap.

Back in Britain, people followed events on the battlefield, thanks to reports by a new kind of journalist—the war correspondent. Readers were shocked to discover how their heroes were suffering, giving impetus to attempts to improve healthcare at the front—from improved hygiene standards to better-trained medical personnel.

Attack on Sevastopol

The event that precipitated the end of the conflict was the Siege of Sevastopol, Russia's Black Sea base in Crimea, by the Allies. Many of the actions during this siege, which lasted from October 1854 to September 1855, were attempts by the Russians to relieve the city. Balaclava had been one; so too was the Battle of Inkerman on November 5. During this battle, the contending armies lost their way in dense fog and had to fight at close quarters. Casualties were heavy.

The Western powers were slowly wearing down the czar's army. The winter took as much of a toll on the Allies as the Russians: disease was rife, and many suffered frostbite. On September 5, 1855, the Allies launched their final assault against Sevastopol, and after bitter fighting, the city fell on September 9. This Russian defeat ended major military operations, and the exhausted sides entered into peace negotiations that concluded in the Treaty of Paris on March 30, 1856. ▪

Combatant care

Between them, Briton Florence Nightingale and Jamaican-born Mary Seacole founded the profession of modern nursing. Their achievements during the Crimean War transformed medical treatment on the battlefield and in hospitals at home.

Nightingale brought order and efficiency to the military hospital at Scutari, on the Turkish mainland, which until then had merely warehoused dying men. An instinctive sense of decency prompted her to tackle the hospital's squalid conditions and to press the authorities to evacuate the sick and wounded quickly and efficiently. Seacole set up the British Hotel near Balaclava, which operated as a canteen for servicemen needing a meal.

Both women saw rest and comfort as key to healing; unfortunately, they were working a decade or so too soon to have the added benefit of antiseptics. On the Allied side, far more soldiers died of disease (120,000) than did in combat (45,000).

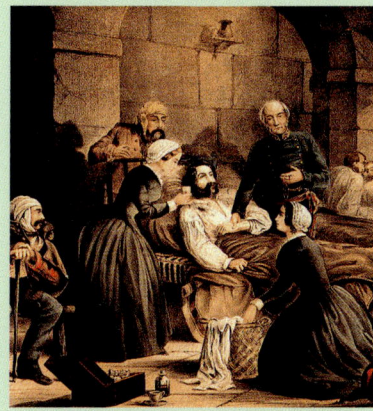

Florence Nightingale tends a wounded soldier in the Scutari hospital, in an image dating from 1855.

ONE FLAG, ONE DREAM
THE WARS OF ITALIAN UNIFICATION (1848–1870)

IN CONTEXT

FOCUS
Garibaldi: Hero of the Two Worlds

BEFORE
1835 Garibaldi fights in Brazil's Ragamuffin War alongside republican rebels. One of their demands is the abolition of slavery.

1843 During the Uruguayan Civil War, Garibaldi lends his support to the liberal Colorado Party and recruits volunteers from the capital's Italian immigrant community.

AFTER
1871 Garibaldi declares his support for the revolutionary Paris Commune.

1880 Just weeks before Italy acquires its first colonial possession in Eritrea, Garibaldi dies.

c. 1922 Italian dictator Benito Mussolini claims to be honoring Garibaldi's patriotic values.

Italy as a unified country came into being as the result of a political movement known as the Risorgimento ("resurgence"). The forces that drove the movement were the political machinations of Victor Emmanuel II, King of Piedmont–Sardinia, and the popular patriotism of General Giuseppe Garibaldi, later known as "Hero of the Two Worlds" because of his campaigning in South America.

A unifying impulse
In the mid-19th century, Italy was a patchwork of separate states. These included Lombardy–Venetia, which was an Austrian possession, and Piedmont–Sardinia in the north. In central Italy's Papal States, the pope held both religious and secular power, while southern Italy and Sicily formed the Kingdom of the Two Sicilies, ruled by relations of the Spanish Bourbons.

In March 1848, among a series of nationalist revolutions taking place across Europe, the people of Milan drove out their Austrian rulers. Piedmont–Sardinia lent its support to the rebels, but the Austrians reestablished their rule after winning the First Battle of Custoza, near Verona (July 22–27).

The following February, Rome also rose up, declaring itself a republic, but future French emperor Napoleon III intervened to restore papal rule. Garibaldi, a career idealist who had been fighting in

---

Much of **Italy** is under the despotic authority of **foreign powers**. → The citizens of **Milan and Rome successfully rise up** against their **rulers**.

↓

Garibaldi helps bring independence to the **Kingdom of the Two Sicilies**. → **Victor Emmanuel II becomes king of a unified Italy.**

REVOLUTIONS AND EMPIRE

See also: The Italian Wars 120–121 ▪ The war of the Austrian Succession 159 ▪ The wars of the French Revolution 180–187 ▪ The rise of Prussia 210–213 ▪ An expanding war 252–255

> I have no other ambition than to be the first soldier of Italian independence. Viva l'Italia!
> **Victor Emmanuel II of Piedmont-Sardinia**

The red shirts of Garibaldi's Thousand made their first appearance in Uruguay. The fabric was originally intended for butchers' overalls, to hide the blood.

South America, returned to Italy to take part in the uprising and to lead the people in resisting the French Siege of Rome. He failed, but Italian patriotism was gaining ground.

Power politics

One of the few states ruled by an Italian dynasty, Piedmont–Sardinia emerged as the natural leader of an independent nation. Victor Emmanuel II enlisted Napoleon III to the Italian cause, despite the latter's 1849 intervention in Rome.

On June 4, 1859, French and Piedmontese troops defeated the Austrian army at Magenta, outside Milan. On June 24, the two sides clashed again at Solferino, near Mantua, where Austria suffered another heavy defeat. Northern Italy was now free of its Austrian rulers but was indebted to Napoleon III.

Redshirts on the march

In the Kingdom of the Two Sicilies, King Francis II had thus far crushed any stirrings of revolt. However, by 1860, his despotism had fueled new unrest in Sicily. In May, Garibaldi landed on the island to support the insurgents. At the head of the Thousand, a troop of soldiers also known as Redshirts, he took Palermo in June, then captured Naples, on the mainland, in September. At this point, the Thousand were 20 times that, but they were still outnumbered at the Battle of the Volturno, north of Naples. A stand-off ensued until Piedmontese forces arrived.

The patriots won, but they had to compromise, acknowledging the sovereignty of the Papal States under Napoleon III's protection. In March 1861, Victor Emmanuel II declared himself King of Italy. True unification came with the outbreak of the Franco-Prussian War in 1870: the French left Rome, and the Redshirts moved in. In 1871, Rome became the capital of Italy. ▪

Garibaldi in Britain

The British people, especially in the industrial regions of the north, followed Garibaldi's struggle closely. In 1854, he received a hero's welcome in South Shields, Tyneside, where he was a guest of left-wing journalist Joseph Cowen Jr., whose trade unionist readers would have respected Garibaldi's radicalism.

Not everybody was in thrall to Garibaldi. Karl Marx believed his idealistic nationalism was "imbecilic," and Queen Victoria considered him a threat to the safety of her realm. Even so, Garibaldi's patriotic project held wide romantic appeal, as did his flamboyant and charismatic personality. When he toured Britain in his later years, he drew large crowds wherever he went.

Garibaldi's legacy in Britain includes the Nottingham Forest football strip, inspired by his Redshirts, and the Garibaldi biscuit. First produced in 1861, it features a layer of currants between twin layers of dough and is fired until golden brown.

TO LEAD THE FATHERLAND ON TO A BLESSED FUTURE

THE RISE OF PRUSSIA (c. 1860–1871)

IN CONTEXT

FOCUS
Burgeoning nationalism

BEFORE
1740–1786 Frederick the Great oversees Prussia's rise to the status of a major power.

1834 The Zollverein, a German customs union, offers a template for wider unification.

1848 Frederick VII of Denmark tries to integrate Schleswig into his kingdom.

1860 Italian Republican Giuseppe Garibaldi leads the Expedition of the Thousand, taking a major step toward Italian unification.

AFTER
1871 Rome becomes the capital city of a united Italy.

1879 Germany and Austria-Hungary sign an alliance treaty; Italy joins in 1882, creating the Triple Alliance.

From 1815, 39 territories—kingdoms, duchies, and city republics—were allied in the German Confederation. The two dominant states were Austria and Prussia, with Prussia the driving force behind the creation of a single German nation state. That goal was not finally achieved, however, until 1871, after three wars.

The 1860s had seen Austria and Prussia vying for preeminence among the German states. By 1866, Prussia had come out on top. Under King Wilhelm I and his "Iron Chancellor" Otto von Bismarck, it cemented this position through diplomacy, threat, and war. A hand-picked general staff drove through

REVOLUTIONS AND EMPIRE 211

See also: The Holy Roman Empire versus the papacy 94–95 ▪ The Seven Years' War 162–165 ▪ The wars of Italian unification 208–209 ▪ World War I: outbreak 242–247 ▪ World War II in Europe 266–271

Otto von Bismarck, who was Prussian prime minister from 1862, believed German unification would be achieved by "blood and iron."

German nationalism

The beginning of the 19th century had been a time of romantic nationalism across Europe. In Germany, however, this movement was arguably triggered by war.

French emperor Napoleon I's victories over various German states, followed by the heavy territorial losses and harsh reparation terms imposed by the Peace of Tilsit of 1807, were deeply humiliating for the Germans, helping to bond and define them against the French.

Germany's dream of a united nation state started to take shape within this context of resentment. In an attempt to distance themselves from French Enlightenment ideas, German nationalists drew inspiration from the Romantic movement in art and literature. Sources ranged from the poetry of 18th- and 19th-century polymaths Novalis and Johann Wolfgang von Goethe, to the folk tales of the Brothers Grimm—authors whose works underlined the shared identity, language, and culture of the German people.

far-reaching organizational and technological reforms in the army to make Prussia a military superpower and, in effect, the leader of a united German nation.

The Elbe duchies

For Bismarck, it seemed an anomaly that the German-speaking "Elbe duchies" of Schleswig and Holstein in southern Jutland should belong to Denmark. The Danes' attempt to integrate Schleswig formally in 1848 had provoked rioting in the duchy and war with Prussia. Unexpectedly, Denmark had won, but other European powers had blocked the annexation.

In 1864, when Denmark tried again, Bismarck worked together with Austria to stage a joint invasion—the Second Schleswig War. The Danes lost this time,

and the Gastein Convention of 1865 determined that Holstein would be administered by Austria, and that Schleswig would become part of Prussia.

Bismarck lost no time in discarding his ally. Before the year's end, he had engineered a dispute with Austria over the administration of Schleswig-Holstein. On June 14, 1866, the Austro-Prussian War (also known as the Seven Weeks' War) began. It ended on August 23, with victory for Prussia. Indeed, the outcome had been clear since Prussian commander-in-chief Helmuth von Moltke's victory at the Battle of Königgrätz, near Sadowa in present-day Czechia, on July 3.

Structures for success

Königgrätz was won through Moltke's talent for organization. He brought his men into the battle zone by train, on six railroad lines. They then converged on the Austrians from three sides. A communications breakdown left one Prussian army stranded some way off, but a frantic forced march by these superbly trained troops got them to the battlefield only a few hours late. »

Wilhelm I is shown on a black horse, flanked by Bismarck, Moltke, and others, as he oversees Prussian victory at the 1866 Battle of Königgrätz, in this work by German artist Georg Bleibtreu.

The victory underlined the value of the *Kriegsakademie* ("war academy") that Moltke had created. Well trained and educated across a range of subjects, its graduates were perfectly equipped to occupy positions in Moltke's general staff, which was recruited on merit and rigorously regulated. So vast were Prussia's armies by this time that it no longer made sense to have a single commander, however brilliant. As long as Prussia's generals worked within the limits of the system overall, they had considerable freedom in the field. While Bismarck was a tyrannical bully—politicians and diplomats across Europe testified to his capricious and overbearing ways—he did not interfere in military decisions. Ultimately, Moltke, his general staff comrades, and every Prussian soldier were trusted servants of their state, and Bismarck respected their expertise and experience.

Prussian generals also had the advantage of the latest military technology, such as breech-loading "needle guns." These rifles could be reloaded much more quickly than the muzzle-loading muskets that the Austrians used at Königgrätz. Prussia's artillery was superior, too; its field guns had rifled barrels—marked by grooves and ridges—rather than smoothbore, giving them much more accuracy at greater range. These technical advances were reflected in the casualty figures at Königgrätz: 9,000 Prussians killed or wounded to 24,000 Austrians.

> The state stands or falls with the army.
> **Helmuth von Moltke**
> Prussian commander in chief

Overall, the Seven Weeks' War cost as many as 65,000 lives, including deaths caused by disease.

Bismarck's master plan

Victory in the Seven Weeks' War secured Saxony, Hanover, and Hesse-Kassel for Prussia, but Bismarck wanted much more: his intention was to unite the whole of Germany. In the short term, however, he made peace, preferring a weakened rather than destroyed Austria over a Central European power vacuum that France or Russia might occupy. With no real alternative available, Austria agreed to dissolve the German Confederation and let Prussia take the lead in German unification. In 1867, Bismarck annexed Schleswig-Holstein and all other territories north of the Main River. They joined a new North German Confederation under Prussian rule.

Friction with France

French emperor Napoleon III had watched Prussia's rise with some concern, fearing that a united Germany could displace France as Europe's leading power. Bismarck was reluctant to start a war against Napoleon—not least in case the recently defeated Austrians should side with France. Instead, he waited

---

Germany's **different states** are divided by **religious** traditions and **dynastic** lines.

Language is the one thing they have **in common**.

Romanticism in **art, poetry, and folklore** nurture **nationalist interest** across much of Europe.

Aspirations for a German nation state are reinforced by the **experience of defeat** in the Napoleonic Wars.

Prussia's success in war unites the country in optimism and pride.

REVOLUTIONS AND EMPIRE 213

Wilhelm I of Prussia was anointed emperor of a unified German state in the Hall of Mirrors, Versailles, Paris, on January 18, 1871, 10 days before the city fell to his armies.

for an opportunity to provoke France into declaring war on Germany, believing that an act of aggression would cause all German states to unite against Napoleon.

He had the excuse he needed in 1870, when Napoleon tried to prevent Prince Leopold von Hohenzollern-Sigmaringen from accepting the vacant throne of Spain when offered it. Although Leopold belonged to the southern, Catholic branch of the Hohenzollern family, he was also related to the Protestant Prussian ruling dynasty, and Napoleon was concerned that this would strengthen Prussian influence. Fearing the French response, Prussia's King Wilhelm I was uneasy about giving his consent, but Bismarck encouraged the match precisely because he knew it would anger Napoleon.

Wilhelm faltered again in July 1870, when Napoleon sent him a message demanding that the king apologize for even having advanced Leopold's claim. Wilhelm drafted a telegram, firmly but tactfully refusing; by the time Bismarck had edited the message, however, it was curt to the point of rudeness. Leaked to the press in Prussia and France, it raised tensions further, and France declared war on July 19.

The Franco-Prussian War

Prussian patriots rushed to volunteer, swelling the ranks of the regular army and reserves. Moltke again made use of the railroads to move troops rapidly into France. One Prussian army moved westward through the valley of the Moselle, another traveled along the Saar Valley, and a third advanced from Bavaria, further south. By contrast, the French mobilization was much slower. Napoleon had big, powerful forces but was unable to get them into the field quickly enough. At Fröschwiller, Alsace, on August 6, 1870, French defenders, outnumbered three to one, found themselves overwhelmed.

By the time of the Battle of Mars-la-Tour, 10 days later, the two sides were evenly matched numerically, and the battle looked as though it would result in a stalemate. However, Marshal François Achille Bazaine's French troops were defeated by Europe's last cavalry charge, with the Prussian riders making their initial advance under the cover of French artillery smoke. Although Bazaine's troops fought bravely at Gravelotte-St. Privat, Metz, on August 18, even coming close to victory, Prussian artillery eventually forced them to surrender.

Prussia prevails

As early French enthusiasm for the war waned, Napoleon decided he had to lead his army into battle like a medieval king. At Sedan, in the Ardennes of northeastern France, on September 1–2, 1870, he joined the battle line. However, the French troops were massively outnumbered and pulverized by 400 powerful and accurate Prussian guns. Eventually, Napoleon's army folded. He and 100,000 of his men were captured. In disgust, French workers rose up, deposed their imprisoned emperor, and proclaimed a Third Republic.

The Prussians continued their westward advance, making short work of several hastily assembled republican armies, before besieging the French capital. Paris held out for four months but was finally starved into submission, falling on January 28, 1871. By that time, Bismarck had already brought together princes from the whole of Germany to proclaim Wilhelm emperor of Germany. Nationalist aspirations had been satisfied, and the German nation state was a reality. ∎

THEY ... ARE AFRAID OF OUR REPEATING RIFLES

THE AMERICAN CIVIL WAR (1861–1865)

THE AMERICAN CIVIL WAR

IN CONTEXT

FOCUS
The first modern war

BEFORE
1853 The British Enfield Pattern rifle-musket is introduced, improving firing range and accuracy.

1857 During the first Indian War of Independence, the new electric telegraph enables the British to defeat an uprising.

1859 The French launch the first steam-powered ironclad warship, the *Gloire*.

AFTER
1866 British engineer Robert Whitehead designs the first self-propelled torpedo.

1901 Italian inventor Guglielmo Marconi transmits the first transatlantic radio message.

1914–1918 Warring nations use machine guns, poison gas, tanks, and aircraft during World War I.

The art of war is simple enough. Find out where your enemy is. Get at him as soon as you can. Strike him as hard as you can.
General Ulysses Grant
at the start of the
Tennessee River Campaign, 1862

Since the American Revolution (1775–1781), "*E pluribus unum*"—"Out of the many, one"—had been the unofficial motto of the US. Yet less than a century later, the young nation tore itself apart in civil war. The conflict was rooted in long-standing regional differences about economic policy and the scope of national as opposed to state sovereignty, but the primary cause was the existence of chattel slavery in the South. In Northern states, where it was largely banned, many people wanted chattel slavery to be abolished throughout the US, including in western territories that had not yet become states. Southern states, whose economies relied on enslaved people's unpaid labor, hoped that expanding slavery into these western territories would help them preserve it.

Ultimately, the extreme tensions between states would erupt in the first modern war, featuring repeating rifles, ironclad warships and submarines, reconnaissance balloons, railroads for the rapid transportation of troops, and the telegraph for communications. The new military technology came at a bloody cost: 620,000 combatants were killed, or one in 50 of the US population.

Lincoln won the 1860 presidential election on the Republican Party's anti-slavery ticket, taking 180 of the 303 members of the Electoral College.

Election and insurrection
By November 1860, the US had become so divided by the slavery debate that four candidates ran in that month's presidential election. The winner, Abraham Lincoln, could claim no popular majority and not a single Electoral College vote from the South. He was chosen, thanks only to northern electors. He had limited military experience but possessed keen judgment and strategic insight. In addition, he had clearly announced his opposition to the extension of slavery.

Distrusting the president-elect's motives, seven Southern states (later increased to 11) seceded from the US and formed the Confederate States of America. Lincoln believed the Union to be indissoluble, and like President Andrew Jackson—who had stared down similar secession threats in the 1830s—he was willing to fight for it.

Lincoln waited for the Southerners to fire the first shot. They did so on April 12, 1861, when the first round hit US government-held Fort Sumter in Charleston, South Carolina. Lincoln then declared the Southern Confederacy to be an insurrection against the legitimate federal authority and called for 75,000 volunteers to invade the rebellious states. Soon, far more than this number of citizen soldiers would be fighting in the Civil War.

Opening phase

The Lincoln administration's overall strategy was to keep foreign nations, especially cotton-hungry Britain, from recognizing the Confederate States as a legitimate nation. The US Navy blockaded Southern ports, making it difficult for them to receive arms and assistance from overseas. Lincoln then hoped to divide the Confederacy by seizing control of the Mississippi River and aiding pro-Union sympathizers in western Virginia, eastern Kentucky, and eastern Tennessee.

The eastern theater of war lay right at the president's doorstep in Washington, DC. After May 8, 1861, when Richmond, Virginia, became the Confederate capital, the principal battleground was the 100 miles (160 km) of forest and farmland separating the two cities, as well as the Shenandoah Valley to the west. That region would become the scene of at least a dozen major battles and countless minor engagements during the four years of war.

The western theater lay mostly in the vast expanse of territory between the Appalachians and the Mississippi River. Generals both north and south studied maps of this sprawling domain and planned similar, if reversed, strategies. Each side hoped to win the border states, especially Kentucky and Tennessee. Even the names of the armies reflected that struggle. »

Lincoln's strategy initially revolves around **preserving the Union** by quelling the insurrection.

→ He plans to squeeze the **Confederacy** via **blockades**, then split it by **controlling the Mississippi River**.

Lincoln then wants to **reclaim** the **border states**, **defeat Lee's army**, and seize Richmond, Virginia.

→ He later adds **opposition to slavery** to his strategy, **aligning the North** with the cause of **freedom**.

Lincoln is victorious and treats the defeated Southerners leniently.

→ Southern states eventually agree to **ratify the 13th Amendment** to the US Constitution, which **abolishes slavery**.

The First Battle of Bull Run in 1861 ended in a humiliating, disorganized retreat by General Irvin McDowell's Union army, leaving almost 3,000 of its men dead, wounded, or missing.

THE AMERICAN CIVIL WAR

The chief Confederate force in the West was the Army of Tennessee, and the principal Union forces were named after rivers: the armies of the Tennessee, Cumberland, and Ohio. Troops from each side soon entered the mountainous regions.

Early struggles

On July 21, 1861, the first major battle of the war was fought at Bull Run, Virginia. This resulted in a big Confederate victory that saw the emergence of a Southern hero, General Thomas J. "Stonewall" Jackson. By early 1862, however, the contest took a favorable turn for Lincoln. Forts Henry and Donelson, commanding respectively the Tennessee and Cumberland rivers, fell to the Army of the Tennessee, led by Major General Ulysses S. Grant, securing two vital waterways for the Union.

By April, two more victories had advanced the Union campaign to seize the Mississippi River: the fall of Confederate Island No. 10, near Memphis, and the capture of New Orleans, the largest city in the South. Soon, only a 110-mile (176 km) section of the river remained in Confederate control—between Port Hudson in Louisiana, and Vicksburg, a well-defended fortress settlement perched high above the river in Mississippi.

The desperate two-day Battle of Shiloh took place on the Tennessee River on April 6–7. It was another victory for Grant, but the scale of the casualties—more than all previous US wars combined—warned of a long, bitter struggle ahead. Matters were different in Virginia, where Jackson's small force in the Shenandoah Valley defeated three larger Union armies.

General Robert E. Lee

In the Seven Days' Battles of June 1862, Southern general Robert E. Lee sent General George McClellan and his large, well-equipped Army of the Potomac reeling back from the gates of Richmond. An impatient Lincoln ordered the Federal Army to fall back on Washington, DC. However, Union armies were winning in the states of Kentucky

The war's most bloody battles—Gettysburg, Seven Days, Chickamauga, Chancellorsville, and Antietam—were fought between June 1862 and September 1863. All but Chickamauga were in the eastern theatre. Some clashes with far fewer casualties were also strategically crucial, including Vicksburg, Fort Henry, and Fort Donelson.

Key:
- Union state
- Border state
- Confederate state
- ✕ Major battle
- Union blockade

and Tennessee. A major Confederate advance into the former ended in defeat at Perryville, and by the end of 1862, a savage battle near Murfreesboro, Tennessee, secured nearby Nashville as a major Union supply base.

Even Lee was nearly undone. He had led his Army of Northern Virginia into Maryland, menacing Washington, DC. On September 17, McClellan and the Army of the Potomac attacked him on the banks of Antietam Creek near Sharpsburg. The fierce encounter was tactically a draw, and strategically a Union victory, but McClellan allowed Lee to escape into Virginia.

Emancipation proclaimed

While the anti-slavery Republican Party held the Senate, it lost control of the House of Representatives in elections held in 1862–1863, in part due to the rise of the "Copperheads," a faction of the Democratic Party who believed in the inalienable rights of individual states, held abolitionists to blame for the war, and wanted an immediate peace settlement. Some of their fears were realized when Lincoln, prompted by the hope of lending his war effort a high moral purpose and the need to boost morale, announced his Emancipation Proclamation. This, on January 1, 1863, freed all 3.5 million enslaved people in the Confederate states, but not the half a million or so still held in Kentucky, Maryland, and Washington, DC—border areas whose loyalty the Union needed.

Changing fortunes

In the meantime, in Virginia, Lee foiled one Union commander after another—McClellan, Pope, Burnside, and Hooker. The president's strategy not only focused on capturing Richmond and destroying Lee's army but also aimed at taking Vicksburg so as to control the Mississippi River, Chattanooga in order to control all of Tennessee, and Charleston to close yet another important Confederate port.

Lee continued his string of victories, though the most daring and decisive one, Chancellorsville, fought in May 1863, came at the cost of losing Stonewall Jackson to a mortal wound. Lee then mounted a second invasion of the North to further damage Union morale, but that ended badly on the fields of southern Pennsylvania. The Battle of Gettysburg of July 1–3 1863, the bloodiest of the war, wrecked many of Lee's finest divisions. It culminated in "Pickett's Charge," when Union troops repulsed 12,000 Confederate infantry, leaving more than 8,000 wounded or dead. Once again, however, Lee managed to extricate many of his troops and return to Virginia.

On July 4, Lincoln received even better news. Grant's brilliantly conducted campaign to capture the Vicksburg stronghold finally ended in its surrender. After the subsequent fall of Port Hudson, the Union had now severed the corridor binding the Confederacy together. »

> Don't forget today that you are from Old Virginia!
>
> **Confederate General George E. Pickett**
> rallying his troops, Battle of Gettysburg, July 1863

Rifles and railroads

While rifle-muskets, railroads, and telegraph lines played important roles in the Crimean War (1853–1856), most military historians consider the US Civil War to be the first modern war. More rifles, used by large armies of citizen soldiers, were available than ever before, and these were deadly at far greater ranges than smoothbore muskets could achieve.

More importantly, the US possessed one of the largest and densest rail networks in the world, with 20,000 miles (32,000km) of track in the North and 9,000 miles (14,500km) in the South. Most of the track was lined with telegraph cables. Since railroads were the most efficient way of moving soldiers, arms, horses, and medical supplies, they defined the geography of the war, determining where campaigns were mounted and even the course of the fighting.

Retreating troops destroyed railway tracks and bridges to slow the enemy's progress. Advancing armies relied on engineers to repair them again.

With Union gunboats now able to patrol the Mississippi's entire length, Arkansas, western Louisiana, and Texas—important sources of Confederate horses, men, and supplies—were completely isolated. In June and July 1863, two major strategic goals were achieved when General William Rosecrans's Army of the Cumberland outmaneuvered Braxton Bragg's Confederate forces in mid-Tennessee, forcing them to retreat to northern Georgia. That pivotal area now seemed clear of organized rebel resistance.

New foes and a new state

Lincoln now had to face another enemy—one within the Union. War weariness had set in and desertion rates had soared, so in March 1863 he had signed the Enrollment Act, the first mass conscription in US history. The reaction in the North was furious, fueled in part by the burden falling on poorer men who could not afford to pay substitutes to take their places. Troops had to quell a three-day draft riot in New York City. Meanwhile, Copperhead Democrats and Confederates were discussing a negotiated peace. Lincoln's prospects for reelection looked increasingly doubtful.

A military setback came in September 1863, when Rosecrans's army was nearly routed at the bloody Battle of Chickamauga in northern Georgia and sent reeling back to Chattanooga. Confederate soldiers advanced and besieged the city, threatening to undo all the gains of the Tennessee campaign. However, in November, Lincoln stood in the rain on the churned-up fields of Gettysburg and transformed a dedication to a cemetery for the slain into a vision of the old republic having to die so that a "new birth of freedom" might rise from mass sacrifice.

As if in response to this inspiring rhetoric, the year ended with a growing tide of Union victories. Confederate forces were defeated in Knoxville, putting most of eastern Tennessee into Union hands. Grant arrived with his unbeaten Army of the Tennessee, broke the siege of Chattanooga, routed the enemy, and drove them back into Georgia. Already, western Virginia had become the new Unionist-leaning state of West Virginia.

The final phase

In March 1864, Grant was placed in command of all Union armies. With Lincoln's approval, he planned a strategy for winning the war that year, based on destroying Lee's Army of Northern Virginia and taking Richmond. Concurrently, in the western theater, Union General William T. Sherman was to invade Georgia and capture Atlanta—the Confederate rail, supplies, and munitions hub. Both offensives started in early May. Southern strategy, conversely, was to play for time in the hope that those Democrats advocating peace with the Confederacy might offer an independence settlement if they could unseat President Lincoln in the November elections.

The inconclusive Battle of the Wilderness began a series of titanic clashes between Lee and Grant in Virginia in May and June. By this stage of the war, engineers on both sides were designing ever more complex defensive and offensive earthworks. These played a part at Cold Harbor, near Richmond, on June 3, when at least 7,000 Union soldiers fell in the first 30 minutes of their attack on entrenched

After taking supreme command of the Union's armies, Ulysses S. Grant accompanied the Army of the Potomac into the field in the so-called Overland Campaign of May and June 1864.

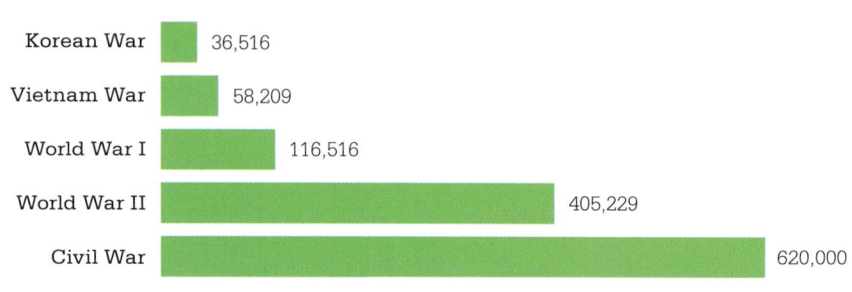

The highest wartime death tolls for the US

Korean War	36,516
Vietnam War	58,209
World War I	116,516
World War II	405,229
Civil War	620,000

At the Battle of the Wilderness in May 1864, Grant refused to order a retreat despite heavy Union losses, with 17,500 killed or wounded within 48 hours. No clear victor emerged.

Confederates. By July, the armies were locked in trench warfare around Petersburg and Richmond, a stalemate that forced Grant to fight a campaign of attrition instead of maneuver. In the neighboring Shenandoah Valley, the back-and-forth struggle would last well into fall, one Confederate advance nearly reaching Washington, DC.

Meanwhile, Sherman's armies fought their way south from Chattanooga toward Atlanta. His opponent, Confederate General Joseph Johnston, erected one series of temporary fortifications after another, but Sherman's divisions eventually outflanked them all, forcing nine major Confederate withdrawals in total. Bloody but inconclusive battles of maneuver delineated the Confederate retreat, and by mid-July the Union soldiers had the spires of Atlanta in sight.

With Grant and Lee deadlocked and Atlanta besieged, Lincoln's reelection chances still looked slim. The 1864 Democratic Convention in Chicago had adopted a Copperhead-influenced platform calling for an immediate cessation of hostilities and a negotiated settlement with the Confederacy, even though the Democrats' candidate, General McClellan, did not endorse it. Then, on September 2, Atlanta surrendered, changing the momentum of the war—and on November 8, 1864, the heartened North reelected Lincoln.

Toward the end
Southern morale quickly collapsed, and Confederate desertion rates soared. Sherman destroyed Atlanta and embarked on a scorched-earth March to the Sea (November 15–December 21), ending at Savannah, Georgia. Victorious Union forces similarly torched the Shenandoah Valley. The Confederate Army of Tennessee, after losing Atlanta, was nearly destroyed south of Nashville, leaving Lee's Army of Northern Virginia as the only major rebel force still in the fight.

By early 1865, Union victory appeared imminent. On April 1, Grant's divisions finally broke Lee's right flank, forcing the threadbare Confederates into a full westward retreat from the Richmond and Petersburg trenches. Lee hoped to join Confederate troops in North Carolina but was surrounded at Appomattox Court House, where, on April 9 1865, he surrendered to Grant. The Union commander in chief, in accordance with Lincoln's wishes, offered generous terms. After stacking arms, the captives were paroled and allowed to return home. Two weeks later, on April 26, in North Carolina, General Joseph Johnston surrendered all remaining Confederate troops east of the Mississippi and received the same terms from Sherman. That effectively ended the war.

Untasted fruits
The principal architect of Union victory in the first modern war would never taste its fruits. Just five days after Appomattox, Confederate sympathizer John Wilkes Booth assassinated Lincoln. In his Second Inaugural Address, only a month before the war's end, the president had said that the time to "bind up the nation's wounds" was nigh. Since he governed only during war and the buildup to it, history will never know what kind of peacetime president he would have made. ∎

> We have devoured the land. All the people retire before us and desolation is behind. To realize what war is, one should follow in our tracks.
> **General William Sherman**
> on the March to the Sea, 1864

MY PEOPLE WISH FOR PEACE
THE CONQUEST OF NORTH AMERICA (c. 1785–1890)

IN CONTEXT

FOCUS
European settlement of the continental United States

BEFORE
16th century European diseases ravage Indigenous populations across the Americas, causing widespread death and depopulation.

1675–1678 King Philip's War is fought between Wampanoag Indians and New England colonists; it is the first major war between Indigenous people and Europeans.

1784 The US becomes a sovereign state, free to set its own boundaries of colonization.

AFTER
1924 US citizenship is granted to all Indigenous peoples in the Indian Citizenship Act.

1968 The Indian Civil Rights Act finally grants Indigenous nations many of the benefits of the Bill of Rights.

In 1890, the US Census Bureau decreed that "the unsettled area has been so broken into by isolated bodies of settlement that there can hardly be said to be a frontier line." The US now stretched across the entire North American continent, having expanded from its original 13 colonies to encompass millions of square miles.

An idealized mythology about "how the west was won" developed alongside this insatiable feat of conquest—a narrative of brave settlers and soldiers triumphing over "savage Indians." For the Indigenous peoples, the long series of so-called Indian Wars constituted a drawn-out genocide.

Independence in 1776 and sovereign statehood eight years later freed the land-hungry American colonists from the limits to westward expansion that were imposed by the more wary British. In the Northwest Territory—the land west of Pennsylvania and east of the Mississippi—settler militias crushed the Northwestern Confederacy of Indigenous peoples at the Battle of Fallen Timbers in 1794 and then crushed the last remnants of resistance at the Battle of Tippecanoe in 1811.

Trails of tears
In the south, Indigenous warriors fought for their lands in the Creek War of 1813–1814 and the drawn-out Seminole guerrilla wars of 1817–1858. Defeated in both conflicts, they lost most of their territory in Alabama, Georgia, and Florida. Following the passing of the Indian Removal Act of 1830, US government agencies forcibly relocated several southern tribes to barren reservations much farther west. Often starving, cold, and prey to diseases, thousands

For shame! For shame! You dare to cry out Liberty, when you hold us in places against our will, driving us from place to place as if we were beasts.
Sarah Winnemucca
Writer, activist, and member of the Paiute tribe, 1883

died along the way. The forced migration of the Cherokee and other peoples in the 1830s became known as the "Trail of Tears" because around a quarter of those moved died while in transit.

Gold and cattle

The discovery of gold in California in 1849 triggered a rapid influx of settlers on the west coast, leading in turn to widespread massacre of the Indigenous population. Murder, enslavement, and disease had reduced it from 150,000 to just 31,000 by 1870.

In the Midwest, the settlers' hunger for new land, especially for rearing cattle, and the desire for transcontinental transportation corridors led to a series of conflicts known as the Plains Wars (1854–1879). Although some Indigenous leaders, such as Sitting Bull and Crazy Horse (who defeated US commander George Custer and his men at Little Bighorn in 1876), achieved successes, it was an unequal conflict, and ultimately US military might prevailed. Also, the wholesale slaughter of buffalo herds devastated the economy and health

The US 7th Cavalry sets up camp after the Wounded Knee Massacre, in which it had shot nearly 300 men, women, and children—ending organized Indigenous resistance.

of Indigenous society. Almost the last act of this brutal sequence of conflicts was the massacre of several hundred Lakota people at Wounded Knee in South Dakota, in 1890. By this time, most of the surviving 300,000 or so Indigenous people of the US were confined to reservations comprising just 2 percent of the nation's land area. ∎

Sarah Winnemucca

Born in present-day Nevada in 1844, Sarah Winnemucca came from a line of Paiute chiefs. She spoke multiple languages and, despite the US cavalry having killed her mother and other family in 1865, worked as an interpreter and negotiator between the army and Indigenous tribes.

After some of her people were forcibly relocated to the Yakima Reservation, in northeast US, Winnemucca became a forceful advocate for Indigenous land rights and welfare. She also focused on the corruption and abuses of government-appointed reservation agents, which she raised in a meeting in 1880 with US president Rutherford B. Hayes. In 1883 she became the first Native American woman to publish a book, *Life Among the Piutes* [sic]: *Their Wrongs and Claims*. Her advocacy helped to wring from the government commitments to reform and promises of land restoration, but these pledges were betrayed. Winnemucca died in 1891.

THE GREAT NAVAL FEAT OF THE ... IRONCLADS
THE PARAGUAYAN WAR (1864–1870)

IN CONTEXT

FOCUS
River warfare

BEFORE
1811 Paraguay declares independence from Spain.

1854 A formidable fortress is built at Humaitá, on the Paraguay River, to stop the Brazilians from invading Paraguay via the river.

1861 During the American Civil War, a "brown-water navy" patrols the Mississippi River.

AFTER
1947 The French navy creates the Dinassaut divisions to patrol the Mekong and Red rivers in French Indochina to combat communist guerrillas.

1965 A US Navy–created brown-water navy patrols rivers during the Vietnam War.

2022– Key battles during the Russo-Ukrainian War take place along rivers such as the Dnipro.

Also known as the War of the Triple Alliance, the Paraguayan War was the deadliest conflict in 19th-century Latin America. It transformed the fortunes of the four countries involved and changed warfare on the continent.

The 1825 fall of the Viceroyalty of the Río de la Plata left Paraguay's riverine borders undefined. In a bid to gain territory, the country declared war on its neighbors: Argentina, Brazil, then Uruguay.

With few roads in the region, most of the fighting took place near rivers that ran through swampy jungles. All sides suffered heavy casualties, though many of the deaths were due to fatal diseases such as cholera, smallpox, and typhoid, which were rife in the subtropical environment.

Profound changes

At the start of the war, the armies were poorly trained and equipped with outdated European firearms. By 1870, they had become better drilled and were using upgraded

Dense jungle vegetation and a damp climate along the Paraguay River led to poor hygiene conditions and the spread of diseases among combatants.

percussion rifles. They also adopted more efficient tactics, such as fighting at strategic river crossings. After a yearlong siege, the fall of the fortress at Humaitá in 1868 marked the beginning of the end for Paraguay's territorial ambitions.

The war profoundly changed Paraguay, which lost 70 percent of its population and had to cede territory to Brazil and Argentina. Brazil realized the importance of controlling the Paraguay River, which was the sole access to its vast territory in Mato Grosso. ■

See also: The European conquest of the Americas 122–125 ▪ The Spanish American wars of liberation 200–203 ▪ Revolution and counterrevolution in Latin America 298–299

REVOLUTIONS AND EMPIRE 225

INDIA WAS THE PIVOT OF OUR EMPIRE
THE BRITISH CONQUEST OF INDIA (1803–1857)

IN CONTEXT

FOCUS
Britain and the sepoys

BEFORE
1600 Queen Elizabeth I approves the establishment of the East India Company (EIC), created to find spices, indigo dye, and cotton in Asia.

1751 EIC troops clash with French forces at Arcot (Tamil Nadu). Both armies are supported by Indian sepoys.

1757 Led by Robert Clive, EIC troops defeat the Nawab of Bengal and his French allies at the Battle of Plassey.

AFTER
1895 Indian soldiers are absorbed into the British Indian Army. They are now allowed to become officers, although in practice this rarely happens.

1947 The Indian subcontinent is partitioned into independent nations: India and Pakistan.

By the 1750s, the British East India Company was competing with French trading companies for control of South Asia's lucrative spice trade. It had fortified its trading depots and set about expanding its territory. The East India Company had also built up its own private army, which comprised locally recruited Indigenous infantry known as sepoys, well drilled in European military tactics and led by British officers. At its peak, the East India Company's army numbered around 300,000, of which more than 95 percent were sepoys.

General Robert Clive's 1757 victory at Plassey consolidated the East India Company as the rulers of South Asia for the next century. Supported by its army of sepoys, the company imposed British law and cultural values, made English the official language, and plundered India's natural resources.

Resistance to the British rulers continued until the princely states of the Punjab were defeated in a series of conflicts, including the Second Anglo-Maratha War (1803–1805), and the two Anglo-Sikh wars (1845–1846 and 1848–1849).

In 1857, increasing resentment of company policies led to a sepoy mutiny that grew into a general uprising against British rule. The Indian Rebellion had some successes, but the harsh British response ultimately led to the deaths of as many as 800,000 Indian people. Thereafter, the British government replaced the East India Company as rulers of India. ∎

The place was literally running ankle deep in blood … I looked down and saw them lying in heaps.
Major George Bingham
on Cawnpore, 1857

See also: The Mauryan Empire 42–43 ▪ The Mongol invasions 96–101 ▪ Timur's conquests 105 ▪ Mughal conquests in India 140–141

THE SCRAMBLE FOR AFRICA
IMPERIAL WARS IN AFRICA
(c. 1880–1900)

IN CONTEXT

FOCUS
Empires in Africa

BEFORE
1482 Portugal founds Elmina, a trading base on the West African coast, marking the start of European encroachment in Africa.

1847 Resettled, formerly enslaved people from the US found the state of Liberia.

AFTER
1935 Fascist Italy invades Abyssinia—the last imperial conquest in Africa.

1956–1968 Independence movements in Africa mark the end of direct colonial rule in many parts of the continent.

1975 Angola and Mozambique are freed from Portuguese rule.

2020 Belgium's King Philippe apologizes for the colonial crimes of his forebear Leopold.

In the early 1880s, rival European powers were alarmed to discover that King Leopold II of Belgium had stealthily carved out for his nation, by subterfuge, diplomacy, trade, and violence, a vast province in the heart of Africa. As a result, in 1884, German chancellor Otto von Bismarck called a meeting of European powers in Berlin, with the aim of formalizing what was later dubbed the "Scramble for Africa," in which the continent was carved up into spheres of European influence. Within a few years, these spheres had crystallized into directly ruled colonial possessions. The entire continent, with the

REVOLUTIONS AND EMPIRE 227

See also: Zimbabwean kingdoms 104 ▪ Warfare in northern Africa 126–127 ▪ The wars of the French Revolution 180–187 ▪ The Second Boer War 234 ▪ The African wars of independence 300–303 ▪ Postcolonial Africa 304–305

> " If I am called upon to conduct operations against the Zulus, I shall … show them how hopelessly inferior they are to us in fighting power.
> **Lord Chelmsford**
> British Army general, 1878 "

exception of Liberia and Abyssinia (now Ethiopia), was conquered by European force of arms.

Creeping partition

European nations had operated zones of influence in Africa for centuries, but direct control had been limited to coastal enclaves. Their desire for greater control was driven by a variety of factors.

In North Africa, the social and political destabilization caused by a century or more of creeping imperialism had left power vacuums in areas previously under the control of the Ottoman Empire. Egypt, for example, became nominally independent as the Khedivate of Egypt in 1867, but it had a weak government and came under British rule in 1882. European imperial powers also sought prestige and strategic advantage through conquest, sometimes allowing territories a degree of autonomy. In northern Nigeria, for example, Britain forged an alliance with the Sokoto Caliphate, allowing it to maintain authority over its subjects as long as it resisted advances from other colonial nations.

European powers' hunger for control in Africa was underwritten by self-serving ideologies: racial and religious prejudices, as well as nationalist sentiment.

Imperial conquests on the continent were supercharged by technological advances in three fields: medicine, transportation and communications, and armaments. European expeditions into the interior of Africa had long been hampered by the risk of tropical diseases; new medicines greatly relieved this problem. In particular, synthesized quinine was developed to treat malaria, a deadly disease borne by mosquitoes. Inventions such as steam-powered boats, railroads, and the telegraph made it much easier and faster to travel and communicate across large distances. The Europeans also had the advantage of better organized military forces, but equally important were their significant developments in arms technology.

Deadly weaponry

By the 1870s, vast numbers of obsolete European guns were circulating in Africa; sought-after trade goods, they were often used to win treaties and concessions from local power brokers. Meanwhile, European armed forces were upgrading to new weapons that would radically change the nature of conflict. Foremost among these were breech-loading rifles. Even when these were traded to Africans—as in 1889, when the British South Africa Company bargained for a concession from Lobengula, king of the Ndebele people in what is now Zimbabwe, by offering him 1,000 of the latest Martini-Henry rifles—European armies retained the technological edge because they had machine »

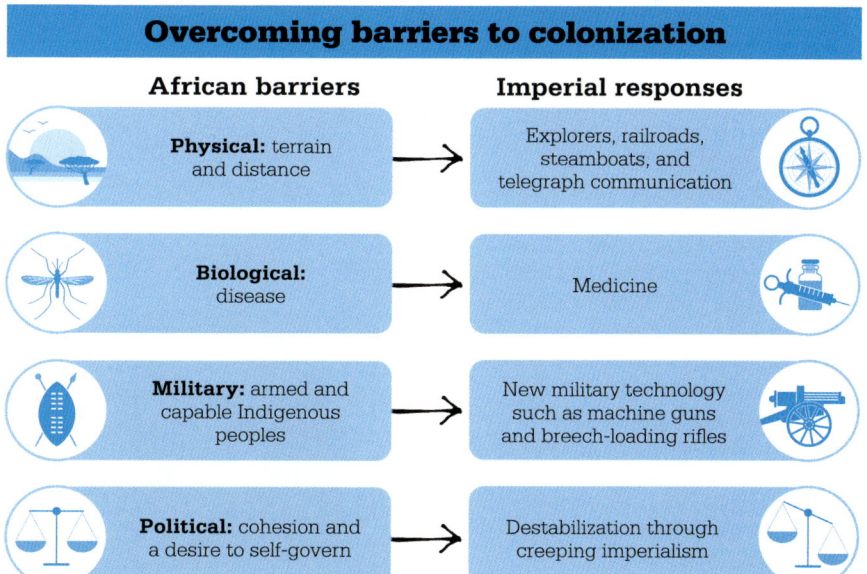

IMPERIAL WARS IN AFRICA

Uereani Maharero

Born in 1856, Uereani Maharero, generally known as Samuel, was the son of a Herero chieftain in what is now Namibia. His father, repeatedly rebuffed by the British when seeking protection, had reluctantly succumbed to German occupation in 1885. Samuel was educated at a German mission school and became chief when his father died in 1890. Initially, he sought German support, conceding land rights to the colonists. However, as the latter increasingly encroached on Herero territory, Maharero rallied support for a rebellion.

In January 1904, Maharero exhorted the Herero people to "rise up … against the Germans … [L]et us die fighting rather than as a result of maltreatment." The revolt came close to success, but a German army under Lothar von Trotha defeated Maharero at the Battle of Waterberg in August 1904. In October of that year, Trotha ordered a genocide against the Herero people. Maharero and about 1,000 of his men fled to exile in the Bechuanaland Protectorate (now Botswana), where he died in 1923.

guns. They were always careful to keep these out of the hands of local forces, prompting French-British poet Hilaire Belloc's 1898 rhyme about the power imbalance between Africans and Europeans: "Whatever happens, we have got / The Maxim gun, and they have not."

The Maxim gun was a recoil-operated, water-cooled, fully automatic machine gun that was developed by American British inventor Hiram Maxim in the 1880s. It became the weapon most associated with the colonization of Africa. Although bulky and awkward to operate, it could fire at least 600 rounds per minute to devastating effect. In the First Matabele War of 1893–1894, a British force of only 700 men, with the assistance of just five prototype Maxim guns, fought off a force of 5,500 Matabele warriors, killing many of them.

French interests

Armed with breech-loading rifles, machine guns, artillery, and steamboats, European powers overcame local resistance wherever they went. The French had annexed Algeria as early as 1830, and by the 1870s they were plotting to link their North African possessions with new territories in West Africa. In the 1892 Dahomey expedition, French forces numbering just 2,000 men under the command of Alfred-Amédée Dodds provided a model of how imperial forces

> [Africa] is now open … [T]ry to make an open path for commerce and Christianity.
> **David Livingstone**
> Scottish explorer, in a speech at Cambridge University, 1857

could fight and win in Africa, even against courageous opponents. They defeated around 12,000 soldiers of the Fon people in what is now Benin, killing 5,000 of them at a cost of just 77 French fighters.

British imperialism

The British Army had become increasingly involved in running the nominally Ottoman territory of Egypt and Sudan. In 1885, an uprising against British rule by Mahdist Sudanese resulted in the death of Governor-General Charles Gordon at Khartoum.

At the other end of the continent, the British struggled to exert control over southern Africa. There, the expansion of the Zulu Kingdom under King Shaka Zulu (r. 1816–1828) had created a powerful adversary for British imperialists, as well as galvanizing other regional powers, such as the Swazi and the Tsana.

Initial Zulu successes against the British in the Anglo-Zulu War of 1879 unleashed the full power

Hiram Maxim produced a prototype of his machine gun in 1884. British forces first used it against the Yoni people of West Africa three years later.

of the imperialist war machine, leading to the decisive defeat of the Zulu Kingdom. The resulting vacuum destabilized the region and helped exacerbate the conflict between the British and the Boers—colonists of Dutch, German, and French descent. This friction had already been triggered by competition to exploit the region's diamond and gold reserves. The British and the Boers fought brutal wars in 1880–1881 and 1899–1902.

Hostile takeovers

Belgium's King Leopold initially carved out a vast colony in the Congo by means of treaties and trade concessions from local leaders. However, when this strategy ran out of steam, his army took territory by force. Leopold's exploitation of the region was brutal and merciless; about half of the population died as a result of Belgian depredations.

Germany seized territory in Cameroon, South West Africa (Namibia), and German East Africa (Tanzania), often with extreme violence. Its troops suppressed the 1904 Herero uprising in South West Africa and the Maji Maji Revolt in German East Africa the following year with horrific brutality. In the former, 75 percent of the Herero people were killed.

Italy was also determined to stake its own claim to African dominions, annexing Eritrea in 1885 and parts of Somaliland in 1889. However, its attempt to conquer Abyssinia was rebuffed with defeat at the Battle of Adwa in 1896. Along with Liberia in West Africa, Abyssinia was the only part of Africa not annexed by European powers by 1914. The rest of the continent was divided into 30 new colonies or protectorates, populated by around 110 million Africans. Imperial contempt for the peoples they subjugated was made graphic on maps of the partitioned continent. Around 30 percent of the borders were straight lines, with no consideration for the boundaries of Indigenous villages, tribes, or kingdoms. ∎

At the Battle of Omdurman, Sudan, in September 1898, General Herbert Kitchener's army sought revenge for the killing of Charles Gordon in the Mahdist uprising.

IF WE MUST PERISH, WHY NOT FIGHT TO THE DEATH?
CHINA IN TURMOIL (1840–1911)

IN CONTEXT

FOCUS
Decline of Qing China

BEFORE
206 BCE–220 CE Under the Han dynasty, China becomes unified, centralized, and rich.

1644 The Qing dynasty takes control of Beijing.

1755–1792 The Ten Great Campaigns of the Qianlong Emperor result in Imperial China's greatest expansion.

AFTER
1937–1945 In the Second Sino-Japanese War, Japan seizes vast areas of China.

1949 Communists defeat the Chinese Nationalist Party, or Kuomintang, after a four-year civil war. The Nationalists retreat to Taiwan, while the Communists control China.

1964 China detonates its first atomic bomb, taking a central spot on the world stage.

Qing-dynasty China was one of the richest nations in the world in the 19th century—and the most populous. However, it was unable to keep pace with the military advances of the West, or with the economic, political, and social developments that underpinned that military strength. A major trigger for future disasters were the Opium Wars of 1839–42 and 1856–60, in which Britain used gunboat diplomacy (the threat of naval force) to impose treaties on Qing China. The wars were caused by Britain wanting to flood Chinese markets with the opium grown in its Indian colonies, even though opium was banned in China.

The First Opium War started when an imperial commissioner confiscated and destroyed opium chests belonging to British traders. In June 1840, 16 British warships took Hong Kong and then sailed up the Bei River to occupy the walled city of Canton (Guangzhou). China was able to regain the city only upon payment of a colossal sum.

The Second Opium War was also known as the Arrow War after Chinese officials boarded and seized

- **Famine**, natural disasters, and foreign interference **destabilize the nation**.
- **Unrest**, insurrection, and **war follow**.
- China is forced to **concede control** to local warlords and **foreign powers**.
- **Qing authority** wanes.
- China is unable to modernize and equip itself to cope with escalating challenges.

See also: Origins of the Chinese Empire 44–47 ▪ The Han Empire 48–49 ▪ The establishment of Manchu China 142–143 ▪ The Ten Great Campaigns 166–167 ▪ The Second Sino-Japanese War 264–265 ▪ The Chinese Civil War 294

The Armstrong artillery gun was used by the British in Beijing in 1860. *The Times* of London correspondent William Bowlby noted that it "smashes whatever it comes into contact with."

a British ship, the *Arrow*, in 1856. Along with French forces, the British launched a military expedition to the north of the country and even went on to occupy Beijing in 1860.

The Taiping Rebellion

Defeat in these conflicts damaged the Chinese economy, exacerbated currency problems, and undermined central authority. Criminal gangs, warlords, and secret societies flourished, while famine and instability ravaged the country. In 1844, a powerful quasi-Christian cult, the Taiping Tianguo, launched a massive rebellion that resulted in one of the bloodiest civil wars in history. Between 1853 and 1860, Taiping territory occupied a vast portion of the Chinese heartland around Jiangxi, Anhui, and Zhejiang, and it took the Western-trained, imperial Ever Victorious Army to subjugate the rebels. The Taiping capital, Nanjing, finally fell in July 1864, but the war and associated famine cost between 20 million and 30 million lives.

A failure to reform

China badly needed to modernize its economy, politics, and military, but under Empress Dowager Cixi, the Qing dynasty tried to cling to power by ceding regional control to warlords and simultaneously encouraging both reformist and nationalist movements.

The inadequacy of attempts to reform the armed forces—notably the Self-Strengthening Movement of the 1860s—was revealed during the First Sino-Japanese War, fought to secure influence in Korea.

Now they have started the aggression, and the extinction of our nation is imminent.
Empress Dowager Cixi
Declaration to Grand Council, 1900

China's much-vaunted Beiyang Fleet was defeated in the Battle of the Yellow Sea in September 1894.

Qing authority was weakened even further, and in desperation, Cixi supported the anti-foreigner Boxer Rebellion, which had started in 1899. Foreign powers allied with local warlords to occupy Beijing and crush the uprising in 1901. Following Cixi's death, reformist and revolutionary movements led to the 1911 Xinhai Revolution that finally ended imperial rule. ■

Empress Dowager Cixi

Born Yehe Nara Xingzhen in 1835, Cixi was the daughter of a middle-ranking Manchu noble. Sent to the imperial palace to become a lowly fifth-rank concubine to the Xianfeng Emperor, she went on to gain great power not only through cunning but also by bearing the emperor's only son.

When the emperor died, in 1861, Xingzhen colluded with imperial princes to overthrow her son's regents and become empress dowager with the name Cixi ("motherly and auspicious").

Chauvinist strictures, however, mandated that she literally had to rule from behind a curtain.

For the rest of the century, Cixi tried to protect her dynastic interests in a delicate balancing act between reformist and reactionary forces, against the backdrop of wars, droughts, floods, famine, encroaching imperialist forces, and economic and religious turmoil. She clung to power until her death in 1908; her last act was to install another child emperor on the throne.

RUSSIA WOULD WIPE US OFF THE MAP
OTTOMAN DECLINE AND RUSSIAN EXPANSION (c. 1790–c. 1890)

IN CONTEXT

FOCUS
Russian-Ottoman rivalry

BEFORE
1681 After a five-year conflict, the Russian and Ottoman empires sign the Treaty of Bakhchisarai.

1783 Catherine the Great annexes the whole of the Crimean Peninsula.

AFTER
1904–1905 Russia is defeated in the Russo-Japanese War. Its commanders fail to understand warfare in the industrial age.

1912–1913 Ottoman military failings lead to the loss of Albania and Macedonia in the Balkan Wars.

1916–1917 Russia's military losses against Germany's modernized war machine in World War I help trigger the Russian Revolution.

Two vast empires that were constantly in conflict with one another in both Europe and Asia, the Ottomans and the Russians faced similar challenges. As well as their size and diversity, both struggled to keep pace with the quickly modernizing economies and militaries of the great powers to the west of their own lands.

Reforms and reorganization

Despite the many problems they faced, both empires made serious attempts to update their armed forces during the 19th century. In this goal they were at least partially successful.

Humiliating defeat in the Russo-Turkish War of 1787–1792, following Russia's annexation of Crimea, had demonstrated to Sultan Selim III that he needed to modernize the Ottoman military and associated bureaucracy. In 1793, he created the *nizam-ı cedid*, or "new order." These troops had modern weapons and foreign advisers (mainly from France), who were also recruited to supervise shipbuilding and the creation of new arsenals and fortifications. However, the Janissary Corps—the Ottoman army's elite infantry—undid Selim's attempted reforms by staging a coup and killing the sultan in 1808.

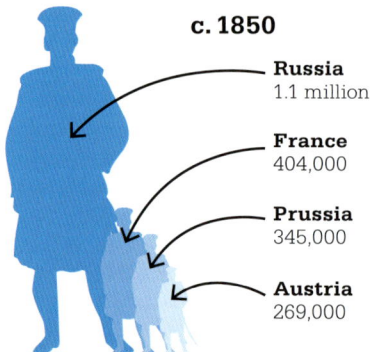

c. 1850
- Russia 1.1 million
- France 404,000
- Prussia 345,000
- Austria 269,000

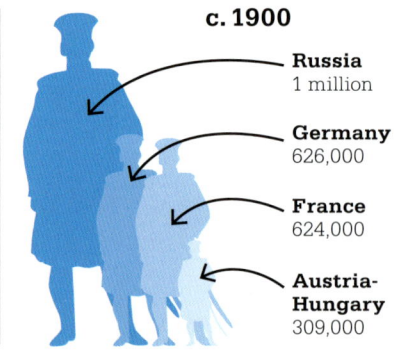

c. 1900
- Russia 1 million
- Germany 626,000
- France 624,000
- Austria-Hungary 309,000

The Russian army decreased in size by almost 10 percent between around 1850 and 1900, while other European nations considerably increased the size of their forces.

REVOLUTIONS AND EMPIRE 233

See also: The rise of the Ottoman Turks 112–113 ▪ The Ottoman Empire 130–133 ▪ The Great Northern War 158 ▪ The wars of Catherine the Great 178–179 ▪ The Crimean War 206–207 ▪ The Russo-Japanese War 235 ▪ Conflict in the Balkans 236–237

Mikhail Skobelev

Born in 1843, Mikhail Skobelev was known as the White General for the white uniform he wore into battle with total disregard for personal safety. He became a hero of the Pan-Slavic movement, which hoped to unite all the Slavic-speaking peoples into one nation state.

In 1873, Skobelev was a commander during a Russian expedition to Central Asia, but he achieved real fame leading a Cossack brigade in the Russo-Turkish War of 1877–78. In battle, he would generally be found where the fighting was fiercest.

Distinguishing himself in battles to liberate Bulgaria from the Ottoman Empire, Skobelev was lionized by Russian newspapers. As a result, his bold tactics became the model for the late-19th-century Russian "bayonets before bullets" battlefield ethos, tactics that were to prove inadequate in the Russo-Japanese War of 1904–05. Skobelev died in 1882.

Seen as a barrier to modernization, the Janissary Corps was crushed by Sultan Mahmud II in 1826, although this failed to prevent the defeat of the Ottomans in the Russo-Turkish War of 1828–29. Mahmud now set about building a new army, trained by Prussian officers.

In Russia, a "revolution in military affairs" took place in the 1860s and 70s, driven by minister of war—and former serving army officer—Count Dmitry Alekseyevich Milyutin. He reorganized the army into autonomous districts, created a system of reserve troops, and introduced universal conscription.

Reshaping the region

In 1877, when Russia was drawn into yet another conflict with the Ottomans in support of its Balkan allies, its army was ready. Using modern communications to coordinate maneuvers, Russia attacked on two fronts: in the Balkans and the Caucasus. One series of battles was fought at the strategically important Shipka Pass in Bulgaria. At the fourth and last battle, in January 1878, Russian commander Mikhail Skobelev cut off the bulk of the retreating Ottoman army. This victory provided an opportunity for Russia to threaten the Ottoman capital Constantinople (modern-day Istanbul).

Ottoman domination of the Balkans was decisively ended, even though it retained much territory, and only the threat of intervention by Western European powers, alarmed by Russian successes, stopped Russia from going further. Russia's victory over the Ottoman Empire transformed the political landscape of the Balkans, formally creating the new state of Bulgaria and helping secure independence for Romania, Serbia, and Montenegro. ■

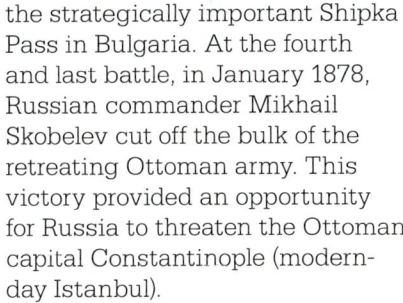

Georgian militiamen pose for a photograph during a quiet period in the 1877–1878 Russo-Turkish War. Georgia had become a part of the Russian Empire by this time.

CASUALTIES OF NEARLY 100,000 MEN
THE SECOND BOER WAR (1899–1902)

IN CONTEXT

FOCUS
British Army reform

BEFORE
1879 During the Anglo-Zulu War, advanced military technology—specifically breech-loading rifles—secures a British victory, fueling assumptions of superiority.

1880–1881 Mobile, disciplined, and organized Boer commando forces defeat Britain in the First Boer War.

AFTER
1910–1914 As part of the Haldane Reforms, Major General Henry Wilson overhauls all aspects of army mobilization, including rail and naval transportation for military personnel and horses.

1914 When World War I breaks out, the British Expeditionary Force is lauded as the best trained, organized, and equipped force that Britain has ever fielded.

Growing tensions between Britain and the Dutch Boer settlers in southern Africa—fueled by the discovery of diamonds and gold on Boer territory—led to the outbreak of the Second Boer War in 1899. British military engagements since the Crimean War of 1853–1856 had largely been against heavily outgunned Indigenous peoples. Now the British army faced a very different kind of opposition. The mounted citizen soldiers of the Boer (known as commandos) were disciplined, hardy, and better armed than the British, having bought thousands of German Mauser rifles in anticipation of the conflict.

Back from the brink

In October 1899, Boer commandos besieged British troops at Mafeking and Ladysmith (in modern-day South Africa). Then, in mid-December, a British force under General Redvers Buller lost three battles. The British brought in reinforcements from across the Empire. By late 1900, an army of 150,000 had beaten the main Boer forces. Boer guerrillas resisted for another two years, which led British General Lord Kitchener to resort to scorched-earth tactics, starvation, and internment in concentration camps.

The Boer War shone a light on the British Army's deficiencies—from antiquated weapons to a shortage of mounted troops. It subsequently prompted a series of military reforms that put it on a sounder footing for World War I. ∎

Let us admit it fairly, as a business people should, / We have had no end of a lesson: it will do us no end of good.
Rudyard Kipling
"The Lesson," 1901

See also: European wars of religion 134–139 ▪ The wars of Louis XIV 152–157 ▪ The Crimean War 206–207 ▪ Imperial wars in Africa 226–229 ▪ An expanding war 252–255

A NEW FORCE HAS BEEN BORN
THE RUSSO-JAPANESE WAR (1904–1905)

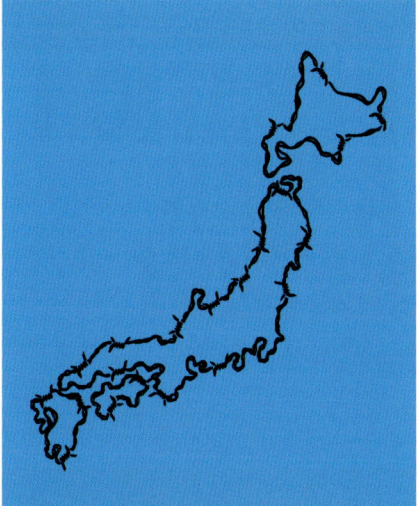

IN CONTEXT

FOCUS
Modern, industrial warfare

BEFORE
1861–1865 The American Civil War is the first industrial war, with railroads, warships, and mass production of weapons.

1868 The Meiji Restoration sets Japan on a modernizing and militaristic path.

AFTER
1912 The First Balkan War breaks out between the Ottoman Empire and the Balkan League. It employs new methods of warfare that will be used in World War I, including aerial bombing.

August 1945 Following the development of nuclear weapons, the US drops the first atomic bombs on the cities of Hiroshima and Nagasaki, precipitating the surrender of the Empire of Japan.

Many of the elements that would later characterize World War I were first seen in the Russo-Japanese War. These include extended fronts and drawn-out battles, trench warfare, barbed wire, machine guns and grenades, indirect fire, submarines and sea mines, and even some forms of electronic warfare.

Russia and Japan were vying for influence over Korea and Manchuria (then northeast China and inner Mongolia). Russia had leased land from China in Korea to establish a warm-water port at Port Arthur (modern-day Lüshun Port), and the imminent completion of the Trans-Siberian Railway had the potential to tip the balance of power in favour of Russia, cementing its presence in the region.

On February 8, 1904, Japan launched a surprise attack on the Russian fleet at Port Arthur, prior to transporting its forces to the Asian mainland. Meanwhile, with the bulk of its army deployed in Europe, Russia was unable to reinforce its troops facing the Japanese in Asia

Japanese soldiers prepare their weapons while holding a trench. This kind of warfare would come to greater prominence a decade later.

sufficiently quickly. As a result, it was forced to conduct a series of retreats that gave Japan a decided territorial advantage.

In January 1905, revolution broke out in Russia, partly in response to the humiliating performance of its army in the conflict against Japan. When the Japanese navy destroyed a Russian fleet at Tsushima in May 1905, Russia felt it had no option but to sue for peace. ∎

See also: Ottoman decline and Russian expansion 232–233 ▪ The Second Sino-Japanese War 264–265 ▪ Japan ascendant 280–283 ▪ Japan defeated 284–285

A WAR OF LIBERATION BECAME ... A WAR OF EXTERMINATION
CONFLICT IN THE BALKANS (1912–1913)

IN CONTEXT

FOCUS
The Balkan powder keg

BEFORE
1389 Ottoman forces defeat Serbian troops in Kosovo and become the dominant power in the Balkans.

1878 The Russo-Turkish War ends with victory for Russia. Some Balkan states, including Romania and Serbia, gain independence from the Ottoman Empire.

AFTER
1914 Instability in the Balkans and the assassination of Austria's Archduke Franz Ferdinand lead directly to the outbreak of World War I.

1918 The National Council of Slovenes, Croats, and Serbs creates the state that will become Yugoslavia.

1991–2001 After the fall of communism, Yugoslavia breaks up and nationalist tensions resurface.

In May 1897, Austria-Hungary and Russia signed a pact in which they agreed to maintain the status quo in the Balkan Peninsula. By keeping their rivalry in check, Austria-Hungary could focus on political unrest at home and Russia on the expansion of Japan.

Centuries of Ottoman rule in the Balkans had both created and suppressed a patchwork of groups with different nationalist, ethnic, and religious aspirations. With the assistance of the great powers (Germany, France, Britain, Austria-Hungary, and Russia), which sought to maintain balance in Europe from the 18th century until World War I, these aspirations had brought into being a number of land-hungry states, such as Serbia, Montenegro, and Romania. At their helm were some ambitious rulers with imperial pretensions of their own. The czar of Bulgaria, for example, dreamed of becoming the leader of a renewed Byzantine empire.

Conflict breaks out

Serbia, Montenegro, Bulgaria, and Greece all united in the Balkan League. They eyed the Ottoman territories in the region eagerly, and uprisings in Macedonia and Albania in 1912 gave them a pretext

Bulgarian soldiers survey the area at the First Battle of Çatalca in November 1912. The battle resulted in victory for the Ottoman Empire.

See also: The Byzantine Empire 70–73 ▪ The rise of the Ottoman Turks 112–113 ▪ The Ottoman Empire 130–133 ▪ Ottoman decline and Russian expansion 232–233

Cameramen are attacked as they film a battle in the First Balkan War in this illustration for a magazine. Up to 300 war reporters are thought to have been active through the two conflicts.

for what became known as the First Balkan War. The League mobilized almost one million men, defeated the Ottomans, and partitioned Macedonia and parts of Thrace.

The tactics and technology deployed in the Balkan conflict were similar to those of the Russo-Japanese War (1904–1905), which foreshadowed much of what was to come in World War I, with extended fronts, wide-scale entrenchments, quick-firing, indirect artillery, armored cars, and widespread use of machine guns. (The Balkan League fielded 480 machine guns, while the Ottoman forces had 340.) In one of the first uses of aircraft in warfare, Bulgarian pilots dropped hand grenades on Ottoman troops in the 1912–13 siege of Adrianople (modern-day Edirne, Türkiye).

Outgunned and marginally outnumbered, the Ottoman troops focused most of their efforts on resisting Bulgarian advances that threatened Constantinople. Eventually, pressure from the great powers reined in the Balkan states, and the war concluded with the expulsion of the Ottomans from the Balkans. They would later regain what is now Turkish Thrace.

From one war to the next

Unhappy with the partition of Macedonia after the First Balkan War, Bulgaria attacked Serbian and Greek positions there in 1913. When Romania and the Ottomans joined the fray of the Second Balkan War, Bulgaria had no choice but to sue for peace. The two Balkan wars left Bulgaria "sore, injured, and despoiled," in the words of British foreign minister Sir Edward Grey.

No amount of fighting could disentangle the ethnic, religious, and nationalist strands in the Balkan Peninsula. It also proved difficult to defuse tensions between the great powers, with the Austro-Hungarian Empire in particular nervous of Serbian aspirations. These tensions would eventually erupt in World War I. ■

The rising nations of South-Eastern Europe are surrounded by … enemies … The outlook is dark.
Edward Freeman
Fortnightly Review, June 1899

Czar Ferdinand I of Bulgaria

A divisive figure, Ferdinand I of Bulgaria today is both lauded as a shrewd hero of his country and condemned as a disastrous and risible failure. Born in Vienna, in 1861, into the German House of Saxe-Coburg-Gotha, he was elected Prince of Bulgaria in 1887. Ridiculed for his flamboyant dress and hedonistic lifestyle, he was nevertheless an astute and capable leader.

In 1908, Ferdinand proclaimed formal Bulgarian independence from the Ottomans, declaring himself tsar. He oversaw Bulgaria's rapid industrialization and military expansion, but his obsession with restoring a Greater Bulgarian kingdom and even a new Byzantine empire, with himself at its head, led him to miscalculate. He was instrumental in triggering the Second Balkan War, which led to a rapid Bulgarian defeat, and he chose to support the Central Powers during World War I.

Forced to abdicate in 1918, Ferdinand moved to Coburg, Germany, where he died in 1948. His remains were moved to Bulgaria in 2024.

THE WOR
AND BEYO
1914–PRESENT

LD WARS
ND

INTRODUCTION

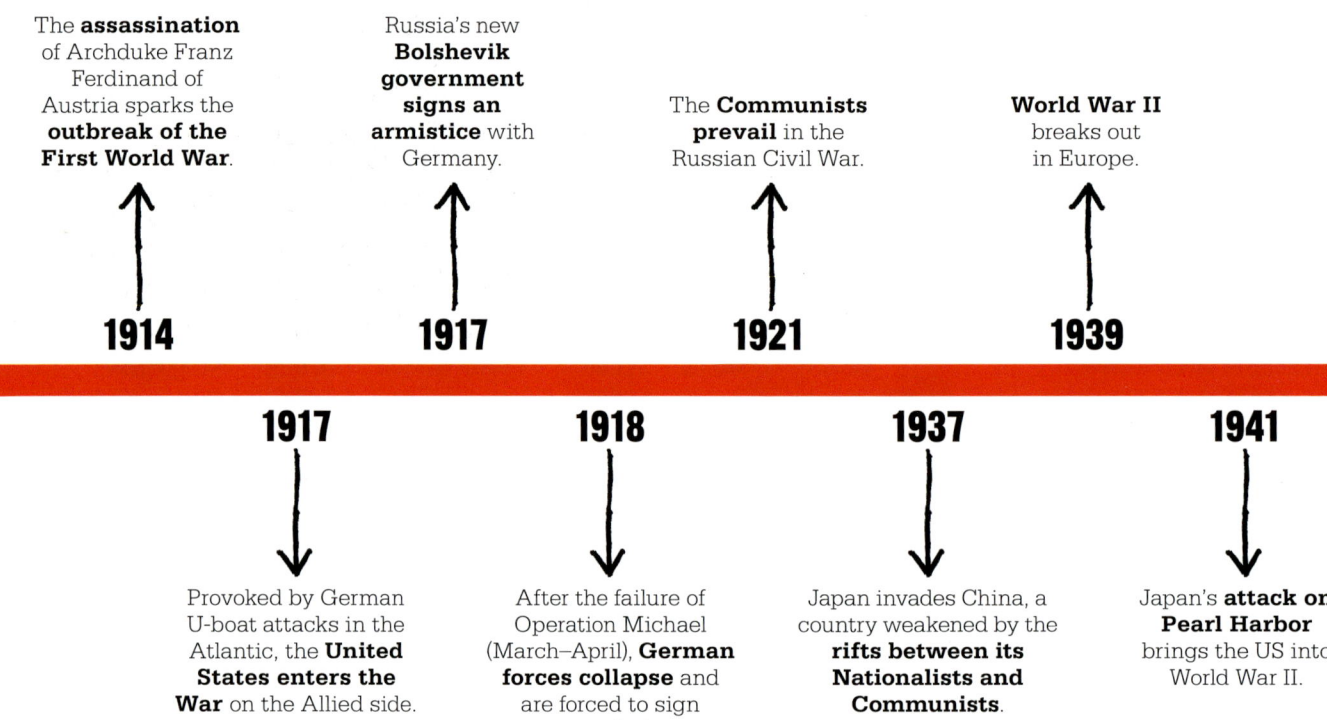

1914 — The **assassination** of Archduke Franz Ferdinand of Austria sparks the **outbreak of the First World War**.

1917 — Russia's new **Bolshevik government signs an armistice** with Germany.

1921 — The **Communists prevail** in the Russian Civil War.

1939 — World War II breaks out in Europe.

1917 — Provoked by German U-boat attacks in the Atlantic, the **United States enters the War** on the Allied side.

1918 — After the failure of Operation Michael (March–April), **German forces collapse** and are forced to sign an armistice.

1937 — Japan invades China, a country weakened by the **rifts between its Nationalists and Communists**.

1941 — Japan's **attack on Pearl Harbor** brings the US into World War II.

In 1905, Britain launched HMS *Dreadnought*, a colossal, yet fast and highly maneuverable warship with big, rapidly reloading guns. Two years later, Germany launched SMS *Nassau*, as formidably armed and larger.

The 20th century had started as it was to go on, in an arms race that would take technology, industrial production, and military organization to unprecedented levels. The war-torn decades that followed produced a stream of innovations from planes, tanks, and submarines, to advanced signaling and communications systems. Radically improved rifles, field guns, giant howitzers, and flame-throwers would transform the battlefields of World War I; even deadlier weapons in World War II and beyond revealed the devastating potential of nuclear power.

Imperial ambitions and alliances between rival European nations had driven the desire to rearm. Germany, Austria-Hungary, and Italy had formed the Triple Alliance in 1882; Britain, France, and Russia had signed the Triple Entente in 1907.

War and its fallout

In mid-1914, the assassination of Archduke Franz Ferdinand, heir to the Austro-Hungarian throne, by a Slav nationalist prompted Austria-Hungary to declare war on Serbia. This triggered a domino effect as Germany declared war on Russia, an ally of Serbia, and began its long-planned invasion of France, drawing Britain into the war.

On the Western Front, the deadly power of newly developed artillery that fired high-explosive shells, shrapnel, and poison gas turned fighting into an entrenched grind of attritional slaughter. The war spread to become the first-ever global conflict, exacting a death toll of up to 22 million. At its end, the punitive conditions imposed on a defeated Germany caused a festering bitterness.

In the years after World War I, communist Russia became the Union of Soviet Socialist Republics (USSR) and Japan emerged as an aggressive expansionist power in the Far East. Germany's sense of grievance gave rise to a defiant, far-right nationalism under Adolf Hitler and his Nazis, who began secretly to rearm their nation.

Germany's strategy in 1939 was Blitzkrieg—lightning war. Though successful at first as its tanks swept through Europe, it foundered with the invasion of the USSR in

THE WORLD WARS AND BEYOND

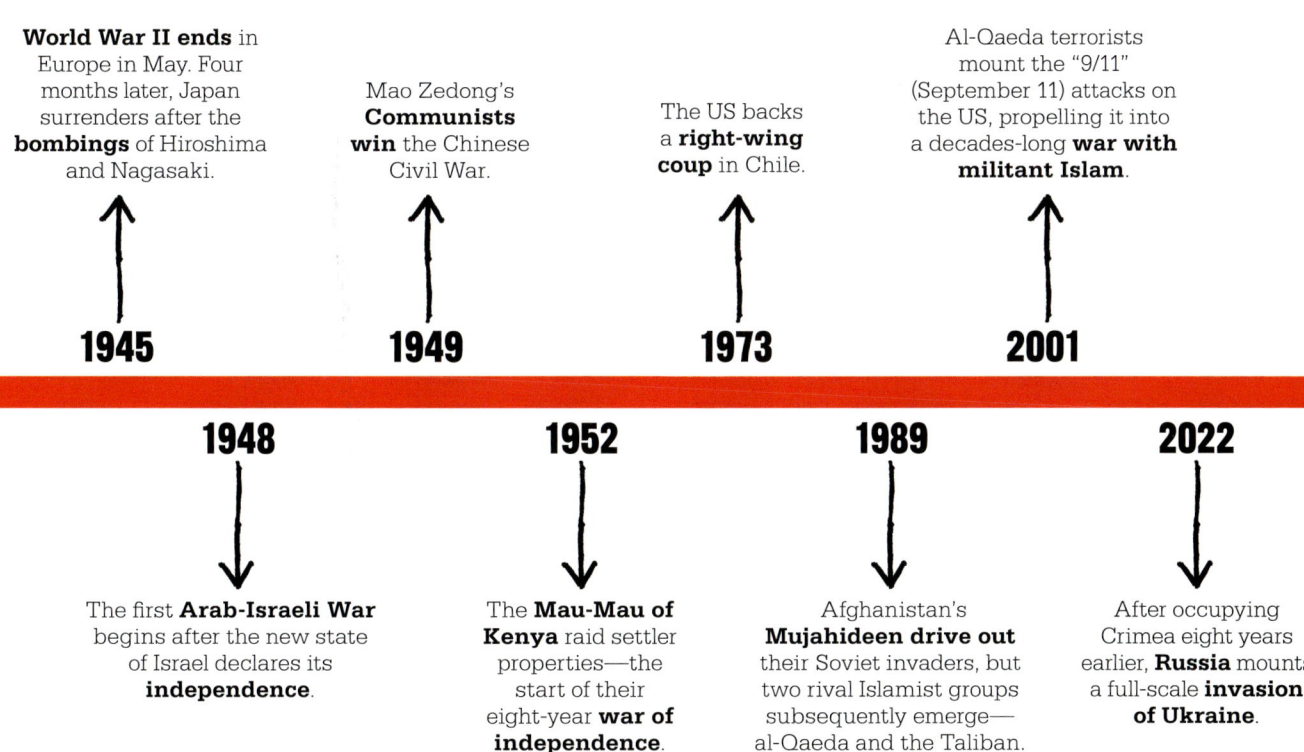

1941. The US, which had supported its allies financially, entered the war after Japan's raid on its Pacific Fleet. America's swift mobilization and the addition of its substantial material and manpower resources tipped the balance in favor of the Allies in Europe. Its development of the first atomic bombs also forced Japan into final defeat.

Cold War and Arab unrest

Victory in World War II left the USSR and US as the world's great superpowers but also bitter rivals, with diametrically opposed political attitudes and economic strategies. The Cold War was a stand-off, but its underlying tenets—communism versus capitalism—fueled wars in China, Southeast Asia, and Latin America and played a role in African struggles for independence.

The Middle East also became a tinderbox. The UN's approval of the partition of Palestine in 1947 to provide a new home for Holocaust victims and other displaced Jewish people was bitterly opposed by Arab states. When Israel declared itself an independent state in 1948, its Arab neighbors invaded in the first of seven Arab-Israeli Wars—the most recent ignited by a brutal, attack on southern Israel in 2023.

Although the Cold War ended in 1991 with the collapse of the USSR, its reverberations have continued. The rise of militant Islamism was unwittingly aided in the 1980s by US support for Muslim Mujahideen guerrillas who were driving Russian troops out of Afghanistan. Islamist terrorists have since launched attacks in the US, Europe, Middle East, Africa, and elsewhere.

In Russia, amid the economic and political chaos resulting from the USSR's implosion, ex-KGB officer Vladimir Putin rose to power. Under his rule, Russia has become involved in proxy conflicts in the Middle East and Asia, and directly in Ukraine as he seeks to regain former Soviet territory.

New military technology

The Ukraine war and also the latest Israeli-Arab conflict have featured thousands of missiles and drones that, combined with AI and military intelligence, take warfare to a new level. While drones are relatively cheap to produce, effective air defense systems are not. The race is now on to find new, affordable, high-tech countermeasures to shield nations and their people from future remote-controlled wars. ∎

THE RUSH TO THE ABYSS
WORLD WAR I: OUTBREAK (1914)

244 WORLD WAR I: OUTBREAK

IN CONTEXT

FOCUS
Who was responsible for the war?

BEFORE
1839 Britain signs the Treaty of London, which pledges to guarantee Belgian neutrality.

1871 The German Empire is established.

1882 The Triple Alliance of Germany, Austria–Hungary, and Italy is formed.

AFTER
July 1, 1916 On the first day of the Battle of the Somme, German artillery and machine-gun fire causes more than 57,000 British casualties.

1930s The German army pioneers the use of tanks and motorized transport in its Panzer divisions.

1939–1945 World War II is a mobile war; trenches are seldom occupied for long.

The lamps are going out all over Europe, and we shall not see them lit again in our lifetime.
Edward Grey,
British Foreign Secretary,
August 3, 1914

British troops exchange rifle fire in their first encounter with German forces, at the Battle of Mons, on August 23, 1914, in a painting by military artist William Barnes Wollen.

Article 231 of the Treaty of Versailles, signed in 1919, blamed the "aggression" of "Germany and her allies" for the outbreak of World War I. As a result, the defeated German nation was forced to pay punitive reparations. Its ally, Austria–Hungary, had indeed initiated the move toward conflict by threatening Serbia. This was in response to a Serbian nationalist assassinating Archduke Franz Ferdinand, heir to the Austro-Hungarian throne, on June 28, 1914. The first nation to order the full mobilization of its armed forces, however, was Serbia, Russia's ally. This in turn triggered the call-up of the German army on August 1.

Whether Germany and Austria–Hungary seized the opportunity provided by the assassination to fight short, preemptive wars against France, Russia, and Serbia—that soon spiraled out of control—has long been debated. Some historians argue that all combatants were to blame, their leaders "sleepwalking" over the abyss into horrific war and dragging their citizens with them.

Germany's strategy

Wherever the blame for the onset of war in August 1914 may lie, once diplomacy had failed to prevent the crisis between Austria–Hungary and Serbia from escalating, Germany took center stage. Its military strategy attempted to minimize the problems of a two-front war against both France and Russia by launching a swift and decisive blow against France before turning to face Russia, whose forces would be slower to mobilize and deploy in the field. Germany's war plan—the Schlieffen Plan—was based on a doctrine that was later called the "cult of the offensive," with victory ensured by one decisive strike. Its model was the 1870–1871 Franco-Prussian War—a war fought well before the advent of automatic weapons and rapid-firing heavy artillery. The result in World War I would be appalling carnage.

The Schlieffen Plan, named for Alfred von Schlieffen, the officer who spent years developing it, aimed to avoid German forces attacking France along the fortified common border. The proposal was to send the bulk of the German army looping west through Belgium,

THE WORLD WARS AND BEYOND 245

See also: The Crimean War 206–207 ▪ The rise of Prussia 210–213 ▪ Ottoman decline and Russian expansion 232–233 ▪ Conflict in the Balkans 236–237

then swinging south on the French army's rear for a final, decisive blow. That would entail violating Belgian neutrality, guaranteed since 1839 by Britain. If Britain, with its powerful navy, could be kept neutral, the chances of overall victory against France and Russia were considered by the German General Staff to be achievable. During the opening stages of the fighting, Britain and its small army would play only a limited part but its vast naval power and economic and trading strength would play a decisive role as the war developed. Many Germans expected Britain to remain neutral, but in the event it stood by its guarantee and chose to fight.

Early exchanges
At first, the Schlieffen Plan worked well. Within 10 days of the German invasion of Belgium on August 4, more than 1 million of its troops were transported to the frontier. Once battle was properly joined, however, the timetable was sorely tested. Where the Schlieffen Plan scheduled two days to take the Belgian fortress city of Liège, it actually took 11. That delay allowed more French divisions and the British Expeditionary Force (BEF) to take up positions in Belgium.

Meanwhile, French forces unleashed a massive assault on German-held Lorraine, lost by France in the Franco-Prussian War. On August 22, 1914, two French armies attacked German positions in the forests of the Ardennes. Wearing blue tunics and scarlet pantaloons, their white-gloved officers gripping sabers, the French soldiers launched their onslaught with confidence, but by the end of that day, 27,000 French soldiers had been killed by artillery and machine-gun fire. »

Soldiers of the Royal Welch Fusiliers and the Cheshire Regiment—part of the British Expeditionary Force—rest in a Belgian town in August 1914 on their way to the battlefront at Mons.

Alfred von Schlieffen

Born in Berlin in 1833, Alfred von Schlieffen was the son of a Prussian general. After a short period training to be a lawyer, he joined the General War School when he was 25. After graduating, he saw active service in the Seven Weeks' War against Austria (1866) and the Franco-Prussian War (1870–1871). Rising through the ranks of the army, he was appointed head of the German General Staff in 1891, a position he held until early 1906. Fascinated by the impact of landscape and weather on war, he finalized the Schlieffen Plan in 1905, shortly before his enforced retirement after being kicked and wounded by a horse.

Schlieffen is a controversial figure today because in 1904 he defended genocidal policies directed against the Herero and Namaqua peoples in Southwest Africa (present-day Namibia). He died in 1913 before seeing his war plan put into operation. However, his ideas outlived him: they influenced not only Germany's invasion of France in 1914, but also both German and Allied strategy in the early years of World War II.

246 WORLD WAR I: OUTBREAK

The machine gun

In 1884, Hiram Maxim, an American-British inventor, produced the first fully automatic portable machine gun, capable of rapid repeating fire. The new weapon was used to devastating effect in the Russo-Japanese War (1904–1905), and deployment of the gun increased rapidly during World War I. In August 1914, the German army had around 12,000 machine guns; by 1918, the number was more than 100,000.

The guns were heavy—65–130 lb (30–60 kg)—and prone to overheating, but they could fire up to 600 rounds per minute as far as 4,400 yd (4,000 m). Few military commanders predicted the weapon's destructive effect on advancing soldiers, which completely undermined classic infantry tactics of a mass of troops advancing in line or in columns. The machine gun became a key component of the defensive, trench-bound tactics that dominated the war on the Western Front.

A French machine gun crew take up a defensive position east of Paris at the First Battle of the Marne in September 1914.

British troops began digging trenches in September 1914—as did their French and German counterparts. Ultimately, trenches stretched from Belgium to the Swiss border.

Less than 24 hours later, at Mons in Belgium, the regular troops of the BEF poured an enormous volume of rifle fire into the massed ranks of attacking Germans but were forced to retreat. Although accurate rifle fire had long been an effective part of infantry assault, of much greater consequence in 1914 was the widespread introduction of machine guns. Alongside artillery, they would become the new measure by which the strength of armies was judged.

War grinds to a halt

Within three weeks of the outbreak of war, the Schlieffen Plan began to unravel. Pressure to keep to rigid timetables led to troop-jammed roads, and delays mounted up. This was accompanied by atrocities against civilians, including the burning of houses and villages, and the summary execution of people deemed to be guerrillas.

The German advance through Belgium and France had been the most massive military offensive in history to date. Millions of soldiers, horses, armament-filled wagons, ambulances, and civilian refugees were pushed south through the hot, dusty days of late August. Allied troops fell back over the entire front, with some French troops holding positions on the outskirts of Paris, fearing for the safety of the capital.

The First Battle of the Marne, beginning on September 5, 1914, then changed the course of events. This tremendous, three-day clash along a 100-mile (160-km) front initially slowed the Germans, then halted them, and finally forced them to retreat. It spelled the end for the Schlieffen Plan. From their

[The whole] history of the First World War ... is the story of the outcome of the Schlieffen Plan.
John Terraine
White Heat, 1982

new positions behind the Aisne River, German forces began to dig entrenchments, and the Allies followed suit to the west.

Making matters worse for Germany was the relative speed of Russia's mobilization, which saw two Russian armies advance into East Prussia. German army commanders in the East began to panic and demand the dispatch of reinforcements otherwise destined for the West. The two-front war, so feared by the German high command, had become a reality.

Fighting on the Eastern Front was just as horrific as in the West, but the battlefield geography precluded continuous trench lines, as the plains and forests were just too vast. Massive encirclement and counter-encirclement battles were fought throughout the fall of 1914, and recurrent onslaughts and scorched-earth retreats continued until the 1917 Bolshevik Revolution ended Russia's war.

Artillery and attrition

While the fighting was fierce in the East, war would ultimately be decided on the Western Front, where the bulk of the German army remained, cooped up in increasingly elaborate networks of trenches. These offered some protection, but not against artillery fire, which killed and wounded even more men than machine guns did. During the 1870–1871 Franco-Prussian War, around 96 percent of German wounds were caused by French rifle bullets. Studies of wounds to British soldiers in World War I, however, found that 59 percent were caused by shell or mortar fire and flying shrapnel, and only 39 percent were bullet strikes. The concussive effects of high explosives also induced shell shock, which took tens of thousands of soldiers out of action.

Artillery was ultimately more versatile than the machine gun as it could hit rear areas as well as front lines. Its weaponry ranged from portable trench mortars to gigantic railway-mounted guns hurling shells over 32 km (20 miles). Increasingly lethal munitions and refinements in bombardment and barrage tactics would make artillery the most destructive of combat arms. Even so, it could not break the stalemate on the Western Front in late 1914. Germany's plans for rapid victories against France and Russian were dead, and the war would drag on for another four devastating years. ∎

When Austria–Hungary declared war on Serbia in July 1914, it set in motion a chain reaction, as Europe's major powers, bound by existing alliances, were drawn into further declarations of war. By the end of 1914, the Ottoman Empire had also joined the conflict, which, after three months of offensive and counteroffensive, had ground to a halt on the Western Front.

Key:
- Central Powers
- Allies
- Neutral countries
- Declaration of war
- -- Western Front

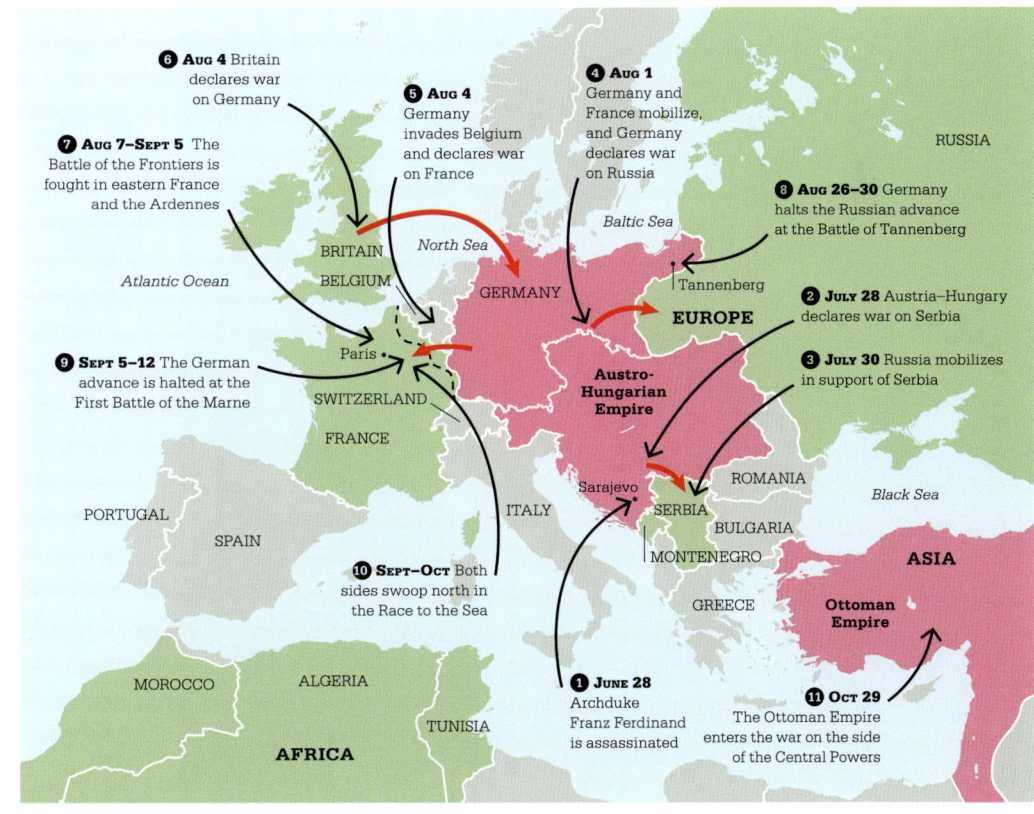

WE CURSED THROUGH SLUDGE

STALEMATE ON THE WESTERN FRONT (1915–1917)

IN CONTEXT

FOCUS
Shell shock

BEFORE
1865 Confederate medical director William Carrington calls for a hospital to treat "lunacy and dementia" arising from the American Civil War.

1901 British Army surgeon Anthony Bowlby recognizes "nervous symptoms" among combatants in the Boer War.

AFTER
1940 Combat stress accounts for about a tenth of admissions to regimental aid posts during the Allied retreat to Dunkirk.

1980 The American Psychiatric Association first uses the term post-traumatic stress disorder (PTSD).

1980s Some 15.2 percent of male Vietnam veterans are thought to suffer from PTSD.

The hundreds of thousands of men who joined the fight in France and Belgium from 1914 could not have imagined the horrors of the Western Front, nor foreseen the drawn-out war of attrition that it would become. All were equally unprepared for the relentless shell bombardments, merciless machine-gun fire, and poisonous gas attacks that would shatter bodies and minds in the rat-infested, mud-soaked trenches.

By December 1914, around 10 percent of British officers and 4 percent of enlisted men were reportedly experiencing "nervous and mental shock." Two months later, the term "shell shock" was

See also: The rise of Prussia 210–213 ▪ The American Civil War 214–221 ▪ The Second Boer War 234 ▪ The Russo-Japanese War 235 ▪ World War I: outbreak 242–247 ▪ The defeat of the Central Powers 258–261 ▪ World War II in Europe 266–271

A soldier affected by shell shock awaits treatment in a Western Front trench. By 1916, more than 40 percent of casualties were victims of the debilitating condition.

coined in the British medical journal *The Lancet* to describe cases characterized by "a loss of memory, vision, smell, and taste." Other symptoms included uncontrollable shivers, recurrent nightmares, and sudden blindness. Mental trauma had been noted in conflicts in both Europe and the US during the 19th century but never on the scale reported during World War I.

Forced to dig in

At the outbreak of hostilities, many strategists had expected a short, sharp war, but Germany's defeat at the First Battle of the Marne in September 1914 thwarted its bid for a swift victory in France. By the end of the year, as casualties on both sides reached the hundreds of thousands, opponents were forced to abandon mobile warfare in the face of huge artillery firepower and dig defensive trenches.

A decade earlier, trenches had featured in the Russo-Japanese War, but the millions of high-explosive shells now unleashed against infantry called for a deeper, more sophisticated system. This consisted mostly of three roughly parallel lines—a forward trench protected by barbed wire and sandbags, backed up by support and reserve trenches, all linked by a communication trench, and with dugouts to allow for some rest and battle planning.

As the conflict became one of slow attrition, digging in became essential, with each side striving to penetrate the other's defenses. The deadlock exacerbated mental distress, as it combined periods of tedium with others of sheer terror when trenches came under fire. The cramped, damp, unsanitary conditions of trench life did nothing to alleviate the troops' spirits.

Even greater terror was inflicted when soldiers were ordered to attack. As they rushed from their trenches ("going over the top"), they met rapid machine-gun fire and flying shrapnel from mortar and artillery shells—the cause of 60 percent of deaths in World War I.

The tactics of attrition

For three years, from 1915 to 1918, positions would shift relatively little along the line of opposing Allied and German entrenchments that stretched 475 miles (765 km) from the North Sea to the Swiss border. The generals on each side sought to break through their opponent's line and cause collapse up and down the sector. Salients—bulges in the line—were the obvious weak points as they provided three sides that could be attacked. Allied strategy was always to keep on the offensive in a bid to regain occupied French territory. German tactics, on the other hand, would vary between attack or, especially when fighting Russian forces on the Eastern Front, stubborn defense of their lines. »

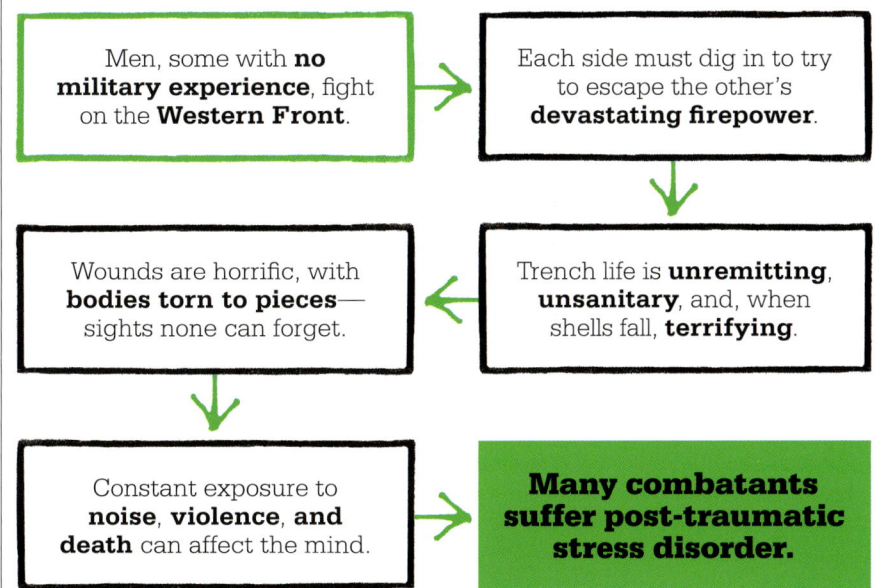

STALEMATE ON THE WESTERN FRONT

German artillery shells explode around French infantry at the Battle of Verdun, the war's longest engagement. Germany's aim was to take the fortress for its strategic and national importance.

We'd rather lose a leg, be wounded, anything but to have shell shock.
Edwin Bigwood
Worcestershire Regiment

In February 1915, the French army attacked the northern sector of the German front line in Artois and the southern sector in Champagne. It continued targeting these sectors throughout 1915, but with little success. German forces countered by attacking the Ypres salient in Belgium, which protected a key road and rail link supplying the British Expeditionary Force (BEF).

At the Second Battle of Ypres (April 22–May 15, 1915), during which nearly 100,000 men died, the Germans introduced a potent new weapon designed to break the stalemate—poisonous chlorine gas, which wafted toward the Allied lines in yellowish green clouds. It proved lethally effective, blistering the skin of panicked Allied soldiers, and burning their throats and lungs. The gas killed hundreds of men and scarred thousands.

In the subsequent Battle of Loos (September 25–October 8), the British (now equipped with masks) also used chlorine gas, but in places it blew back into their lines. Loos added to the troops' sense of helplessness. It cost the British some 60,000 casualties for almost no gain as every advance was repelled by German forces.

The longest battles

As 1916 dawned, Germany planned a campaign designed to "bleed France white" by luring its forces into a trap at Verdun, an ancient fortress city on its eastern border. It became a titanic 10-month struggle that ended with no breakthroughs, no territory gained by either side, and more than 700,000 deaths.

The battle at Verdun was still raging when the British, hoping to alleviate the pressure on the French, launched an offensive designed to break the German line at the Somme River. After a weeklong Allied bombardment of the German defenses, some 100,000 British and other Allied troops crossed into no-man's-land on July 1, 1916. They expected no resistance, but deep trenches had helped the German forces survive. Then, under accurate German artillery and machine-gun fire, advancing British troops sustained 57,000 casualties in what became the bloodiest single day in the history of the British Army.

The bruising Somme campaign lasted nearly five months, costing more than 1 million casualties on all sides. The Allies advanced just 6 miles (10 km). Not all the injuries were physical; as many as a fifth of the wounded—up to 63,000 men—may have had to endure disabling psychiatric disorders.

Futile actions

At the start of 1917, Allied generals persisted with the same positive expectation of a breakthrough and victory being only months away—but they were soon to suffer further setbacks. In April, a major French assault near Reims was repulsed. Learning in advance of the massive French bombardment, German forces had taken cover in their deep dugouts, then mowed down the advancing French infantry. With no end to the war in sight and morale collapsing, French troops began to mutiny along the Western Front. Ultimately, the high command suppressed the mutiny, and 629 men were sentenced to death, of which 49 were actually executed.

Meanwhile, German forces had pulled back the central part of their defenses to what the Allies came to call the Hindenburg Line, a 90-mile (145 km) zone anchored in Ypres to the north and Lorraine in the southeast. In July 1917, the BEF sought to strengthen its hold on its key Ypres salient by seizing a German-held ridge 2 miles (3 km) to the east across a plain and crowned by a hamlet called Passchendaele.

Passchendaele would come to rival the Somme as a symbol of the tragedy, waste, and futility of war. Over the next three months, 300,000 British soldiers were killed or wounded on the waterlogged plain, as the fall rains came early and persisted, turning the battlefield into a sea of mud, blood, and corpses. Although the hamlet was finally taken on November 6, the gaining of such little territory had come at a terrible cost.

Despite the horrors of the battle, the British Army recorded only 5,346 shell-shock casualties—widely believed to be a considerable underestimation given the terrible conditions experienced. Official attitudes to the syndrome had hardened after the Battle of the Somme, when the British director-general of the army medical service, Lieutenant-General Sir Alfred

It was mud, mud, everywhere ... a sea of filthy, oozing mud.
John Palmer
British gunner, Battle of Passchendaele

Keogh, declared that such cases were "under no circumstances to be recorded as a battle casualty."

An end—for some

Within a year of Passchendaele, the stalemate on the Western Front had eventually ended. The massive German Spring Offensive in March 1918 broke the lines of the Allies, who fought back in August and, now with US troops arriving in large numbers, finally breached the Hindenburg Line. Germany was exhausted, while the Allies had momentum and the resources they needed—and in November, the war ended on their terms.

For many soldiers, however, the war never left them. Thousands endured permanent debilitating physical injury, but many also paid a high psychological price. During the course of the war, more than 600,000 German troops had been treated in military hospitals for "nervous diseases," and 80,000 British combatants were diagnosed with "war neurosis." More than a decade after the end of the war, Britain's Ministry of Pensions was still providing support for around 75,000 neurologically damaged veterans. Thousands more were likely suffering in silence. ∎

Recognizing shell shock

Charles Myers, a captain in the Royal Medical Corps from 1915, used the term "shell shock" to describe three cases he had studied in 1914. Appointed consultant psychologist to the British armies in 1916, he set up four specialist units for lesser cases and sent those affected more severely to base hospitals.

After the bloody battles of 1917, incidences of shell shock escalated, causing panic among the military authorities, which feared a collapse in troop morale.

Myers, however, persuaded the War Office to fund courses on military psychiatry, and a few specialist hospitals were established. Early therapies included the use of anesthetics and electric shock treatment, but British neurologist William Rivers at Craiglockhart War Hospital in Scotland better understood the effects of trauma and began to use a talking cure. Decades later, shell shock was recognized as a type of post-traumatic stress disorder (PTSD).

ONE VAST BATTLEFIELD
AN EXPANDING WAR (1915–1917)

IN CONTEXT

FOCUS
Call of empire

BEFORE
1756–1763 In the Seven Years' War, Britain and France fight over land claims in North America and the Caribbean.

1871 Germany starts to build an overseas empire.

1885 At the Berlin Conference, European powers carve Africa into colonies.

1912–1913 The Ottoman Empire loses territory as the Balkan Wars reshape boundaries in southeastern Europe.

AFTER
1919 The Treaty of Versailles strips Germany of colonies in Africa, China, and the Pacific.

1920 As the Ottoman Empire falls, France takes control of Syria and Lebanon; and Britain, Palestine and Mesopotamia.

The outbreak of war in Europe in 1914 had quickly enveloped all the major imperial powers, making it a global conflict. Colonies were called upon to supply raw materials, food, and huge pools of manpower. The war would mark the demise of the German, Ottoman, Russian, and Austro-Hungarian empires, while the surviving French and British colonies would soon begin to seek their own identity and destiny— and independence.

Britain's dominions

In 1914, the British Empire was the world's largest, covering nearly a quarter of the world. Its main

THE WORLD WARS AND BEYOND

See also: The Crusades 88–93 ▪ The Ottoman Empire 130–133 ▪ The Seven Years' War 162–165 ▪ The Crimean War 206–207 ▪ Imperial wars in Africa 226–229 ▪ The Second Boer War 234 ▪ World War II in Europe 266–271 ▪ The defeat of Germany 276–279

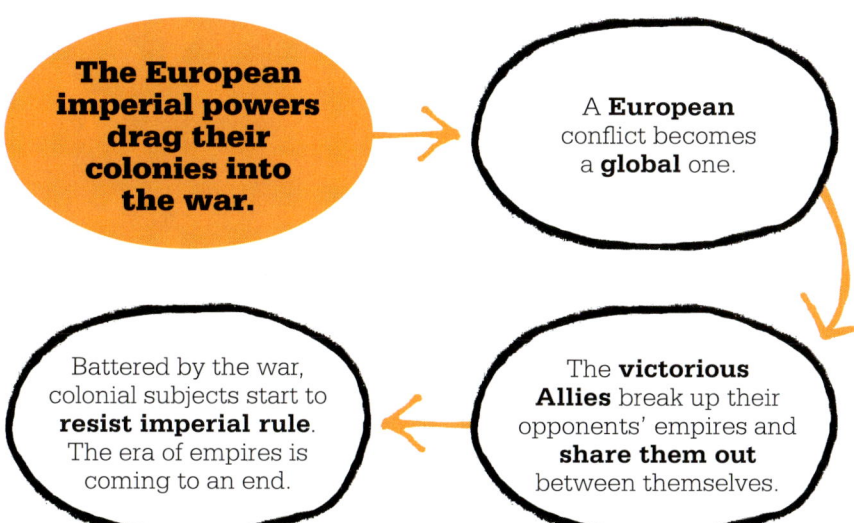

sources of military recruits were India and the self-governing imperial dominions of Canada, Australia, New Zealand, and the Union of South Africa. The young men of the dominions, which were mainly populated by people of Anglo-Saxon descent, rallied to the British cause. Depots and training camps were established, and the first new recruits began to arrive in the principal theaters of war from late 1914.

Canadians were shipped directly to the Western Front, where they fought with such tenacity at the Somme, Vimy Ridge, and Passchendaele in 1916–1917 that British Secretary of State for War David Lloyd George called them the empire's "storm troops." Members of the Australian and New Zealand Army Corps (known as Anzacs)

Sikh cavalry from the Army of India ride close to the Franco-Belgian border in 1915. The previous year, many Sikh cavalrymen had been killed at the First Battle of Ypres.

crossed the Indian Ocean to train in Egypt. In one of the war's most devastating campaigns, they were then deployed in April 1915 at Gallipoli, a peninsula flanking the narrow Dardanelles Strait connecting the Aegean Sea and the Sea of Marmara in northwest Türkiye. Hemmed in by steep cliffs on shallow beachheads, Anzacs, together with British, Indian, French, and colonial African troops, fought valiantly for eight months in heat and disease-ridden conditions against unrelenting Ottoman opposition until withdrawn by the Allied high command in December. By 1916, most Anzacs had been redeployed to the Western Front, while some remained in the Middle East, fighting principally in Egypt and Palestine from 1917 to 1918.

India's crucial role

Imperial Britain drew on India to supply its largest reserve of troops. When war broke out, the Army of India included more than 78,000 British troops and 154,000 Indian soldiers, whose numbers would swell to 573,000 in 1918. Over half of the Indian soldiers were from the northern Punjab region—Sikhs, Gurkhas, Muslims, and others perceived by the British as "martial" races. Infantry and cavalry units of the Indian Expeditionary Force A were fighting at Ypres in Belgium by October 1914, and then at the Battle of Neuve Chapelle in March 1915. Indian cavalry regiments remained on the Western Front until the end of the war, but Indian infantry »

254 AN EXPANDING WAR

divisions, which were poorly equipped and unaccustomed to European conditions, were transferred to Mesopotamia in October 1915, joining the main mission of the Army of India to protect key British oil installations around Basra at the head of the Persian Gulf.

The success of Indian army advances up the Euphrates and Tigris rivers in 1915 encouraged an unsuccessful offensive against Baghdad; it ended in ignominious surrender to the Ottomans after a 147-day siege at Kut al-Amara. Baghdad was taken in March 1917, at a cost of many Indian casualties. Of the 675,000 Indian troops who landed at Basra before the end of 1918—five times the number that went to France—more than 32,000 were wounded and close to 30,000 died.

Some 144,000 Indian troops were also involved from 1915 in the campaigns against Ottoman forces in Palestine and Egypt, fighting alongside British, French, Anzac, and Arab forces. By September 1918, Indians made up two-thirds of the British-controlled infantry and a third of the cavalry that crushed Ottoman and German forces at the Battle of Megiddo, which spelled the end of the war in the Middle East and further splintered the Ottoman Empire.

French Empire troops

France had the second largest world empire and had recruited Indigenous people into its colonial forces since 1750. At the start of World War I, it mobilized them en masse, including 175,000 Algerians, 80,000 Tunisians, and 40,000 Moroccans from North Africa, plus 180,000 men from its eight colonies in French West Africa. More than 38,000 men were recruited from French Guiana, Guadeloupe, Martinique, and Réunion, and a further 43,000 came from Indochina (and even more Indochinese people arrived to work in French munition factories). By the war's end, France had mobilized some 600,000 colonial troops.

Most Indigenous soldiers from the French colonies were *tirailleurs* (riflemen), while Algerians of French descent served in the cavalry regiments of *Chasseurs d'Afrique* ("hunters of Africa") and in infantry units known as the Zouaves. Many Africans were dispatched to the Western Front, but some served at Gallipoli in 1915, and in the Balkans from 1915 to 1918. The Senegalese *tirailleurs* fought across all fronts. Forced conscription prompted uprisings across French West Africa in 1915

A wartime poster entitled "Day of the African army and colonial troops" by French artist Lucien-Hector Jonas (1880–1947) glorifies the fighting prowess of recruits from Africa.

Lawrence of Arabia uses traditional Arab clothes both as a disguise and as an act of identification with the Arab people involved in the revolt.

The Arab Revolt

In June 1916, Hussein bin Ali, emir of Mecca, on the Arabian peninsular, declared a revolt against the Ottoman Empire. He did so against a backdrop of growing Arab nationalism, famine, and imperial repression. Behind the action were promises from Britain that, once the Ottomans were defeated, an independent Greater Arabia would be established.

Coordinated in part by British officer Captain T.E. Lawrence ("Lawrence of Arabia"), the Arabs launched raids from desert strongholds to divert Ottoman troops from other fighting fronts, seized the port of Aqaba, and destroyed much of the Ottoman railroad system in Arabia and Sinai. The Arab army continued to engage Ottoman forces up until the end of the war, aiding the Allied advance through Palestine and into Syria. When hostilities ended, hopes for a Greater Arabia were dashed when Britain and France, protecting their own colonial interests, secured control over much of the Middle East.

Askari soldiers of the German East African Schutztruppe stand to attention before an officer in 1914. By the end of 1916, more than 11,000 *askaris* had been recruited to the German forces.

and 1916, but by offering social benefits to African soldiers and their families, the French government attracted 72,540 new recruits in four months of 1918.

Like Britain during this era, France held the racist view that Indigenous people in its colonies were inferior. Africans, deemed fiercer and less susceptible to pain than white Westerners, were used as frontline shock troops; one international study calculated that more than 71,000 French colonial soldiers died in the war.

War in Asia and Africa

Most of the German Empire's overseas possessions were lost soon after the start of the war. The Asia–Pacific region was the largest theater of action in World War I but was also its least bloody and destructive. By the end of 1914, New Zealand, Australian, and Japanese forces had taken German Samoa, German New Guinea, the

The black troops ... have ... the instinct for combat, the absence of nervousness, and an incomparable power of shock.
General Charles Mangin
Advocate of West African recruitment
La Force Noire, 1910

Bismarck Archipelago of Papua New Guinea, and the Mariana, Caroline, Marshall, and Palau island chains, together with the fortified port of Tsingtao in eastern China.

The Allies attacked all four German colonies on the African continent—Togoland (Togo), Kamerun (Cameroon), German Southwest Africa (Namibia), and German East Africa (Tanzania). Togoland surrendered in August 1914. Then, in January 1915, the largely white Union Defence Force (UDF) of South Africa invaded German Southwest Africa, defeating its defenders within six months. In Kamerun, the Schutztruppe—the German colonial army of mostly *askaris* (native African soldiers)—held out until February 1916. Fighting continued in German East Africa until late 1918 as the colony's vast expanses of bushland favored the guerrilla tactics of German general Paul von Lettow-Vorbeck. With a tiny army a 20th the size of his Allied opponents, he held out with his *askaris* until November 25, 1918, a fortnight after the war finished.

An end to empires

By 1918, Russia had gone through a Marxist revolution. The German, Austro-Hungarian, and Ottoman empires had disintegrated in defeat and were divided up by the victors at subsequent peace conferences. Britain and France would soon face new challenges as their colonial subjects began to resist imperial rule. Within 50 years, and after a second world war, their colonies would vanish as nations fought for and won their full independence. ∎

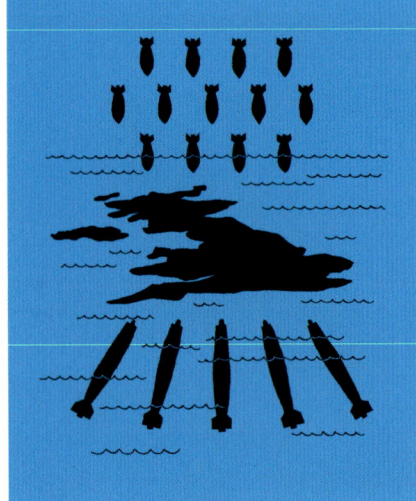

THE BIGGEST MENACE … IN THIS WAR
THE WAR AT SEA AND IN THE AIR (1914–1918)

IN CONTEXT

FOCUS
Submarines and bombers

BEFORE
1864 During the American Civil War, *H. L. Hunley* becomes the first submarine to sink an enemy ship in combat.

1906 Germany launches its first *Unterseeboot* (U-boat).

1911 An Italian pilot drops grenades from his plane during the Italo-Turkish War—the first aerial bomb attack.

AFTER
1937 German planes attack Guernica in northern Spain during the Spanish Civil War, blanket-bombing civilians.

1939–1945 During World War II, Germany builds more than 1,000 U-boats and sinks around 3,000 Allied ships.

1945 US Air Force B-29 aircraft drop 1,667 tons of incendiary bombs on Tokyo, Japan, killing more than 100,000 people.

The naval arms race between Britain and Germany that preceded World War I had focused on dreadnoughts: giant battleships with huge, heavy guns. It was the submarine, however, that was to seize the strategic initiative.

In 1914, Britain's navy blockaded the English Channel and the strait between Scotland and Norway, in order to cut the flow of supplies to Germany and its allies via the North Sea. Germany reacted in February 1915 by threatening to attack ships heading for British or French ports.

The submarine menace
With its surface fleet bottled up, Germany turned to its submarines, known as U-boats, and in mid-1915, they attacked Allied ships in the North Atlantic. The British hit back with Q-ships, warships disguised as civilian vessels, which lured U-boats to the surface and sank them. In response, U-boats attacked without warning while submerged, contrary to the previously accepted

British dreadnought HMS *Monarch*, pictured here in 1914, took part in the Battle of Jutland in 1916. Fought close to Denmark in the North Sea, it was the only major naval battle of the war.

THE WORLD WARS AND BEYOND

See also: The Russo-Japanese War 235 ▪ An expanding war 252–255 ▪ The defeat of the Central Powers 258–261 ▪ The war at sea 272–273 ▪ The air war 274–275

Development of the submarine

1776 *Turtle*: The first submersible craft used in action—against HMS *Eagle* in the American Revolution (1775–1781)

1864 *Ictíneo II*: The first combustion-powered submarine, designed by Spanish engineer Narcís Monturiol

1897 USS *Holland* (SS-1): The first submarine to be commissioned by the US Navy

1902 HMS *A-1*: The first British-designed submarine; sank after a collision during training exercises

1914 *U-35*: The most successful U-boat of World War I, sinking 226 merchant ships

1959 USS *George Washington*: The first nuclear-powered ballistic missile submarine

---

rules of engagement. These tactics raised an outcry when a U-boat sank British-owned passenger liner RMS *Lusitania* off the coast of Ireland on May 7 1915, killing 1,198 people, including 128 Americans.

Turning points

To avoid provoking the US further, U-boats left the Atlantic for the Mediterranean in late 1915. They sank more than 400 vessels there in 1916, but the Allied blockade held. By late 1916, food riots had erupted in Austria-Hungary and Germans were starving. U-boats renewed their Atlantic attacks, sinking 430 Allied and neutral ships in April 1917 alone.

From May 1917, Britain—now also close to starvation, because of the U-boat campaign against merchant shipping—set up a new system. Convoys of merchant ships were escorted across the Atlantic by British warships, equipped with depth charges (underwater bombs) and painted in "dazzle" patterns of abstract shapes to disorient U-boat crews. The effect was dramatic. Shipping losses dropped from 20 percent to less than 1 percent.

As soon as the US declared war on Germany, on April 6, 1917, the Allies set up a maritime transport pool, which carried 10 million tons of food across the Atlantic between July 1917 and July 1918. Meanwhile, German citizens struggled to find enough food. Allied victory was now almost inevitable—but German submarine tactics had revolutionized naval warfare. ■

The strategic bomber

During World War I, the development of military and naval aircraft was even faster than that of submarines. Little more than 10 years after the American Wright Brothers had taken the first heavier-than-air flight in 1903, single- and double-winged planes with machine guns fitted were fighting midair battles. It was as bombers, however, that aircraft acquired the most strategic significance, with their ability to strike beyond enemy lines to target industry and civilians.

In August 1914, German zeppelin airships attacked the Belgian cities of Liège and Antwerp. Zeppelins had targeted Paris and London by spring 1915, but by 1917, their raids diminished. Airships were replaced with the Gotha G.IV heavy bomber, which killed 162 people in London in June 1917. British, French, and Italian heavy bombers soon followed.

The technology continued to develop: in early 1918, crews were using bombsights and pulling wires to release bombs from racks. Raining explosives from the air would become a defining feature of future warfare.

The Zeppelin–Staaken R.VI heavy bomber, with a wingspan of 138 ft (42 m), joined Gotha G.IV bombers on raids over Britain and France from mid-1917.

WE ARE AT THE END OF OUR RESOURCES
THE DEFEAT OF THE CENTRAL POWERS (1918)

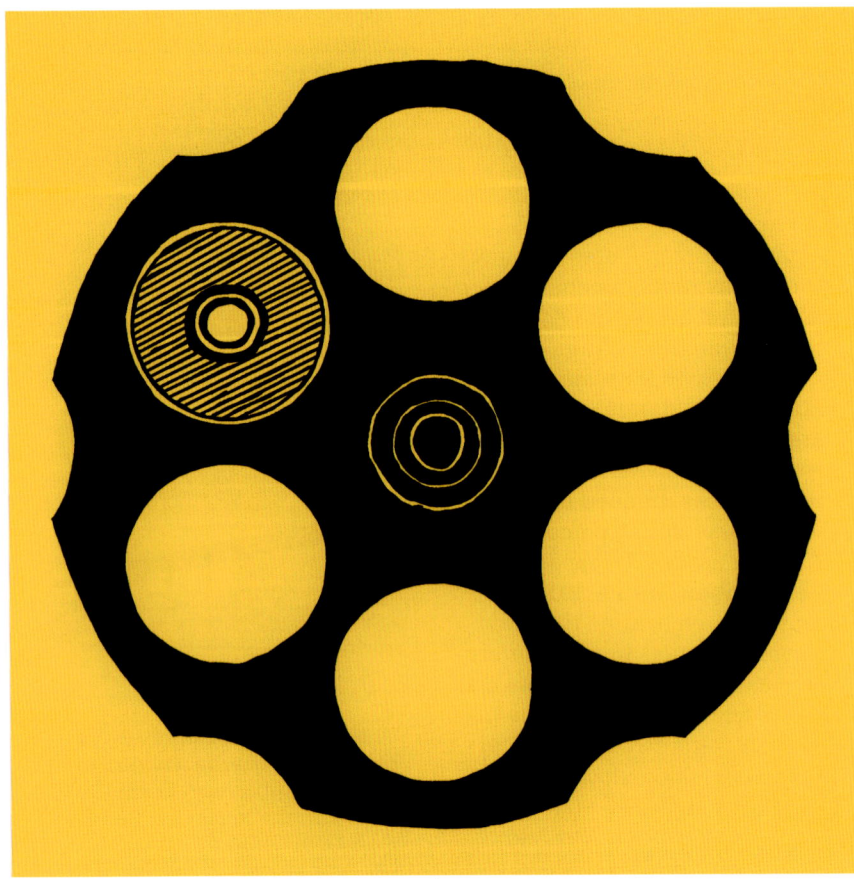

IN CONTEXT

FOCUS
Home front morale

BEFORE
1914 The Central Powers start to suffer food shortages when Britain blockades their ports.

1916–1917 In the Turnip Winter, a poor potato harvest brings Germany close to starvation.

1917 The Russian Revolution inspires socialists in Germany and elsewhere.

AFTER
1919 A revolt by the Marxist Spartacus League fails, ending hopes of revolution in Germany.

1920 The Paris peace treaties dismantle the Ottoman and Austro-Hungarian empires.

1941 The Nazis devise the Hunger Plan to starve people in the Soviet Union and create a food surplus in Germany.

The most effective weapon in total—unrestricted—warfare is one that attacks the foundations of society, such as food, work, and living conditions. The failure of a government to provide the most basic needs undermines a nation's civilian morale—and weakens the will of its military forces to fight.

Crises on the home front

In early 1918, every combatant nation in World War I had a shortage of both food and labor, but the Central Powers faced the bleakest situation. Effectively surrounded, and their ports tightly blockaded, both Austria-Hungary and Germany

See also: World War I: outbreak 242–247 ■ Stalemate on the Western Front 248–251 ■ An expanding war 252–255 ■ The Russian Civil War 262–263 ■ World War II in Europe 266–271 ■ The defeat of Germany 276–279 ■ The Cold War 286–293

Most **citizens** are not in the **armed forces**.

Ample food and other **basic provisions** are needed to **maintain civilian morale**.

Collapse of morale on the Central Powers' home front leads to unrest and revolution.

Combatants **depend on civilian support**, which relies on **high morale**.

Allied **blockades** of the Central Powers and **bad harvests** create **hunger** and **civil unrest**.

---

had imposed food rationing by the middle of 1916, and Germany was left reeling under a failed potato crop that fall. At the same time, famine was raging through parts of the Ottoman Empire. By contrast, Britain and France, having overcome the German U-boat threat to merchant shipping, did not have to introduce rationing until early 1918, and then only in a limited form.

Feeding millions of troops was the first priority for the Central Powers, while civilians went increasingly hungry. With so many working men conscripted into service, farmlands often went untended. Crop yields in Germany were half their prewar level by 1918, and meat consumption had fallen nearly 80 percent.

The continuing deterioration in living conditions fueled discontent on the home front. In January 1918, following the halving of flour rations, hundreds of thousands of workers went on strike across Austria-Hungary, where the many mutually hostile nationalities comprising the empire began to talk openly of secession, peace, and independence. In the same month in Berlin, nearly half a million German workers, increasingly attracted to the left-wing Social Democratic Party or the more radical, Marxist-inspired Spartacus League, went on strike, demanding an end to the war.

Last hopes
Another crisis facing German military commanders in 1918 was the ever-diminishing availability of soldiers, with around 6 million already killed or wounded. However, the withdrawal of Russia from the war in March meant that nearly 50 divisions—around 1 million soldiers—could now be transferred to the defensive Hindenburg Line, snaking 90 miles (145 km) across France and Belgium. This gave the Germans a numerical advantage—at least until troops began to arrive in force from the US, which had entered the war in April 1917.

With Austria-Hungary splitting along ethnic lines, the Ottoman Empire losing ever more troops to desertion, and Bulgaria—the fourth Central Power—convulsed by demands for peace, Germany might have only one more chance to win the war. But it would have to strike hard—and soon.

Offensive and counterstroke
On March 21, 1918, German artillery launched what the generals called the *Kaiserschlacht* ("Kaiser Fight") with more than 1 million shells—the largest bombardment of the war. Squads of highly mobile, well-armed stormtroopers, trained to infiltrate »

German women scour through a Berlin refuse tip looking for scraps of food during World War I. In 1918 alone, more than 290,000 Germans died of starvation and hypothermia.

260 THE DEFEAT OF THE CENTRAL POWERS

German prisoners—some of the more than 29,000 captured during the Battle of Amiens in August 1918—await transit to a PoW camp. Mass surrender seriously depleted German fighting power.

opposition positions, caused havoc deep behind Allied lines, and the three-year stalemate on the Western Front was broken. For two weeks, the fierce battle (later known as the Spring Offensive) resembled the conflicts of August 1914, a ceaseless motion of attack and retreat leaving confusion and isolated pockets of troops in its wake.

Operation Michael, the first and largest German attack, aimed to drive British forces back to their lifeline, the ports of Calais, Boulogne, Dunkirk, and Dieppe. The Allies continued to regroup, however, and this and several subsidiary attacks ground to a halt. Germany had advanced up to 40 miles (64 km) but also suffered 240,000 casualties, with teenage conscripts the only likely replacements.

By July, the arrival of around 10,000 fresh US troops each day began to give the Allies numerical advantage, while Germany's reserves were exhausted. The decisive counterstroke came on August 8, when British Empire and French forces broke through German defenses near Amiens, in northern France, capturing thousands of demoralized soldiers. The next month, German commander Erich Ludendorff ordered his forces to withdraw to the Hindenburg Line, from where he believed the German army could still launch attacks.

A domino effect

Bulgaria, a kingdom that had only entered the war reluctantly, was the first Central Power to break. A desire for peace had swept through its army, which, on September 15, was overrun on the Macedonian Front by the multinational Allied Army of the Orient. Mutiny in the Bulgarian ranks swelled into revolution against the government of Czar Ferdinand I. On September 29, his emissaries signed the Armistice of Salonica, taking Bulgaria out of the war.

Bulgaria's withdrawal alarmed Germany, which dispatched forces to protect captured Romanian oil wells. It also unnerved Ottoman Türkiye. With the bulk of its diminished forces spread thinly across the Caucasus, Mesopotamia, and Palestine fronts, there was little to stop the Army of the Orient from advancing on Constantinople.

September also saw troops of the American Expeditionary Forces (AEF) and the French army fighting a grim battle against German troops in northeastern France. On September 26, a gas attack and artillery bombardment marked the start of the Meuse–Argonne Offensive, and within days Allied armies were attacking up and down the Hindenburg Line. British, Australian, and American troops made the first breach in the line at St. Quentin Canal on September 29, and soon those Germans not surrendering were retreating further east. On October 3, the Allied offensives finally convinced the German commanders of their inevitable defeat, prompting a diplomatic overture to US President Woodrow Wilson.

Meanwhile, the Austro-Hungarian Empire was fracturing rapidly, as industrial strikes and socialist uprisings added to its

> Had [the Hindenburg Line] been defended by the Germans of two years ago, it would certainly have been impregnable.
>
> **General Sir Henry Rawlinson**
> **Commander, British Fourth Army at St. Quentin Canal, 1918**

divisions along ethnic lines. Hungary had already severed formal relations with Austria when, on October 24, Italy launched a decisive offensive against the Austro-Hungarian Empire's starving and demoralized troops at Vittorio Veneto, north of Venice. Rioters swarmed the streets of Vienna, the Austrian capital, and Czechoslovak independence was proclaimed in Prague on October 28. The following day, the South Slavs united as the State of Slovenes, Croats, and Serbs (the future Yugoslavia). The Austro-Hungarian Empire had collapsed.

Germany's revolution

The German Empire was also tottering, although—unlike the Austro-Hungarian and Ottoman empires—it avoided breaking up into multiple states. In mid-October 1918, fighting was still flaring along the length of the Western Front, and transatlantic diplomacy was mired in disagreements over the future of Wilhelm II, the German kaiser. Socialists within the Reichstag (Germany's parliament) were now growing more influential in their demands to end the war.

> Workers and soldiers! The killing is over. … Long live the Republic!
> **Philipp Scheidemann**
> Proclamation of the Republic, November 9, 1918

On October 24, when the German High Seas Fleet was ordered (without government approval) to steam into the North Sea and attack the British Grand Fleet, its crews rebelled rather than comply with such a suicidal directive. Their action sparked a revolt that quickly spread through Germany, sweeping through streets of starving people. By November 3—the day Austria signed the Armistice of Villa Giusti with Italy and four days after the Ottomans had signed the Armistice of Mudros with Britain—revolution had engulfed most German cities.

On November 9, Wilhelm II was forced to abdicate and fled to the Netherlands. Philipp Scheidemann and Karl Liebknecht, leaders of the Social Democratic Party and the Spartacus League, respectively, proclaimed that Germany was now a republic and asked for an immediate armistice. This was signed in a train carriage in the Forest of Compiègne, north of Paris, on November 11, 1918, marking Germany's defeat and the end of World War I.

Home front lessons learned

Despite the surrender, many Germans believed that their army could have continued fighting and that defeat lay in a lack of patriotism at home. One of the disillusioned was Adolf Hitler, returning from the Western Front as a German soldier. He never forgot the crippling effect on national morale of a lack of life's basic necessities or Germany's failure to prepare its civilian population for a protracted war. As leader of the German Third Reich (1933–1945), he took measures—often drastic, murderous ones—to ensure that the German people would not starve again. ∎

Women handle shells at a British factory in 1915. By 1918, almost 1 million women in Britain worked in the manufacture of munitions.

Women at war

Although not allowed to fight in the forces of most combatant nations, women still played a vital part at the front. They served as nurses—a role that had been expanding since the Crimean War (1853–1856)—and ambulance drivers, and also carried out administrative, catering, and other support work as "auxiliaries"— including up to 50,000 active in the Austro-Hungarian army by 1918.

At home, many of the jobs left vacant by the millions of civilian men conscripted into the armed forces were filled by women, including heavy industrial and agricultural labor. In Germany's massive Krupp steelworks, in Essen, women were rarely seen on the factory floor before the war. By 1917, they made up nearly 30 percent of the 175,000 employees, working shifts around the clock. Almost 1.5 million women worked in the German war effort's labor force. Russia was the only nation to deploy an all-female combat unit, the 2,000-strong Women's Battalion of Death, which fought in the 1917 Kerensky Offensive.

YOU WILL BE SHOT LIKE PARTRIDGES
THE RUSSIAN CIVIL WAR (1917–1921)

IN CONTEXT

FOCUS
Red Terror

BEFORE
1903 The Russian Social Democratic Labor Party (RSDLP) splits into Bolsheviks and less radical Mensheviks.

1905 On January 22 (Bloody Sunday), in St. Petersburg, 200 peaceful protesters are killed, sparking revolution in Russia.

March 1917 After a series of strikes and protests, Czar Nicholas II abdicates, but Russia continues to fight in World War I.

AFTER
1922 The Union of Soviet Socialist Republics (USSR) is formed from the remnants of the Russian Empire.

1936–1938 In the "Great Purge," Soviet leader Josef Stalin has around a million opponents killed, including old allies and high-ranking military officers.

On March 3, 1918, four months after coming to power, Russia's Bolshevik government, led by Vladimir Lenin, made peace with Germany, signing the Treaty of Brest-Litovsk. In the process, it signed away swathes of Russian territory, including Ukraine and Finland.

The treaty was not the end of conflict within Russia. The revolutionary regime of the "Reds" faced a ferocious fightback from the "Whites," who included supporters of the Russian czar, liberals, and even socialists. The Whites had strong support from France, Britain, the US, Japan, and other states who felt communism was a threat to capitalist democracies. Backed by their Red Army of peasants, industrial workers, and some former imperial officers, the Bolsheviks had to fight to survive. In the name of ideological purity, they attacked their political opponents and cowed the country into submission via a campaign of violence and intimidation known as the "Red Terror."

A merciless civil war

Across the old Russian Empire, a full-scale civil war began to unfold. Britain and France each sent several thousand troops to help the Whites, who until 1919 controlled vast areas of southern Russia and had a powerful presence in Siberia and the Far East. The Bolsheviks, however, held the industrial and

On a recruitment poster of 1920, the question "Have you signed up yet?" is posed, urging citizens to join the Red Army to fight in the Russian Civil War.

THE WORLD WARS AND BEYOND

See also: The defeat of the Central Powers 258–261 ▪ World War II in Europe 266–271 ▪ The defeat of Germany 276–279 ▪ The Cold War 286–293

> The Bolsheviks believe **the Russian proletariat has been repressed and exploited** by the old "bourgeois" order.

> For the **Bolshevik revolution to succeed,** that old order has to be **utterly destroyed**.

> **"Bourgeois" elements**, such as czarist loyalists and foreign infiltrators, **threaten the revolution**.

> **Only a reign of terror can destroy the "bourgeoisie," galvanize the people, and save the revolution.**

---

transport core of Russia around Petrograd (St. Petersburg) and Moscow, allowing them to strike out at the more scattered White forces.

The conflict also spread through neighboring countries. The Treaty of Brest-Litovsk had left Bolsheviks smarting from their country's loss of territory and, with their support, communist revolutions flared in Finland, Lithuania, Latvia, Estonia, Belarus, Ukraine, Moldavia, and the Caucasus. The Reds annexed the nations under their control; where the Whites prevailed, as in Finland and Baltic areas, independent states resulted.

Poland fights back

In February 1919, a newly founded Second Polish Republic invaded Ukraine, and with the aid of local Whites came close to taking the capital Kyiv. The Red Army quickly counterattacked and seemed likely to conquer Poland but was finally turned back at the Battle of Warsaw in August 1920. By the end of the year, the Poles had recovered most of the territory lost to the Red Army's forces in 1919.

The Peace of Riga (1921) divided Belarus and Ukraine between Poland and Bolshevik Russia, but by this point the civil war was effectively over, as the Red Army had defeated the last significant resistance from White troops in the Crimea in November 1920. Victory for the Red Army, however, came at a huge cost—Russia's industry and agriculture were devastated and up to 10 million people, most of them civilians, had died as a result of famine, disease, and massacres on both sides. ∎

Red Terror

The Whites' fightback against repressive Bolshevik Reds took a dangerous turn in 1918. On August 30, a military cadet murdered Moisei Uritsky, head of Petrograd's secret police (the Cheka), and SR (Social Revolutionary) member Fanya Kaplan shot and seriously wounded Vladimir Lenin. The Bolshevik newspaper, *Pravda*, urged its readers to "crush the bourgeoisie," and in early September, the government sanctioned the Red Terror to be used against its foes.

To root out these enemies, the Cheka secret police (forerunner of the KGB) grew massively over the next four years. After a purge of SR members, hundreds of whom were executed and thousands sent to labor camps, all possible Bolshevik opponents were targeted. The clergy, czarists, liberals, *kulaks* (landowning peasants), and even striking workers were hunted down, and some were tortured and killed. By 1922, the White forces were defeated, and the new state of the USSR was born.

Lenin addresses his supporters in Sverdlov Square, Moscow, on May 5, 1920. He was renowned for his passionate oratory.

ATROCIOUS CRIMES AGAINST HUMANITY
THE SECOND SINO-JAPANESE WAR (1937–1945)

IN CONTEXT

FOCUS
Massacre in China

BEFORE
1894–1895 Japan defeats China in the First Sino-Japanese War, a conflict over influence in Korea, and emerges as a major world power.

1912 Rebellions prompt China's final emperor, Pu Yi, to abdicate, marking the end of the Qing dynasty.

1928 Chinese Nationalists under Chiang Kai-Shek form a new government and partially reunify the nation.

AFTER
2014 Hospitals in Shanghai, China, launch a joint project to help surviving victims of germ warfare by Japan's Unit 731.

2015 Japanese prime minister Shinzo Abe expresses regret—but does not apologize—for the mass rape and killings of Chinese citizens and soldiers in Nanjing, China, in 1937.

In 1937, Chinese and Japanese forces exchanged fire on the Marco Polo Bridge near Beijing, igniting a regional conflict that would last until 1945, merge with World War II, and come to involve Allied and Axis forces. It would also result in some of the worst atrocities of the world war.

Japan was an expansionist and resource-hungry power, keen to take advantage of the internal unrest that had fractured China, its regional rival, since the collapse of the Qing dynasty in 1912. In 1931, Japan had seized and occupied Manchuria, in northeast China. For the next six years, its troops skirmished with Chinese forces, taking more land in the north.

Chinese resistance
A few months before the 1937 Marco Polo Bridge incident, China's ruling Kuomintang Nationalists (KMT), under Chiang Kai-shek, had reluctantly combined forces with their rivals, Mao Zedong's Chinese Communist Party (CCP), to form the United Front. Germany had helped Chiang to train the Nationalist troops, but they were no match for the Japanese, who soon took Beijing and the port city of Tianjin. In August 1937, Japan called for the withdrawal of Chinese troops from Shanghai. Chiang refused, and a bitter three-month battle ensued.

Horrors of war
The Chinese initially held their own but were finally overcome by the superior numbers of the Japanese air, naval, and ground forces. The Imperial Japanese Army advanced on the Chinese capital, Nanjing, capturing it on December 13, and unleashing horrific atrocities. Over a three-month period, they looted,

Let our people realize to the full the meaning of 'the limit of endurance,' and the extent of sacrifice implied. For once that stage is reached, we can only sacrifice and fight to the bitter end.
Chiang Kai-shek
July 17, 1937

See also: China in turmoil 230–231 ▪ The Russo-Japanese War 235 ▪ Japan ascendant 280–283 ▪ Japan defeated 284–285 ▪ The Chinese Civil War 294

destroyed property, and raped and killed indiscriminately. Estimates vary, but some historians believe that the troops raped as many as 80,000 people and murdered up to 300,000—events sometimes referred to as the Nanjing Massacre.

By early 1938, Japan dominated China's seas and skies, bombing cities at will. Japanese blockades starved China of essential supplies, but Chinese forces still fought on, using guerrilla tactics.

Peace remains elusive

After the attack on Pearl Harbor, Hawaii, in 1941 prompted the US to declare war on Japan, the Sino-Japanese War was subsumed into World War II. With Allied support, China's Nationalist government survived until 1945, despite a huge Japanese offensive—Operation Ichigo—the previous year. By the end of the war, China had suffered an estimated 15–20 million deaths. Even the end of World War II did not bring peace: the KMT were soon plunged into a four-year war against Mao Zedong's CCP for control of China. It was a battle that the Communists were to win.

War crimes

In 1948, 25 high-ranking Japanese defendants were convicted of war crimes, including inhumane treatment of both prisoners of war and civilians. Japan's ministers have apologized for some of these atrocities. In 2002, for the first time, a Tokyo court admitted biological warfare by Japan's Unit 731, based in northeast China. This included vivisection (dissecting live victims) and dropping plague-infected fleas on villages. The court did not award compensation to victims. ■

Soong Mei-ling (Madame Chiang)

Born in 1898, the daughter of a wealthy Shanghai businessman, Soong Mei-ling was educated in the US, before returning to China in 1917. In 1927, she became the second wife of Chinese Nationalist (KMT) leader Chiang Kai-shek. She soon played an active role in Chinese politics, assisting her husband in his bid to unify China politically and culturally.

At the beginning of the Sino-Japanese War, Madame Chiang rallied Chinese women to support the KMT cause, helped to establish women's battalions, and coordinated international relief efforts. Celebrated for her charm, courage, and diplomacy, she traveled to the US during World War II to lobby support for China. She spoke at rallies and, alongside her husband, was featured on the cover of *Time* magazine. After the KMT's defeat in the Chinese Civil War in 1949, she fled with Chiang Kai-shek to Taiwan, where she worked with several international charities. On her husband's death in 1975, she moved back to the US. She died in New York City in 2003, aged 105.

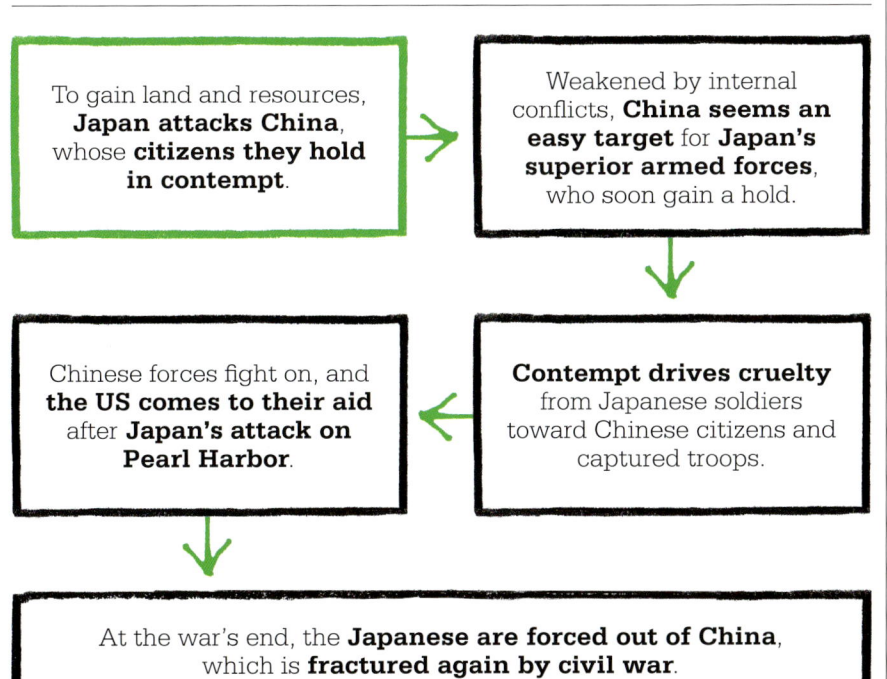

THE NAZI WAR MACHINE

WORLD WAR II IN EUROPE (1939–1943)

IN CONTEXT

FOCUS
The triumph of Blitzkrieg

BEFORE
1914 As World War I begins, Germany attempts a modified version of its 1905 Schlieffen military strategy for a swift victory in France. It fails.

1933 Nazi Party leader, Adolf Hitler, is appointed chancellor of Germany.

1936 Germany reoccupies Rhineland, a demilitarized area on its western borders, and annexes Sudetenland in northern Czechoslovakia.

AFTER
June 1944 Allied forces land in Normandy, France—the D-Day landings—and press forward, gaining aerial supremacy and outgunning the Germans.

April–May 1945 Hitler commits suicide, and Berlin falls to the Soviet Red Army.

German forces launched a long-planned assault on Poland on September 1, 1939, triggering the start of World War II. Over the next two years, they would achieve one stunning victory after another, making Germany supreme in continental Europe. Initial success was due to well-planned, rapidly executed strategies, later known as Blitzkrieg ("lightning war"), that surprised and overpowered its opponents.

Poland is seized
In 1935, German chancellor Adolf Hitler had announced his intention of reintroducing conscription and rearming Germany. The Allies and League of Nations deplored his actions but did nothing to stop them, despite limits imposed at the end of World War I by the Treaty of Versailles, whose terms Germany judged humiliating. Hitler began to build a new air force (Luftwaffe) with fast, modern fighter planes, and to supply his armed forces with advanced weaponry and the latest communications equipment. Their deployment would be guided by a key strategy based on much earlier thinking within the German Army

Rotterdam burns after an aerial bombardment by the Luftwaffe on May 14, 1940. Threatened with the destruction of other cities, the Netherlands surrendered a day later.

High Command—that enemy forces should be attacked rapidly at their weakest points, leaving no time or space for retaliation. A flexible command system capable of initiative and quick reactions was also introduced.

In September 1939, Germany put its theories into practice in Poland, attacking with tank brigades, infantry, and artillery supported by the Luftwaffe. Poland fell in five weeks. The British and

Heinz Guderian

Born in Kulm, West Prussia (now Poland), in 1888, the son of a Prussian officer, Heinz Wilhelm Guderian fought in World War I, rising to the rank of infantry battalion commander. One of 4,000 officers allowed to serve in the *Reichswehr*, Germany's reduced postwar army, he studied armored warfare tactics and helped illicitly to develop mobile armored forces, especially Panzer divisions, and pioneered their wireless communication system. In 1936, Guderian wrote a book about motorized warfare entitled *Achtung—Panzer!*, and he soon put its theories into practice— in Poland in 1939 and France in 1940. Impatient and sometimes insubordinate, Guderian was popular and liked by Hitler, who appointed him inspector general of armored troops in 1943.

Guderian steered clear of a plot to kill Hitler in 1944 and then headed a court that sent those involved to be judged and executed. He avoided conviction as a war criminal in 1945 but was interned for three years. In retirement, Guderian remained an ardent nationalist. He died in 1954, in Schwangau, Germany.

THE WORLD WARS AND BEYOND

See also: The Seven Years' War 162–165 ▪ The rise of Prussia 210–213 ▪ Stalemate on the Western Front 248–251 ▪ The war at sea and in the air 256–257 ▪ The defeat of the Central Powers 258–261 ▪ The defeat of Germany 276–279

French had no time to come to its aid, and the Nazi-Soviet pact divided the country between Germany and the USSR.

Following Poland's collapse, the so-called Phoney War began—an uneasy pause when the Allies relied on the strength of their fortified lines to discourage German ambitions. Conflict continued at sea, with German U-boats and warships pitted against Allied vessels in the Atlantic, but it was not until April 1940 that the land war in Europe erupted again. German forces seized Denmark and attacked Norway—both neutral—rebuffing a poorly planned British response. One consequence of this was the collapse of British prime minister Neville Chamberlain's government, and the arrival of Winston Churchill as Britain's war leader.

The German trap

After several revisions over the winter of 1939–1940, the German plan for its attack in the west (*Fall Gelb* or Plan Yellow) was accepted by Hitler. It called for a powerful but subsidiary offensive through the Netherlands and into Belgium, while the main thrust—spearheaded by Panzer (armored) divisions—would be made further south through the wooded Ardennes region of southern Belgium. The German intention was to divide and then encircle the Allied armies.

On May 10, German forces invaded the neutral Netherlands, taking it in a week. Within hours of this attack, as anticipated, Allied forces began moving into Belgium to confront their opponents. Further south, Panzer divisions erupted from the forest terrain of the Ardennes, having crossed from Belgium via

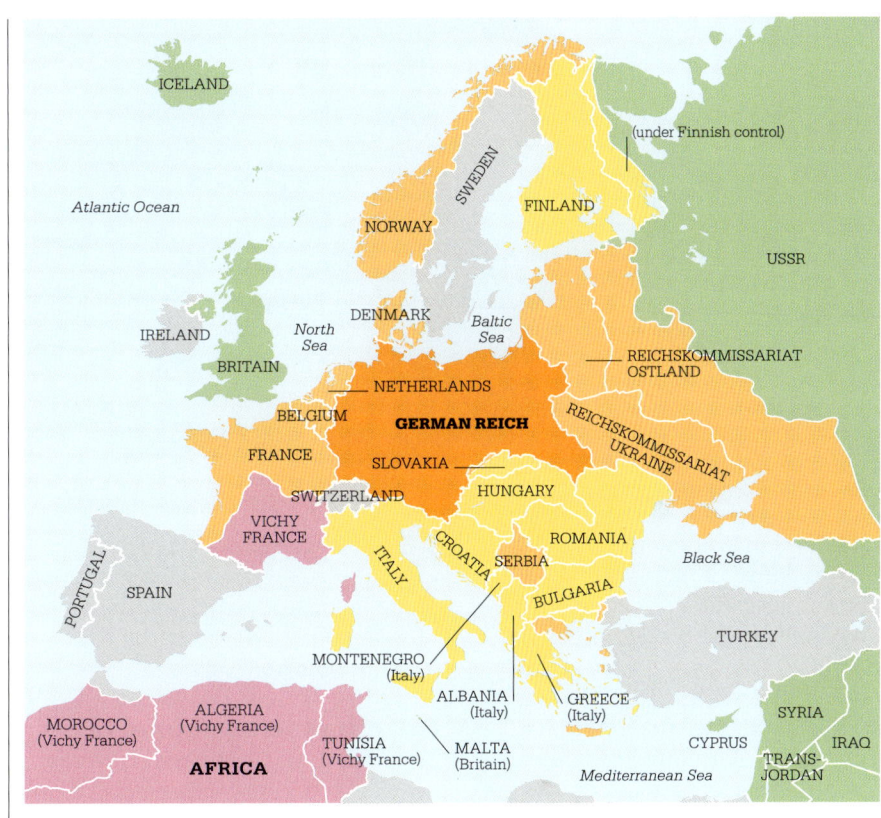

The German Reich rapidly dominated Europe in the early years of World War II. By mid-1941, the Reich and its Axis allies controlled some 1.3 million sq miles (3.28 million sq km) of land—more than nine times the area of modern Germany. Of all its European counterparts, the Reich was now at war only with Britain and the USSR.

Key:
- German Reich
- Areas occupied by Germany
- German allies, co-belligerents, and puppet states
- Nominally unoccupied
- Allied-held areas
- Neutral countries

a weak northern extension of the Maginot Line (France's border fortifications). Supported by dive bomber aircraft, German battalions broke through French lines and hurtled toward the coast to cut off the Allied troops in Belgium. Panzer commander Heinz Guderian ignored orders to halt his advance and, by May 20, his division arrived at Abbeville, near the mouth of the Somme River. He then advanced up the English Channel coast toward Calais and Dunkirk.

German troops now began to surround the Allied divisions, whose only means of escape was via the Channel. Transported by naval vessels and hundreds of civilian boats, more than 338,000 men were evacuated from Dunkirk, although thousands of British troops still »

The German Panzerjäger 1 was a converted Panzer 1, its chassis mounted with a powerful Czech anti-tank gun. Some 200 were built in 1940–1941 and used to destroy heavy French tanks.

remained in France. The French had lost most of their tanks and other military vehicles in Belgium. Plan Yellow cost the Allies 61 divisions; Germany's forces rapidly gained ground, and its Luftwaffe soon established air supremacy. On June 9, German forces moved toward Paris, advancing across the Seine and Aisne rivers with relays of fresh tanks, supported by dive bombers that destroyed much of the remaining French resistance.

France falls

The next part of Germany's plan—*Fall Rot* (Plan Red) for the conquest of France—was now underway. On June 10, Italy also declared war on the Allies, intent on grabbing French territory before the war was over. The following day, the French government abandoned Paris in a bid to spare its destruction. Three-fifths of the city's population also fled, joining millions of other refugees crowding the roads, in what became known as *L'Éxode* (the Exodus). France officially surrendered on June 22. German forces now occupied 60 percent of France; the other 40 percent was to be ruled by a collaborationist, quasi-fascist government under Marshal Philippe Pétain, based in Vichy, central France.

Britain resists, others fall

After Dunkirk and further Channel evacuations, Hitler expected Britain to negotiate peace terms. Churchill's refusal prompted Germany to consider invading Britain, although this was not part of its grand plan. The Luftwaffe, confident that it could pave the way by destroying the Royal Air Force (RAF)—targeting planes, aircraft production factories, and other infrastructure—began attacking Britain in 1940. However, Britain's fighter planes— powerful Hurricanes and agile Spitfires—proved a match for the Luftwaffe's aircraft, which included Junkers Ju-87 (Stuka) dive bombers and Messerschmitt Bf-109 fighters. British radar and ground defenses helped complete an effective air defense network.

By the end of October 1940, the RAF had lost 1,744 planes and the Luftwaffe 1,977. Britain had won the Battle of Britain. Night attacks on cities—the Blitz—continued, but the RAF retained its air superiority over Britain, and Germany decided to abandon its invasion plans.

Hitler remained master of much of Western Europe. In 1941, he added Greece and Eastern Europe to his conquests, although these gains were not precisely planned. Without alerting Germany, Italy had invaded Greece and met strong resistance from the Greeks and Britain's RAF, which provided air cover. Meanwhile, Yugoslavia's pro-British ruler Prince Paul had refused to join Eastern European and Balkan neighbors in a pact with Germany. In response, Hitler ordered air and ground attacks on Greece and Yugoslavia and, with Italian assistance, secured both by the end of April 1941.

By June, German air strikes had driven Allied forces out of Crete and the eastern Mediterranean.

We have now to face the task of cutting up the giant cake according to our needs, in order to be able: first, to dominate it; second, to administer it; and third, to exploit it.
Adolf Hitler
July 16, 1941

THE WORLD WARS AND BEYOND

Opposition to Europe's Nazi occupation now came only from national resistance groups, sometimes working with agents from Britain's Special Operations Executive in acts of sabotage, raids, espionage, and guerrilla warfare.

The Eastern Front

Despite the Nazi-Soviet pact of August 1939, by the end of 1940 Hitler was planning a full-scale invasion of his mighty eastern neighbor in a bid to seize its coveted resources and the space—*lebensraum*—he sought for a greater Germany. In June 1941, Germany launched Operation Barbarossa, involving more than 3.5 million Axis troops in 148 divisions, including a vanguard of 17 Panzer divisions with 3,400 tanks and 2,700 fighter aircraft in support. Three army groups advanced along a 1,800-mile (2,900 km) front: Army Group North from East Prussia toward Leningrad (St. Petersburg); Army Group South heading for Ukraine and the Black Sea; and Army Group Center, which included Guderian's armored force, whose ultimate goal was the capture of Moscow.

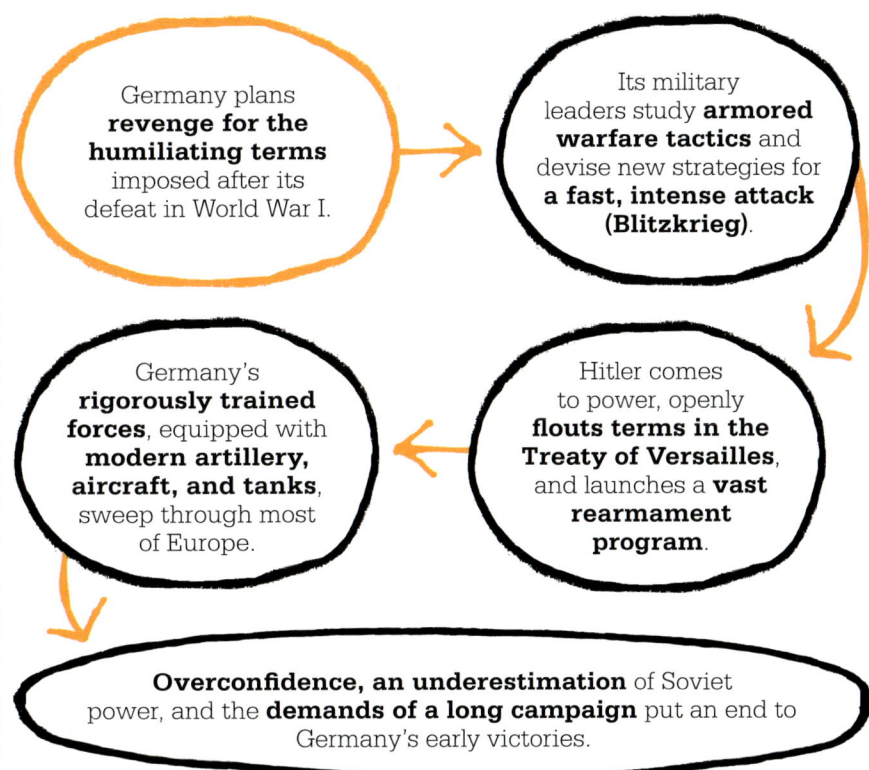

Germany plans **revenge for the humiliating terms** imposed after its defeat in World War I.

Its military leaders study **armored warfare tactics** and devise new strategies for **a fast, intense attack (Blitzkrieg)**.

Hitler comes to power, openly **flouts terms in the Treaty of Versailles**, and launches a **vast rearmament program**.

Germany's **rigorously trained forces**, equipped with **modern artillery, aircraft, and tanks**, sweep through most of Europe.

Overconfidence, an underestimation of Soviet power, and the **demands of a long campaign** put an end to Germany's early victories.

Italian dictator Benito Mussolini addresses Italian forces sent in August 1941 to assist German troops in Operation Barbarossa, Hitler's campaign against the USSR.

Caught by surprise, as the Luftwaffe bombed their airfields, artillery, and troops, the Russians offered little resistance. By mid-July, Army Group North was closing in on Leningrad, and by the month's end, Army Group Center had encircled five Russian armies, taking more than 600,000 prisoners. Army Group South faced tough resistance, but by early August it had captured 100,000 Russians and besieged the Black Sea port of Odessa.

Soviet fightback

By fall 1941, the Germans began to face supply problems. In September, its northern force began its siege of Leningrad, but the city would hold out for an epic 890 days and was never taken. The battle for Moscow began in October, but despite initial gains, Army Group Center were soon mired in the mud of fall, allowing the Russian troops time to reinforce. Freezing weather then arrived, and German forces became trapped in deep snow just 12 miles (19 km) from the capital. Soviet troops led by Marshal Georgy Zhukov forced them to retreat 150 miles (240 km).

In 1942, Axis forces penetrated deep into the Caucasus but failed to seize Stalingrad in January 1943. In July, the Soviets triumphed at Kursk in the largest tank battle in history, and the next month Zhukov won back Kharkov, lost to Germany 22 months earlier. The Germans were forced to beat a bloody retreat, pursued by the Russians. Hitler had grossly underestimated the USSR's capacity for counterattack and the superiority of its tanks, now being produced in increasing numbers. Germany's military strategies were beginning to fail. ∎

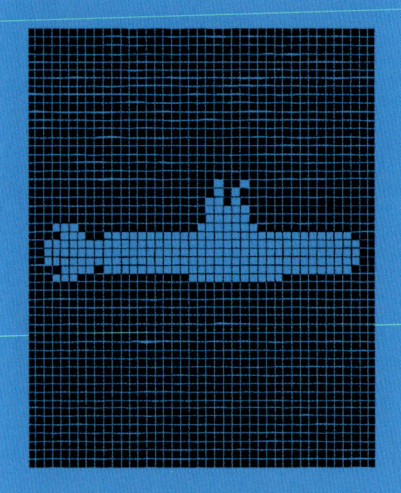

THE U-BOAT … MUST BE HUNTED
THE WAR AT SEA (1939–1943)

IN CONTEXT

FOCUS
Code breaking

BEFORE
1917 During World War I, German U-boat attacks almost paralyze Britain's economy.

1935 The Anglo-German Naval Agreement allows Germany to build submarines.

July 1939 Polish code breakers pass their knowledge of the German Enigma code to British intelligence.

AFTER
June 1944 Cryptographers at Bletchley Park support the D-Day landings by deciphering German messages.

August 1944 Most U-boats leave Lorient, their largest base in France, when the port is surrounded by the Allies.

1945 By the end of World War II, women make up nearly 70 percent of the US Army's 10,500 code breakers.

On land, Nazi Germany's invasion of Poland in September 1939 was followed by a period of stalemate, but conflict was soon underway at sea. Within nine hours of the declaration of war, a German *Unterseeboot* (U-boat) submarine had torpedoed the British liner SS *Athenia* off the coast of Ireland with the loss of 117 passengers. Within six weeks, Britain's Royal Navy was shaken by the sinking of aircraft carrier HMS *Courageous*, as well as the battleship HMS *Royal Oak* at Scapa Flow in Scotland's Orkney Islands, with the loss of 835 crew members. It looked like the sea war would hinge on the success of U-boats, but the key weapon in the Battle of the Atlantic would prove to be cryptography—the science of deciphering codes.

The U-boat threat

When Germany went to war in 1939, its navy had not yet completed a planned expansion of its surface fleet, and it was unable to match the strength of the Royal Navy. German naval leaders instead concentrated on deploying their U-boats. Each side had a similar strategic aim—to impose a blockade that would starve the enemy of the resources necessary to prosecute war or even survive. For the German navy, this meant using the stealth, surprise, and destructive power of U-boats to sink British ships crossing the Atlantic—an initially successful tactic, with more than 140 ships sunk from September 1939 to February 1940.

The German occupation of Norway, Denmark, the Low Countries, and France in April to May 1940 offered new Atlantic-facing naval bases for the U-boat fleet to penetrate deep into the Atlantic. German naval strategy relied increasingly on submarines,

The enemy knows all our secrets and we know none of his.
Admiral Karl Dönitz
Commander, German submarine fleet
12 November 1943

THE WORLD WARS AND BEYOND

See also: The war at sea and in the air 256–257 ▪ The defeat of the Central Powers 258–261 ▪ World War II in Europe 266–271 ▪ The defeat of Germany 276–279

The crew of a German U-boat line up on deck at the Kiel naval base in Germany. Of 1,162 U-boats built during World War II, 632 were sunk at sea by Allied surface ships and aircraft.

especially after the British navy eliminated key German warship threats, including the *Admiral Graf Spee* at the Battle of the Plate River (December 1939) and the *Bismarck* (May 1941). The Battle of the Atlantic, between Allied shipping convoys and U-boat "wolfpacks," continued to rage through 1942. The balance shifted in favor of one side, then the other, as new technologies and tactics came into play, such as escort ships loaded with fighter aircraft and daring U-boat nighttime surface attacks.

Breaking the codes

The real key to success in the sea war, however, rested on the ability of each side to decode the other's encrypted communications. In 1941, the British "Ultra" decryption operation broke the German Enigma code, enabling the Allies to follow German naval movements, so saving hundreds of ships. German intelligence services achieved major success in February 1942 when they partially broke the Allies' Naval Cipher No. 3—the code used for the control of convoys. In that same month, an enhanced M4 Enigma machine with an additional rotor foiled Ultra for nine months, leading to a series of devastating U-boat attacks on convoys in the North Atlantic and the Arctic. More than 1,000 Allied merchant ships—double the previous year's total—were sunk in the North Atlantic in 1942, the vast majority hit by U-boats. As a result, the Allies were forced to suspend Arctic convoys to the USSR in late 1942.

By the end of 1942, however, Enigma had been broken again, and momentum swung decisively against the U-boats. Allied shipping losses fell dramatically in 1943, and by September of that year, more U-boats were being sunk than Allied ships. No one can know for sure, but many historians believe that the breaking of the Enigma code shortened World War II by months, if not years. ▪

Ultra and Enigma

For all the valor and sacrifice of the naval personnel on both sides, possibly the three most decisive acts in the Battle of the Atlantic were the captures of German Enigma coding machines, code books, and code rotors (wheels) from U-boats *U-33* (February 1940), *U-110* (May 1941), and *U-559* (October 1942). The Enigma device used an ingenious combination of rotors to encode messages. Both sides had long thought it to be unbreakable, but the British Ultra code breaking operation based at Bletchley Park—a house in Buckinghamshire, England—made a series of breakthroughs, thanks in part to information supplied by Polish intelligence before the start of the war.

The German navy confused Ultra by adding a fourth rotor to Enigma in February 1942, but British cryptographers, with intelligence secured from the daring raid on the stricken *U-559* (carried out as it was sinking), were still able to decrypt transmissions sent to and from the German submarines. The British used these to redirect convoys and interceptor forces.

The Colossus computer, which operated at Bletchley Park from 1944, accelerated code breaking enormously, but additional, human "hand breakers" were still vital.

BOMBING THEM … AROUND THE CLOCK
THE AIR WAR (1939–1944)

IN CONTEXT

FOCUS
Precision versus area bombing

BEFORE
1911 Over Libya, an Italian airman carries out the first aerial bombing mission.

November 21, 1914 British planes carry out the first strategic bombing raid when they attack Zeppelin sheds in Germany.

1922 The Japanese navy commissions the first purpose-built aircraft carrier, *Hōshō*.

1937 German and Italian planes bomb Guernica, Spain.

AFTER
1945 US B-29 Superfortress bombers drop atomic bombs on two cities in Japan—Hiroshima and Nagasaki.

1991 Over a six-week period in Operation Desert Storm, the US and its allies drop 88,500 tons of bombs on Iraqi targets.

Air power had been in its infancy at the end of World War I, but aircraft technology had made huge advances by 1939. The Luftwaffe (German air force), already used to devastating effect during the Spanish Civil War (1936–1939), spearheaded Germany's Blitzkrieg ("lightning war") strategy of fighter and bomber air support acting in concert with mobile armor to overwhelm any opposition. Air superiority would prove vital in deciding the outcome of war, but it was strategic bombing—concentrated attacks on a country's infrastructure, industry, and population—that left the most devastating mark on history.

Winning in the air
At the beginning of World War II, Germany had as many aircraft as Britain and France combined. In addition, German planes such as the Messerschmitt Bf 109 fighter and Junkers Ju 87 (Stuka) battlefield dive bomber were more technically advanced than most Allied aircraft.

This aerial force played a vital role in Germany's ability to conquer western Europe in May 1940. However, in the first major air battle of the war, the Battle of Britain (July–October 1940), the Luftwaffe was limited by the fuel capacity of its planes, which allowed only for short-range missions. It also struggled with the introduction of the British Supermarine Spitfire fighter, which could match the Messerschmitt Bf 109 for speed and maneuverability. Britain, free of the threat of invasion, could turn its attention to strategic bombing.

On the Eastern Front, Germany employed the Blitzkrieg strategy ruthlessly, destroying 1,800 Soviet planes on the first day of its

The Nazis entered this war under the rather childish delusion that they were going to bomb everyone else, and nobody was going to bomb them.
Arthur "Bomber" Harris
Newsreel message, 1942

See also: An expanding war 252–255 ▪ The war at sea and in the air 256–257 ▪ World War II in Europe 266–271 ▪ The defeat of Germany 276–279 ▪ Japan ascendant 280–283 ▪ Japan defeated 284–285 ▪ Independence in Southeast Asia 296–297

invasion of the USSR on June 22, 1941. The Luftwaffe quickly gained the upper hand but over time it lost ground, as the vastness of the battlefront and drawn-out attritional struggles, such as the Battle of Stalingrad (July 1942–February 1943), took their toll on its resources.

Like Germany, Japan sought air dominance, amassing around 1,500 combat aircraft by 1941 and using them to sow havoc at the US naval base at Pearl Harbor in December 1941. For two years, the Japanese dominated the skies over the Pacific Ocean, aided by highly agile, heavily armed, long-range Mitsubishi A6M "Zero" fighter planes. By late 1943, however, the US had overtaken the Japanese in both plane numbers and aircraft quality, with the Zero meeting its match in the Grumman F6F Hellcat fighter plane.

Strategic bombing

After its land forces were expelled from France in 1940, Britain turned to strategic bombing to hit back at Germany. When, at first, British long-range bombers suffered terrible losses in daylight raids against specific military targets, air marshal Arthur "Bomber" Harris ordered night raids and "area bombing" against German cities. Tons of incendiary bombs were dropped, igniting raging fires that inflicted widespread random damage to the population as well as infrastructure. The first "1,000-bomber raid" hit Cologne on May 30, 1942, killing more than 450 people and making 45,000 civilians homeless. It was followed by others.

Harris's controversial approach was rejected by the US, which from the summer of 1942 insisted on daytime "precision bombing" of German targets. Flying by day was especially dangerous, leading to the loss of large numbers of American aircraft and crew. The strategy was saved in December

American B-17 Flying Fortress bombers attack the Messerschmitt aircraft factory near Vienna, Austria, on a daylight precision raid in November 1943.

1943, however, by the introduction of heavily armed, long-range P-51 Mustang fighters, which acted as escorts for the bombers. Proving more than a match for Luftwaffe aircraft, they secured much greater survival rates and Allied control of German airspace by late 1944. Both area bombing and precision bombing—in practice, not very precise—both continued until the end of the war in Europe. ∎

The pilot and navigator of a Night Witch aircraft receive last-minute instructions before setting off on a new bombing mission.

The "Night Witches"

Of the 800,000 women who volunteered for the Soviet Red Army in World War II, perhaps the most remarkable were the 1,000 or more who served in the air force as pilots, navigators, and ground crew. In 1941, navigator Marina Raskova persuaded Soviet leader Josef Stalin to allow her to form three female air combat regiments.

One women's unit, the 588th Night Bomber Aviation Regiment, was commanded by Soviet pilot Yevdokiya Bershanskaya and flew flimsy, canvas and plywood Polikarpov Po-2 biplanes. Flying low, at night, in formations of three, the pilots cut their engines and glided toward their targets as they dropped bombs, making an eerie whooshing sound that earned the pilots and navigators the German nickname *Nachthexen* (Night Witches). Between 1942 and 1945, the Night Witches dropped more than 3,300 tons of bombs and 26,000 incendiary shells on 23,000 missions, hitting bridges, railroad lines, and other vital German infrastructure.

THE WAR IN EUROPE IS OVER

THE DEFEAT OF GERMANY (1944–1945)

IN CONTEXT

FOCUS
An extended war

BEFORE
September 1914 Allied victory at the First Battle of the Marne ends Germany's hopes of a rapid end to World War I.

1920 The Treaty of Versailles imposes punitive restrictions on the German military.

1933 Adolf Hitler and the Nazi Party seize power in Germany.

1942 Nazi Germany reaches the peak of its military success, controlling most of Europe.

AFTER
August 1945 Three months after the end of the war in Europe, Japan surrenders and World War II finally ends.

1990 After the collapse of the USSR, West Germany and East Germany join to form a reunited Germany.

By the late spring of 1944, Germany was beginning to lose the advantage in World War II. Although its armies had stalled Allied offensives in the Mediterranean, defeats at Stalingrad and Kursk on the Eastern Front had finally reversed the German tide of victories and put it on the defensive. In the skies above German cities, new long-range fighters successfully escorted the US bomber fleets to daylight targets in Germany, while the British RAF pounded German cities by night.

On June 6, 1944, the Allies opened a long-expected second front. Operation Overlord, or D-Day, the largest amphibious operation in history, landed more than 150,000 troops on five Normandy beaches in northern France. With forces and equipment increasing by the day, on June 12, the Allies consolidated their gains into one beachhead—a coastal stronghold from where they could launch attacks inland. Meanwhile, British commandos, American special forces, and French resistance fighters worked behind the German lines, attacking gun batteries and blowing up bridges and railroad lines to disrupt counterattacks.

The position looked bleak for Germany, but its refusal to surrender and insistence on continuing the fight through a series of increasingly desperate measures meant the war would drag on for almost another year. This period proved to be the bloodiest of the war for Germany, accounting for nearly half of all its military losses and 60 percent of all the bombs dropped on its cities.

Operation Valkyrie

In July 1944, the Nazi regime faced a serious threat at home from a group of German army officers. Although many attempts had been made on Hitler's life, the officer-backed plot—Operation Valkyrie—promised the best chance of a coup d'état and end to the war, as the plotters included senior figures in the *Ersatzheer* (Replacement Army). This reserve force, based within Germany, had the potential to seize key domestic targets and suppress public opposition.

On July 1, one of the plotters, Colonel Klaus von Stauffenberg, was made the *Ersatzheer* chief of staff, giving him access to meetings at Hitler's *Wolfsschanze* (Wolf's Lair) headquarters in East Prussia. At a meeting on July 20, Stauffenberg, on the signal of Major General Henning von Tresckow—a senior officer in Germany's Eastern Front armies and mastermind of Valkyrie—planted a bomb hidden in a briefcase under a table next to Hitler. Once the bomb exploded, the Replacement Army network went into action—only to discover that Hitler had survived, shielded from the blast by a heavy table leg.

German prisoners of war captured in the Falaise Pocket are marched away from Normandy in August 1944, watched by British troops waiting to advance further into France.

Within a day, Tresckow died of suicide and Stauffenberg was killed by a firing squad.

In the wake of the assassination attempt, around 200 plotters were rounded up and shot or hanged—including Stauffenberg's brother, Berthold, whose drawn-out death was filmed for Hitler to watch. In the ensuing reign of terror, up to 7,000 "enemies of the Reich" were killed or sent to concentration camps.

Refusal to give in

In late summer 1944, the Allies broke out of their beachhead and swept across Normandy, destroying much of the German Seventh Army and Fifth Panzer Division at the Falaise Pocket and capturing up to 50,000 »

I know I will be able to justify … what I did in the struggle against Hitler.
Henning von Tresckow
1944

soldiers. On the Eastern Front, German forces lost 300,000 troops in a massive victory for the Soviet army in Operation Bagration. Faced with such huge losses, in the fall, the Nazi regime created additional *Volksgrenadier* (Citizen Grenadiers) divisions—improvised formations made up of men with previous military experience—and formed a new militia, the *Volkssturm* (People's Storm), composed of a poorly trained and armed males aged 16 to 60.

Despite its diminishing pool of fighting men, Germany could still muster formidable weaponry. Britain had been attacked by the first of more than 6,500 V-1 missiles in June 1944, followed from September by around 500 V-2 rockets. Terrifyingly random in their targeting, the weapons caused more than 30,000 British civilian casualties.

German land forces also fought back. An attack in September by Allied paratroops on vital supply bridges on the Dutch–German border, at Arnhem, was overrun by German tanks. Three months later, more than 200,000 German troops, backed by nearly 1,000 tanks,

launched a massive offensive in the wooded Ardennes region of Belgium, aiming to smash through the Allied lines and capture the port of Antwerp. At first, the Allied defenses buckled, but in late December, the sheer weight and number of American forces pushed the German army into retreat.

By the end of 1944, Germany was running out of time, space to maneuver, and both military and domestic supplies. Under Hitler's dictatorship, any opposition that might have harnessed discontent had been eradicated. The failed Valkyrie plot had only enhanced the power of the fearsome SS—the elite Nazi guard led by Heinrich Himmler—which stood between an increasingly erratic Hitler and the German army's leaders, each side detesting the other.

Germany's enemies close in

For much of the war, especially on the Eastern Front, German armies had the advantage of interior lines of supply and communication. By early 1945, however, daily aerial Allied assaults had wrecked much of the German rail system, as well as canals and roads. Supplies of steel, coal, and oil were running short.

German women clear debris after a Berlin bombing raid in early 1945. The heaviest attack on Berlin occurred on March 18, 1945, when 1,221 US Air Force bombers targeted the city.

With the Red Army bearing down on Germany, Minister of Propaganda Josef Goebbels whipped up citizens' fears of Soviet retribution for German actions. He warned that Bolshevik hordes were about to sweep from the east and annihilate the German people, raping women, pillaging, and carrying off survivors to labor camps. Tens of thousands of refugees from the German-settled Baltic states and East Prussia began to reach German-held territory. Thousands more died attempting to flee, many when ships crammed with refugees, such as the *Wilhelm Gustloff* and *General von Steuben*, were torpedoed in the Baltic Sea by Soviet submarines. More than 9,500 drowned on the *Wilhelm Gustloff*—the worst ever maritime disaster.

At least 100,000 refugees were crowded into Dresden when, on February 13–15, 1945, Allied aircraft firebombed the city, killing nearly 25,000 people. At the same time, Budapest fell to the Soviet army, and by early March, the Western

Volkssturm members gather on a German city street in March 1945, each armed with a *Panzerfaust* anti-tank weapon. A black armband indicates their *Volkssturm* identity.

> Only those who are inferior will remain ... for the good have already been killed.
> **Adolf Hitler**
> to Albert Speer, Minister of Armaments, 18 March 1945

Allies were crossing the Rhine and fighting their way into Germany. As the vice tightened, on March 19, Hitler—now lying low in his Berlin bunker—issued a scorched-earth decree ordering the demolition of all remaining German transportation and industrial infrastructure to prevent it falling into Allied hands.

The sight of men executed as defeatists, their bodies hanging from lampposts, was an effective spur to continue fighting. Fear—of Allied retribution and severe penalties for desertion—kept German soldiers under arms. On April 16, the Red Army began its devastating assault on Berlin, the city's defense force including Hitler Youth as young as 12 and around 40,000 *Volkssturm* troops, many old and infirm. Fighting was fierce, with more than 80,000 Red Army soldiers killed in the two weeks it took to seize the city.

The finale

Hitler died by suicide on April 30, a day after SS commander Karl Wolff had surrendered all Axis forces in Italy. Admiral Karl Dönitz, Hitler's chosen successor as head of state, surrendered unconditionally to the Allies a week later. Dönitz's delay was prompted by fears of reprisals from the advancing Red Army and the need to get as many refugees, citizens, and military forces as possible to western Germany, behind the protection of American and British armies. Nevertheless, after the formal capitulation took effect on May 8, 1945 (Victory in Europe Day), millions of soldiers and civilians were still trudging westward. By the end of 1945, those still east of a line running from the Baltic to Czechoslovakia would face a far different future from those to the west of it. ∎

Germany divided

In 1945, the Allies could all agree on one thing: Germany must never again threaten the peace of Europe. That prompted the creation of four Allied Zones of Occupation. These areas largely mirrored where the respective armies were by May 8: the British in the north, the Americans in the south, the French in the southwest, and the Soviets in the east. The immediate rise of Cold War tensions, however, led to a change of plan. By 1947, Britain and the US joined their sectors to create a single "Bizone" (two zones), which the French joined in 1948.

In June 1948, the USSR began to blockade West Berlin. The Allies' response—the Berlin Airlift, a 15-month relief operation—hardened a desire for western German union as a defense against communism. In 1949, two new Germanys emerged: the Federal Republic of Germany (West Germany) and the German Democratic Republic (East Germany)—now a Soviet satellite.

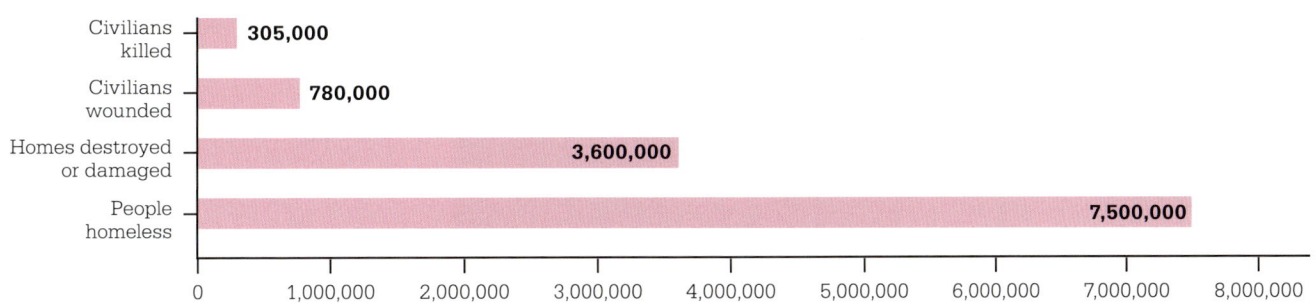

The US Strategic Bombing Survey for Europe, published in September 1945, showed the impact of Allied air raids on Germany (excluding figures withheld by Soviet-occupied eastern Germany). The attacks cost the lives of 79,265 American and 79,281 British airmen.

EIGHT CORNERS OF THE UNIVERSE UNDER ONE ROOF

JAPAN ASCENDANT (1941–1943)

IN CONTEXT

FOCUS
The end of "European supremacy"

BEFORE
1854 The US and Japan sign the Treaty of Kanagawa, which paves the way for new trading relations between the nations.

1860 At the end of the Second Opium War, the West imposes humiliating terms on China.

1894–1895 Japan defeats China in the First Sino-Japanese War and emerges as a world power.

AFTER
August 15, 1945 Japan's surrender marks the end of World War II.

1952 The Allied occupation of Japan ends. The nation starts to rebuild a powerful economy.

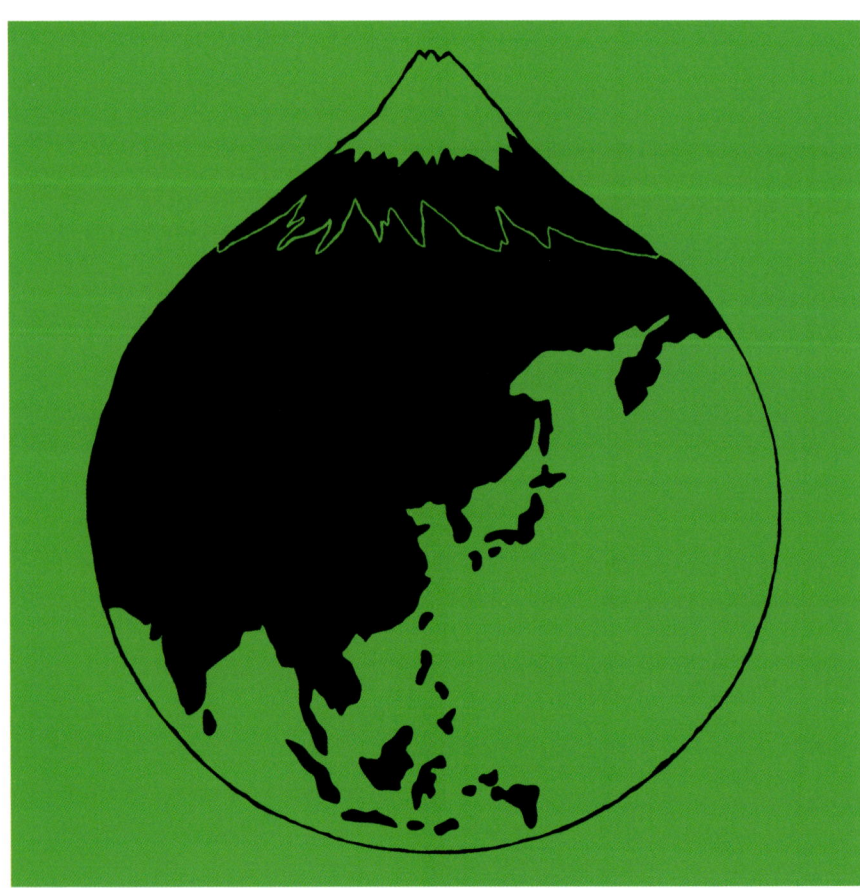

As Chinese influence in Southeast Asia declined in the 19th century under the weak Qin dynasty, Western powers grew bolder. Together with their directly ruled colonies, such as the Dutch East Indies, French Indochina, and British-held Singapore and Malaya, several European countries began creating free trade zones in China that they controlled.

Japan resisted any Western-imposed limitations on its power and pursued its own imperial ambitions, steadily developing the industrial and military resources it needed to achieve those goals. As it lacked the raw materials to sustain the long-term economic expansion envisaged, the country set about gaining ground in neighboring China. Japan's spectacular military

THE WORLD WARS AND BEYOND **281**

See also: Japan in the Sengoku era 128–129 ▪ China in turmoil 230–231 ▪ The Russo-Japanese War 235 ▪ The Second Sino-Japanese War 264–265 ▪ The air war 274–275 ▪ Japan defeated 284–285 ▪ Independence in Southeast Asia 296–297

victories exposed the fallacy of the West's belief in white supremacy and had long-lasting consequences across East and Southeast Asia.

The southern road

By 1941, Japan had already spent many years battling China. Its seizure of Manchuria, northeast China, in 1931, had been followed six years later by a full-scale invasion, launching the Second Sino-Japanese War. In 1940, Japan proposed a pan-Asian union—the Greater East Asia Co-Prosperity Sphere—a clear indication of its desire to drive Western colonial powers out of Southeast Asia. In June 1940, when France fell to Germany, Japan made its move in French Indochina, demanding—with menaces—the closure of supply routes to China from the south, and then the right to set up air bases and station troops in Indochina. Its declared *nanshin-ron* ("southern road") doctrine for expanding trade in Southeast Asia was now clearly militaristic. On September 27, 1940, Japan signed the Tripartite Pact, allying itself with Germany and Italy. In April 1941, Japan also agreed to a Neutrality Pact with the USSR, giving it the security in the north to pursue its southern goals.

Pearl Harbor

Japan's actions were met with growing disapproval in the US, which began to embargo exports to Japan and freeze Japanese assets in American banks. Japan refused to accept the US government's demand for its withdrawal from

The USS *Arizona* battleship is bombed from the air and sunk during Japan's attack on Pearl Harbor. A memorial to the 1,177 crew who died was built where the ship went down.

China and decided to attempt a swift strike to strengthen its position in Southeast Asia by temporarily disabling the US Navy.

On December 7, 1941, Japan launched a surprise attack on the US naval base at Pearl Harbor, Hawaii. Torpedo-carrying planes from Japanese aircraft carriers destroyed 188 aircraft and sank or damaged all eight American battleships and seven other warships, although they failed to sink any US aircraft carriers, as they were out of port. It was a tactical victory for the Japanese, »

JAPAN ASCENDANT

The rise of nationalism

Japan's military successes in Southeast Asia encouraged anti-colonialist parties in the region. A few welcomed its forces but soon recognized that Japan's overriding goals were supremacy and the exploitation of their natural resources. Sukarno, who led the independence movement in the Dutch East Indies, acted as an adviser to the Japanese, then pressed for independence when Japan was defeated. In Burma, Aung San secured Japan's support for his nationalist army, which aided Japanese forces when they invaded, then led his country to independence after the Allies' victory in 1945.

Communist leaders of nationalist parties resisted Japan from the first. In 1941, Ho Chi Minh founded the Viet Minh to oppose Japanese forces in French Indochina (modern Vietnam, Cambodia, and Laos). He liaised with Mao Zedong, who led the Chinese Communist Party and headed the People's Republic of China from 1949. Indochina's nations and China itself were later caught up in violent struggles between East and West—the aftermath of Japan's ambition and European colonial rule.

To mark 10 years of the People's Republic of China in 1959, Russian premier Nikita Khrushchev and Ho Chi Minh join Mao Zedong (center).

Japanese soldiers wade across a river as they advance toward Singapore in 1942. Alhough guarded by 85,000 British troops, the city-state fell to a Japanese force of 35,000 men.

but it immediately drew the US into World War II. The US declared war on Japan the following day.

Pressing its advantage

With British forces tied up in Europe and the Americans yet to mobilize, Japan began to rampage through Southeast Asia. Although it had no great advantage over the Allies in troop numbers, Japan, crucially, gained control of the air and sea. On December 8, Japanese bombers destroyed 100 American aircraft on the ground in the Philippines and two days later stunned the Royal Navy by sinking the battleship HMS *Prince of Wales* and the battlecruiser HMS *Repulse* north of Singapore. Japanese troops quickly defeated Thailand and overran Allied forces in Malaya, and in February 1942, Singapore fell with relatively little resistance. By May, Japan also controlled the Dutch East Indies, the Solomon Islands, and most of New Guinea and had expelled the US from the Philippines.

Meanwhile in Burma, which Japan invaded at the end of 1941, British forces had to undertake the longest retreat in their military history—their front line pushed to the mountainous border with India. Western prestige in Southeast Asia was suffering an irreversible blow.

Japan's audacity and success emboldened Southeast Asia's anti-colonial nationalists. Some looked toward the Japanese as possible liberators, while others, such as the Viet Minh, established by Ho Chi Minh in Indochina in 1941, adopted communist ideals.

A huge death toll

Japan's treatment of captured soldiers and conquered civilians appalled its opponents. Japanese troops invading the Malay Peninsula had been ordered not to take prisoners. Soldiers who surrendered, both wounded and uninjured, were murdered, some by being doused with gasoline and set alight. Local people who aided British forces were tortured and killed.

After its victory in Singapore, Japanese forces killed tens of thousands of Chinese living there and also patients and medical staff at the Alexandra Military Hospital. Many of the soldiers and civilians taken prisoner were forced to labor on the yearlong construction of the Burma–Thailand railroad.

More than 60,000 British, Dutch, Australian, and American prisoners of war and 200,000 civilians worked on the 258-mile (415 km) line, dubbed the Death Railway. Of this enormous workforce, more than 12,000 POWs and about half of the civilians perished due to starvation, disease, and mistreatment.

Two Pacific sea battles
After Japan's success in Southeast Asia, its bid to strengthen its position in the Pacific proved more difficult. The Battle of the Coral Sea in early May 1942—the first naval battle in which vessels never came in sight of each other—ended inconclusively. Both sides suffered serious losses, and the encounter served to check Japan's southward advance by foiling its plans to occupy Port Moresby on New Guinea and establish air bases that would threaten Australia. More importantly, serious damage to two Japanese aircraft carriers prevented them from joining the Battle of Midway, the strategic turning point of the Pacific war.

> When you encounter the enemy … think of yourself as an avenger coming face to face at last with his father's murderer. Here is a man whose death will lighten your heart.
> **Japanese Army manual**
> 1941

Japan was eager to grab Midway Atoll, a strategically important island halfway between North America and Asia. It hosted a US airbase, whose capture would help Japan protect its homeland and dominate the western Pacific. On April 18, 1942, 16 American B-25 bombers launched from the aircraft carrier USS *Hornet* had carried out the Doolittle Raid, the first American attack on Tokyo and other targets on the Japanese mainland. Little damage was done to strategically important targets, but the raid boosted morale in the US—still smarting from the Pearl Harbor attack—and deeply upset Japan's government and its public.

In response, the Japanese navy, under Admiral Isoroku Yamamoto, planned to seize Midway Atoll in a surprise attack, knock out the US aircraft carrier threat, and secure a conclusive victory in the Pacific. A fleet of Japanese warships was sent toward the island, but American intelligence had deciphered the Japanese code for their target. US admiral Chester Nimitz devised a response. At a key moment during the five-day battle in June, American dive bombers attacked Japanese aircraft carriers as their planes were refueling and sunk all four, wiping out most of their frontline naval aviators, crew, and aircraft. After this defeat, Japan never recovered its strategic initiative in the Pacific. ∎

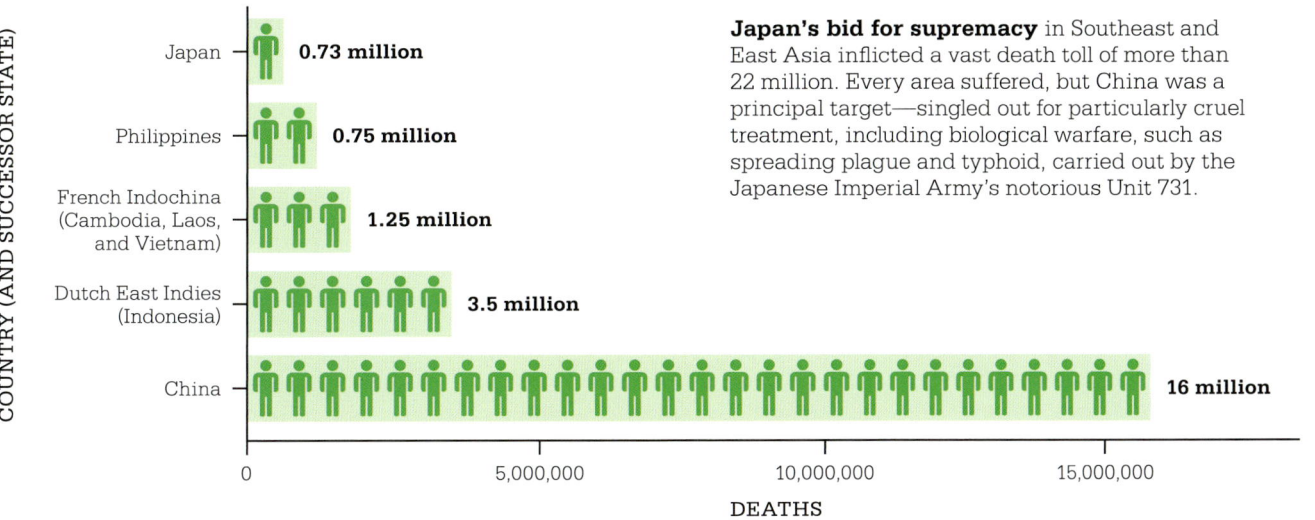

Civilian deaths in East and Southeast Asia during World War II

Japan's bid for supremacy in Southeast and East Asia inflicted a vast death toll of more than 22 million. Every area suffered, but China was a principal target—singled out for particularly cruel treatment, including biological warfare, such as spreading plague and typhoid, carried out by the Japanese Imperial Army's notorious Unit 731.

- Japan: 0.73 million
- Philippines: 0.75 million
- French Indochina (Cambodia, Laos, and Vietnam): 1.25 million
- Dutch East Indies (Indonesia): 3.5 million
- China: 16 million

WE DEVOUTLY HOPED THAT THE JAPANESE WOULD HEED OUR WARNING
JAPAN DEFEATED (1943–1945)

IN CONTEXT

FOCUS
The decision to use the atomic bomb

BEFORE
1938 German chemists Otto Hahn and Fritz Strassmann discover nuclear fission—splitting the atom to release huge amounts of energy.

1939 German-born physicist Albert Einstein warns US president Franklin D. Roosevelt that Germany could develop an atomic bomb.

1941 The Japanese attack on Pearl Harbor, Hawaii, brings the US into World War II.

AFTER
1949 The USSR tests its first atomic bomb. Three years later, Britain tests an atomic bomb on uninhabited islands off Australia.

2006 North Korea becomes the ninth nation to possess nuclear weapons.

Once the US put its economy on a serious war footing from December 1941, its military power soared. Munitions production rapidly accelerated, easily outstripping that of Japan, and the whole country leaned into the war effort. The goal was total victory in the Pacific.

Allied forces under US Army general Douglas MacArthur in the southwest Pacific and US admiral Chester Nimitz in the central Pacific targeted Japanese-held islands in both areas from early 1942. The Allies aimed to retake them one by one until heavy American bombers were within range of the four main islands of Japan.

MacArthur's Australian and US troops had begun the reconquest of occupied New Guinea in 1942. Victory was not complete until the war ended but was largely secured by October 1944, when MacArthur moved on to the Philippines. In the Battle of Leyte Gulf—the largest-ever naval battle—MacArthur and Nimitz combined forces. Japan lost most of its remaining fleet as it sought to prevent the amphibious assault on Leyte—the springboard island for MacArthur's campaign. In March 1945, MacArthur took the Philippine capital Manila and mostly completed his reconquest of the islands by June.

Meanwhile, US naval forces under Nimitz had won the Battle of the Philippine Sea in June 1944, and by August, the capture of islands such as Guam in the Marianas had put Japan's home islands within range of the new American B-29 Superfortress bombers. In late 1944, the planes began to launch the first devastating firebombing attacks on Japanese cities. Already, millions of civilians and soldiers had died in

If [the Japanese] do not now accept our terms they may expect a rain of ruin from the air, the like of which has never been seen on this earth.
Harry Truman
White House statement,
August 6, 1945

See also: Japan in the Sengoku era 128–129 ▪ China in turmoil 230–231 ▪ The Russo-Japanese War 235 ▪ The Second Sino-Japanese War 264–265 ▪ The air war 274–275 ▪ Japan ascendant 280–283 ▪ The Cold War 286–293

the Asian conflict. In the first six months of 1945, Japanese kamikaze attacks and further costly fighting on islands such as Iwo Jima and Okinawa convinced the US that a planned invasion of the Japanese mainland could involve hundreds of thousands of casualties.

Utter destruction

On the night of March 9–10, 1945, 279 B-29 bombers dropped deadly incendiaries on residential areas of Tokyo in Operation Meetinghouse. The death toll was estimated at 110,000 but may have been much higher. Still, there was no Japanese surrender. Accordingly, Harry S. Truman, US president following Franklin D. Roosevelt's death in April 1945, decided to use the atomic bomb, recently developed by physicist Robert Oppenheimer and

Hiroshima's devastation is clear from a photograph taken after the atomic bombing. Those within 1,000 yd (1 km) of its epicenter died; survivors suffered extreme burns and radiation sickness.

Controversial decision

The atomic bombing of Japan still provokes controversy. One camp defends it as a military necessity, while opponents call it a war crime or even genocide. When Japan surrendered in 1945, a Gallup poll in the US revealed that 85 percent of Americans supported the bombings. The figure dropped to 56 percent in a 2015 survey, when a younger generation was more influenced by the destruction and suffering inflicted by the bombs.

US president Truman considered invading Japan instead. On June 15, 1945, a Joint War Plans Committee memo advised him that possible casualties would vary from 132,500 to 220,000, or up to 500,000 in a worst-case scenario. Since the troops of the Imperial Japanese Army had pledged to fight to the death, an invasion could have proved the costliest invasion for US troops in the war. In the event, it was Japanese civilians who paid the price.

the Manhattan Project team at the Los Alamos Laboratory in New Mexico. On July 26, shortly after a successful test of the bomb, the Allies issued the Potsdam Declaration, demanding that Japan surrender unconditionally or face "prompt and utter destruction." Japan did not respond. On August 6, the bomb nicknamed Little Boy was dropped on the city of Hiroshima, instantly killing at least 70,000 people. The second bomb—Fat Man—released over Nagasaki three days later, killed around 40,000 people. On August 15, in spite of resistance from his military leaders, Japanese emperor Hirohito announced his acceptance of the Potsdam Declaration's terms. Japan's surrender was formally confirmed on September 2, 1945. ■

AN IRON CURTAIN HAS DESCENDED

THE COLD WAR (1945–1991)

288 THE COLD WAR

IN CONTEXT

FOCUS
Spy vs. spy

BEFORE
1920 British statesman Winston Churchill states that "a Bolshevist peace is only another form of war."

1924 The *Daily Mail* publishes the Zinoviev Letter—a forged plea to British communists to pressure the Labour Party into backing an Anglo-Soviet treaty.

1938 The House Un-American Activities Committee is formed to investigate suspected communist subversion in US government and public life.

AFTER
1995 In Russia, the Federal Security Service (FSB) succeeds the Soviet KGB.

1998 In May, both India and Pakistan carry out nuclear bomb tests, provoking outrage around the world.

In 1945, World War II gave way to an uneasy confrontation between the communist USSR (or Soviet Union) and the capitalist US. Given that the US already had nuclear weapons and the USSR was sure to follow suit—detonating its first atomic bomb in September 1949—all-out war was going to mean mutual suicide.

With the threat of nuclear weapons ever-present, both sides entered a five-decade period of ideological conflict that stopped short of open warfare between the two superpowers. Fueled by paranoia and increasingly complex intelligence gathering systems—based on spying—this left its mark on everything from civil rights and personal liberties to sport and culture. Writing in 1945, the British author George Orwell called this stand-off a "cold war."

East and West take sides

After 1945, the USSR's influence and control spread across much of Eastern Europe, creating a "Soviet Bloc" of nations—Czechoslovakia, Poland, Hungary, Romania, Bulgaria, and Albania—that now lay behind what Winston Churchill in 1947 had described as an "iron curtain." Defeated Germany had been divided into two, a communist East and a capitalist West, with a new capital in Bonn. The former capital, Berlin—itself divided into western and eastern sides—formed an enclave within the East. When, in June 1948, the communist authorities cut off road and railroad links with West Berlin, the US and its allies organized a major airlift to deliver everything the city needed, from food to coal.

The Western alliance was formalized in 1949 with the North Atlantic Treaty, its signatories promising to come to each other's aid against communist attack. West Germany's admission to the North Atlantic Treaty Organization (NATO) in 1955 prompted the communists—including East Germany—to sign their own defense treaty, the Warsaw Pact.

A nuclear arms race

Although a nuclear attack was, in theory, unthinkable, the US and USSR proceeded to build their arsenals. By far the richer nation, the US had an estimated 299 atomic bombs by 1950, while the USSR had

Berlin Wall

The ideological divide between East and West found physical expression in the steel and concrete of the Berlin Wall. The East German authorities began to build it during the night of August 12–13, 1961. The stream of defectors heading into West Berlin to escape what was supposed to be a workers' paradise had been embarrassing East Germany—and the USSR.

The "wall" was actually two concrete walls, up to 12 ft (3.6 m) high, between which lay a "death strip," protected by alarmed, electrified fences, and patrolled by border guards with dogs. The wall ran for 27 miles (43 km) between East and West Berlin, stretching beyond both with a total length of 96 miles (155 km). From its watch-towers, armed soldiers looked out for anyone trying to get to the West. Up to 5,000 succeeded during the 28 years of the wall's existence, but some 140 were killed in the attempt, more than half shot by guards. The Berlin Wall came to symbolize the grim realities of the Cold War, and its demolition by a rapturous crowd in 1989 signaled a new beginning.

THE WORLD WARS AND BEYOND 289

See also: The Russian Civil War 262–263 ▪ The defeat of Germany 276–279 ▪ The Korean War 295 ▪ Independence in Southeast Asia 296–297 ▪ Revolution and counterrevolution in Latin America 298–299 ▪ Conflict in Afghanistan 312–313

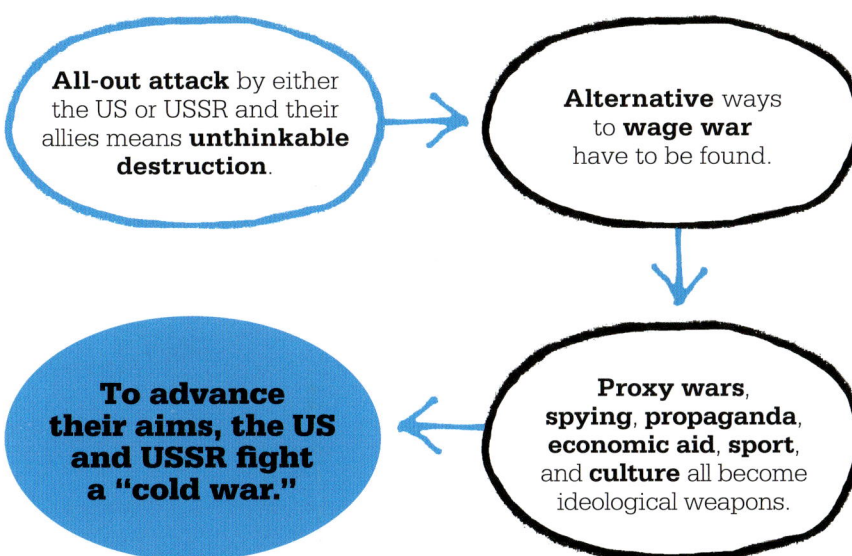

All-out attack by either the US or USSR and their allies means **unthinkable destruction**.

Alternative ways to **wage war** have to be found.

Proxy wars, **spying**, **propaganda**, **economic aid**, **sport**, and **culture** all become ideological weapons.

To advance their aims, the US and USSR fight a "cold war."

only five. The imbalance between the two rivals continued to grow, although sheer numbers were less important than the fact that only a limited number of nuclear blasts would cause global catastrophe.

In 1952, the threat became even graver after the successful testing by the US of the first hydrogen, or H, bomb, which combined the effects of nuclear fission—the power behind the atomic bomb—with those of fusion. To achieve nuclear fission, scientists in the 1930s had found a way to "split the atom"—breaking up the nucleus to release enormous amounts of energy. Then, immediately after World War II, US investigators had discovered that the forcing together (fusion) of radioactive hydrogen nuclei produced a chain reaction that unleashed destructive power a thousand times more powerful than that of the bomb dropped on Hiroshima, Japan, in 1945. Modes of weapon delivery were also changing, as aircraft-carried bombs were supplemented by intercontinental ballistic missiles (ICBMs), from 1958 in the USSR and from 1959 in the US.

By 1960, the US still had overwhelming superiority over the USSR, with Britain also fielding more than 100 nuclear weapons. Despite this reality, there was a growing fear in the US of a "missile gap"—a more than 10 times advantage enjoyed by the USSR in the number of ICBMs. The fear was stoked by opponents of US President Dwight D. Eisenhower, eyeing an impending national election, and by those in business and the military—what Eisenhower described as the "military-industrial complex." For these people, it was important to keep the idea of the Soviet threat alive in Americans'

An Atlas ICBM, the first American ICBM, is tested at Cape Canaveral, Florida. This missile could deliver a nuclear warhead over a distance of more than 6,200 miles (10,000 km).

minds to assure their continuing support for a huge program of spending on weapons.

Proxies and propaganda

While nuclear war seemed impossibly remote, there was still scope for smaller-scale conflict. Once World War II had ended, the US and USSR used "proxy wars"—conflicts in which they could interfere as third parties—to undermine each other's ideology and strategy. The Greek Civil War (1944–1949) had set the template, pitting left-wing partisans, who wanted a socialist state, against conservatives seeking a restoration of Greece's monarchy. In 1947, US President Harry S. Truman gave his support to the royalists, preventing Greece from becoming a socialist state.

It became commonplace for the USSR to support left-wing "liberation struggles" around the »

Julius and Ethel Rosenberg, shown here in police mugshots, were the first Americans to be executed for spying. Soviet records released in the 1990s appeared to confirm their guilt.

world, while the US backed those opposing them in the name of "freedom." In 1950, communist North Korea benefited from Soviet support when it invaded South Korea, which in turn was aided in the ensuing war (1950–1953) by more than 1 million US troops. The USSR also helped left-wing insurgents in Laos and Vietnam resist France's attempts to restore its colonial occupation from 1946 to 1954.

On the home fronts of the US and USSR, different battles were taking place to mobilize and manage public opinion. Soviet communism had always harnessed propaganda to underpin its ideology, utilizing the press, broadcasting, arts, and cinema as instruments of the state. The American media, including newspapers, radio, and television, although theoretically independent, was soon caught up in anti-communist fear and suspicion—the "red scare"—stirred up from the late 1940s by government bodies.

What do you think spies are: priests, saints, and martyrs? They're a squalid procession of vain fools.
John le Carré
The Spy Who Came in from the Cold, **1963**

From 1950, Joseph McCarthy, a US senator from Wisconsin, began to target people working within government that he claimed were communists secretly subverting the American system. The intensity of his interrogations—which reached a peak in 1954 with 36 days of televised hearings—led to the coining of a new word, "McCarthyism," for the excessive pursuit of unsupported accusations.

At the same time, the House Un-American Activities Committee (HUAC), a US government body formed in 1938.found a new lease on life investigating alleged communists and left-wing "fellow travelers" in government, the media, and entertainment, including Hollywood directors and actors. The anti-communism fever stoked by such scaremongering helped ensure support for the US government's program of nuclear armament as well as the wholesale reinforcement of conventional forces.

The spying game
National intelligence services had existed, especially in Europe, since the 19th century, but ideological battles on a global level now called for new organizations. President Truman founded the Central Intelligence Agency (CIA), the first of its kind in the US, in 1947, while the USSR restructured its various agencies into the Soviet Committee for State Security (KGB) in 1954, which worked alongside the Red Army's intelligence organization (GRU). Both sides employed extensive levels of espionage.

Sometimes spying fears were justified. In the US, Julius and Ethel Rosenberg, a married couple, were arrested in 1950 and executed for spying three years later. Julius had been a government scientist; Ethel had helped him pass nuclear secrets to the USSR—aiding its atomic bomb development. In fact, several of the scientists who worked on the Manhattan Project that developed the first US atomic bomb, in 1945, had also shared some of their discoveries with the USSR, fearing how the US might use a monopoly of nuclear might.

Many idealists had been drawn to what still seemed the utopian project of Soviet communism. In the 1930s, some of the brightest students at Britain's Cambridge University had formed connections with Soviet intelligence officers and went on to divulge state secrets to them as they rose in Britain's intelligence services and wider establishment.

During a war of stalemate in which each side was always looking for an "edge," however tiny, that could damage the opposition, espionage became feverishly intense. Both sides recruited "assets"—spies or informants—from almost every walk of life, from government and the military to industry and education, going to endless trouble, not just to spy themselves, but to thwart (or even "turn") each other's agents.

Enormous effort and ingenuity went into projects such as Operation Gold in 1954–1955, in which agents of the CIA and MI6 (Britain's intelligence service) tunneled deep under East Berlin to tap into phone calls to and from the Soviet army headquarters. So great was the atmosphere of deceit that, when the operation was revealed to KGB agents by George Blake, a "mole," or informant, within MI6, they decided to ignore it for fear of jeopardizing Blake's role.

The endless twists and turns of espionage were so compelling that they generated a boom in novels, and films of those novels, based on Cold War life, including the works of British writers Ian Fleming and John le Carré. Both men were former intelligence officers—Fleming working in naval intelligence and le Carré serving not only in MI6 but also in Britain's counterintelligence security service MI5.

Communist coups

While the Cold War was fought largely without tangible combat gains, the forces of communism were able to score some public victories that at least embarrassed the West. In 1960, Soviet air defenses shot down an American Lockheed U-2 spy plane over the USSR's Ural Mountains and captured the pilot, Gary Powers.

Typically for the time, the propaganda potential was as important as the strategic facts of the mission and the capture. Both the USSR and the US vied to profit from the incident. The downing of a U-2 flying at a height of more than 69,000 ft (21,000 m) reflected well on the Soviets' surface-to-air missile, and the arrest of a US pilot was an obvious coup, with Powers's court trial televised. The US took comfort »

The Cold War divided most of Europe into two military alliances. NATO represented the capitalist West, while the Warsaw Pact held together the communist East. Both were based on the concept of collective security—an attack on one state is an attack on all.

Key:
- Founding members of NATO, 1949
- Newer NATO members: Greece and Türkiye (1952), West Germany (1955), Spain (1982)
- Founding members of the Warsaw Pact, 1955
- Newer Warsaw Pact member: East Germany (1956)
- Warsaw Pact withdrawal: Albania (1968)

> In accepting them [the missiles], we would be reinforcing the socialist camp the world over.
> **Fidel Castro**
> to *Le Monde*, March 1963

from the fact that earlier U-2 planes had entered Soviet airspace largely unhindered, which was humiliating for the USSR. In 1962, the incident was closed when Powers was exchanged for the Soviet agent Rudolf Abel—the first of many spy exchanges during the Cold War.

How events such as the U-2 incident were presented to the wider world was hugely important. The US and USSR were in an endless struggle to either save face or undermine their opponent's ideologies. In 1959, the victory of Marxist revolutionary Fidel Castro on the Caribbean island of Cuba was a huge boost to the communist cause. The heroic glamour of Castro and his supporters, including the photogenic Argentinian guerrilla leader Che Guevara, held a strong appeal for young students in the East and West, and for minority communities, which had not felt fairly represented in political life.

Arriving to address the UN in New York City in September 1960, Castro stayed in Cuba's consulate in the Harlem district. There, he hosted meetings with leaders of America's emerging Civil Rights movement, including Malcolm X. The implication was that Castro cared more about Black Americans than the US government did. He had struck a blow for the global left.

The Cuban crisis

Cuba was the scene of further embarrassment for the US in 1961, when a small invading army of Cuban exiles was easily crushed at the Bay of Pigs on the southwestern coast of Cuba. John F. Kennedy, elected US president in 1960, had inherited the plan but scaled back the level of US support, dooming a risky strategy to abject failure. The incident was seen as a personal humiliation for the president.

Much more than a loss of face was at stake the following year, when a U-2 flying over Cuba photographed facilities being built for the launch of Soviet-supplied missiles. Eager to redeem his reputation, Kennedy placed the entire island under naval quarantine and demanded the removal of the missiles. The leader of the USSR, Nikita Khrushchev, was unwilling to comply, especially because the US had just placed a similar missile site in eastern Türkiye. Nuclear war seemed closer than it had ever done, but after six days Khrushchev relented and removed the missiles. As part of the deal, however, he won a concession from the US that it would dismantle its own missiles in Türkiye and Italy.

"Soft" power struggles

Unlike other large-scale conflicts, the Cold War was waged with an array of "soft," nondestructive weapons. For both sides, generosity proved a potent source of strength and allegiance. In 1948, the US enacted the Marshall Plan—named for its inaugurator, US secretary of state George C. Marshall—which provided $13.3 billion (around $170 billion today) to 16 European countries. The plan helped build a

US President Kennedy signs the Interdiction of the Delivery of Offensive Weapons to Cuba proclamation, enforcing a naval blockade of Cuba, on October 23, 1962.

THE WORLD WARS AND BEYOND

The Aswan Dam, funded by the USSR, takes shape in January 1965. It controls flooding by regulating the flow of the Nile River and supplies water for the irrigation of Egypt's crops.

new Europe that was affluent, democratic, and oriented toward the US. In turn, the USSR helped its allies with major development projects, such as the construction of Egypt's Aswan Dam in the 1960s.

Culture was another battlefront as each side began to weaponize anything that could influence minds and suggest that its way of life was more conducive to thought and creativity than the other's. From 1953, the CIA, under the guise of the Congress for Cultural Freedom, sponsored *Encounter*, an influential political and literary journal published in Britain. The CIA also lobbied the Royal Swedish Academy of Sciences to award the 1958 Nobel Prize for Literature to Russian author Boris Pasternak, whose 1957 novel, *Doctor Zhivago*, the USSR had suppressed for its bleakly pessimistic portrait of Soviet life. With Nobel endorsement, it became a global bestseller, but Pasternak had to decline his Nobel Prize at the behest of the irritated Soviet authorities. The USSR also countered with tours by Moscow's Bolshoi Ballet and the Kirov Ballet from Leningrad (now St. Petersburg).

Sport was weaponized too; the US and USSR both used the Olympic Games in particular to score ideological points. In 1980, the US boycotted the Moscow games, and the USSR retaliated four years later by staying away from the Los Angeles games. From 1974, communist East Germany went as far as encouraging its athletes to take drugs, especially steroids, in order to ensure Olympic glory.

The most spectacular Cold War rivalry was expressed in the space race—essentially an extension of the two countries' weapons programs. The first ICBM, the R7 Soviet rocket, began the race in 1957, launching the satellite Sputnik 1 into space. A related Soviet rocket sent the first human, Yuri Gagarin, into space in 1961. The US rushed to compete, hastily developing new rockets for its Apollo program. Ultimately, however, the "race" became a battle for prestige, with the US eventually taking the lead in 1969 when its Apollo 11 mission placed the first man on the moon.

End game for the East

In the 1970s, the Cold War eased a little, as the US and USSR began to discuss arms control, a process known as "detente." Relations cooled again in 1979 when the USSR invaded Afghanistan, but from 1985, Soviet leader, Mikhail Gorbachev, engaged in talks with US President Ronald Reagan to reduce each nation's nuclear weapons, which together totaled more than 60,000. International pressure and the cost of the war forced a Soviet withdrawal from Afghanistan in 1989, while Gorbachev's policy of *perestroika* ("restructuring") was moving the USSR away from communism. Destabilized by internal unrest, communist governments across Eastern Europe began to fall. East and West Germany soon reunited, and in 1991 the USSR finally collapsed, bringing the Cold War to an end. Ultimately, the sheer economic might of the US had prevailed, with the USSR unable to sustain the kind of commitment that Cold War rivalry required. ∎

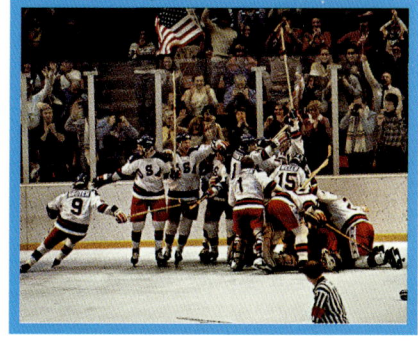

The US ice hockey team celebrate after beating—against the odds—the USSR 4–3 to win the gold medal at the 1980 Winter Olympics, held at Lake Placid, New York State.

THE SKY CANNOT HAVE TWO SUNS
THE CHINESE CIVIL WAR (1945–1949)

IN CONTEXT

FOCUS
Harnessing the masses

BEFORE
1921 The Chinese Communist Party (CCP) is founded.

1927 An armed conflict begins between the CCP and the Kuomintang (KMT).

1934–1935 Mao Zedong's Red Army makes the Long March—6,000 miles (9,600 km) across China—pursued by the KMT.

1937–1945 The Second Sino-Japanese War ends with the surrender of Japan.

AFTER
1954 The US signs a Mutual Defense Treaty, guaranteeing Taiwan's security from China.

1966–1976 Mao's Cultural Revolution sees millions of the urban young sent to rural areas to be "reeducated."

2010 China overtakes Japan to become the world's second largest economy.

The invasion of China by Japan in 1937 had pushed the Kuomintang (KMT)—China's ruling nationalists, under Chiang Kai-shek—and the Chinese Communist Party (CCP), led by Mao Zedong, into an uneasy alliance. Once Japan was defeated, in 1945, hostilities between the two factions renewed, and by summer 1946, China had descended into civil war. The CCP had an army of more than 1.2 million, backed up by a militia twice as big, but were initially overwhelmed by KMT forces and driven back into their northeastern stronghold of Manchuria.

Vital peasant support

In 1947, Mao Zedong's army went on the offensive, using guerrilla tactics to harass the armies of the KMT and surrounding its major cities. Mao, realizing the importance of the vast peasant majority in China, won their support with promises of agricultural reform, better living conditions, and the redistribution of land. He argued that his guerrilla forces would "swim" among the peasant masses like fish in the sea, fighting superior forces until the Chinese people had been won over.

Mao's strategy worked, as the communist forces (now called the People's Liberation Army, or PLA) defeated the KMT in Manchuria in October 1948, drove into northern China, and entered Beijing on January 21, 1949. Nanjing and Shanghai fell in April. In October, Mao proclaimed the People's Republic of China (PRC), and his victory was complete when the KMT fled to Taiwan in December. ■

Political power grows out of the barrel of a gun.
Mao Zedong
November 1938

See also: China in turmoil 230–231 ▪ The Second Sino-Japanese War 264–265 ▪ Japan ascendant 280–283 ▪ Japan defeated 284–285 ▪ The Korean War 295

THE WORLD WARS AND BEYOND

OUR BIG GENERAL ... MUST BE RECALLED
THE KOREAN WAR (1950–1953)

IN CONTEXT

FOCUS
Civilian military control

BEFORE
1787 The US Constitution states that "The President shall be the Commander in Chief" of all US military forces.

1832 Prussian general Carl von Clausewitz argues in his book *On War* that the military is the servant of political aims.

1947 US president Harry S. Truman vows to support "free peoples who are resisting attempted subjugation."

AFTER
1954 After the First Indochina War, Vietnam is divided between the communist north and the US-backed south.

1957 In his book *The Soldier and the State*, American political scientist Samuel Huntington calls for "objective civilian control" of a highly professionalized military that can act as it deems best.

In 1945, the Korean peninsula, formerly part of the Japanese empire, was divided along the 38th parallel—a line of latitude—into the USSR-backed Democratic People's Republic of Korea (North Korea) and the pro-Western Republic of Korea (South Korea). Tensions escalated and, on June 25, 1950, the North's Korean People's Army (KPA) invaded South Korea, seizing Seoul, the capital, within three days. The United Nations Security Council denounced the action and sent a United Nations force, led by US general Douglas MacArthur, to support South Korea.

Questioning authority

MacArthur reversed the North Korean advance and, following an amphibious landing at Inchon, liberated Seoul in September 1950. By October, he had advanced into North Korea. Communist China now intervened, sending in its army and forcing the UN troops back south.

MacArthur wanted to take the fight to China—blockading its ports and bombing strategic targets.

UN forces withdraw from North Korea in December 1950. The border—the 38th parallel—was established after World War II to split Korea into two separate states.

When President Truman gave notice of a peace proposal in 1951, MacArthur publicly threatened the Chinese, shattering ceasefire plans. Truman, as commander-in-chief of US forces, dismissed MacArthur, stating the military "must be controlled by civilian authority."

The war settled into a costly stalemate. After failed peace talks, the two sides signed an armistice on July 27, 1953, accepting that Korea would remain divided. ■

See also: China in turmoil 230–231 ▪ Japan ascendant 280–283 ▪ The Cold War 286–293 ▪ The Chinese Civil War 294 ▪ Independence in Southeast Asia 296–297

RAISE ALOFT THE BANNER OF INSURRECTION
INDEPENDENCE IN SOUTHEAST ASIA (1945–1975)

IN CONTEXT

FOCUS
Asymmetric warfare

BEFORE
1602 The Dutch East India Company is formed to protect Dutch trade in Asia.

1619 Batavia (now Jakarta, Indonesia) becomes the capital of the Dutch East Indies.

1858 The Cochinchina Campaign marks the beginning of French imperial encroachment in Indochina.

1941 Japanese forces conquer most of Southeast Asia.

AFTER
1975 Destabilized by the Vietnam War, Cambodia is taken over by Khmer Rouge.

1978 Vietnamese forces invade Cambodia to drive out the Khmer Rouge.

1979 Robert Garwood, said to be the last American prisoner of war in Vietnam, returns to the US.

World War II had reshaped the global order, straining to breaking point the empires of the Western powers. In some parts of Southeast Asia, the old colonial overlords, including France in Indochina—today's Cambodia, Laos, and Vietnam—tried to reassert their imperial dominance, but met with fierce resistance.

During the war, Southeast Asia's Indigenous peoples had suffered Japanese attacks and invasions that European colonial powers had failed to resist, shattering claims of Western superiority. Now, these populations believed increasingly that they should take charge of their futures. The US disengaged from the Philippines, which was granted independence in 1946, but elsewhere Indigenous peoples had to use asymmetrical warfare to win their nations' freedom.

Colonial war spreads
Conflict erupted in most colonized countries in Southeast Asia. In Indonesia, the Dutch relinquished control in 1949, after heavy fighting, while the British successfully suppressed a communist insurgency between 1948 and 1960 in Malaya, which went on to join North Borneo, Sarawak, and Singapore to become independent Malaysia in 1963.

The heaviest fighting was in what had been French Indochina. In the First Indochina War, the Viet Minh independence movement, led by communist revolutionary Ho Chi Minh, expelled the French in an eight-year campaign, culminating in the decisive defeat of French forces at Dien Bien Phu in 1954. As part of the resulting Geneva Accords, the US forced France to withdraw its troops, giving independence to Laos and Cambodia, and partitioning Vietnam into a communist-led North and an independent South, the latter backed by the US.

We are fighting a war with no front lines, since the enemy hides among the people.
General William C. Westmoreland
US Army Chief of Staff, 1967

See also: The Second Sino-Japanese War 264–265 ▪ Japan ascendant 280–283 ▪ Japan defeated 284–285 ▪ The Cold War 286–293 ▪ The Chinese Civil War 294 ▪ The Korean War 295

Viet Cong bicycle porters, steering with a pole mounted on the handlebar, carry heavy loads to the front near Saigon in 1972. Bicycles were a vital means of supply for the Viet Cong.

In the Second Indochina War, or Vietnam War, American forces were drawn into indirect and, from 1964, direct conflict with insurgent communist forces in South Vietnam. Later known as the Viet Cong, the insurgents were backed by the army of the North. By the end of 1967, with an increasing number of ground forces and massive aerial bombardment of the North, supported by superior technology and firepower, the US seemed to be winning the war.

Whenever US and Viet Cong forces clashed in direct combat, the Americans usually prevailed, but the Viet Cong and its northern support, under the direction of Vo Nguyen Giap, followed a simple principle: all they had to do to win was to survive. They succeeded in weathering the American assault through guerrilla tactics, knowledge of local terrain, embedding their forces in local populations, and retreating to hideouts across the border. This was a classic example of asymmetric warfare.

An escape route

On January 30, 1968, communist forces that had infiltrated deep into South Vietnam launched the Tet Offensive—a series of coordinated attacks across the country. It was beaten back, but the effect on American public opinion was so damaging that US leaders began to seek ways out of the conflict. This culminated in US military withdrawal after the Paris Peace Accords of January 1973. These soon broke down, leading to a humiliating evacuation of American personnel from the southern capital, Saigon, as communist forces overran South Vietnam in 1975. ▪

A US Air Force Fairchild UC-123K Provider plane sprays the Soai Rap river delta, southeast of Saigon, with Agent Orange around 1970.

Agent Orange

A key asset in the Viet Cong's asymmetric warfare was their ability to use the jungle terrain of Vietnam to counter or negate American military advantages, which included air, armor, and superior firepower. The Viet Cong could follow concealed routes through the jungle to carry out ambushes, move troops, and transport supplies.

To counter this threat, the US Air Force launched Operation Ranch Hand to defoliate vast areas of forest and destroy crops. Pursued from 1962 to 1971, the operation involved spraying areas with an estimated 19 million gallons (86 million liters) of herbicides. The chemical mixtures, named for the colors of the containers in which they were shipped, included Agent Orange, which turned dense forest into a mass of barren trees. Operation Ranch Hand was largely ineffective in military terms but caused huge ecological damage and terrible consequences for the health of Vietnamese civilians and combatants on both sides.

A COUNTRY FREE FROM FOREIGN INTERFERENCE
REVOLUTION AND COUNTERREVOLUTION IN LATIN AMERICA (1953–1990s)

IN CONTEXT

FOCUS
Castro, Guevara, and the Cuban Revolution

BEFORE
1902 Cuba gains formal independence from Spain following the Cuban War of Independence (1895–1898).

1909–1913 Under its "dollar diplomacy" policy, the US lends money to Latin American states in exchange for political control.

1933 US president Franklin Roosevelt's Good Neighbor Policy prioritizes trade and cooperation over military action in Latin America.

AFTER
2002 The US is accused of involvement in a failed coup against Hugo Chávez, president of Venezuela.

2018 Miguel Díaz-Canel succeeds Raúl Castro as president of Cuba.

As the US became more economically powerful at the start of the 20th century, it began to intervene in the domestic affairs of its Latin American neighbors, sometimes militarily, and usually in order to protect its commercial interests. In the 1930s, the US pursued a less interventionist policy, but fear of the spread of communism after World War II led it to take action against any left-leaning Central American or South American country—nations in its own "backyard." The extent of this interference varied.

The United States was not merely 'doing business' in Latin America but was fighting a war there against communism.
Dwight D. Eisenhower
US president, 1954

Apart from three full-scale military invasions—of the Dominican Republic in 1965, Grenada in 1983, and Panama in 1989—the US primarily followed a strategy of covert action, such as influencing politicians and training and equipping foreign troops. Through its Central Intelligence Agency (CIA), it orchestrated revolutions and coups led by local opposition groups across Latin America, including Bolivia (1971) and Nicaragua (1979). The US failed, however, to reverse the communist revolution that began in 1953 on one of its nearest islands—Cuba—which, led by Fidel Castro from 1959, would remain a thorn in its side for the rest of the century.

Protecting business
Business interests were often at the root of American intervention. By the 1940s, the Boston-based United Fruit Company controlled nearly half of the land of Guatemala, in Central America, and owned all its banana production, telephone and telegraph system, and most of the railroads. In 1951, army colonel Jacobo Arbenz was elected president, with a radical plan of action, including expropriating 40 percent of the

See also: The European conquest of the Americas 122–125 ▪ The Spanish American wars of liberation 200–203 ▪ The American-Mexican wars 204–205

United Fruit Company's land. In support of US business interests, President Dwight D. Eisenhower backed a CIA-led coup in 1953. Arbenz was deposed a year later.

In 1959, revolutionary leader Fidel Castro and his followers, including Argentinian guerrilla leader Ernesto "Che" Guevara, overthrew Cuban president Fulgencio Batista. The US accepted the new government at first, but when Cuba expropriated American assets, including mines, railroads, and sugar plantations, Eisenhower broke off diplomatic relations. The CIA planned an invasion by Cuban exiles. This took place in 1961 at the Bay of Pigs on Cuba's southwestern coast, with the assent of newly elected President John F. Kennedy. Cuba's 20,000-strong army crushed the 1,400 invaders, leaving Castro's regime entrenched and firmly allied with the USSR.

Sowing unrest

In 1965, US president Lyndon B. Johnson, fearing a communist takeover, ordered the invasion of the Dominican Republic. The subsequent US occupation lasted for eight years. In 1973, the CIA helped overthrow Chile's socialist president Salvador Allende. Six years later, the US intervened again, when Nicaragua's socialist Sandinista National Liberation Front (FSLN), supported by Cuba and the USSR, ousted the nation's US-backed dictator Antastasio Somoza. The US sent military aid to the Contras, right-wing Nicaraguan rebels, who launched a counterrevolution from neighboring Honduras. Conflict between US-backed, right-wing factions and left-wing activists also engulfed Guatemala and El Salvador in civil wars until the 1990s. ∎

Cuban militiamen celebrate their victory over the invasion force, trained and equipped by the US, that landed at the Bay of Pigs in April 1961.

Fidel Castro

Born in southeastern Cuba in 1926, Fidel Castro studied law and was heavily involved in student activism. When Fulgencio Batista seized power in 1952, Castro began to plot an uprising and in 1953 led a failed attack on an army barracks. Released from prison two years later, Castro traveled to Mexico, where he met fellow revolutionary Che Guevara and planned a return to Cuba. After a disastrous landing on the eastern coast, Castro fled to the mountains, where he built an 800-strong guerrilla force that in 1958 defeated a government army numbering 30,000.

Taking control from Batista in January 1959, Castro became increasingly radical, and many middle-class Cubans fled the country. When Castro entered a trade pact with the USSR in February 1960, the US severed diplomatic ties. Ruling as a dictator, Castro put down any political dissent. Although many Cubans benefited from his social reforms, he failed to grow the economy, which was further damaged by the collapse of the USSR in 1991. Castro handed power to his brother, Raúl, in 2006, and died in 2016.

WE DO NOT WANT SOMEBODY ELSE'S NATIONALISM
THE AFRICAN WARS OF INDEPENDENCE (1952–1990)

IN CONTEXT

FOCUS
The end of colonial rule

BEFORE
1884–1885 At the Berlin Conference, European powers divide Africa into colonies, to be governed by force.

1910 The Union of South Africa wins some independence from Britain but is ruled by a white minority government.

1945 At the fifth Pan-African Congress, held in Britain, leading African politicians demand an end to colonial rule.

AFTER
1994 Apartheid ends in South Africa. ANC leader Nelson Mandela becomes the nation's first Black president.

2013 The British government agrees to pay £20 million in compensation to Mau-Mau survivors tortured by British forces in the 1950s.

African independence movements had begun to emerge in the early 1900s, spurred by the cruelties and racism of colonial rule across the continent. Between 1885 and 1909, as many as 10 million Africans died as a result of colonial exploitation in the Belgian Congo Free State. In German Namibia, an estimated 100,000 Indigenous Herero and Nama peoples died between 1904 and 1908, after they rebelled against the colonists' appropriation of their land and cattle. Many were put in concentration camps, where they were executed or perished from overwork and ill-health. Hundreds

THE WORLD WARS AND BEYOND

See also: The Spanish American wars of liberation 200–203 ▪ The American-Mexican wars 204–205 ▪ Imperial wars in Africa 226–229 ▪ Postcolonial Africa 304–305

of their skulls were sent to Germany for examination by eugenicists seeking evidence of racial inferiority in Indigenous African people.

Winds of change

The colonial map changed little during the first half of the 20th century. In 1941, British prime minister Winston Churchill and US president Franklin D. Roosevelt had co-signed the Atlantic Charter, whose provisions included "the right of all peoples to choose the form of government under which they will live." Churchill, however, claimed that the clause did not apply to British colonies. Of greater significance was the interplay of economic factors.

World War II had depleted the coffers of major European powers, who found it increasingly difficult to afford the cost of running their colonies. Simultaneously under pressure from African nationalist movements, some started to consider the idea of giving up control. A few African colonies

Suspected Mau-Mau supporters, imprisoned in camps across Kenya, faced extreme heat, torture, sexual assault, and malnutrition at the hands of British-led soldiers.

won independence without a large-scale military conflict. Ghana, led by Kwame Nkrumah, largely fought for its freedom with strikes and boycotts and gained independence from Britain in 1957. Other nations faced violent battles.

Detention and warfare

For decades in British Kenya, white settlers had seized land previously inhabited and farmed by Africans. In 1952, frustrated by such losses, the Kenya Land and Freedom Army (KLFA), also known as the Mau-Mau, began raiding white settler properties, leading Britain to declare a state of emergency. During a war that raged for eight years, anyone suspected of having Mau-Mau sympathies was put in prison, tortured, and often killed. More than 1 million people were »

The Suez Crisis

In July 1956, Gamel Abdel Nasser, Egypt's president, nationalized the British- and French-owned Suez Canal Company. The move infuriated Britain, which had continued to control this key shipping route after Egypt achieved its independence in 1922. France and Britain quickly hatched a plot and enlisted Israel's help to execute it.

In line with the plan, Israel invaded Egypt via Sinai in October 1956, giving Britain and France the pretext they required to retake control of the canal and "defend" it. The plot misfired when the US and USSR appealed to the UN, which sent in a special force to ensure that all British, French, and Israeli troops left Egyptian territory. The Suez incident humiliated France and Britain but enhanced Nasser's status in the Arab world. He seized British, French, and Jewish assets, expelled 12,000 British and French citizens, deported Israelis, and interned some 3,000 Egyptian Jews in four detention camps.

French troops arrive in the Port Fuad area of Port Said, with orders to join British troops to occupy the Suez Canal zone.

THE AFRICAN WARS OF INDEPENDENCE

> After decades of **repression and exploitation** by colonial powers, **African people form resistance** groups.

> When **colonial powers fail to negotiate** and meet their demands, they resort to **guerrilla tactics**.

> **African countries gain their freedom and independence.**

> Their leaders employ **peaceful strategies**—strikes and boycotts—to press their **demands for independence**.

> Facing **economic constraints**, and worn down by **violence and international condemnation**, the colonial powers finally capitulate.

herded into camps, where many reported physical abuse. Up to 100,000 Kenyans were detained without trial, and at least 20,000 Mau-Mau supporters were executed, including 1,000 who were publicly hanged. Civilian African deaths included at least 7,000 Kenyan women and 26,000 children aged under 10 years.

In 1960, Britain finally started to negotiate Kenyan independence, which was granted in 1964. When, in 2011, survivors attempted to sue the British government, it emerged that documents relating to abuses in Kenyan detention camps had been systematically destroyed for fear they "might embarrass Her Majesty's government."

Violence on all sides

Algeria in North Africa suffered a brutal war of independence from 1954 to 1962, as its largely Muslim population fought against France and 1 million white French settlers (pied-noirs) for the greater self-rule promised after World War II. Algeria's National Liberation Front (FLN) carried out its first guerrilla attacks in 1954. It also appealed to the United Nations (UN) for support, as France was then in the process of granting independence to Algeria's neighbors, Morocco and Tunisia—achieved in 1956. France ignored FLN demands and sent in thousands of troops to tackle FLN strongholds, instituting a violent crackdown that included torture and summary executions.

The FLN did not give up. Its attacks erupted in battles around Algiers in 1956 and 1957. Fearing that France might cede self-rule, dissident French army officers and the pied-noirs staged a counterrevolt in 1958. As French and international criticism of the war steadily swayed French president Charles de Gaulle

> We do not govern the indigenous people [of Algeria], we command them.
> **Adolphe Messimy**
> French Minister of War, 1913

in favor of independence, the Organisation de l'armée secrète (OAS), a terrorist group supported by the pied-noirs, formed in 1961 to disrupt the process with bombings and murders in France and Algeria. After independence was granted in 1962, most pied-noirs fled to France, fearing reprisals.

Long-fought campaigns

Portugal, the first European nation to gain territory in Africa, was the last to leave its colonies—Angola, Guinea-Bissau, Cape Verde, and Mozambique. Revolts against forced labor on Angolan coffee plantations in 1961 left 50,000 native Angolans dead, eventually prompting a long guerrilla war waged by three militias—the National Front for the Liberation of Angola (FNLA), the National Union for the Total Independence of Angola (UNITA), and the Popular Movement for the Liberation of Angola (MPLA).

In Guinea-Bissau, where the Portuguese had carried out brutal "pacification" measures, nationalist movements that had won support after World War II united as the African Party for the Independence of Guinea and Cape Verde (PAIGC) in 1956 and launched an armed campaign against the Portuguese in 1963. By the early 1970s, the PAIGC had gained control of much of the country. The Mozambique Liberation Front (Frelimo) formed in Tanganyika (now Tanzania) and launched its first attacks on Portuguese Mozambique in 1964, fighting a guerrilla war that would frustrate Portuguese armed forces for the next decade.

In 1974, the Carnation Revolution, a left-wing military coup in Lisbon, the Portuguese capital, ushered in independence for all four colonies. In Angola, Portugal withdrew its war-weary forces without any formal handover of power, and the MPLA took charge. Conflicts in Guinea Bissau, Cape Verde, and Mozambique also ended.

Last vestiges of colonialism

The white settlers of Mozambique's neighbors—Southern Rhodesia (Zimbabwe), South Africa, and South West Africa (Namibia)—held out far longer onto rule by a minority over the majority Black population. The white government of Southern Rhodesia firmly resisted the idea of majority Black rule and declared their own independence in 1965. Two communist-backed African nationalist parties waged a long guerrilla war in pursuit of a more democratic system of government, which, together with other political and economic pressures, forced Southern Rhodesia to capitulate finally in 1979. In elections held in 1980, Robert Mugabe came to power in newly named Zimbabwe.

Algerian freedom fighter Ali Boumendjel was tortured and killed by French forces in 1957 (a death passed off as suicide), as admitted in 2021 by French president Emmanuel Macron.

Meanwhile, despite military and economic sanctions and repeated UN condemnations of its apartheid policies, South Africa maintained its minority-white rule. However, the African National Congress (ANC), which had long waged a diplomatic and guerrilla war, gained increasing international support throughout the 1980s. In 1990, ANC secretary-general Nelson Mandela was released from life imprisonment. A year later, he and South Africa's white president F. W. de Klerk signed the National Peace Accord that brought about South Africa's transition to majority Black rule.

Namibia was gradually ceded by South Africa from 1978 and gained full independence in 1990—a victory for the freedom fighters of its South West Africa People's Organization (SWAPO). Africa had finally thrown off its colonial chains, although foreign powers and companies would continue to influence its nations' politics and economies. ∎

Amílcar Cabral

Born in Guinea-Bissau in 1924, Amílcar Cabral attended school in Cape Verde, then studied agronomy in Lisbon, Portugal, where he developed his nationalist ideas. In 1956, with five associates, he founded the African Party for the Independence of Guinea and Cape Verde (PAIGC), and the same year co-founded the People's Movement for the Liberation of Angola (MPLA) with poet and politician Agostinho Neto.

After Portuguese officers fired on demonstrators during a dockworkers' strike in 1959, Cabral arranged for his PAIGC members to attend military training camps in Ghana to prepare for an open war against the Portuguese authorities. Launched in 1963, this proved highly effective.

As the PAIGC—backed by the USSR—gained ground, Cabral began to visualize his dream for Guinea-Bissau. In 1972, he created the Guinean People's National Assembly, a basis for a new independent government, but in January 1973 he was assassinated by a PAIGC member thought to have been working with the Portuguese.

POVERTY CONTINUES TO BREED CONFLICT

POSTCOLONIAL AFRICA (1960–PRESENT)

IN CONTEXT

FOCUS
Foreign complicity in African conflict

BEFORE
1922 Britain declares Egypt an independent foreign state but continues to station troops there and to control the Suez Canal.

1950s France faces violent campaigns for freedom in Algeria, Morocco, Tunisia, Cameroon, and Mauritania.

1957 Ghana achieves its independence from Britain. It is the first African country to break away from a European colonial power.

AFTER
April 2023 Civil war erupts in Sudan. In a single year, thousands die and millions are displaced or flee the country.

June 2024 The Geneva Academy of International and Humanitarian Law reports more than 35 conflicts across the African continent.

Following Ghana's lead in 1957, 17 African nations gained independence from European powers in 1960, dubbed the Year of Africa. More followed—Zimbabwe, in 1980, was the last. Independence brought political and cultural recognition, but many nations' troubles were not over. The colonial powers had imposed borders and hierarchies that ignited rivalries between ethnic groups; upon independence, tensions rose as they competed for control.

Civil war

After achieving independence in 1960, Nigeria comprised three areas, dominated respectively by the Yoruba, Igbo, and Hausa-Fulani ethnic groups. Following a military coup in 1965, and a countercoup in 1966, the large Igbo community in the east seceded in 1967 to form a new country called Biafra, sparking a bitter three-year civil war.

During the conflict, the Nigerian federal government received arms from Britain and, indirectly, the USSR; unofficially, France supplied arms to Biafra. To break the initial stalemate, Nigeria imposed a blockade that led to the death by starvation of up to 2 million Biafrans. The war was televised, which inspired the birth of aid organizations such as Médecins Sans Frontières (Doctors Without Borders). By mid-January 1970, Nigerian forces had compelled the Biafrans to accept defeat.

Genocide

In 1962, Ruanda-Urundi, until then administered by Belgium, was split into the independent nations of Rwanda and Burundi. Belgium's

A terrified Biafran mother and her child lie on the ground. Images such as this, showing malnourished Africans caught up in civil war, shocked the world in the 1960s.

THE WORLD WARS AND BEYOND

See also: Warfare in northern Africa 126–127 ▪ Imperial wars in Africa 226–229 ▪ The Cold War 286–293 ▪ The African wars of independence 300–303

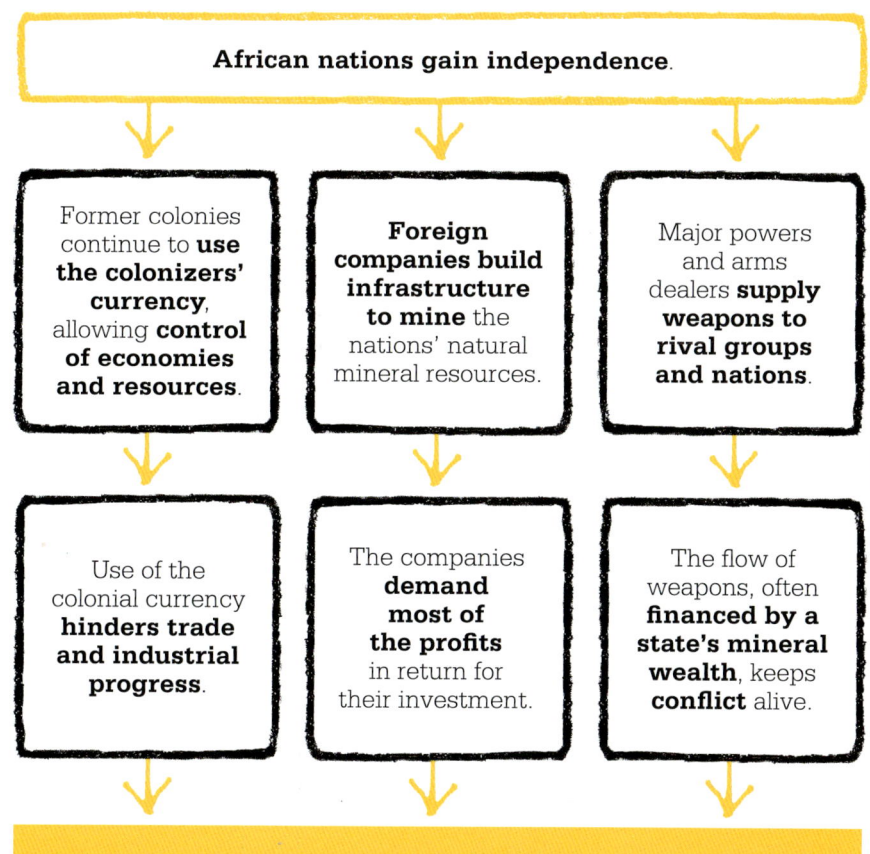

The Wagner Group

Around 2014, the Wagner Group took shape as a pro-Russian fighting force in eastern Ukraine, directed by oligarch Yevgeny Prigozhin, then a close associate of Russian president Vladimir Putin. Its activities expanded into the Middle East and African states, including the Central African Republic (CAR), Mali, Mozambique, and Sudan. The group offers its military support to governments in exchange for mineral concessions, but it has been accused by UN human rights campaigners of involvement in crimes against civilians, including torture, rape, and mass executions.

Since Prigozhin's challenge to Putin in 2023, and his subsequent death, the group was renamed the Africa Corps. Now controlled by the Russian government, its forces, which are present across West Africa, have largely replaced those of France. Its services are still paid for in mineral wealth; between 2022 and 2024, Russia reportedly secured $2.5 billion (£2 billion) worth of African gold.

overt encouragement of the Hutu ethnic group's domination in Rwanda frightened and angered the Tutsi ethnic group, many of whom fled to Burundi and Uganda.

Belgium's colonial influence had lasting consequences. Incursions by Tutsis from Burundi precipitated a massacre of Rwandan Tutsis in December 1963. Tensions simmered for 30 years, with periodic coups, assassinations, and massacres in both countries. In 1994, a plane carrying Rwandan president Juvénal Habyarimana and Burundian president Cyprien Ntaryamira—both Hutus—was shot down near Rwanda's Kigali airport. In response, Hutus in Rwanda murdered up to 1 million Tutsis in a 100-day genocide, sparking a humanitarian crisis.

Catalysts for conflict

Corruption and manipulation by those keen to profit from Africa's abundant raw materials, such as oil, cobalt, lithium, diamonds, and gold, remain potent factors in the continent's postcolonial conflicts. Leaders have used their positions to siphon wealth into the pockets of supporters or favored ethnic or tribal groups, perpetuating already high rates of poverty. Private interests, often linked to foreign powers, also vie for control of resources. They demand a major share of profits from, for example, mining, but frequently either ignore or perpetrate collateral violence, exploitation, and environmental damage. The presence of players such as the paramilitary Wagner Group seems unlikely to further Africa's progress toward peace. ∎

ENOUGH OF BLOOD AND TEARS. ENOUGH

THE ARAB-ISRAELI CONFLICTS (1948–)

THE ARAB-ISRAELI CONFLICTS

IN CONTEXT

FOCUS
Two-state solution?

BEFORE
1897 In Basel, Switzerland, the first Zionist Congress launches the Jewish Zionist movement.

1917 The Balfour Declaration states British support for a Jewish homeland in Palestine.

1922 The League of Nations' Mandate for Palestine confirms British control of the territory.

1930s Thousands of European Jews migrate to Palestine as a result of Nazi persecution.

1936–1939 Palestinian Arabs, fearing mass displacement from their homeland, revolt against British control.

1947 As Britain tries to limit illegal Jewish immigration to Palestine, its troops intercept SS *Exodus 1947* and take its Jewish passengers—including many Holocaust survivors—to detention camps in Cyprus.

Since the creation of Israel in 1948, a succession of wars, insurgencies, and armed incursions involving the new state and its neighbours have caused repeated unrest in the Middle East. Tensions had increased from the 1920s, when Western plans for a new Jewish homeland in Arab-populated Palestine began to emerge in response to the tens of thousands of Jewish people fleeing persecution. In 1947, the United Nations (UN) approved the partition of Palestine into two countries (one Jewish and one Arab)—a move that was strongly opposed by Palestinians and all Arab nations.

Israel expands

In May 1948, as British troops left Palestine, the new state of Israel declared its independence, and nearby Arab nations—Egypt, Iraq, Jordan, Lebanon, and Syria—launched an invasion. While the US State Department had embargoed arms sales to Palestine and its Arab neighbors, Czechoslovakia, sanctioned by the USSR, which supported the partition of Palestine, had supplied arms to the newly established Israel Defense Forces (IDF). As a result of this support

Palestine is the cement that holds the Arab world together, or it is the explosive that blows it apart.
Yasser Arafat
PLO leader, 1974

and the lack of coordination and cooperation between the Arab armies, the Israeli forces prevailed and increased their proportion of Palestinian territory from the 55 percent allocated by the UN to 75 percent in 1949. More than 700,000 Palestinians were forced out or fled, a process known as the Nakba ("catastrophe").

War resumes

In 1956, Israel colluded with an ill-fated Franco-British scheme to seize back control of the Suez Canal, which Egyptian president Gamal Abdel Nasser had nationalized. Israeli forces advanced into Gaza and the Sinai Peninsula—both held by Egypt—and gained control of the Straits of Tiran, gateway to the Gulf of Aqaba and the Red Sea. The US forced Israel to withdraw from its newly occupied land, but Israeli ships were subsequently permitted through the straits, which had previously been denied to them.

Many thousands of Palestinians flee their homes after the creation of Israel in 1948, seeking safety in Arab parts of Palestine or neighboring Jordan, Lebanon, and Egypt.

See also: The Ottoman Empire 130–133 ▪ Ottoman decline and Russian expansion 232–233 ▪ An expanding war 252–255 ▪ World War II in Europe 266–271 ▪ The Cold War 286–293 ▪ The Gulf Wars 314–315 ▪ Conflict in Iraq 317

An uneasy peace prevailed until 1966, when Israeli forces responded to incursions by Palestinian guerrillas with violent reprisals, including strikes on Jordan and Syria. By this time, US president Lyndon Johnson had supplied Israel with M48A3 tanks and A-4 Skyhawk aircraft in the belief that a show of military superiority would deter attacks from adjacent Arab powers.

In the event, Israel struck first, in 1967—an "offense is defense" tactic that has often characterized its strategy toward hostile near neighbors. Nasser, in support of Syria, had blocked Israeli access to the Straits of Tiran, which Israel saw as an act of war. It launched what became known as the Six-Day War with crippling, preemptive strikes on Egyptian airfields and Syrian planes. Jordan entered the fight, attacking West Jerusalem, but Israel drove out its forces and took much of the West Bank.

By the end of the war, Israel had complete control of Jerusalem and occupied 100 percent of the prepartition territory of Palestine, as well as Egypt's Sinai Peninsula and the Golan Heights, taken from Syria to the north. In November 1967, the UN passed Resolution 242, which acknowledged Israel's right to live in peace but called for it to withdraw from its newly occupied territory. Israel did not comply and, as a consequence, had more than a million additional, embittered Palestinians under its rule.

In the wake of the crushing defeat of Arab forces, the Palestine Liberation Organization (PLO), a militant nationalist faction formed in 1964, became more prominent. After initial attacks on Israel and Western targets, the PLO gained international legitimacy under Yasser Arafat—the leader from 1969—achieving UN observer status in 1974 and full membership of the Arab League in 1976.

US and Soviet involvement

Hostilities between Israel and Egypt, which by now had support from the USSR, had continued along the Suez Canal after 1967. Nasser died in 1970, but his successor as Egyptian president, Anwar Sadat, remained determined to regain the Sinai Peninsula. When Israel rejected a peaceful solution, Sadat devised a military strategy acting in concert with Syria, Jordan, and Iraq. The resulting conflict—the Yom Kippur War—began on October 6, 1973, when Syria attacked the Golan Heights while Egypt advanced across the Suez Canal into the Sinai Peninsula, rebuffing an Israeli counterattack. The USSR was arming both Egypt and Syria, to the alarm of the US, which began airlifting weapons to Israel, with the first arriving on October 14.

As the IDF regained ground, Sadat pressed for a resolution. US secretary of state Henry Kissinger flew to Moscow in a bid to secure a ceasefire, which the UN adopted on October 23. Israel, however, was still pursuing victory in the Sinai Peninsula, prompting a Soviet threat to send troops to Egypt to enforce the ceasefire. In response, »

In the Six-Day War, Israeli soldiers advance on East Jerusalem, then held by Jordan as part of the West Bank. Since the war's end, all of Jerusalem has been under Israeli rule.

THE ARAB-ISRAELI CONFLICTS

Hanan Ashrawi

Born in Nablus, Palestine (now the West Bank), in 1946, Hanan Mikhail, as she then was, settled with her family in Ramallah in 1950. Her father, physician Daoud Mikhail, a founding member of the PLO, encouraged her education. She studied at the American University of Beirut, became active in Palestinian politics, and worked in refugee camps. She completed her studies in the US, returning to the West Bank as a professor and later dean at Birzeit University, before its closure in 1988 during the First Intifada.

At the same time, Ashrawi came to worldwide attention as an articulate and passionate advocate for Palestinian rights. In 1991, she was appointed as the Palestinian delegation's spokesperson at the peace talks that led to the Oslo Accords and later worked with the Palestinian Authority. In 2003, she was awarded the Sydney Peace Prize.

Disillusioned with the PLO, in 2005 Ashrawi set up Third Way, an alternative to the Fatah party and Hamas. Ashrawi continues to advocate for a two-state solution that safeguards the rights of both Israelis and Palestinians.

on October 25, the US put its nuclear forces on worldwide alert; within the day, Israel had accepted a revised UN resolution. Its forces had gained another victory, but the confrontation between the US and the USSR now emphasized the much wider implications of the conflict, as did the imposition of oil embargoes by oil-producing Arab states against countries that supported Israel. In 1979, Israel and Egypt signed a peace deal and the Sinai Peninsula was returned to Egypt in 1982.

Meanwhile, PLO guerrillas were sporadically attacking Israel, mainly from southern Lebanon. In June 1982, Israel's IDF invaded the country, ostensibly to create a "security zone" on the Lebanese side of the border. It paused in Lebanon's Bekaa Valley to destroy Syrian anti-aircraft missile batteries used to thwart its attacks on PLO targets, then pressed on to West Beirut.

Atrocities occurred along the way. The massacre of Palestinian refugees in the Sabra and Shatila camps by the Phalange, a Lebanese Christian militia under the auspices of the IDF, in mid-September caused international outrage, prompting the US to send in Marines as part of a multinational peacekeeping force. The IDF finally withdrew from Beirut in September 1983. The following month, 241 American troops were killed in Beirut by suicide bombers with suspected links to Syria's ally Iran. Israel kept forces in southern Lebanon until 2000, often clashing with Hezbollah, a Shia militia force, which in 2006 crossed into Israel and took two Israeli soldiers hostage. Israel invaded Lebanon again. A 34-day war erupted and left more than 1,000 Lebanese civilians dead.

Intifadas and Gaza

Most of Israel's wars had been waged with Arab neighbors, often on their soil. However, since it had occupied Gaza and the West Bank, Israel had faced almost continuous Palestinian opposition that flared up periodically into crises known as intifadas, from the Arabic for

Fighting breaks out in the West Bank town of Ramallah in 2000 during the Second Intifada. The violence was prompted by the death of a 14-year-old boy, killed in clashes with Israeli troops.

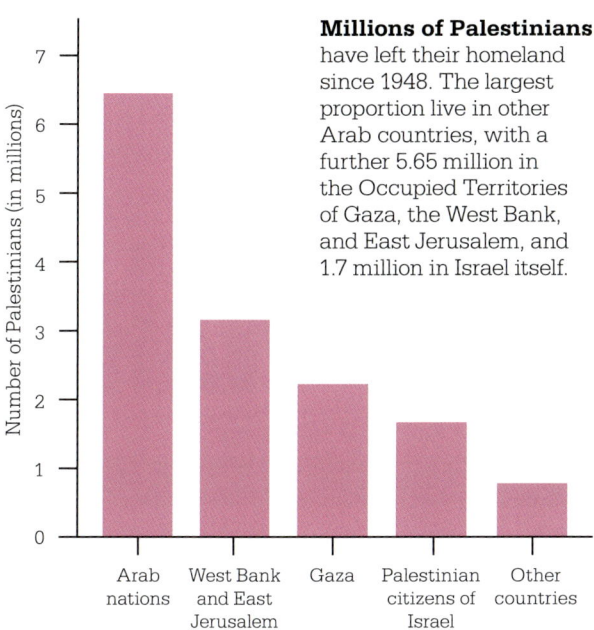

Millions of Palestinians have left their homeland since 1948. The largest proportion live in other Arab countries, with a further 5.65 million in the Occupied Territories of Gaza, the West Bank, and East Jerusalem, and 1.7 million in Israel itself.

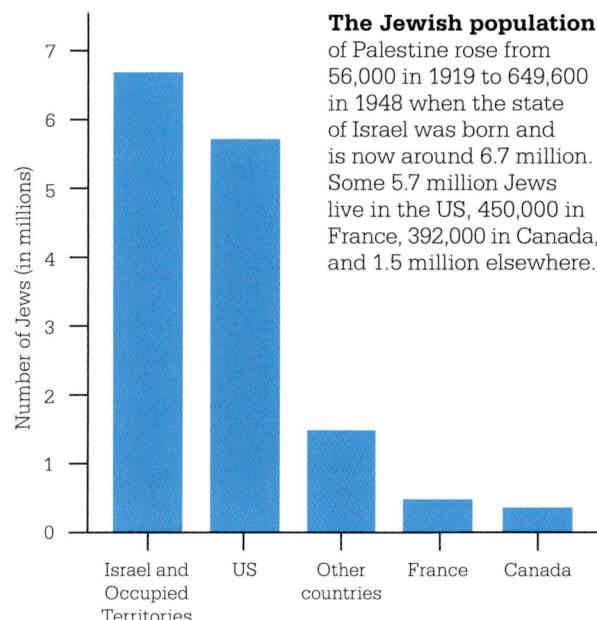

The Jewish population of Palestine rose from 56,000 in 1919 to 649,600 in 1948 when the state of Israel was born and is now around 6.7 million. Some 5.7 million Jews live in the US, 450,000 in France, 392,000 in Canada, and 1.5 million elsewhere.

"uprising." The First Palestinian Intifada (1987–1993) involved protests, strikes and other civil disobedience, and violence—from stone throwing to suicide bombs. Israel's military response led to the deaths of more than 1,000 Palestinians, while around 160 Israelis were killed.

Despite or perhaps because of the troubles, Palestinian and Israeli leaders moved toward a diplomatic settlement, with international backing. Peace talks began in 1991, with Hanan Ashrawi heading the Palestinian delegation. The resulting 1993 Oslo Accords between PLO leader Yasser Arafat and Israeli prime minister Yitzhak Rabin set out the path toward a two-state solution in which most of the West Bank and the Gaza Strip would return to Palestinian control, as a prelude to full statehood. However, crucial issues, such as the right of return of refugees and the status of Jerusalem, were not settled, which undermined the chances of a durable peace, as did the assassination of Rabin by a Jewish extremist in 1995.

In 2000, after the breakdown of further peace talks, for which each side blamed the other, a Second Intifada flared up, lasting until 2005. That year, Israel withdrew its forces from the Gaza Strip and evacuated its settlements, leaving a power vacuum, which the militant Islamist group Hamas quickly filled. In 2006, Hamas surprisingly beat the

We must share this land as one state or two states or five states. Otherwise, we will share this same piece of land as the graveyards of our kids.
Bassam Aramin
Combatants for Peace
2023

previously dominant Fatah political party to win a majority of seats in the Palestinian Legislative Council (PLC) and seized power in Gaza in 2007, prompting crippling blockades from both Egypt and Israel. Over the next 16 years, multiple cycles of Hamas assaults and retaliatory and preemptive Israeli raids followed.

On October 7, 2023, Hamas and other Palestinian groups in Gaza launched a ruthless, surprise attack on southern Israel, killing at least 1,200 people and taking more than 240 hostages. Israel retaliated with a massive and ongoing assault on Gaza, destroying its infrastructure and killing tens of thousands of people. Tensions with Hezbollah escalated, leading to Israeli forces bombing targets in southern Lebanon and assassinating Hassan Nasrallah, the Hezbollah leader, in September 2024. A two-state solution seems further away than ever, although many Palestinians, Israelis, and other powers still believe that it is the only viable path to a just, lasting peace. ■

THERE WAS A GOOD WAR ... AND A BAD WAR
CONFLICT IN AFGHANISTAN (1979–2021)

IN CONTEXT

FOCUS
Supporting the mujahideen

BEFORE
1921 Afghanistan wins independence from Britain after the Third Afghan War.

1950s Zahir Shah, king of Afghanistan, receives Soviet funding for his country's infrastructure and builds his army with Soviet help.

1973 Mohammad Daoud Khan deposes Zahir Shah in a bloodless coup and becomes Afghanistan's first president.

AFTER
2022 A suicide bombing claimed by Islamic State (IS) kills six people, including two Russians, at the Russian Embassy in Kabul.

2023 The UN Assistance Mission in Afghanistan (UNAMA) documents scores of illegal killings, arrests, and torture of detainees since 2021.

In April 1978, Mohammad Daoud Khan, Afghanistan's president, was killed in a communist-led coup. Tensions between Khan's government and the Marxist-Leninist People's Democratic Party of Afghanistan (PDPA) had escalated, and the PDPA had taken control of Afghan forces. After a period of repression, unrest, and instability, the USSR invaded Afghanistan—to support the pro-communist government. To counter the Soviet influence, the US Central Intelligence Agency (CIA) worked with neighboring Pakistan to arm and fund resistance fighters—the Afghan mujahideen, who were variously motivated by Islamic fervor, nationalism, opportunism, and anti-communism. Among the mujahideen was Osama bin Laden, later to found the Islamic terrorist group al-Qaeda.

A losing battle

Tens of thousands of Soviet troops, flown into Kabul, the Afghan capital, took control of the city and portions of the country in December 1979. Although heavily armed with fighter bombers, helicopters, and tanks, the Soviet forces struggled to operate in Afghanistan's rugged, mountainous terrain, which had historically made the country so difficult to unify or conquer. Scorched-earth tactics and persistent bombing of guerrilla mountain strongholds only hardened the mujahideen's resolve. The CIA's covert program, called Operation Cyclone, also armed the group with

A Soviet tank crew prepare to leave Afghanistan in April 1988. The next month, Afghanistan, the US, and the USSR signed an agreement to end foreign intervention in the country.

THE WORLD WARS AND BEYOND 313

See also: The rise of Islam 76–81 ▪ Mughal conquests in India 140–141 ▪ The British conquest of India 225 ▪ The Cold War 286–293 ▪ Conflict in Iraq 317

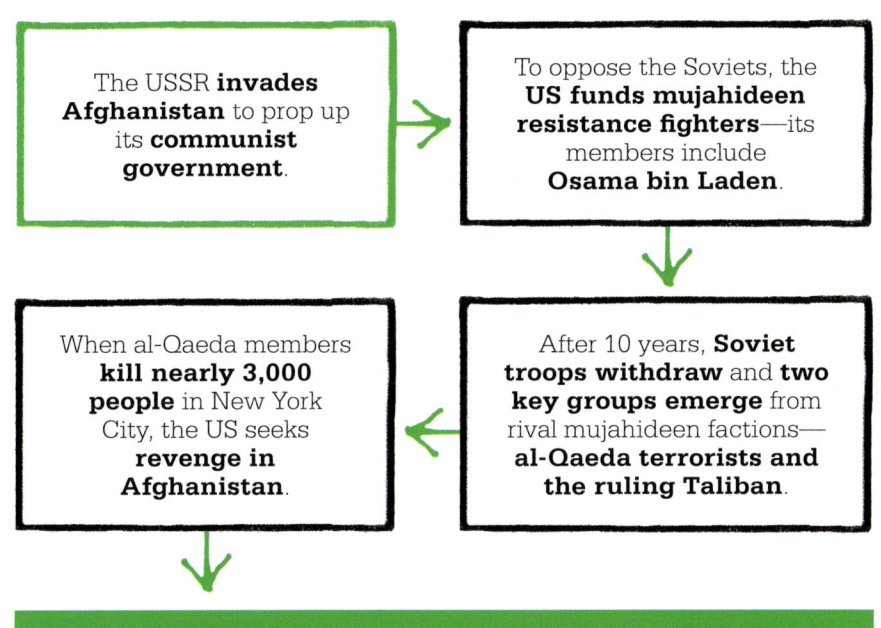

The USSR **invades Afghanistan** to prop up its **communist government**.

To oppose the Soviets, the **US funds mujahideen resistance fighters**—its members include **Osama bin Laden**.

After 10 years, **Soviet troops withdraw** and **two key groups emerge** from rival mujahideen factions—**al-Qaeda terrorists and the ruling Taliban**.

When al-Qaeda members **kill nearly 3,000 people** in New York City, the US seeks **revenge in Afghanistan**.

In 2021, US and other Western troops withdraw, and the Taliban returns.

the latest American equipment and weaponry, including Stinger missiles to bring down the Soviet Mi-24D helicopter gunships widely used to bomb the guerrillas.

The unexpected length of the costly war contributed to the USSR's economic problems. In 1989, Soviet leader Mikhail Gorbachev ordered the withdrawal of Soviet troops.

Fighting the Taliban
The mujahideen extended its influence, but rivalries developed among its different factions, including the Taliban, which took power in 1996 and imposed strict Islamic sharia law. The Taliban's aims were regional, unlike the wider ambitions of bin Laden's al-Qaeda, which began to plan strikes from its Afghan base against the US, including the 9/11 attacks in 2001.

In October 2001, the US launched Operation Enduring Freedom to avenge the al-Qaeda assaults and to capture bin Laden in his Afghan sanctuary. By December, US forces and their Western allies had toppled the Taliban regime, but they then failed to defeat its supporters in the countryside and build effective democratic institutions.

Bin Laden was found and killed in 2011, and in 2013 the role of coalition forces in Afghanistan shifted to security, training, and counterterrorism. They remained, however, mired in an endless cycle of mujahideen guerrilla attacks, and by 2021 the Afghan government had collapsed. The Taliban took charge, and coalition forces ended their involvement, evacuating more than 120,000 troops and allied personnel. ∎

Operation Neptune Spear

In 2011, the US finally cornered architect of the 9/11 attacks Osama bin Laden. Informant evidence, wiretaps, and observation from drones confirmed that a man who fitted bin Laden's description regularly paced around—but never left—a walled residence in Abbottabad, northeast Pakistan, and was visited by al-Qaeda couriers. An airstrike on the compound in its densely populated area was dismissed as unviable as its force could also make identification of a body difficult.

Instead, a group of US Navy SEALs (special-operations troops) rehearsed a carefully planned raid—Operation Neptune Spear—at mock sites in North Carolina and the Nevada desert. On May 1, without informing Pakistan's government, whose secrecy was not trusted, the SEALs were flown in at night from Afghanistan by Black Hawk helicopter. They secured the compound in 40 minutes, shooting dead bin Laden, a woman, and three men, before escaping with bin Laden's body—later fully identified and buried at sea.

Osama bin Laden sits in the library of his Tora Bora cave hideout in the mountains of eastern Afghanistan around 2001.

DEEP ATTACK AND DECISIVE MANEUVER
THE GULF WARS (1980–1991)

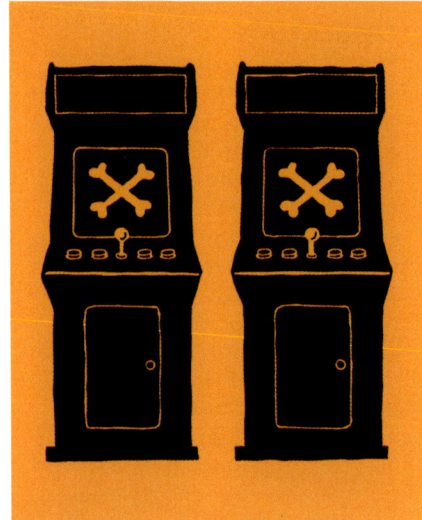

IN CONTEXT

FOCUS
AirLand Battle

BEFORE
1976 US military consultant John Boyd delivers his "Patterns of Conflict" briefing. This forms the basis of the AirLand Battle strategy adopted six years later.

1979 The Iranian revolution brings Ayatollah Ruhollah Khomeini to power.

1979 Saddam Hussein becomes president of Iraq.

AFTER
2001 The US Army adopts Full Spectrum Operations as its primary battle plan.

2014 US president Barack Obama announces the return of US aerial forces to Iraq to combat Islamic State (IS).

2021 US president Joe Biden concludes his nation's combat mission in Iraq, pulling out most of the American troops.

After the withdrawal of British military forces from the Gulf states in 1971, local conflicts that the British had once arbitrated began to resurface, exacerbated by disputes over areas with oil deposits. While the bitter Iran–Iraq War of 1980–1988 was largely a battle over borders, the Gulf War of 1990–1991, when Iraq invaded Kuwait, was a squabble over oil production—and the US intervened. Kuwait's terrain and situation presented an ideal opportunity for the US Army to employ AirLand Battle concepts, defined by the American military in 1986 as focusing on unity of effort, targeting enemy vulnerabilities, and anticipating battlefield events.

In 1980, Saddam Hussein sent Iraqi troops to attack Iran's western border, taking advantage of the nation's instability after its 1979 revolution. He hoped to regain land conceded in the 1970s and wanted to preempt any unrest that Iran's new Shi'ite regime could spark in Iraq. After initial success, his troops were beaten back. Iran insisted on pursuing its advantage, but on its home soil Iraq fared better. The

Disputes in the oil-rich Gulf

When Britain pulled its troops out of the Gulf in 1971, the political landscape quickly changed. In August, Bahrain became independent, and Qatar followed in September. Abu Dhabi, Dubai, Sharjah, and four other emirates formed the United Arab Emirates (UAE) in December. The emirates had ruled three islands—Abu Musa and the Greater and Lesser Tunbs—in the Persian Gulf's Strait of Hormuz, a strategically important waterway that most oil tankers in the area pass through. In November 1971, Iran sent its navy to seize the islands. Despite UAE protests, Iran still controls them.

From 1974 to 1975, Iran and Iraq fought over Iran's support for an independent Iraqi Kurdish state. Tensions also resurfaced between the UAE and Saudi Arabia over the oil-rich Buraimi Oasis on the border of Oman and the UAE. A 1974 treaty was designed to settle the issue, but the dispute rumbles on.

THE WORLD WARS AND BEYOND 315

See also: Mesopotamia and Ancient Egypt 18–21 ▪ Persia 23 ▪ The rise of Islam 76–81 ▪ The Crusades 88–93
▪ An expanding war 252–255 ▪ The Arab-Israeli conflicts 306–311 ▪ Conflict in Afghanistan 312–313 ▪ Conflict in Iraq 317

Destroyed Iraqi tanks litter the desert after the US air strikes that prefaced Desert Storm and killed up to 12,000 Iraqi troops. As many as 100,000 Iraqis died in the ground war.

conflict became a protracted, bloody stalemate as Iran sent in untrained conscripts and Iraq unleashed chemical weapons. Despite this, Western regimes armed Saddam, fearing an Iranian victory. Fighting continued until a UN-brokered ceasefire in 1988.

AirLand Battle in operation

In August 1990, Saddam's troops invaded Kuwait. After months of diplomacy to force Iraq to withdraw, the US launched Operation Desert Storm in January 1991. An initial six-week bombing campaign was followed by a short but brutal 100-hour land campaign, in which coalition forces under US command destroyed most of the Iraqi army and had Saddam at their mercy. Fears of destabilizing the Iraqi regime led the US to halt the war, leaving Saddam still in charge.

Our strategy to go after this [Iraqi] army is very simple. First we are going to cut it off, and then we're going to kill it.
Colin Powell
US general
Pentagon press briefing, 1991

The AirLand Battle doctrine the US Army followed was a successor to the Active Defense doctrine of 1979, both developed in the context of a possible war with the USSR in Europe. Active Defense focused on activities at the front line, while AirLand Battle anticipated the battlefield, with the use of advance airpower to degrade the enemy's capabilities and destroy reserve and reinforcement units deep inside enemy territory. A subsequent combined air and land operation, using advanced technology such as powerful mobile armor and attack helicopters, could then punch through front lines and create havoc across a deep battlefield area.

Under US commander Norman Schwarzkopf's direction, advance helicopters launched missiles and rockets to clear out air defense installations in Kuwait, opening an air corridor through which fighter planes, cruise missiles, and other weapons destroyed a huge range of targets. Next, Schwarzkopf launched a classic encirclement operation, drawing Iraqi attention to the south while a mobile armor force swung around from the west. Ground-attack airpower then devastated Iraqi formations attempting to retreat.

Full Spectrum Operations

By 2003, when the US and Britain invaded Iraq in the Iraq War, the role of overwhelming military power and advanced weapons technology formed part of a new American battlefield doctrine called Full Spectrum Operations. Employed by the US-led coalition forces, the strategy succeeded in quickly deposing Saddam, but its other objectives, such as building new infrastructure and establishing a stable government, were never fully realized before American troops withdrew at the end of 2011. ▪

THIS CONFLAGRATION WILL SPREAD
POST-COMMUNIST WARS (1991–)

IN CONTEXT

FOCUS
Russia's Caucasus strategy

BEFORE
1817–1864 In various brutal conflicts, Russia conquers the peoples of the Caucasus.

1922 Following each nation's brief independence after World War I, Armenia, Georgia, and Azerbaijan are grouped together as Transcaucasia, a republic under Soviet control.

1936 Armenia, Georgia, and Azerbaijan become separate republics under the USSR's second constitution.

1988 Violence erupts in the mainly Armenian enclave of Nagorno-Karabakh, Azerbaijan, as Armenia seeks to reclaim it.

1989 In Tbilisi, the Soviet Army kills unarmed Georgian independence protesters.

1989 Azerbaijan imposes a blockade on Armenia that devastates its economy.

The collapse of the USSR in 1991 resulted in a series of conflicts in regions ranging from the Balkans to Central Asia, as different ethnic, nationalist, and sectarian groups competed for dominance. Russia's primary focus was and remains its strategy in the Caucasus, where it seeks to preserve its historic influence and strengthen political and economic ties in the resource-rich but volatile region.

Politics and muscle

Lying between the Caspian Sea and the Black Sea on the Europe–Asia border, the Caucasus includes the nations of Georgia, Armenia, and Azerbaijan. After the breakup of the USSR, declining Russian power unleashed intense volatility in areas that had long resented Soviet rule. In the North Caucasus, Russia fought two long and bloody wars (1994–1996 and 1999–2009) to suppress the predominantly Islamic people of Chechnya.

Russia has also played South Caucasus neighbors Azerbaijan and Armenia off against each other by arming both. In 1992, Armenian separatists seized the Armenian-populated enclave of Nagorno-Karabakh in Azerbaijan. Peace brokered by Russia largely held until 2020, when Azerbaijan took the territory back in a violent conflict that Russia did not oppose, though it again played peacemaker.

Georgia's desire post-1991 to align with Europe upset Russia, which invaded it in 2008. Russia still strongly deters Western influence. ■

The North Caucasus ... which post-Soviet Russia sees as key to the integrity of the Russian state.
Philip Remler
former US diplomat, 2020

See also: Conflict in the Balkans 236–237 ▪ The Russian Civil War 262–263 ▪ The Cold War 286–293 ▪ The Russian invasion of Ukraine 318–321

THE WORLD WARS AND BEYOND

CORRUPTION IS MORE DANGEROUS THAN TERRORISM
CONFLICT IN IRAQ (2003–2011, 2014–2019)

IN CONTEXT

FOCUS
The rise of radical Islam

BEFORE
1989 Soviet forces withdraw from Afghanistan, driven out by the radical Islamist mujahideen whose numbers include al-Qaeda founder, Osama bin Laden.

1991 The US and its allies expel Iraqi forces from Kuwait in the Gulf War.

2001 Islamist terrorists perpetrate the 9/11 attacks on targets in the US.

AFTER
2019 US-supported Syrian forces defeat IS fighters at the Battle of Baghuz Fawqani in Syria, marking the end of IS as a territorial entity.

2023 The Global Terrorism Index states that, in 2022, IS and its affiliates remained the deadliest terrorist group for the eighth successive year, with attacks in 21 countries.

In the aftermath of the 9/11 attacks in 2001, US president George W. Bush highlighted the threat of hostile nations. His first target was Saddam Hussein's regime in Iraq, said to be hiding "weapons of mass destruction" (WMDs), including chemical and nuclear devices, in defiance of UN resolutions. Coalition forces, mainly American and British, invaded in March 2003 and quickly overcame Iraqi resistance. Bush declared major combat operations over by the beginning of May.

Breeding ground for terror

The occupation of Iraq by the US and its attempts to construct a stable government proved far more problematic. American, British, and Iraqi troops battled insurgencies from Islamic militia, bringing about widespread destruction and misery for the Iraqi people. Divisions between Sunni and Shia Muslims increased, corruption thrived, and radical Islam spread amid the chaos. Opinion in the US now favored withdrawal, and most of the British troops left in 2009. When the US reduced troop numbers in the early 2010s, it left a power vacuum, soon exploited by Islamic State (IS). In 2014, IS overran much of Iraq and areas of neighboring territories, declaring a caliphate—a strictly religious Islamic state. A five-year struggle to destroy IS as a territorial force ended in Syria in 2019, but its violent ideology had by then been exported to Sub-Saharan Africa, Central Asia, and Indonesia. ∎

An Iraqi woman and children flee Basra, southern Iraq, as elements of the British Army head toward the burning city in March 2003.

See also: The rise of Islam 76–81 ▪ An expanding war 252–255 ▪ The Arab-Israeli conflicts 306–311 ▪ Conflict in Afghanistan 312–313 ▪ The Gulf Wars 314–315

THE FIRST DRONE WAR
THE RUSSIAN INVASION OF UKRAINE (2022–)

IN CONTEXT

FOCUS
Drone warfare

BEFORE
1917 The first radio-controlled unmanned aircraft—the Aerial Target—is tested in Britain.

1964–1975 The US Air Force AQM-34 Firebee drone flies more than 34,000 surveillance missions over Southeast Asia.

1982 Israeli Air Force drones play a key reconnaissance role in the destruction of Syrian air defenses in the Lebanon War.

1991 Ukraine declares its independence following the collapse of the USSR.

2001 A US Predator drone fires a Hellfire tactical missile at a target in Afghanistan—the first armed UAV attack.

2019 Iranian-made Shahed "kamikaze" drones hit two Saudi oil installations.

In February 2022, Russia invaded Ukraine, unleashing a brutal and enduring war combining old-fashioned attritional fighting—with infantry attacks, supported by tanks and heavy artillery—and combat driven by modern technology, such as long-range missiles, cyberattacks, and unmanned aerial vehicles (UAVs), or "drones." Russian president Vladimir Putin expected Ukraine to rapidly collapse, but his optimism was unfounded.

A resurgent Russia
Russian claims on Ukraine date back more than 1,000 years. After the USSR collapsed in 1991, Russian

THE WORLD WARS AND BEYOND

See also: The Crimean War 206–207 ▪ Ottoman decline and Russian expansion 232–233 ▪ The Russian Civil War 262–263 ▪ World War II in Europe 266–271 ▪ The Cold War 286–293 ▪ Post-communist wars 316

An engine from a downed Russian jet fighter lies in a residential area of Chernihiv in northern Ukraine, in April 2022. Russia lost close to 300 aircraft in the first month of the war.

leaders watched in trepidation as former Soviet states and satellites, such as Poland, Hungary, and Latvia, sought to guarantee their future security by joining the North Atlantic Treaty Organization (NATO). Putin—president from 2000—fueled the sense of betrayal and resolved to restore Russia's dominance in what he saw as its rightful sphere of influence.

Putin set his sights on Ukrainian territory, and in 2014 annexed the strategically important Crimea peninsula and seized territory in the Donbas region. The full-scale invasion of Ukraine in 2022 was the most aggressive military action in Europe since World War II.

The battle for Kyiv

With up to 190,000 troops amassed in Belarus on the northern Ukraine border, Putin hoped to seize the capital, Kyiv, and quickly neutralize the Ukraine government. The plan depended on initial deception—attacking in the south and east to divert Ukrainian forces away from Kyiv, while striking at the city and seizing the key Antonov and Vasylkiv airfields. Putin expected to control and annex the country within 10 days.

With Ukrainian forces vastly outnumbered, the deception appeared to work at first, but events soon turned against the invaders. The Russian advance was slowed down by fierce resistance from the Ukrainian Armed Forces (UAF), who since 2014 had benefited from NATO-aided training and stocks of weaponry supplied by the West. Russian paratroops seized the Antonov and Vasylkiv airfields, but only after fierce fighting prevented the landing of vital reinforcements and supplies. Russian attacks were then either brought to a standstill or beaten back.

A grinding war of attrition

Lacking any backup plan for such a slow advance, Russian forces mostly withdrew from northern Ukraine, concentrating instead on the east and south. There, they resorted to more traditional warfare, using massed artillery to bombard opposition areas and unleashing huge numbers of infantry troops, an approach that led to casualty rates up to six times higher than those of the Ukrainian army.

Russian forces took the key southern port of Mariupol in May 2022, but their slow progress was thrown into reverse by a Ukrainian counterattack from September 2022, which relieved pressure on the beleaguered cities of Kharkiv in the northeast and Kherson in the south. One of the few places where Russia remained on the offensive was in and around the eastern city of Bakhmut, the scene, from August 2022, of a 10-month street-by-street struggle—the bloodiest infantry battle since World War II, claiming up to 100,000 Russian casualties.

To spearhead the assault on Bakhmut, Putin, frustrated by the failures of his conventional forces, »

Every day, every meter is given by blood.
Valerii Zaluzhnyi
Ukrainian general
The Washington Post, June 2023

turned to the mercenary soldiers of the Wagner Group, a paramilitary organization founded by Russian businessman Yevgeny Prigozhin. Wagner troops—many recruited from prisons—were generally better organized, equipped, and led than the Russian army. Bakhmut was eventually taken but at the cost of around 20,000 Wagner soldiers.

Reaching stalemate

Following a massive conscription program in fall 2022, which recruited 200,000 more troops, the Russians were able to stabilize their lines. Exploiting delays in Ukrainian efforts to rearm and upgrade their forces, the Russians built deep defenses, enabling them to frustrate a Ukrainian offensive in June 2023. In particular, they took advantage in late 2023 of a six-month delay in US government approval of a new round of military support for Ukraine.

By February 2024, Ukrainian forces were rationed to firing just 2,000 artillery rounds per day, compared to the 10,000 rounds fired daily by the Russians. That same month, Russian forces seized the industrial city of Avdiivka, capital of the heavily industrialized Donbas region in southeastern Ukraine and the first significant Russian gain since Bakhmut.

The belated arrival of aid for Ukraine from the US—part of a $61 billion package—stabilized the situation, but Russia continued to take advantage of its greater air power and bombing resources, using a variety of missiles, bombs, and guided munitions to target Ukrainian infrastructure and cities. Facing an extended conflict, and with sanctions and blockades affecting its ability to produce high-tech weapons, Russia turned to relatively low-cost but still devastating military strategies. These included fitting wings and satellite navigation to its huge stockpile of "dumb bombs" to turn them into smart, highly destructive "glide bombs," and, above all, using mass drone attacks.

A Ukrainian emergency services worker helps evacuate a woman from Toretsk, an industrial city in the Donetsk region, under heavy fire from Russian forces in July 2024.

Drone power

The term "drone" describes a range of technology, from basic off-the-shelf consumer units to AI-enabled craft capable of making in-flight decisions. First designed for target practice and then reconnaissance missions, drones have since the early 2000s been equipped to carry explosives and hit enemy targets, guided by remote control and satellite navigation.

Thousands of drones have been launched in the Ukraine war. On the front line, each side routinely uses first-person view (FPV) drones to spot enemy formations and artillery, guide counterstrikes, and attack infantry and vehicles. FPV drones include small commercially available models to which an explosive device is attached.

Yevgeny Prigozhin

Born in St. Petersburg in 1961, Yevgeny Prigozhin left school at 16 and fell into a life of petty crime, including fraud and burglary, spending nine years in prison. After his release in 1990, he entered the catering business, moving from selling hot dogs to running a chain of restaurants, where he mixed with the St. Petersburg elite, including Vladimir Putin. This earned him the nickname "Putin's chef."

A wealthy and shrewd businessman, Prigozhin took advantage of the Russian invasion of Crimea to found the private mercenary army Wagner Group, which fought in the Donbas region of Ukraine from April 2014 and extended its activities into Africa and Syria. Prigozhin also created one of the world's biggest internet "troll farms," disseminating pro-Russian propaganda and interfering in Western elections. The Ukraine war further elevated his profile, but his increasingly vocal antipathy toward the Russian military drove him to launch a coup against Putin in June 2023. Prigozhin died in a mysterious plane crash two months later.

THE WORLD WARS AND BEYOND

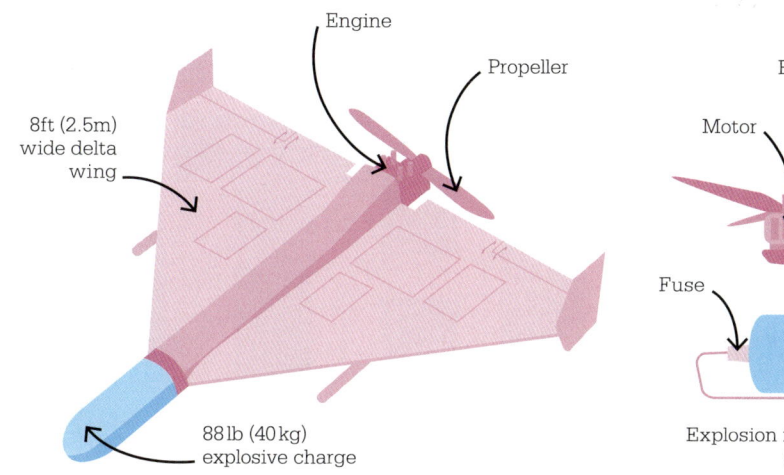

The Shahed-136 drone is 11.5 ft (3.5 m) long, delta-winged, and weighs around 440 lb (200 kg). It can carry a high-explosive warhead up to 1,550 miles (2,500 km), at a fraction of the cost of a guided missile.

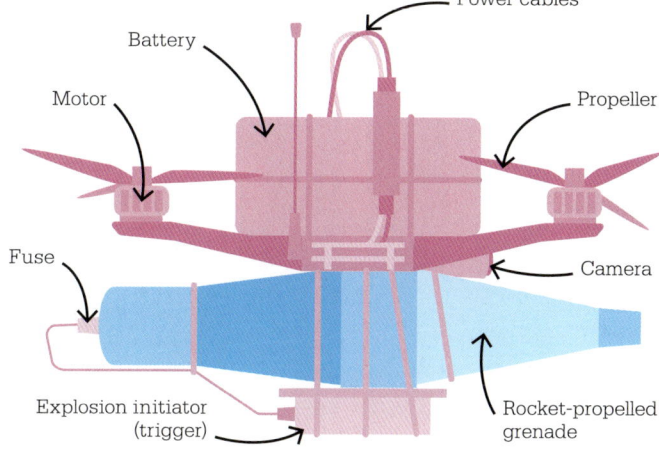

The battlefront FPV drone has a range of up to 12.5 miles (20 km) and is operated by a soldier on the ground using a remote-control unit or laptop computer and a headset linked to the drone's camera.

Russia and Ukraine also send an ever-increasing variety of explosive-laden drones into each other's territory. By February 2024, Russia had used more than 4,600 Iranian-designed Shahed-136 "kamikaze" drones against Ukraine. Their slow top speed of 115 mph (186 km/h)—and the increasingly effective use of radar and sensors to locate drones—mean that 75–95 percent of Shaheds are shot down. However, even if only a small number get through, they can still wreak havoc.

Drones have brought new dimensions to warfare. Their relatively low cost—as little as $20,000 to produce a long-range drone, compared to as much as $500,000 for a surface-to-air missile—allows forces with limited funds to drain the resources of a much richer adversary. Drones can also be deployed far more quickly than piloted aircraft or artillery batteries, and their ability to stop, hover, and change direction while seeking out a target injects a new level of terror into the battlefront.

Breaking the deadlock

By summer 2024, the Ukraine front lines remained largely unchanged. Then, on August 6, 2024, Ukraine surprised its allies—and Russia—by attacking the Kursk region, in the first invasion of Russian territory since World War II. Despite the attack's success, Russian forces continued to advance in the east. After 18 months and an estimated 500,000 Russian casualties, an end to the war still seemed far off, as Ukraine and Russia poured ever more soldiers, missiles, and drones into the bitter conflict. ∎

A Ukrainian soldier prepares to pilot an FPV drone loaded with explosives. By March 2024, the Ukrainian army was launching around 50,000 FPVs a month.

DIRECTO

RY

DIRECTORY

The history of warfare dates back millennia, as rock art and other archaeological evidence testify. This book traces its development over 4,500 years, examining a broad range of conflicts from across the world in detail, while others are more briefly described below. Each entry outlines the triggers for war, which have varied remarkably little over time. Nations fight for land, wealth, power, and resources. The oppressed revolt and fight back, ethnic groups clash, and the defense or advancement of religious beliefs sparks violence. However, industrialization and new technology have radically changed the nature of modern warfare. Armies still fight on the ground, but tactics are increasingly informed by military intelligence, and lethal weapons can be remotely and distantly controlled.

CELTIC INVASION OF THE BALKANS
(281 BCE)

The Celtic civilization emerged in the 1st millennium BCE in central Europe then expanded north and west. From 281 BCE, Celts advanced southeast into the Balkans, which had suffered unrest since the death of Alexander the Great in 323 BCE. A huge force swept through Thrace into northern Greece, sacking the shrine of Delphi in 279 BCE, before the Greeks repelled them. Some Celts pushed east into Asia Minor as raiders, then mercenaries for local kings, finally settling in a highland area of present-day Türkiye, later called Galatia.

MACCABAEAN REVOLT
(167–63 BCE)

In 167 BCE, Palestinian Jews under the Hellenistic rule of Seleucid monarch Antiochus IV revolted. They rebelled against the king's suppression of Jewish culture and sacred rituals, and his introduction of Greek rites in their Temple of Jerusalem. Among them was Judas, nicknamed Maccabeus ("the hammer") for his militancy, who became the rebel leader. The insurrection spread, and in 164 BCE, Jewish rites in the Temple were restored. Maccabean successors of Judas extended their territory and achieved political independence, creating a kingdom in 104 BCE, which lasted until the Romans took over Palestine in 63 BCE.

ROME'S SERVILE WARS
(135–32 BCE, 104–100 BCE, 73–71 BCE)

From 135 BCE, the discontent often simmering under Roman rule at times boiled over. Much of it arose among the Republic's slaves, the *servi* whose forced labor had largely built Rome's prosperity. In 135 BCE, there were major uprisings in Sicily and in Cilicia, western Türkiye, and further unrest followed in 104 BCE, again in Sicily. In 73 BCE, Spartacus, a slave and gladiator, led a large uprising on the mainland, which, before its final suppression, threatened Rome itself.

GOGURYEO–SUI WAR
(598–614 CE)

After uniting China in 589 CE, the Sui dynasty sought to extend its northeastern region into Goguryeo, the largest, most northern of Korea's Three Kingdoms (the other two being Silla and Baekje). In 598, a 300,000-strong Sui army invaded Goguryeo but became bogged down in mud from heavy rains. After this, the Sui sent out its naval force, which was also defeated. The Sui took time to plan and consolidate their strength—even constructing the Grand Canal to transport soldiers and supplies—before mounting a major land and sea attack in 612, yet this, too, was finally repelled.

THE RISE OF KHMER
(802–1431)

The kingdom of Khmer rose out of Chenla, a region of rival dominions in what is now Cambodia, during the reign of Jayavarman II (r. 802–835). He made Indrapura his capital and fought rival kingdoms to establish Cambodia as the dominant power in Southeast Asia. His successors extended the empire and built impressive temples and palace complexes around the later capital Angkor, among them Angkor Wat, a Buddhist temple constructed by Suryavarman II in the 12th century. The capture of Angkor by the forces of Thailand's Ayutthaya kingdom in 1431 ended Khmer supremacy.

GORYEO-KHITAN WARS
(993–1019)

By 936, Wang Kon, king of Goryeo (formerly Goguryeo), had succeeded in uniting Korea's Three Kingdoms and had also extended Goryeo's boundaries to the north, bringing him into conflict with the Liao dynasty, descended from the nomadic Khitan tribes of what are now Manchuria and Mongolia. The Liao launched frequent raids, and in 993, an army of 800,000 invaded Goryeo. The result was indecisive, but the Liao invaded again in 1009 and 1018. Both sides recognized by 1019 that neither could win a conclusive victory. They agreed to a peace treaty in 1022.

EDWARD I'S CONQUESTS OF WALES AND SCOTLAND
(1282–1296)

When, in 1282, Prince of Wales Llywelyn ap Gruffudd refused to pay homage to Edward I of England, the king invaded Wales and imposed his authority by force. He ringed the north of the country with castles and installed English colonists to keep the peace. Scotland had been an independent realm, but Edward took advantage of a succession dispute to invade the country in 1296. His victory at Dunbar temporarily ended Scottish independence, but the Scots would restore it in 1314 at Bannockburn, during the reign of Edward's son, Edward II.

FORTY YEARS' WAR
(1385–1423)

From the 9th to the 12th centuries, until Mongol invasions fragmented it, the Pagan Kingdom had covered much of the area of modern-day Myanmar (formerly known as Burma). Subsequent anarchy was gradually brought under control by the rival Ava and Hanthawaddy kingdoms. The Ava kingdom was dominant in the north and center, while the Hanthawaddy kingdom lay around the Irrawaddy Delta in the south. An attempt by Ava to seize its rival's land in 1385 went on for almost four decades, interrupted by monsoon seasons and lengthy truces. It ended inconclusively.

THE ANGLO-DUTCH WARS
(1652–1674)

Two major Protestant colonial powers—England and the Dutch Republic—became trading rivals in the 17th century. Weakened by its recent civil war, England first tried to gain an advantage by introducing legislation to penalize the importation of goods on any but English ships. The two nations clashed—mostly at sea. Mutual exhaustion rather than decisive outcomes divided the conflict into three periods (1652–1654, 1665–1667, and 1672–1674). By the early 18th century, Britain would surpass the Netherlands as the region's major naval and economic power.

GLORIOUS REVOLUTION/ WILLIAMITE WAR
(1688–1691)

Within three years of Catholic King James II's accession to the English throne in 1685, his policies had so upset the nobility that it plotted to oust him in favor of the Dutch Protestant prince William of Orange. Invited by a group of English peers, the prince invaded in fall 1688. Deserted by his supporters, James fled to Catholic Ireland, where he attempted a fight back. Irish Protestants held Derry in 1689, buying William time to bring an army to Ireland and defeat James at the Battle of the Boyne in July 1690. James's forces were defeated at Aughrim in July 1691, crushing any hopes of his return to power.

THE HAITIAN REVOLUTION
(1791–1804)

Since 1697, Haiti (then named Saint-Domingue) had been a French colony, where periodic rebellions of enslaved people had been severely put down. In 1792, inspired by the French Revolution, Toussaint Louverture, a formerly enslaved man, led a successful revolt. French troops reconquered Haiti in 1801, deporting Toussaint in 1802, but the colony soon rose up again. Its Black army emerged victorious in 1804 and renamed the island Haiti (Ayiti). France finally recognized its independence in 1825, but only in exchange for hefty compensation. French warships arrived at the capital Port-au-Prince to demand 150 million francs— a debt that would cripple Haiti's economy for more than a century.

GREEK WAR OF INDEPENDENCE
(1821–1829)

After the Ottomans conquered Greece in 1460, its people rebelled periodically, but without success. The formation of the secret Greek *Philikí Etaireía* ("Society of Friends") in 1814, however, gave their cause momentum. An uprising in 1821 was put down, but it led to revolts across Greece, from Macedonia to the island of Crete. Fighting continued until 1827, when fleets from Russia, France, and Britain destroyed the Ottoman navy at the Battle of Navarino. The defeat forced the Ottomans to give Greece the independence it had long sought.

EUROPEAN GAINS IN THE FAR EAST
(1823–1904)

The Monroe Doctrine, proclaimed by US president James Monroe in 1823, designated the Americas as a distinct sphere of the US. The move encouraged European powers to look eastward and establish their own spheres of influence. Dislodged from India by Britain, France pursued new colonial interests in Indochina. In Indonesia, the Dutch expanded their trading posts into colonies, strengthening their hold with wars in western Sumatra (1821–1837), Java (1825–1830), and Aceh, northern Sumatra (1873–1904).

THE FRENCH IN MEXICO
(1861–1867)

Alarmed by Mexico's increasing foreign debt under President Benito Juárez, Britain, France, and Spain sought to collect what they were owed. French emperor Napoleon III sent out an expeditionary force, which overthrew Juárez in 1864 and made the Austrian archduke Maximilian emperor of Mexico. The nation's republicans fought back. The US, embroiled in its own civil war, later intervened to help reinstate Juárez. Maximilian was executed by firing squad in 1867.

MOROCCAN CRISES
(1905–1911)

An Anglo-French agreement over areas of influence in North Africa, signed in April 1904, angered Germany. Kaiser Wilhelm II visited Morocco in March 1905, promising its ruler, Sultan Abdelaziz, his support in resisting French control. Opposed by France, Britain, and their allies, Germany backed down but sparked a new Moroccan crisis by sending its gunboat *Panther* to waters off Agadir in July 1911. In November, a face-saving exchange was agreed; Germany withdrew from Morocco and was assigned a territory in Equatorial Africa to add to its protectorate in Cameroon.

THE EASTER RISING
(1916)

On Easter Monday, 1916, Pádraig Pearse's nationalist Irish Volunteers and James Connolly's Irish Citizen Army occupied Dublin's General Post Office (GPO), and outside it, they proclaimed Ireland a republic. Five days of fighting followed, with hundreds killed, as the British fought to reassert their authority. Initially unsympathetic to the rebels, the wider Irish public was shocked and angered when the British executed key leaders by firing squad. The men's deaths fueled support for the Irish Republican Army (IRA) in its War of Independence (1919–1921).

THE SPANISH CIVIL WAR
(1936–1939)

In July 1936, a military uprising in Spain's garrison towns and other territories failed to overthrow the Republican government but sparked a bloody civil war in the chaos that ensued. Monarchists and other right-wing groups came together as Nationalists under General Francisco Franco to oppose the Republicans. Both sides fought a bitter conflict, including brutal tit-for-tat massacres. Volunteer fighters from around the world served in the Republican ranks, and the USSR sent arms and supplies. However, supported by Nazi Germany and Fascist Italy, Franco's Nationalists were ultimately victorious.

INDO-PAKISTAN CONFLICTS
(1947–1971)

In 1947, Britain's solution to growing dissent in British India was to divide the country, creating a Hindu India and, to its northwest and east, two Muslim states: West Pakistan (later simply Pakistan) and East Pakistan (later Bangladesh). This crude partitioning triggered mass religious migration of up to 14 million people, and as many as 2 million died in violent clashes. With a mostly Muslim populace and a ruling Hindu elite, Kashmir proved a source of conflict that has still to be resolved. India and Pakistan fought over the region in 1965, 1971, and 1999.

THE WESTERN SAHARA CONFLICT
(1975–1991)

Morocco has long claimed rights over the desert region to its south—land occupied by the nomadic Sahrawi people. In 1975, 350,000 Moroccan civilians, accompanied by 20,000 troops, staged a Green March to press their claim. Militant Sahrawi nationalists—the Polisario Front—sought independence and resisted the Moroccans, while neighboring Mauritania attacked from the east and south to stake its own claim. The International Court of Justice supported the Sahrawi, but thousands died before the UN brokered a ceasefire in 1991. The dispute remains unresolved.

INDONESIAN OCCUPATION OF EAST TIMOR
(1975–1999)

After a short civil war in 1975, the left-wing Revolutionary Front for an Independent East Timor (Fretilin) seized power in the former Portuguese colony and declared independence. In December 1975, purportedly to oppose communism, Suharto, Indonesia's president, sent forces to invade East Timor, and Fretilin fought back. More than 100,000 people died during the fighting, its accompanying famine, and atrocities carried out by Suharto's forces.

THE FALKLANDS CONFLICT
(1982)

Although 8,000 miles (13,000 km) from Britain, the Falkland Islands have been a British colony since 1840. The closest mainland, some 300 miles (480 km) to the west, is Patagonia, part of Argentina, which calls the islands Islas Malvinas and has long claimed them as its own. Encouraged by the scaling down of Royal Navy patrols around the islands, Argentina invaded them in April 1982. A small force overran the British garrison, and thousands of Argentinian troops followed; Britain sent a naval task force in response. On May 2, a Royal Navy submarine torpedoed and sank the cruiser *General Belgrano*; two days later, an Argentinian Exocet rocket sank HMS *Sheffield*. Gradually, British troops secured control of the air and sea around the islands then launched an amphibious assault, securing victory in the 74-day war.

SRI LANKAN CIVIL WAR
(1983–2009)

The majority Sinhalese people, who outnumber the Tamil ethnic group by about eight to one, had come together with the Tamils in 1948 to win independence for Sri Lanka (formerly British Ceylon), but old tensions between them later resurfaced. From 1983, the Tamil Tigers guerrilla organization fought a full-scale civil war against the Sri Lankan government, hoping to form a breakaway Tamil state. While Sinhalese forces carried out periodic anti-Tamil pogroms, the Tamil Tigers, weaker in both numbers and firepower, often resorted to terrorist attacks such as suicide bombing. In 2009, the Sri Lankan government finally crushed the rebels, forcing them to disband. The Tamils finally had to accept the legitimacy of the Sri Lankan state.

WAR IN THE FORMER YUGOSLAVIA
(1991–2001)

After World War II, authoritarian communist rule had held the ethnic groups of Yugoslavia together. When that rule collapsed, the country fell apart. In 1991, Croatia, Slovenia, and Macedonia seceded from Yugoslavia, and Bosnia's Muslims sought their freedom too. Feeling threatened, the Serb minority in Bosnia tried to stop its breakaway, and Croatia intervened on behalf of Bosnia's Croats. Atrocities were committed on all sides, and up to 250,000 people died. Further killings followed when Kosovo's Albanians broke free in 1995. In 2001, an uneasy peace was achieved.

THE SYRIAN CIVIL WAR
(2011–)

During the Arab Spring of 2011, peaceful protests began in Syria, challenging the totalitarian government of its president Bashar al-Assad. The regime reacted by killing hundreds of protesters and imprisoning many more, sparking a civil war that set the Alawite Muslim ruling class against the majority Sunni Muslims. Western nations opposing al-Assad's actions supported the rebels, while Russia and Iran lent him their support, and Islamic State moved in to seize land. In 2024, al-Assad was still president, and most fighting had ended, but the war has cost at least 500,000 lives.

INDEX

Page numbers in **bold** refer to main entries.

9/11 attacks 241, 313, 317

A

Abbasid dynasty 78, 79, 81, 83, 100
Abd al-Rahman I, Emir 81
Abdülmecid, Sultan 206
Abe, Shinzo 264
Abel, Rudolf 292
Abu Bakr 78, 79, 81
Abyssinia 226, 227, 229
Achaemenid Empire 23, 34, 70
Actium, Battle of 55
Active Defense doctrine 315
Ad Decimum, Battle of 72
Adal sultanate 127
administrative class 19
Adrian IV, Pope 95
Adrianople, Battle of 64
Adrianople, Siege of 237
Adrianople, Treaty of 178
Adwa, Battle of 229
Aegospotami, Battle of 31
Afghan Wars 312
Afghanistan, conflict in 241, 293, **312–13**, 317
Afonso I of Asturias 110
Afonso VI of León and Castile 111
Africa
   foreign influence/involvement in conflicts **304–5**
   imperial wars in **226–9**
   postcolonial **304–5**
   wars of independence 226, **300–303**, 304
   World War I 255
Agent Orange **297**
agriculture
   Fertile Crescent 18–19
   Maya 74–5
Agrippa, Marcus Vipsanius 57
Aigun, Treaty of 166
air warfare
   World War I 13, **257**, 274
   World War II 13, 268, 270–71, **274–5**, 284–5
AirLand Battle doctrine **314–15**
Akbar the Great 140–41
Akkadian Empire 12, 16, 20
al-Abbas, Muhammad ibn Ali ibn 81
al-Andalus 73, 81, 83
al-Arabi, Suleyman 83
al-Qadisiya, Battle of 80
al-Qaeda 241, 312, 313, 317
Alamo, Battle of the 204
Alaric I of the Visigoths 64
Albania 112, 232, 236, 288
Albigensian Crusade 102–3, 192
Alcácer Quibir, Battle of 127
Aleppo, sack of 73
Aleppo, Siege of 99
Alesia, Battle of 54
Alexander the Great 12, 16, 17, 18, 22, 23, 24, **32–9**, 40, 42, 70, 71
   successors of **40–41**

Alexander I, Czar 189, 195
Algeria 133, 228, 254, 302, 304
Ali, Caliph 81
Allende, Salvador 299
Allia River, Battle of 50
Alma, Battle of the 206
Almoravid dynasty 126
ambulances 195, 197
Amda Seyon I of Ethiopia 127
American Civil War 28, 171, 182, 186, 194, **214–21**, 224, 235, 248, 256
American Revolution 160, 170, **172–7**
Amida, Siege of 62, 63
Ammianus Marcellinus 62, 63, 64
Amphipolis, Battle of 30
Anatolia 18, 21, 23, 34, 35, 36, 73, 91, 112, 130, 132, 133
Anglo-Dutch Wars 149, 198, **325**
Anglo-French (Bourbon) War 176
Anglo-Maratha Wars 225
Anglo-Sikh Wars 225
Anglo–Zulu War 228, 234
Angola 226, 302, 303
Antietam, Battle of 219
Antigonus/Antigonid dynasty 40, 41
Antioch 41
Antioch, Siege of 91
Antipater 40, 41
antiseptics 206, 207
Antony, Mark 55
Antwerp, sack of 138
Anzacs 253
apartheid 300
Apollodorus of Damascus 57
Appomattox Court House, Battle of 221
Aquinas, Thomas 144
Aquitaine 69, 107
Arabs
   Arab League 309
   Arab Revolt **254**
   Arab-Israeli Conflicts 241, **306–311**
   Arab–Byzantine Wars 72, 79–80
   rise of Islam 12, **76–81**
Arafat, Yasser 308, 309, 311
Arausio, Battle of 52
Arbenz, Colonel Jacobo 298–9
archers 85, 99, **106–9**
Archidamus II of Sparta 29, 30
Archimedes 53
Arcot, Battle of 225
Ardennes offensive 278
Argentina 201, 204, 224
Argos 30–31
Aristotle 34, 144
Armenia 316
Armistice (World War I) 240, 261
armor
   Crusader 92
   samurai 87
Arrow War 230–31
Art of War, The (Sunzi) 17, 44, 45–7
Asculum, Battle of 51
Ashikaga shogunate 128
Ashoka the Great 17, 42, 43
Ashrawi, Hanan **310**, 311
Ashurbanipal of Assyria 22
Ashurnasirpal II of Assyria 22
askaris 255
Askia Ishaq II of Songhai 127

Aspern-Essling, Battle of 191
Assyrian Empire 12, 16, **22**, 23
Aswan Dam 293
asymmetric warfare **296–7**
Atahualpa 125
Athens 16–17, 24, 26–7, 28–31, 34, 56
Atlanta, Siege of 221
Atlantic, Battle of the 269, 272–3
Atlantic Ocean
   maritime trade 198
   U-boat campaigns 256–7, 272–3
Atlantic Triangular Trade 126
atomic bombs 13, 230, 235, 240, 241, 274, **284–5**, 288–9, 290
atrocities **105**, **192–3**
Attila the Hun **65**
attrition, war of **28–31**, 221, 247, 248, 249–50, 275, 319
Auerstadt, Battle of 190
Augsburg, Peace of 94, 137
Augustine of Hippo, St 94, 144
Augustus, Emperor 17, 54, 55, 56
Aung San 302
Aurangzeb, Emperor 119, 141
Austerlitz, Battle of 170, 189–90
Australia
   World War I 253, 255
   World War II 283, 284
Austria
   French Revolutionary Wars 184, 185–6
   Napoleonic Wars 188, 189, 190, 191, 196–7
   Seven Weeks' War 211–12, 245
   Seven Years' War 162, 163, 164, 165
   Succession issues **159**
   Wars of Italian Unification 208, 209
Austria-Hungary 210, 240
   Balkan conflict 236, 237
   collapse of 255, 258, 261
   World War I 244, 247, 252, 259, 260–61
Austro–Turkish War 130
Avars 72
Ayacucho, Battle of 203
Azerbaijan 316
Azincourt, Battle of 109
Aztec civilization 69, **114–15**, 118, **122–5**, 123

B

Babur 118, 140, **141**
Babylon/Babylonians 12, 16, 21, 22, 23, 38, 41
Badajoz, Siege of 193
Badr, Battle of 78
Baghdad 81, 100, 254
Baghuz-Fawqani, Battle of 317
Bailén, Battle of 193
Bakhchisarai, Treaty of 232
Balaclava, Battle of 207
Balfour Declaration 308
Balkans 233, **236–7**
   Balkan Wars 232, 235, 252
   Celtic invasion of **324**
Banu Hud dynasty 111
Bapheus, Battle of 113
barbarian migrations **58–65**, 71, 73, 82
Barbary pirates 84

Basel, Council of 103
Basil II, Emperor 73
Basques 83
Batavia 296
Batavian Republic 183
Batista, Fulgencio 299
battle formations
   Alexander the Great 35, 41
   Franks 82
   maniple infantry formation 50, **51**, 52
   Normans 85
   pike and shot formation 121
   Prussian 164–5
Bavaria 157, 162, 186, 189, 191
Bay of Pigs 292, 299
Bazaine, Marshal François Achille 213
Bechuanaland Protectorate 228
Beirut 310
Bela IV of Hungary 100
Belarus 263, 319
Belgian Congo 229, 300
Belgium
   African colonies 226, 229
   loss of colonies 300, 304–5
   World War I 244, 245, 246
   World War II 269
Belgrade, Siege of 131, 132
Belisarius, Flavius 71–2
Benin 228
Berbers 126–7
Berlin
   Cold War 288, 291
   fall of 268, 279
Berlin Airlift 279
Berlin Conference 252, 300
Berlin Wall **288**
Bermúdez, José 202
Bershamskaya, Yevdokiya 275
Bessus 39
Beyazid I, Sultan 113
Beyazid II, Sultan 132, 140
Bi, Battle of 44
Biafra 304
Biden, Joe 314
Bimbisara 42
bin Laden, Osama 312, 313, 317
Bindusara 42, 43
Bismarck, Otto von 210–213, 226
Black Death 108–9
Bleda 65
Blenheim, Battle of 157
Bletchley Park 272, 273
Blitzkrieg 240, **268–71**, 274
blockades 37, 72, 101, 113, 164, 165, 198, 217, 256, 257, 258–9, 265, 272, 279, 304, 311, 316, 320
Blücher, Gebhard Lebrecht von 197
Boabdil 111
Boers/Boer Wars 229, **234**, 248
Bohemia 103, 164, 165
Bohemian Revolt 119, 145
Bohemond of Taranto 91
Bolesław the Pious 140
Bolívar, Simon 170, 200, **201**, 202–3, 204
Bolivia 203, 298
Bolsheviks 240, 247, 262–3, 288
bombing campaigns
   Vietnam War 297
   World War I 256, **257**

INDEX

World War II **274–5**, 276, 277, 278, 279
Booth, John Wilkes 221
Borneo, North 296
Borodino, Battle of 195
Bosnia 112, 192, 327
Boston Tea Party 174
Boyacá, Battle of 202
Brandywine Creek, Battle of 175
Brasidas 30
Brazil
   independence movement 200, 203
   Paraguayan War 224
   Ragamuffin War 208
Breitenfeld, Battles of 146, 147
Brest-Litovsk, Treaty of 262, 263
Brihadratha 43
Britain
   American Revolution **174–7**
   Arab–Israeli Conflicts 308
   army reform **234**
   Boer Wars **234**
   British Civil Wars 119, **148–9**
   Cold War 288, 289, 291
   conquest of India 171, **225**
   Crimean War **206–7**
   French Revolutionary Wars 184–5
   Garibaldi in **209**
   Glorious Revolution/Williamite War **325**
   Gulf Wars 314, 315
   imperialism in Africa 227, 228–9
   Iraq War 317
   loss of colonies 300, 301–2, 303, 304
   Napoleonic Wars 188, 190–91, 197
   in North America 119, 150–51, 160–61, 170, 222
   Opium Wars 230–31
   in Palestine and Mesopotamia 252, 254
   Peninsular War 191, 192–3, 197
   Roman conquests 57, 60, 62
   and the Sepoys **225**
   Seven Years' War 162, 164, 165, 252
   and South American wars of liberation 201, 203
   Viking raids 84
   War of 1812 **198–9**
   World War I 234, 240, 244–51, 252–4, 256–7, 259, 260
   World War II 269–70, 272–9, 282, 283
   see also England; Scotland; Wales
Britain, Battle of 270, 274
British East India Company 165, **225**
British Empire 252–4, 280
British Expeditionary Force 234, 244, 245, 246
Buena Vista, Battle of 205
Bulgaria 233, 236, 237, 260, 288
Bulgars/Bulgar Empire 73
Bull Run, Battles of 217, 218
Buller, General Redvers 234
Burgoyne, General John 175–6
Burma (Myanmar) 167, 282, 325
bushido 86, 87
Bussaco, Battle of 193
Buyid dynasty 78
Byzantine Empire 65, **70–73**, 79–80, 83, 85, 90
   Ottomans defeat 69, 112, 113, 130
Byzantium 60, 68, 70–71, 73

C

Cabral, Alíĺcar **303**
Caesar, Julius 54, **55**, 56, 57, 105
Cajamarca, Battle of 125
Calais, Siege of 108
California gold rush 223
Callias, Peace of 24, 27
Callinicum, Battle of 71
Callixtus II, Pope 95
Campo Formio, Treaty of 184
Canada
   French and Indian Wars **160–61**, 174
   War of 1812 199
   World War I 253
Cancha Rayada, Battle of 202
Cannae, Battle of 53
Cape St Vincent, Battle of 186
Carabobo, Battle of 203
Cardigan, Lieutenant General Lord 207
Carnot, Lazare 183
Carolingian Empire **82–3**
Carrera, General Rafael 204
Carthage/Carthaginians 17, 22, **52–3**, 71, 127
Caste War of Yucatán 74
Castillon, Battle of 109
Castro, Fidel 204, 292, 298, **299**
Castro, Raúl 298, 299
casualties, battlefield 171, **184–7**, **206–7**
Çatalhöyük 18
Cathars 102–3, 192
Catherine the Great of Russia 140, 165, 170, **178–9**, 232
Caucasus 178, 179, 316
cavalry
   Crusader 93
   limitations of 102
   Mongol 99
   Norman **85**
   Ottoman 132
   Seljuk Turks 93
Celts 105
   invasion of the Balkans **324**
Central African Republic 305
Chacabuco, Battle of 202
Chaeronea, Battle of 34, 35
Chaldiran, Battle of 132
Chamberlain, Neville 269
Chandax, Siege of 72, 73
Chandragupta Maurya 42–3
Changping, Battle of 47
Charge of the Light Brigade 207
chariots 20, **21**
Charlemagne, Emperor 68, **82–3**
Charles, Archduke of Austria 157
Charles the Bold, Duke of Burgundy 102
Charles Emmanuel II of Savoy 136
Charles I of England 119, 148–9
Charles II of England 148, 149
Charles II of Spain 157
Charles III, Duke of Bourbon **121**
Charles III, Emperor 82
Charles V, Holy Roman Emperor 124, **137**
Charles VII of France 108, 154
Charles XII of Sweden 119, 158
Charles Martel 81, 82
Charles the Simple of France 85
Charleston, Siege of 176
Chattanooga, Siege of 220
Chávez, Hugo 298
Chavín de Huántar 114
chemical warfare 297, 315, 317
Chesapeake, Battle of the 177
Chesma, Battle of 178
Chiang Kai-Shek 264, 265, 294
Chickamauga, Battle of 220
Chile 122, 202, 241, 299
Chimayó Rebellion 150
China
   boundary issues **167**
   Chinese Civil War 230, 241, **294**
   Chinese Revolution 142
   communist 282
   decline of Qing **230–31**, 280
   Goguryeo–Sui War **324**
   Han Empire 17, **48–9**
   Korean War 295
   military technology 49
   Mongol invasions 98, 99, 101, 142
   northern frontier **142–3**
   origins of Chinese Empire **44–7**
   Sino-Japanese Wars 171, 230, **264–5**, 280, 281, 294
   Ten Great Campaigns 119, **166–7**, 230
   World War II 265
Chirino, José Leonardo 200
Christianity
   in the Americas 123
   The Crusades **88–93**
   European conversions to 82, 85
Chu state 44, 45, 47, 48
Church and state **94–5**, 136
Churchill, Winston 269, 270, 288, 301
CIA (Central Intelligence Agency) 290, 291, 293, 298, 299, 312
Cimbrian War 52
city-states
   Greek 23, 24, 26, 28–9
   Italian 95, 120
Ciudad Rodrigo, Siege of 193
Civil Rights movement 292
civil wars **128–9**
   American **214–21**
   British **148–9**
   postcolonial African 304
civilian military control **295**
Clausewitz, Carl von 189, 295
Clement III, Pope 95
Cleopatra VII 40, 55
Clermont, Council of 90
Clinton, Lieutenant General Henry 176–7
Clive, Robert 165, 225
Clovis I of the Franks 78, 82
Cochinchina Campaign 296
Colbert, Jean-Baptiste 155
Cold Harbor, Battle of 220
Cold War 13, 241, 279, 284, **286–93**
Cologne 275
Colombia 200, 201, 202, 203
colonialism
   American Revolution **74–7**
   call of empire (World war I) **252–5**
   China 160–61
   discontent with **174–7**
   end of 255, **300–303**, 304
   independence in Southeast Asia **296–7**
   Scramble for Africa **226–9**
   South American wars of liberation **200–203**
Columbus, Christopher 110, 122
comitatenses 60
Commonwealth, English 149
communications **56–7**, 216, 219
Communism
   Afghanistan 312
   China 166, 230, 241, 264, 265, 294
   coups 291–2
   Russia/USSR 133, 240, 255, 258, 262–3, 288, 290–91, 293, 316
   US fear of 290
Concord, Battle of 174, 176
condottieri 120
Confederate States 171, 217–21
Confederation of the Rhine 190
confessional war **136–9**
conscription 47, 158, 163, 233
   mass **182–7**, 188, 220
Constance, Council of 103
Constans, Emperor 61
Constantine I, Emperor 60, 62, 68, 70, 71
Constantine II, Emperor 60–61
Constantinople 60, 65, 68, 70, 71, 73, 90, 130, 233, 237
   Arab siege of 72, 73, 81
   falls to Ottomans 69, 112, 113, 130
   sack of (1204) 73
Constantius II, Emperor 61–2
Continental Congresses 174, 175, 198
Copenhagen, Battle of 186
Coral Sea, Battle of the 283
Corinth, League of 34
Corinthian War 28
Cornwallis, General Charles 175, 177
Cortenuova, Battle of 95
Cortés, Hernán 118, **124**, 125
Corunna, Battle of 193
Cossacks 70, **179**
Covenanters 148
Crassus, Marcus Licinius 54
Crécy, Battle of 85, 108
Creek War 222
Cresson, Battle of 102
Crimea 98, 179, 232, 263, 319, 320
Crimean War 90, 171, **206–7**, 234, 261
Crockett, Davy 204
Cromwell, Oliver 148, **149**, 182, 192
Cromwell, Richard 148
Crusades 12, 56, 68, 69, 73, **88–93**, 101
   European Crusades (1209–1434) **102–3**
cryptography 272, **273**
Cuauhtémoc 124–5
Cuba 122, 124, 204
   Cuban Revolution 292, **298–9**
   Cuban War of Independence 298
cult of the offensive 244
cultural influence 292–3
Cultural Revolution 294
cultures, clash of **90–93**
Cusco, Siege of 125
Custer, George 223
Custoza, Battle of 208
Cyprus 68, 112, 133
Cyrus II of Persia 23
Czechoslovakia 261, 288, 308
   World War II 268, 279

D

D-Day landings 52, 268, 272, 276–7
Dahomey, Kingdom of 126, 228
daimyos 86, 128, 129
Dan-no-ura, Battle of 87
Daoud Khan, Mohammad 312
Dara, Battle of 71
Darius I (the Great) of Persia 23, 26, 27, 70
Darius III of Persia 16, 23, 36, 38–9
Davy, Sir Humphrey 206
de Gaulle, Charles 302
de Klerk, F.W. 303
deception 46
Declaration of Independence 175
Declaration of the Rights of Man and the Citizen 183
Defenestration of Prague 119, 145
Delhemma 79
Delhi, sack of 105, 141
Delian League 29, 30, 31
Denmark, Schleswig Wars 210, 211
Diadochi, Wars of the 34, 39, **40–41**
Dien Bien Phu, Battle of 296
Dieppe Raid 52
Diplomatic Revolution 159, 162

disease 118, 123, 124, 125, 194, 206, 207, 222, 227
Dodds, Alfred-Amédée 228
Dominican Republic 298
Dönitz, Admiral Karl 279
Dos de Mayo uprising 192
drone warfare 241, **318–21**
Drummer's War 160
Dunant, Henri 171
Dunkirk, retreat 248, 269–70
Dutch East Indies 280, 282, 296
Dutch Revolt 138–9
Dzungar nomads 166

E

East Timor, Indonesian occupation of **327**
Eastern Front
    World War I 246, 247, 249
    World War II 271, 274–5, 276, 278
Eastern Roman Empire 60, 61–2, 65, 68
    see also Byzantine Empire
Ecbatana, Battle of 40
Edward, the Black Prince 108
Edward I of England 91, **325**
Edward III of England 107, 108
Egypt
    Alexander the Great 37–8, 40
    Ancient 16, 18, **20–1**, 22, 23, 55
    Arab–Israeli Conflicts 308, 309, 310
    Aswan Dam 293
    European imperialism and 227, 228
    Islamic conquest 73, 80
    Napoleon's expedition 185
    Suez Crisis **301**
    world War I 253, 254
Eighty Years' War 138–9
Eisenhower, Dwight D. 13, 289, 298, 299
El Cid (Rodrigo Díaz de Vivar) **111**
Elam 16, 19
elephants, war **42–3**
Elizabeth I of England 139, 225
Elster, Battle of 94
Emancipation Proclamation 219
encomienda 125
England
    Anglo-Dutch Wars **325**
    Edward I's conquests of Wales and Scotland **325**
    English Civil War 119, **148–9**
    Hundred Years' War **106–9**
    Norman conquest 85
    Spanish Armada 139
Enigma Code 272, **273**
Epaminondas 34
espionage **288–93**

F

Falaise Pocket 277
Falklands Conflict **327**
Fallen Timbers, Battle of 222
famine 258, 259, 263
Far East, European gains in **326**
Fatima, Princess **79**
Fatimid Caliphate 90
Federal Security Service (USSR) 288
Ferdinand I, Emperor 137
Ferdinand II of Aragon 68, 111, 140
Ferdinand II, Emperor 145–6, 147
Ferdinand III, Emperor 147
Ferdinand VII of Spain 192
Ferdinand, Czar of Bulgaria 236, **237**, 260
Fertile Crescent 16, 18, 19
firearms see weapons

Fleurus, Battle of 183
flintlock muskets **163**
flower war **115**
foederati 62, 63, 65, 72
Fontainebleau, Edict of 136
Fort McHenry, Battle of 199
fortifications
    castles 91
    Chinese 47
    Vauban's 154, 155
Forty Years' War **325**
France
    African colonies 170, 228
    American Revolution **174**, 176–7
    colonial empire 280, 290, 296, 326
    colonial troops 254–5
    Crimean War 206
    Franco-Prussian War 171, 194, 213, 244, 245, 247
    French and Indian Wars 119, **160–61**, 174
    French Revolution 170, 182, 183
    French Revolutionary Wars 170, 174, **180–3**, 188
    Hundred Years' War **106–9**
    and India 225
    Italian Wars 120–21
    Italian Wars of Independence 208, 209
    loss of colonies 200, 302, 304
    Napoleon at bay/defeat of **194–7**
    Napoleon triumphant **188–91**
    in North America 160–61
    Peninsular War 170, 192–3
    Seven Years' War 162, 164, 165, 252
    in Syria and Lebanon 252, 254
    Thirty Years' War 147
    wars of Louis XIV **152–7**
    Wars of Religion 78, 118, 119, 137–8
    World War I 154, 240, 244–51, 252, 254–5, 259, 260
    World War II 269–70, 274, 275, 276–7, 279, 281
Francis I, Emperor 190
Francis I of France 121
Francis II of the Two Sicilies 209
Franco, Francisco 110
Franks 62, 68, 78, 81, 82
Franz Ferdinand, Archduke 236, 240, 244
Frederick I (Barbarossa), Emperor 95
Frederick II, Emperor 93, 95, 103
Frederick II (the Great) of Prussia 159, 162, **163**, 164–5, 210
Frederick V of the Palatinate (Frederick I of Bohemia) 145
Frederick VII of Denmark 210
Frederick William I of Prussia 162, 163
Fredriksten, Siege of 158
Friedland, Battle of 190
Fronde uprisings 154
Fröschwiller, Battle of 213
Fulcher of Chartres 90, 91
Full Spectrum Operations 314, 315

G

Gagarin, Yuri 293
Gaixia, Battle of 48
Gallipoli campaign 253
Gallus Caesar 61
Gaozu (Liu Bang), Emperor 48–9
Garibaldi, Giuseppe 171, **208–9**, 210
garrisons 62
Gates, General Horatio 175–6, 177
Gaugamela, Battle of 23, 38
Gaul/Gauls, Romans and 50, 52, 54–5, 56–7, 60, 62, 63, 65, 105

Gaza 37, 310–311
Gaza, Battle of 40
Geneva Conventions 144, 147, 192
Genghis Khan 69, 98–9, 101, 105, 141, 142
Genpei War 69, 87
Geok Tepe, Battle of 233
George II of the United Kingdom 164
germ warfare 264, 265
German Confederation 210
German East Africa 229
Germanic tribes 52, 54, 60, 62–5, 68, 71–2, 82
Germany
    African colonies 226, 228, 229, 244, 300–301
    Cold War 279, **288**, 293
    loss of colonies 252, 255
    Nazi regime 258, 261
    postwar division **279**, 288
    reunification 276
    rising nationalism **210–213**
    Thirty Years' War **144–7**
    unification 211, 212, 213
    wars of religion 136–7
    World War I 232, 240, 244–7, 248–51, 255, 258–61, 276
    World War II 240, 256, 258, 268–79, 281
    see also Prussia
Gersdorff, Hans von 206
Gettysburg Address 220
Gettysburg, Battle of 219
Ghent, Treaty of 199
Global Terrorism Index 317
Glorious Revolution/Williamite War **325**
Go-Toba, Emperor 87
Godfrey of Bouillon 90, 91, 92
Goguryeo–Sui War **324**
Golan Heights 309
Gorbachev, Mikhail 293, 313
Gordon, General Charles 228, 229
Goryeo–Khitan Wars **325**
Goths 63–4, 68, 71, 72
Graeco-Persian Wars 26
Gran Colombia 203
Granada, Siege of 111
Grand Alliance 119, 157
Grand Armée 154, 187, **188–91**, 194, 196
Granicus, Battle of the 35–6
Grant, General Ulysses S. 28, 216, 218, 220–21
Grasse, Lieutenant General Comte de 177
Gratian, Emperor 64
Gravelotte, Battle of 213
Graves, Admiral Thomas 177
Great Conspiracy 62
Great Northern War **158**
Great Purge 262
Great Wall of China **143**
Great Zimbabwe 69, **104**
Greece
    Alexander the Great **34–9**
    ancient 16–17, 23, **24–7**, **34–9**, 51, 70, 78
    Balkans conflict 236, 237
    Greek Civil War 289
    Greek War of Independence **326**
    World War II 270
Greene, Nathanael 177
Gregory VII, Pope 68, 94, 95
Gregory IX, Pope 103
Grijalva, Juan de 124
Grijó, Battle of 193
Grotius, Hugo **147**
Grouchy, Marshal Emmanuel de 197
Guderian, Heinz **268**, 269
Guernica 256, 274

guerrilla warfare 150, 151, **192**, 224, 255, 271, 294, 297, 302, 303, 313
Gulf Wars **314–15**, 317
guns see weapons

H

Habsburg dynasty 119, 121, 133, 136, 137, 145–7, 157, 159
Hague Conventions 144, 147
Haitian Revolution 200, **325**
Halicarnassus, Siege of 36
Hamas 310, 311
Han Empire 17, **48–9**, 167, 230
Han state 44, 46, 47
Harold Godwinson, King of England 85
Harris, Arthur "Bomber" 274, 275
Hastings, Battle of 85
Hattin, Battle of 102
Hellenism 39, **40–41**, 71
Henry II of France 137
Henry III of France 137, 138
Henry IV, Emperor 68, 90, 94–5
Henry IV of France 138
Henry V, Emperor 95
Henry V of England 109
Heraclea, Battle of 51
Herero people 228, 229
heresy 78, 102–3, 192
hetairoi 35, 36, 38, 39
Hezbollah 310, 311
Hideyoshi, Toyotomo 128–9
Hindenburg Line 251, 260
Hirohito, Emperor 285
Hiroshima 13, 235, 241, 274, 285, 289
Hitler, Adolf 240, 261, 268, 269–71, 276, 277, 278, 279
Hittites 21, 22
Hohenlinden, Battle of 186
Hohenzollern dynasty 213
Holocaust 308
Holy Land 12, 68, 90, 93, 102
Holy League 90
Holy Roman Empire 68, 83, 103, 136, 137, 144
    Napoleon dissolves 190
    and Papacy **94–5**
Home Front (World War I) **258–61**
hoplites 12, 13, 17, **25**
House Un-American Activities Committee 288, 290
Howe, General Sir William 175
Huayna Capac 125
Huguenots 78, 118, 119, 136, 137–8
Hui people 166
Hull, General William 199
Hülegü 100
human sacrifice **74–5**, 115
Humayun, Emperor 141
Hundred Years' War 69, **106–9**
Hunger Plan 258
Huns 60, 61, 63, 64–5
Huntington, Samuel 295
Hus, Jan/Hussite Wars **103**, 136
Husayn ibn Ali 81
Hussein, Sadam 314–15, 317
Hydaspes River, Battle of the 39
Hyksos 16, 20–21
hypaspistai 35, 36, 37

I

Iberian War 71
Ibrahim Khan Lodi 140, 141
Ice, Battle on the 103

Ieyasu, Tokugawa 118, 128–9
Inca civilization 69, **114–15**, 118, **122–5**
India
    Alexander the Great 39, 40, 42
    British conquest 171, **225**
    Indian Rebellion 216, 225
    Indo-Pakistan conflicts **326–7**
    Mauryan Empire 17, **42–3**
    Mongol invasions 99
    Mughal conquests 118–19, **140–41**
    nuclear tests 288
    partition 225
    Seven Years' War 164, 165
    World War I 253–4
Indian Citizenship Act (US, 1924) 222
Indian Civil Rights Act (US, 1968) 222
Indian Removal Act (US, 1830) 222
Indigenous peoples
    disease ravages 123, 124, 125, 222
    and European conquests/settlers 118, 123, **150–51**, **222–3**
    and European imperialism 229
    exploitation of 198, 199
    French and Indian Wars **160–61**
    genocide 223
    Southeast Asia 296
Indochina Wars 295, 296–7
Indonesia 296, **327**
industrial warfare **235**
infantry, rise of 12, **102–3**
Inkerman, Battle of 207
Innocent III, Pope 102, 192
International Court of Justice 192
International Criminal Court 144
International Red Cross 171
Investiture Controversy 95
Ipsus, Battle of 41
Iran 314–15, 318
    Iran–Iraq War 314
Iraq 314–15, 317
    Arab–Israeli Conflicts 308, 309
    conflict in 317
    Iran–Iraq War 314
    Iraq War 274, 315, 317
Ireland
    Easter Rising **326**
    Irish Confederate Wars 148, 149, 192
    Viking raids 84
irregular warfare 119, **160–61**
Isabella I of Castile 68, 111, 140
Islam
    The Crusades **88–93**, 102
    forcible conversions 131
    and Graeco-Roman culture 92
    Mongols and 100–101
    preventing spread of 82, 83
    radical 241, **317**
    religious tolerance 140–41
    rise of 68, 72, 73, **76–81**
    slavery **127**
    Spanish Reconquista **110–111**, 140
Islamic State (IS) 317
Ismail, Shah 105
Israel, Arab-Israeli Conflicts 241, 301, **306–311**
Issus, Battle of 36, 37
Istanbul 130
Italy
    imperialism in Africa 226, 229
    Italian Wars 118, **120–21**
    Italo-Turkish War 256
    Napoleon's Italian campaign 184, 188
    Wars of Italian Unification 171, **208–9**, 210
    World War I 244, 261
Ivan IV (the Terrible), Tsar 158, 178
Izmail, Siege of 179

J

Jackson, General Thomas J. "Stonewall" 218, 219
Jacobite rising 159
Jahangir, Emperor 141
James I of Aragon 111
James IV of Scotland 106
Jamestown (Virginia) 119, 150
Jan Sobieski of Poland 133
Janissary Corps 118, **130–33**, 232, 233
Jao Modo, Battle of 142
Japan
    kamikaze pilots **101**, 285
    Russo-Japanese War 171, 232, 233, **235**, 237, 249
    samurai 69, **86–7**
    Sengoku Era 118, **128–9**
    Sino-Japanese Wars 171, 230, **264–5**, 280, 281, 294
    World War I 255
    World War II 235, 240, 241, 265, 274, 275, 276, **280–85**, 296
Jay Treaty 198
Jena, Battle of 189, 190
Jerusalem
    Arab–Israeli Conflicts 309
    Crusades 90, 92, 93
    falls to Arabs 80
    Seljuks take 90
Jews
    Jewish homeland 308
    Jewish Revolt (66–74 CE) 61
    religious tolerance 140
jihad 79
Jin dynasty 44, 48, 142
Joan of Arc 12, **108**, 109
John I Tzimiskes, Emperor 73
John II of France 109
John VI of Portugal 203
Johnson, Lyndon B. 299, 309
Johnston, General Joseph 221
Jomini, Antoine-Henri 189
Jordan 308, 309
Joseph I of Spain 192
Jovian, Emperor 62
Judar Pasha 127
Julian, Emperor 62
Jumonville Glen, Battle of 160
Jurchen 142
just war **144–7**
Justinian I, Emperor 60, 68, 71, 72

K

Kadesh, Battle of 21
Kagul, Battle of 178
Kalinga 17, 42, 43
Kamakura Shogunate 86, 87
kamikaze pilots **101**, 285
Kampala 74
Kanagawa, Treaty of 280
Kanno disturbance 128
Karamanid dynasty 130
Karbala, Battle of 81
Karnal, Battle of 141
Kautilya (Chanakya) 42–3
Kazan, Battle of 179
Kennedy, John F. 292, 299
Keogh, Lieutenant-General Sir Alfred 251
KGB 288, 290, 291
khanates, Mongol 101
Kharkov, Battle of 271
Khartoum, Siege of 228
Khmer Kingdom, rise of the **324–5**

Khmer Rouge 296
Khomeini, Ayatollah Ruhollah 314
Khrushchev, Nikita 282, 292
Khwarazmian Empire 99
King Philip's War 151, 222
King William's War 160
Kitchener, General Lord Herbert 229, 234
Kleidion, Battle of 73
knights 13, 85, 109
    Crusades 90–93, 102
Knights Hospitaller 91, 102
Knights' War 136
Knoxville, Battle of 220
Kojima, Battle of 87
Kongzi (Confucius) 46
Königgrätz, Battle of 211–12
Korea 235, **324**, **325**
    Korean War **295**
Krak des Chevaliers **91**
Kunersdorf, Battle of 165
Kuomintang Nationalists 166, 230, 264, 265, 294
Kurikara Pass, Battle of 87
Kursk, Battle of 271, 276
Kut al-Amara, Siege of 254
Kutná Hora, Battle of 103
Kuwait 314, 315, 317
Kyiv 100, 263, 319

L

La Salle, Robert 160
Lade, Battle of 26
Ladysmith, Battle of 234
Lafayette, Marquis de 174
Lake Erie, Battle of 199
Landsknechts 120
Larga, Battle of 178
Larrey, Dominique-Jean 171, 194, 195, **196**, 197
Lawrence, Captain T. E. **254**
Le Tellier, Michel 154
League of Nations 268, 308
Lee, General Robert E. 218–19, 220
Legnano, Battle of 95
Leipzig, Battle of 188, 196
Lenin, Vladimir 262, 263
Leningrad, Siege of 271
Leo I, Emperor 94
Leo I (the Great), Pope 94
Leo III, Pope 68, 83
Leonidas I of Sparta 27
Leopold II of Belgium 226, 229
Leopold von Hohenzollern-Sigmaringen 213
Lepanto, Battle of 90, 118, 133
Letterman, Jonathan 194
Lettow-Vorbeck, Paul von 255
Leuthen, Battle of 164
levée en masse **182–3**, 186, 188, 194
Lexington, Battle of 174, 176
Leyte Gulf, Battle of 284
Li Yuan 48
Lian Po 47
Liberia 226, 227, 229
Ligny, Battle of 197
Lincoln, Abraham 216–17, 218, 219, 220, 221
Lines of Torres Vedras 193
Lingqu Canal 48
Little Bighorn, Battle of 171, 223
Lobengula, King of the Ndebele 227
Lombard League 95
Lombards 72, 82
Lombardy, Wars of 120

Lombardy-Venetia 208
London, Treaty of 244
Long Island, Battle of 175
Long March 294
Loos, Battle of 250
Louis the Pious, King of the Franks 82
Louis XIV of France 119, 136, **152–7**
Louis XVI of France 174, 176
Louis XVIII of France 197
Louvois, Marquis of 154–5, 156
Luther, Martin 94, 103, 136, 137
Lützen, Battle of 146, 147
Lyons-Seward Treaty 198

M

Ma'arra, Siege of 91
Maastricht, Siege of 154
MacArthur, General Douglas 284, 295
Maccabaean Revolt **324**
McClellan, General George 218, 219, 221
Macedon 34–9, 40, 41
    Macedonian Wars 34
Macedonia 232, 236, 237
Maedi, revolt of the 35
Mafeking, Battle of 234
Magadha 42
Magdeburg, Siege of 146
Magnentius 61
Maharero, Uereani **228**
Mahdist uprising 228, 229
Mahmud II, Sultan 130, 233
Maipú, Battle of 202
Maji Maji Revolt 229
Malcolm IV of Scotland 84
Malcolm X 292
Mali Empire 126, 127
Maling, Battle of 46
Mamluks 127, 132, 185
Manchu dynasty 119, **142–3**, 166
Manchuria 166, 235, 264, 281, 294
Manco Inca 125
Mandela, Nelson 300, 303
Manhattan Project 285, 290
Mantinea, Battle of 31
Manzikert, Battle of 90, 112
Mao Zedong 241, 264, 265, 282, 294
Mapungubwe, Kingdom of 104
Marathon, Battle of 16, 26–7
March to the Sea 221
Marconi, Guglielmo 216
Marengo, Battle of 185, 186
Maria I of Portugal 192
Maria Theresa of Austria 159
Marignano, Battle of 121
Marne, Battles of the 246, 247, 249, 276
Mars-la-Tour, Battle of 213
Marshall Plan 292–3
Masts, Battle of the 80
Matabele Wars 228
Matthias Corvinus of Hungary 120
Mau-Mau 241, 300, 301–2
Mauryan Empire 17, **42–3**
Maxentius, Emperor 60
Maxim, Hiram 228, 246
Maya civilization 68, 69, **74–5**, 115
Mazarin, Cardinal Jules 154
Mecca 78, 132
medicine
    in Africa 227
    battlefield 171, **194–7**, **206–7**
Medina 78, 80, 132
Megiddo, Battle of 16, 21, 22, 23, 254
Mehmed II, Sultan 102, 112, 113, 130
Meiji dynasty 86
Meiji Restoration 235

332 INDEX

mercenaries **120–21**
  barbarian 62
  Norman 85
  Thirty Years' War 145, 182
Mesoamerica
  Aztec and Inca civilizations 69, **114–15**
  Maya civilization 69, **74–5**
  see also South America
Mesopotamia 12, 16, **18–21**, 38, 61–2, 100–101, 252, 253, 260
Meuse-Argonne Offensive 260
Mexico
  Aztec civilization 69, 118, 123, 124–5
  French in **326**
  Mexican War of Independence 204
  Mexican-American Wars 170, 171, 194, **204–5**
MI5 291
MI6 291
Midway, Battle of 283
migrations **58–65**, 71, 73, 82, 112
Mikatagahara, Battle of 129
military theory **44–7**
Milyutin, General Dimitry 233
Minamoto clan 69, 87
Ming dynasty 98, 142–3, 167
Miranda, Francisco de 200, 201, 203
Mochihito, Prince 87
Moctezuma II 122, 124
modern warfare **216–21**
Mohács, Battle of 132
Mohi, Battle of 100
Moldavia 178, 206, 263
Moltke, Helmuth von 211–12, 213
monarchy, versus parliament **148–9**
Möngke Khan 100, 101
Mongol invasions 69, **96–101**, 142
Monmouth, Battle of 176
Monroe Doctrine 326
Mons, Battle of 244, 246
Mons Seleucus, Battle of 61
Montcalm, General Louis-Joseph de 161
Montenegro 233, 236
Montreal campaign 161
Moors 68, 83, 110
morale, home front (World War I) **258–61**
Morat, Battle of 102
Moreau, General Jean 186
Morocco 118, 126, 127, 302, 304
  Moroccan Crises **326**
  Western Sahara Conflict **327**
Moscow
  retreat from 195–6
  Tatars sack 98
Moscow, Battle of 271
Mozambique 226, 302, 303, 305
Mughal Empire 118–19, **140–41**, 165
Muhammad, the Prophet 68, 78, 79, 80, 90
Mühlberg, Battle of 137
Mujahidden 241, **312–13**, 317
Münster, Peace of 139
Murad I, Sultan 113, 130
Murad III, Sultan 133
Mursa, Battle of 61
Mussolini, Benito 208, 271
Mutapa people 104
Muwatalli, High Prince 21
Mycale, Battle of 27

N

Nagasaki 13, 235, 241, 274, 285
Nagashino, Battle of 129
Nagorno-Karabakh 316
Nanda dynasty 42
Nanjing massacre 264, 265
Nantes, Edict of 138
Naples, Kingdom of 120, 121
Napoleon I, Emperor
  at bay/defeated 170, **194–7**
  French Revolutionary Wars 182, 184–7
  Grand Armée 154, 187, **188–91**
  Peninsular War 192–3, 203
  triumphant 12, 170, **188–91**, 211
Napoleon III, Emperor 208, 209, 212–13
Nara, Siege of 87
Naseby, Battle of 149
Nasser, Gamal Abdel 301, 308
nationalism
  African 301
  German **211**
  rise of **282**
NATO 288, 319
naval power
  ancient Greeks **24–7**
  Arab 80
  Athenian 29
  British 13, 157, 164, 185, 186–7, 198–9, 240
  Chinese 231
  French 186–7
  Japanese 235
  Mongol **101**
  Ottoman 133
  Roman 53
  Russian 158, 235
  US 199, 281–2
  Vikings **84**
  World War I **256–7**, 261
  World War II **272–3**
Nazi regime 240, 258, 261, 268, 276, 278, 308
Nazi-Soviet Pact 269, 271
Nelson, Admiral Horatio 185, 186–7
Netherlands
  Anglo-Dutch Wars **325**
  Boer Wars 234
  colonial empire 280, 282, 296
  Dutch Republic 139
  Dutch Revolt 119, 138–9
  Louis XIV's wars 156
  World War II 269, 282, 283
Nevsky, Prince Alexander 103
New Model Army (NMA) 148, 149, 182
New Orleans, Battle of 199
New Zealand, World War I 253, 255
Ney, Marshal Michel 197
Ngoc Hoi Đong Đa, Battle of 167
Nicaea, Siege of 91
Nicias, Peace of 30
Nightingale, Florence 171, 207
Nile, Battle of the 185, 186
Nimitz, Admiral Chester 283, 284
Nine Years' War 119, 154, 157
Nineveh, Battle of 16, 72
Niš, Treaty of 178
Nobunaga, Oda 118, 128–9
Norman conquests 68, 69, **85**
North Africa
  15th and 16th century warfare **126–7**
  Alexander the Great 39
  colonialism in 227, 228
  independence movements 302
  Islamic conquests 81
  Punic Wars **52–3**
  Roman province 71, 72
  Vandal kingdom 64, 65
North America
  European settlement **222–3**
  French and Indian Wars **160–61**
  Seven Years' War 164, 165, 252

warfare (c. 1610–80s) **150–51**
  see also Canada; Mexico, United States
North German Confederation 212
North Korea 284, 290
Northern Han dynasty 48
nuclear arms race 288–93, 317
Nyatsimba Mutota, Prince of Great Zimbabwe 104

O

Ochakov, Siege of 179
Octavian see Augustus, Emperor
Odoacer 65, 68, 71, 82
Ögedei Khan 100
Olmecs 74
Omdurman, Battle of 229
Onin War 128
Opechancanough 251
Operation Desert Storm 274, 315
Operation Enduring Freedom 313
Operation Neptune Spear **313**
Operation Valkyrie 277, 278
Opium Wars 170, 230–31, 280
Oppenheimer, Robert 285
Orhan I, Sultan 113
Orléans, Siege of 108, 109
Osman I, Sultan **112–13**
Osman II, Sultan 133
Ostrogoths 63, 68, 71, 72
Ottoman Empire 70, 73, 90, 102, 118, **130–33**, 140, 162
  and the Balkans 232, 233, 235, 236–7, 252
  collapse of 252, 255, 258, 261
  Crimean War **206–7**
  Napoleon and 185
  rise of the Ottoman Turks 69, **112–13**, 118
  rivalry with Russia 133, 170, 171, 178, 179, **232–3**
  World War I 247, 252, 254, 259, 260
Ötzi the Ice Man 106

P

Pacific Ocean, World War II 275, 282–3, 284–5
Pakistan
  Indo-Pakistan conflicts **326–7**
  nuclear tests 288
  partition of India 225
Palestine
  Arab conquest 80
  Arab-Israeli Conflicts 241, 308–311
  Maccabaeuan Revolt **324**
  World War I 253, 254, 260
Palestine Liberation Organization (PLO) 309
Pan-African Congress 300
Panama 200, 202, 298
Panipat, Battle of 140
Papacy **94–5**
Papal States 120, 208, 209
Paraguayan War 171, **224**
Paré, Ambrose 194
Paris Commune 208
Paris, fall of 270
Paris Peace Accords 297
Paris peace treaties 258
Paris, Siege of 213
Paris, Treaty of (1783) 174
Paris, Treaty of (1815) 197
Paris, Treaty of (1856) 207

Parliament, king versus **148–9**
Parma, Alexander Farnese, Duke of 138–9
Parthian Empire 40, 57
Paschal II, Pope 95
Passchendaele, Battle of 251, 253
Pasternak, Boris 293
Pasteur, Louis 206
Paul I, Czar 178
Pavia, Battle of 121
Pearl Harbor 240, 265, 275, 281–2, 284
Peasants' War 136–7
Pedro I of Brazil 203
Pelagius of Asturias 110
Peloponnesian League 28–9, 30
Peloponnesian Wars 16, 24, **28–31**
Peninsular War 170, 191, **192–3**, 197, 203
Perryville, Battle of 219
Persia/Persian Empire 16–17, **23**, 24, 26–7, 28, 29, 31, 34, 70, 100–101
  Alexander the Great and 16, 35–6, 37, 38–9
  and Byzantine Empire 71, 72
  Ottomans and 132, 133
  and Russia 178
  Timur and 105
  wars with Romans 61–2, 63
  see also Achaemenid Empire; Iran; Safavid dynasty; Sasanian Empire
Pétain, Marshal Philippe 270
Peter I (the Great), Czar 119, 158, 178
Peter III, Czar 165, 178
phalanxes 12, 16, 35, 41, 50
Philip II of Macedon **34**, 35, 40, 154
Philip II of Spain 137, 138, 139
Philip VI of France 69, 107, 108
Philip, Duke of Anjou 157
Philippe of Belgium 226
Philippine Sea, Battle of the 284
Phoney War 269
Pichincha, Battle of 203
Picts 62, 63
Piedmont-Sardinia 208, 209
Pius VI, Pope 184
Pizarro, Francisco 118, 125
Plains of Abraham, Battle of the 161
Plains Wars 223
Plassey, Battle of 165, 225
Plataea, Battle of 27
Poitiers, Battle of (732) 81
Poitiers, Battle of (1356) 109
Poland 162, 164, 238
  Jews in 140
  Mongol invasions 100
  and Ottomans 133
  Partitions of 179
  Russian Civil War 263
  World War II 268–9, 272
Polk, James K. 170, 205
Poltava, Battle of 158
Port Arthur, Battle of 235
Porto, Battle of 193
Portugal
  and Africa 104, 127, 226
  conquests in the Americas 122
  loss of colonies 200, 203, 302–3
  Peninsular War 170, 191, 192–3
Porus, King 39
post-traumatic stress disorder (PTSD) 248, 249, 251
Potemkin, Marshal Grigory 179
Potsdam Declaration 285
Powell, Colin 315
Powers, Gary 291–2
Powhatan, Chief 150–51
Powhatan people 119, 150–51

INDEX

Praetorian Guard 60
Pragmatic Sanction 159
Prague, Peace of 147
Prigozhin, Yevgeny 305, **320**
prisoners of war 192
    Japanese 283
    Vietnamese 296
propaganda
    Cold War 290, 291
    World War II 278
Protestantism 78, 94, 103
    European wars of religion **136–9**
    Thirty Years' War 119, 145
proxy wars 289–90
Prussia
    conscription 182
    Franco-Prussian War 171, 194, 213, 244, 245, 247
    Napoleonic Wars 188, 189, 190, 196–7
    rise of 158, **162–5**, 171, **210–213**
    Seven Weeks' War 211–12, 245
    Teutonic Knights 103
    War of the Austrian Succession 159, 162, 163
Ptolemy/Ptolemaic dynasty 40–41, 55
Pu Yi, Emperor 231, 264
Pueblo Revolts 150, 151
Puerto Rico 122
Pugachev, Yemelyan 179
Punic Wars 17, 22, **52–3**
Punjab 39, 42, 225
Putin, Vladimir 241, 305, 318, 319–20
Pydna, Battle of 40
Pyrrhus of Epirus 51

Q

Qianlong Emperor (Hongli) 119, **166–7**
Qin dynasty 17, 44, 45, 47, 48, 154
Qin Er Shi (Ying Huhai), Emperor 44
Qin Shi Huang (Ying Zheng), Emperor 17, 47, 48
Qing dynasty 119, 142, 143, 166–7, 192, **230–31**, 264
Quatre Bras, Battle of 197
Quebec, Battle of 161

R

Rabin, Yitzhak 311
Ragamuffin War 208
Rameses II, Pharaoh 21
Rameses XI, Pharaoh 18
Ramillies, Battle of 157
Red Army (People's Liberation Army) 154, 294
Red Terror **262–3**
Redshirts 171, 209
Reformation 94, 103, 119, **136–9**, 145
Reign of Terror 182, 183
religion
    Crusades 68, 69, **88–93**, **102–3**
    European Wars of **134–9**
    God versus king **94–5**
    religious tolerance as state policy 119, **140–41**, 147
    Spanish Reconquista **110–111**
    and warfare 68–9, **78–81**
Rhodes, Siege of 102, 131, 132
Richard I (the Lionheart) of England 92
Riga, Peace of 263
Risorgimento 208
River Plate, Battle of the 273
river warfare **224**
Rochambeau, Comte de 176–7

Rogers, Robert/Rogers' Rangers 160, **161**
Roman Catholic Church **84–5**
    European wars of religion **136–9**
    Thirty Years' War 119, 145
Romania 233, 236, 288
Romanos II, Emperor 73
Romanov dynasty 158
Romans
    annexation of Egypt 40
    Belisarius recaptures Rome 72
    conflict with Greece 51
    Constantine's reorganization of army 60
    decline and fall of Western Empire 17, 54, **58–65**, 70, 71
    from republic to empire **54–5**
    infrastructure of empire 17, **56–7**
    Macedonian Wars 34, 40
    Punic Wars 17, 22, **52–3**
    rise of Rome **50–51**
    Servile Wars **324**
    sieges and sackings of Rome 16, 17, 50, 52, 64, 95, 121, 209
Romulus Augustulus, Emperor 54, 65, 68, 71, 82
Roncesvalles, Battle of **83**
Roosevelt, Franklin D. 284, 285, 298, 301
Rosas, Juan Manuel de 204
Rossbach, Battle of 164
Rubicon, crossing the 55
Rudolf of Rheinfelden, Duke of Swabia 94
Rumyantsev, Field Marshal Pyotr 178
Russia
    Balkans conflict 233, 236
    Caucasus strategy **316**
    Crimean War **206–7**
    invasion of Ukraine 224, 241, **318–21**
    Mongol invasions 99, 100
    Napoleonic Wars 188, 189, 190, 194–7
    and Ottoman Empire 133, 162, 171, 178, 179, **232–3**
    rise of **158**
    Russian Civil War 240, **262–3**
    Russian Revolution 158, 232, 240, 247, 255, 258, 262
    Russo-Japanese War 171, 232, 233, **235**, 237, 249
    Russo–Turkish War 130, 162, 170, 178, 232, 236
    Seven Years' War 162, 164, 165
    Teutonic Knights 103
    wars of Catherine the Great **178–9**
    World War I 232, 240, 244, 246, 247, 252, 261, 262
    see also USSR

S

Saadian dynasty 127
Sacred Wars 78
sacrifices, human **74–5**, 115
Sadat, Anwar 309
Safavid dynasty 105, 118, 132, 133, 178
Salah ad-Din (Saladin) 92
Salamanca, Battle of 193
Salamis, Battle of 26, 27
Samnites 51, 52
samurai 69, **86–7**, 106, 128
San Jacinto, Battle of 205
San Martín, José 202, 203
Santa Anna, Antonio López de 204–5
Saratoga, Battle of 176
Sargon I of Akkad 12, 16, 20
Sasanian Empire 18, 43, 61–2, 63, 68, 71, 72, 80
Saxony/Saxons 63, 82, 94, 163, 164

scalping 151
Scchwarzkopf, Norman 315
Scheidemann, Philipp 261
Schleswig Wars 210, 211
Schlieffen, Alfred von/Schlieffen Plan 244, **245**, 246, 247, 268
Schmalkaldic Wars 137
Scholae Palatinae 60
Scipio Africanus **53**
scorched-earth tactics 158, 195, 221, 234, 247, 279, 312
Scotland
    Covenanters 148–9
    Edward I's conquest **325**
    Jacobites 159
Scramble for Africa **226–9**
Seacole, Mary 171, 206, 207
Sedan, Battle of 213
Sekigahara, Battle of 129
Seleucus I Nicator/Seleucid dynasty 40, **41**, 324
Seljuk Empire 90, 91, 92, 93, 112
sepoys **225**
Serbia 112, 233, 236, 237, 240, 244, 247
Sevastopol, Siege of 171, 207
Seven Days' Battles 218
Seven Weeks' War (Austro-Prtussian War) 211–12, 245
Seven-Years' War 159, 160, **162–5**, 252
Shah Jahan 141
Shaka Zulu 228
Shalmaneser III of Assyria 22
Shang Yang 47
Shapur II of Persia 61
shell shock 247, **248–51**
Sherman, General William T. 220, 221
Shi'a Islam 78, 81, 317
Shiloh, Battle of 218
Shipka Pass, Battle of 233
ships
    Greek triremes 25–6
    ironclad warships 13, 216, 224
    Viking longships **84**
Shun dynasty 143
Sicily 2–8, 31, 52, 53, 73, 85, 95, 121, 209
siege warfare 13, **22**, 49, 63, 93, 99–100, 108, 109, 112, 131
Silesia 159, 162, 163, 164–5
Silva Xavier, Joaquim José da 200
Sima Yan 48
Sinai Peninsula 308, 309, 310
Sino-Japanese Wars 171, 230, **264–5**, 280, 281, 294
Sivas, Siege of 105
Six Secret Teachings (T'ai Kung) 45
Six-Day War 309
skirmishers **186**
Skobelev, Mikhail **233**
slavery
    abolition of 171, 208, 216, 217, 219
    slave trade 198
    slave wars **126–7**
Slavs 72, 103
Sluys, Battle of 107
Snowshoes, Battle on 161
socialism 258, 259, 261
Sokoto Caliphate 227
Solferino, Battle of 171, 209
Somali pirates 84
Somerled, Lord of the Isles 84
Somme, Battle of the 28, 244, 250–51, 253
Somoza, Anastasio 299
Song dynasty 101
Songhai Empire 118, 126, 127
Soong Mei-ling (Madame Chiang) **265**
South Africa 300, 303

Boer Wars 229, **234**, 248
World War I 253, 255
South America
    European conquest 69, **122–5**
    Garibaldi in 208–9
    wars of liberation 170, **200–203**, 204
    see also Mesoamerica
Southeast Asia
    independence movements **296–7**
    World War II **280–85**
Southern Rhodesia 303
Soviet Bloc 279, 288, 293, 319
Soviet Union *see* USSR
space race 293
Spain
    conquests in Mesoamerica 110, 114, 118, **122–5**
    Dutch Revolt 138–9
    Islamic 73, 81, 83, 110
    Italian Wars 121
    loss of colonies 170, 298
    Louis XIV's wars with 119, 155–6
    in North America 150
    Peninsular War 170, 191, **192–3**
    reconquista 68, **110–111**
    Romans 60, 64
    South American wars of liberation **200–203**
    Spanish Armada 119, 139
    Spanish Civil War 256, 274, **326**
    Thirty Years' War 146, 147
    War of the Spanish Succession 157, 174
Sparta 16, 24, 25, 26–7, 28–31, 34, 56
Spartacus 54
Spartacus League 258, 259, 261
Special Operations Executive (SOE) 271
Sphacteria, Battle of 30
Spring and Autumn Period 45, 46
Spring Offensive 260
Srebrenica 192
Sri Lankan Civil War **327**
St. Bartholomew's Day massacre 119, 138
Stalin, Josef 262
Stalingrad, Battle of 275, 276
standing armies **154–7**
starvation 258–9
state, Church and **94–5**, 136
Stauffenberg, Klaus von 277
strategic bombing 274, **275**, 279
submarines
    World War I **256–7**
    World War II **272–2**
Sucre, Antonio José de 203
Sudan 228, 229, 304
Suez Crisis **301**, 308
Sui dynasty 48, 324
Sukarno 282
Suleiman I (the Magnificent), Sultan 118, **131**, 132–3
Sulla, Lucius Cornelius 55
Sumer/Sumerians 12, 16, 19–20, 21
Sun Bin 46
Sundiata Keita of Mali 126
Sunni Islam 81, 317
Sunzi 44, 45–7
supplies 163
Surorov, General Alexander 178, 179
Swiss Guard 120
Syracuse 31, 53
Syria 36–7, 40, 72, 73
    Arab conquest 80
    Arab–Israeli Conflicts 308, 309
    Syrian Civil War 317, 318, **327**

334 INDEX

T

T'ai Kung 45
Taiho Code 86
Taika Reform 86
Taiping Rebellion 231
Taira clan 69, 87
Taiwan 166, 167, 230, 294
Takakura, Emperor 87
Talavera, Battle of 193
Taliban 241, 313
Tang dynasty 48
Tangut people 98, 99
tank warfare 244, 268, 269, 278
Tattooed Serpent 74
Tecumseh 198, **199**
Ten Great Campaigns 119, **166–7**, 230
Tenochtitlan 123, 124
Teotihuacán 114
Terracotta Army **47**
Teutoburg Forest, Battle of 52
Teutonic Knights 69, 103
Thames, Battle of the 199
Thermopylae, Battle of 27
Thirty Years' War 78, 119, 120, **144–7**, 182
Thrace 112, 113, 237
Three Kingdoms of China 49
Thutmose III, Pharaoh 16, 21
Tiglath-pileser I of Assyria 22
Tiglath-pileser III of Assyria 22, 23
Tilsit, Peace of 190, 211
Timur/Timurid Empire 69, **105**, 141
Tippecanoe, Battle of 222
Tokugawa shogunate 129
Tokyo, World War II 283, 285
Toltec Empire 114
Tordesillas, Treaty of 122
Torwa dynasty 104
Toulouse, Battle of 193
Tours, Battle of 82
trade/trade routes 57
    Great Zimbabwe **104**
    India 225
    Japan 128
    Silk Road 48
    slave trade 126–7
Trafalgar, Battle of 170, 186–7, 190
Trail of Tears **222–3**
Trajan, Emperor 17, **57**
Trans Siberian Railway 235
transportation **56–7**, 216, **219**
Trasimene, Battle of 53
Trench, Battle of the 78
trench warfare 221, 235, 237, 244, 246, 247, 248–51
Trenton, Battle of 175
Triple Alliance 210, 240, 244
Troy, Siege of 84
Truman, Harry S. 284, 285, 289, 295
Tsushima, Battle of 235
two-state solution **308–311**
Tyre, Siege of 22, 24, 37

U

U-boats 198, 240, 256–7, 259, 269, 272–3
Ubu Abkr 78, 79
Uhud, Battle of 78
Uji, Battle of 87
Ukraine 262, 263
    Russian invasion of 224, 241, **318–21**
Ulm, Battle of 189
Ultra code breaking operation **273**
Umar ibn al-Khattab 78–9
Umayyad caliphate 72, 79, 80, 81, 83

Union States 217–21
United Nations
    peacekeeping operations 23
    Universal Declaration of Human Rights 140
United States
    aid to Ukraine 320
    American Civil War 28, 171, 182, 186, 194, **214–21**, 224, 235, 248, 256
    American Revolution 160, 170, **172–7**
    American-Mexican Wars 170, 171, 194, **204–5**
    Arab–Israeli Conflicts 308, 309–310
    Cold War 241, 288–93
    conflict in Afghanistan 312–13, 318
    and Cuba 298–9
    Gulf Wars 314–15, 317
    highest wartime death tolls 220
    interventions in Latin America 298–9
    Iraq War 317
    Korean War 295
    and opening of Japan 128
    settlement of North America 171, **222–3**
    Vietnam War 296–7
    War of 1812 **198–9**
    World War I 240, 259, 260
    World War II 240, 241, 256, 277, 278, **280–85**
Urban II, Pope 69, 90
Urdaneta, Rafael 202
Uruguay 114, 201, 224
    Uruguayan Civil War 208
Uruk 16, 19
Ushant, 4th Battle of 186
USSR
    Arab–Israeli Conflicts 308, 309–310
    Cold War 241, 284, 288–93
    collapse of 241, 276, 316
    conflict in Afghanistan 312–13, 317
    formation of 262, 263
    Korean War 295
    World War II 240–41, 258, 259, 269, 271, 274–5, 278, 279, 281
    see also Russia
Uthman ibn Affan 80
Uyghur people 167
Uzbek Khan 105

V

Valdivia, Pedro de 122
Valens, Emperor 63–4
Valentinian I, Emperor 63
Valentinian III, Emperor 65
Valley Forge 176
Valmy, Battle of 182
Vandals 64, 65, 68, 71–2
Varangian Guard 73, 84
Vauban, Sébastien Le Prestre, Marquis of **154**, 155, 157
Velázquez de Cuéllar, Diego 124
Venezuela 298
    independence movement 170, 200, 201, 202–3
Venice, and Ottoman Empire 112, 130, 133
Verdun, Battle of 28, 250
Verdun, Treaty of 82
Versailles, Palace of 156
Versailles, Treaty of 244, 252, 268, 276
Vicksburg campaign 219
Victor Emmanuel II of Piedmont-Sardinia (later Italy) 208, 209
Vienna, Napoleon occupies 191
Vienna, Siege of (1529) 90, 118, 131, 132–3
Vienna, Siege of (1683) 133

Vienna, Treaty of 159
Vietnam 167, 282, 290, 295, 296–7
    Vietnam War 224, 248, 296–7
Vikings 68, 69, 73, **84**, 85
Visigoths 17, 62, 63, 64, 65, 78
Vlad III (the Impaler) of Wallachia 105
Volturno, Battle of the 209

W

Wabanaki Confederacy 160
Wagner Group **305**, 320
Wagram, Battle of 191
Waldensians 136
Wales, Edward I's conquest **325**
Wallachia 206
Wallenstein, Albrecht von 146, 147
walls, defensive 47, 62, 63, **143**
Wampanoag people 151, 222
Wang Mang 49
War of 1812 13, **198–9**
War of the Austrian Succession **159**, 162, 163
War of the Bavarian Succession 162
war crimes 265
War of Devolution 156
War of the First Coalition 182
War of the Reunions 156
War of the Second Coalition 185–6
War of the Spanish Succession 157, 174
War of the Third Coalition 189
War of the Triple Alliance 171, **224**
Warring States Period 45, 46
Warsaw, Battle of 263
Warsaw Pact 288
Washington, George 160–61, 175, 176
Waterberg, Battle of 228
Waterloo, Battle of 170, 197
Wayna Daga, Battle of 127
weapons
    Arab 79, 80
    Aztec 114, 115
    cannons 13, 106, 109, 113
    Chinese 46, 49
    Colt revolver 171, **205**
    crossbows 108, 109
    Crusaders 93
    European in Africa 227–8
    flintlock muskets **163**
    Greek fire **73**
    Hundred Years' War **106–9**
    Inca 115
    Indigenous peoples 150, 151
    intercontinental ballistic missiles 289
    Japanese 128, **129**
    longbows 13, 107–8, 109
    Maxim gun 171, 228, 246
    Maya 75
    Mongols 99–100
    Ottoman 131, 132
    rifle-muskets 13, 216, **219**
    Roman 63
    samurai 86–7
    Seljuk Turks 93
    torpedoes 216
    trebuchets 93, 99–100, 101
    V-1 and V-2 rockets 278
    weapons of mass destruction (WMDs) 317
    see also chemical warfare; drone warfare; germ warfare; nuclear arms race
Wei state 46, 47, 48
wellington, Arthur Wellesley, Duke of 193, 197

Western Front (World War I) 244–7, **248–51**, 253, 260, 261
Western Roman Empire 60, 62, 64–5, 70, 71, 72
Western Sahara Conflict **327**
Westphalia, Peace of 147
White Mountain, Battle of the 145, 146
Whitehead, Robert 216
Wilderness, Battle of the 220, 221
Winnemucca, Sarah 222, **223**
Wolfe, General James 161
women
    at war **261**
    code breakers 272
    "Night Witches" **275**
World War I 23, 28, 216, 235, 236, 237, 268
    defeat of Central Powers (1918) **258–61**
    expanding war (1915–17) **252–5**
    outbreak 240, **242–7**
    sea and air warfare 13, 198, **256–7**, 274
    stalemate on Western Front **248–51**
World War II
    air war 13, **274–5**
    defeat of Germany (1944–45) **276–9**
    defeat of Japan (1943–45) **284–5**
    in Europe (1939–43) **266–71**
    Japan ascendant (1941-43) 240, **280–83**
    mobile war 244
    war at sea **272–3**
Wounded Knee, Battle of 223
Wudi, Emperor 49

X

Xerxes I of Persia 27
Xiang Yu 48
Xin dynasty 49
Xinhai Revolution 231
Xiongnu 48–9

Y

Yamamoto, Admiral Isoroku 283
Yamen, Battle of 101
Yangzhou massacre 143
Yarmuk River, Battle of the 79, 80
Yazid I, Caliph 81
Yorimasa, Monamoto no **87**
Yoritomo no Minamoto 87
York, Battle of 199
Yorktown, Siege of 170, 177
Yoshimasa, Ashikaga 128
Yoshinaka, Minamoto no 87
Ypres, Second Battle of 250
Yuan dynasty 101, 167
Yugoslavia 236, 261, 270
    war in the former **327**

Z

Zahir Shah 312
Zama, Battle of 53
Zeppelins 257, 274
Zhao state 45, 47
Zhou dynasty 45, 46
Zhu Yuanzhang 98
Zhukov, Marshal Georgy 271
Zinoviev Letter 288
Zionist movement 308
Zosimus 60
Zouaves 254
Zulu Kingdom 228–9, 234
Zuo Zhuan 46

QUOTE ATTRIBUTIONS

ANCIENT WARFARE

18 Enheduanna of Akkad, Sumerian priestess
22 Sennacherib, Assyrian king
23 Cyrus the Great, founder of the First Persian Empire
24 Thucydides, Athenian historian
28 Archidamus, Spartan king
32 Alexander the Great, Macedonian emperor
40 Antonis Chaliakopoulos, archaeologist
42 Purushottam Lal Bhargava, Indian historian
44 Sunzi, Chinese military theorist
48 Zhuge Liang, Chinese military strategist
50 Virgil, Roman poet
52 Polybius, Roman historian
54 Julius Caesar, Roman dictator
56 Proverb, first recorded in writing by Alain de Lille, French theologian and poet
58 Lord Byron, British poet

WAR IN THE MIDDLE AGES

70 Laws of Justinian I, Eastern Roman emperor
74 *Popul Vuh*, Maya sacred text
76 The Qur'an
82 Einhard, Frankish historian
84 Dudo of St. Quentin, French historian
85 William of Poitiers, Norman chronicler
86 Yamamoto Tsunetomo, Japanese philosopher
88 Crusader rallying cry
94 Frederick Barbarossa, Holy Roman Emperor
96 Genghis Khan, founder of the Mongol Empire
102 Pope Innocent III, leader of the Catholic Church
104 Thomas Streissguth, US writer
105 Sharaf al-Din Ali Yazdi, Persian scholar
106 William Shakespeare, English playwright
110 Peter of Quintana, Spanish secretary of state
112 Urban, Transylvanian cannon maker
114 Aztec prayer to the god Tezcatlipoca

EARLY MODERN WARFARE

120 Jan Westcott, US novelist
122 Simon Sebag Montefiore, British historian
126 Leo Africanus, Andalusian scholar and traveler
128 Tokugawa Ieyasu, Japanese shogun
130 Gábor Ágoston, US historian
134 Treaty of Westphalia
140 Principle of Akbar the Great, Mughal emperor
142 *The Old Manchu Chronicles*, c. 1775
144 Gustav Freytag, German journalist
148 Charles I, English king
150 Unnamed Indigenous American fighter in King Philip's War
152 Philippe-Henri de Grimoard, French military historian
158 Inscription on Russian naval medal, 1702
159 Frederick the Great, Prussian emperor
160 Robert Rogers, founder and commander of Rogers' Rangers
162 Honoré-Gabriel Riqueti, comte de Mirabeau, French politician and orator
166 Hongli, Chinese emperor

REVOLUTIONS AND EMPIRE

172 Patrick Henry, US lawyer and politician
178 Catherine the Great, Russian empress
180 French declaration of war on Austria, 1792
188 Friedrich Nietzsche, German philosopher
192 Joseph de Naylies, French officer
194 Unnamed infantry lieutenant
198 Flag raised on the US frigate *Essex*, July 1812
200 Peruvian Declaration of Independence, 1821
204 Will Fowler, political historian
206 Florence Nightingale, British nurse and social reformer
208 Italian national anthem
210 Wilhelm I, German emperor
214 Theodore F. Upson, US Union soldier
222 Tecumseh, Shawnee chief
224 *Glasgow Daily Herald*, 1868
225 Lord Curzon, British statesman
226 *The Times*, 1884
230 Cixi, Chinese empress dowager
232 Enver Pasha, Ottoman war minister
234 Spencer Jones, historian and author
235 Konstantin Ippolitovich Vogak, Russian military attaché to Japan
236 Sir Edward Grey, British foreign minister

THE WORLD WARS AND BEYOND

242 Basil H. Liddell Hart, British military theorist and historian
248 Wilfred Owen, British poet and soldier
252 Winston Churchill, British politician and author
256 John Arbuthnot Fisher, British admiral and First Sea Lord
258 Wilhelm II, German emperor
262 Bolshevik government warning to the Soviet port city of Kronstadt, 1921
264 *Journal of the History of Medicine and Allied Sciences*, January 2022
266 Winston Churchill, British prime minister
272 Winston Churchill, British prime minister
274 Ira C. Eaker, US general
276 Winston Churchill, British prime minister
280 Japanese political slogan, 1930s–1940s
284 James Francis Byrnes, US secretary of state
286 Winston Churchill, British leader of the opposition
294 Chiang Kai-Shek, Chinese statesman
295 Harry S. Truman, US president
296 Ho Chi Minh, Vietnamese revolutionary and politician
298 Ernesto "Che" Guevara, Argentinian revolutionary and guerilla leader
300 Jomo Kenyatta, Kenyan president
304 Mohamed ElBaradei, winner of the Nobel Peace Prize
306 Yitzhak Rabin, Israeli prime minister
312 Turki al-Faisal al-Saud, Saudi prince and former head of intelligence
314 *FM 100-5 Operations*, US Army field manual, 1982 edition
316 Aslan Maskhadov, Chechen politician and military leader
317 Haider al-Abadi, Iraqi prime minister
318 Seth Cropsey, US political researcher and writer

ACKNOWLEDGMENTS

Dorling Kindersley would like to thank Vanessa Hamilton for additional illustrations; Mark Cavanagh for design assistance; Alice Hughes and Laura Sandford for editorial assistance; Oliver Drake for proofreading; and Helen Peters for indexing. DK Delhi would like to thank Shipra Jain for design assistance; Kanika Kalra, Mohd. Zishan, and Priyal Mote for additional illustrations; and Samrajkumar S. for picture research assistance.

PICTURE CREDITS

The publisher would like to thank the following for their kind permission to reproduce their photographs:

(Key: a-above; b-below/bottom; c-center; f-far; l-left; r-right; t-top)

20 Alamy Stock Photo: Science History Images (t). **21 Alamy Stock Photo:** Prisma Archivo (br). **Dreamstime.com:** Radiokafka (bl). **23 Alamy Stock Photo:** CPA Media Pte Ltd / Pictures From History (cra). **25 Alamy Stock Photo:** George Atsametakis (br). **26 Alamy Stock Photo:** Cola Images (tl). **30 Bridgeman Images:** Look and Learn (br). **Getty Images:** Bettmann (tl). **31 Alamy Stock Photo:** De Luan (tl). **34 Alamy Stock Photo:** Chronicle (bl). **37 Alamy Stock Photo:** Adam Eastland (b). **39 Alamy Stock Photo:** Atlaspix (tr). **Bridgeman Images:** Look and Learn / Illustrated Papers Collection (bl). **40 Alamy Stock Photo:** Sunny Celeste (br). **41 Alamy Stock Photo:** Adam Eastland (tr). **42 Alamy Stock Photo:** Tuul and Bruno Morandi (br). **45 Alamy Stock Photo:** YA / BOT (tl). **46 123RF.com:** Bakai (crb). **47 Alamy Stock Photo:** Ming WU (tl). **48 Alamy Stock Photo:** CPA Media Pte Ltd / Pictures From History (br). **49 Gary Lee Todd, Ph.D, Professor of History Sias University Xinzheng, Henan, China:** (br). **50 Shutterstock.com:** Morphart Creation (br). **52 Alamy Stock Photo:** Heritage Image Partnership Ltd / Docutres (br). **53 Alamy Stock Photo:** Interfoto / Personalities (tr). **54 Alamy Stock Photo:** Volgi archive (br). **55 Alamy Stock Photo:** IanDagnall Computing (tl). **57 Alamy Stock Photo:** Adam Eastland (bl); Jon Arnold Images Ltd (tr). **60 Getty Images:** De Agostini / De Agostini Picture Library (tr). **61 Getty Images:** Corbis Historical / Stefano Bianchetti (bl). **63 Bridgeman Images:** Look and Learn (tr). **64 Getty Images:** Moment / Mikroman6 (t). **65 Alamy Stock Photo:** GRANGER - Historical Picture Archive (bl); Pictorial Press Ltd (tr). **71 Getty Images / iStock:** DigitalVision Vectors / Duncan1890 (br). **72 Alamy Stock Photo:** The Picture Art Collection (b). **73 Alamy Stock Photo:** Niday Picture Library (br). **74 Getty Images:** Universal Images Group / Werner Forman (c). **75 Alamy Stock Photo:** Heritage Image Partnership Ltd / Index (tc); J Marshall - Tribaleye Images / Ethnografia (br). **78 Alamy Stock Photo:** CPA Media Pte Ltd / Pictures From History (bl). **79 Alamy Stock Photo:** Florilegius (tl). **81 Alamy Stock Photo:** Gibson Green (tr). **83 Alamy Stock Photo:** GRANGER - Historical Picture Archive (br); Science History Images / Photo Researchers (tl). **85 Alamy Stock Photo:** Forget Patrick (br). **87 Alamy Stock Photo:** The Picture Art Collection (bl). **Bridgeman Images:** Boltin Picture Library (tr). **90 Alamy Stock Photo:** Album (bl). **91 Getty Images:** De Agostini / Dea / G.dagli Orti (br). **92 Alamy Stock Photo:** CPA Media Pte Ltd / Pictures From History (bl). **93 Alamy Stock Photo:** Science History Images / Photo Researchers (br). **94 Alamy Stock Photo:** Interfoto / Personalities (bc). **95 Alamy Stock Photo:** Sunny Celeste (tr). **99 Alamy Stock Photo:** Interfoto / Fine Arts (br). **100 Alamy Stock Photo:** Abu Castor (bl). **101 Alamy Stock Photo:** Classic Image (bl). **103 Alamy Stock Photo:** Heritage Image Partnership Ltd / © Fine Art Images (tl); World History Archive (br). **104 Alamy Stock Photo:** Christopher Scott (bc). **107 Alamy Stock Photo:** Heritage Image Partnership Ltd / Fine Art Images (tr). **108 Alamy Stock Photo:** Classic Image (bl). **109 Alamy Stock Photo:** GRANGER - Historical Picture Archive (bl). **111 Alamy Stock Photo:** CPA Media Pte Ltd / Pictures From History (tr); Prisma Archivo (bl). **113 Istanbul Metropolitan Municipality - Kültür A - Panorama 1453 History Museum:** (br). **115 Alamy Stock Photo:** IanDagnall Computing (bl); Niday Picture Library (br). **121 Alamy Stock Photo:** Art Collection 2 (tr); Historimages Collection / Yolanda Perera Sánchez (bl). **123 Alamy Stock Photo:** Travelpix (t). **124 Alamy Stock Photo:** Classic Image (tl). **125 Getty Images:** De Agostini / Dea / A. Dagli Orti (tl). **127 Depositphotos Inc:** Piccaya (tl). **129 Alamy Stock Photo:** The Picture Art Collection (tr); Zoom Historical (b). **131 Alamy Stock Photo:** IanDagnall Computing (tr); Mccool (bc). **132 Alamy Stock Photo:** The Picture Art Collection (tc). **133 Getty Images:** De Agostini / Dea / A. Dagli Orti (br). **137 Alamy Stock Photo:** Classic Image (bl). **Getty Images / iStock:** DigitalVision Vectors / ZU_09 (tr). **138 Alamy Stock Photo:** GRANGER - Historical Picture Archive (b). **140 Alamy Stock Photo:** The Picture Art Collection (bc). **141 Alamy Stock Photo:** Archivah (tr). **143 Alamy Stock Photo:** CPA Media Pte Ltd / Pictures From History (tc); Jon Arnold Images Ltd / Alan Copson (br). **145 Bridgeman Images:** National Gallery of Victoria, Melbourne / Brozik, Vaclav (Wenzel von) (br). **146 Getty Images / iStock:** DigitalVision Vectors / ZU_09 (b). **147 Alamy Stock Photo:** Classic Image (tl). **149 123RF.com:** Candyman (bl). **Alamy Stock Photo:** World History Archive (tr). **150 © The Trustees of the British Museum. All rights reserved:** (bc). **154 Alamy Stock Photo:** History_Docu_Photo (bl). **155 Alamy Stock Photo:** Heritage Image Partnership Ltd (tc). **156 Alamy Stock Photo:** Realy Easy Star (bl). **157 Getty Images:** De Agostini / Dea Picture Library (tr). **158 Alamy Stock Photo:** GL Archive (crb). **161 Alamy Stock Photo:** Artgen (bl); World History Archive (tr). **163 Alamy Stock Photo:** IanDagnall Computing (tr). **164 Alamy Stock Photo:** Sunny Celeste (bl). **165 Alamy Stock Photo:** Heritage Image Partnership Ltd / Fine Art Images (tr). **167 Alamy Stock Photo:** Maidun Collection (tl). **174 Alamy Stock Photo:** GRANGER - Historical Picture Archive (tr); Incamerastock / ICP (bl). **175 Alamy Stock Photo:** Rana Royalty free (br). **177 Alamy Stock Photo:** Everett Collection Inc / Ron Harvey (bl). **178 Alamy Stock Photo:** Album (bc). **179 Alamy Stock Photo:** Album (bl). **182 Alamy Stock Photo:** GL Archive (tr). **183 Alamy Stock Photo:** World History Archive (bl). **184 Alamy Stock Photo:** Josse Christophel (bl). **185 Alamy Stock Photo:** Pictorial Press Ltd (br). **187 Alamy Stock Photo:** Shawshots (tr). **189 Alamy Stock Photo:** Niday Picture Library (br). **190 Alamy Stock Photo:** GL Archive (b). **191 Alamy Stock Photo:** Lanmas (tl). **193 Alamy Stock Photo:** Niday Picture Library (tl). **195 Alamy Stock Photo:** Album (br); Artgen (tl). **196 Alamy Stock Photo:** Penta Springs Limited (tl). **197 Alamy Stock Photo:** CBW (tr). **199 Alamy Stock Photo:** IllustratedHistory (br); YA / BOT (tl). **201 Alamy Stock Photo:** Chronicle (tl). **202 Alamy Stock Photo:** Heritage Image Partnership Ltd / Index (bl). **203 Getty Images:** De Agostini / Dea / M. Seemuller (tl). **204 Alamy Stock Photo:** North Wind Picture Archives (bc). **205 Alamy Stock Photo:** Science History Images / Photo Researchers (bl). **207 Alamy Stock Photo:** Historic Illustrations (tl); Science History Images (br). **209 Alamy Stock Photo:** Interfoto / Personalities (tr). **211 Alamy Stock Photo:** IanDagnall Computing (br); World History Archive (tl). **213 Alamy Stock Photo:** Interfoto / Fine Arts (tl). **216 Alamy Stock Photo:** Hi-Story (tr). **217 Alamy Stock Photo:** North Wind Picture Archives (bl). **219 Alamy Stock Photo:** Ivy Close Images (br). **220 Alamy Stock Photo:** Everett Collection Historical (tr). **Statista 2024:** United States; US Department of Defense; American Battlefield Trust; 1775 to 2024 / Data of The highest wartime death tolls for the US (b). **221 Alamy Stock Photo:** Stocktrek Images, Inc. (tr). **223 Alamy Stock Photo:** GRANGER - Historical Picture Archive (t); IanDagnall Computing (bl). **224 Dreamstime.com:** Tifonimages (cra). **228 Alamy Stock Photo:** Stocktrek Images, Inc. / Vernon Lewis Gallery (bc). **Getty Images:** Ullstein Bild (tl). **229 Alamy Stock Photo:** Science History Images / Wellcome Images (b). **231 Alamy Stock Photo:** Ann Ronan Picture Library / Photo12 (bl). **Science Photo Library:** CCI Archives (tl). **233 Alamy Stock Photo:** UtCon Collection (bl); World of Triss (tr). **235 Alamy Stock Photo:** GRANGER - Historical Picture Archive (cr). **236 Shutterstock.com:** Everett Collection (br). **237 Alamy Stock Photo:** Chronicle (tr); World History Archive (tl). **244 Alamy Stock Photo:** Lebrecht Music & Arts (tr). **245 Alamy Stock Photo:** PA Images (bl). **Getty Images:** Ullstein Bild (tr). **246 Alamy Stock Photo:** Royal Armouries Museum (tr). **Bridgeman Images:** Galerie Bilderwelt / Gervais-Courtellemont, Jules (1863-1931) (bl). **249 Alamy Stock Photo:** CBW (tl). **250 Alamy Stock Photo:** Science History Images / Photo Researchers (tl). **253 Alamy Stock Photo:** Historical Images Archive (br). **254 Alamy Stock Photo:** Chronicle (bl). **Shutterstock.com:** Everett Collection (tr). **255 Alamy Stock Photo:** The Print Collector (tr). **256 Alamy Stock Photo:** Chronicle (br). **257 Alamy Stock Photo:** Chronicle (br). **259 Alamy Stock Photo:** Heritage Image Partnership Ltd / Historica Graphica Collection (bc). **260 Alamy Stock Photo:** Pictorial Press Ltd (tr). **261 Alamy Stock Photo:** Shawshots (bl). **262 Alamy Stock Photo:** Colaimages (bc). **263 Alamy Stock Photo:** Pictorial Press Ltd (br). **265 Alamy Stock Photo:** CPA Media Pte Ltd / Pictures From History (tr). **268 Alamy Stock Photo:** Sueddeutsche Zeitung Photo / Scherl (bl). **Shutterstock.com:** Everett Collection (tr). **270 Getty Images:** Corbis Historical / Michael Nicholson (tl). **271 Getty Images:** Popperfoto (bl). **273 Alamy Stock Photo:** Science History Images (br); Süddeutsche Zeitung Photo / Scherl (tl). **275 Alamy Stock Photo:** American Stock / Camerique (tr). **Mary Evans Picture Library:** Media Drum Images (bl). **277 Alamy Stock Photo:** Associated Press (tr). **278 Alamy Stock Photo:** akg-images (bl); Interfoto / History (tr). **281 Alamy Stock Photo:** Shawshots (t). **282 Alamy Stock Photo:** Japanese Military Photo Archives (tr). **Getty Images:** Corbis Historical / George Rinhart (bl). **283 Statista 2024:** Worldwide; National WWII Museum; Various sources; 1939 to 1945 / Data of Civilian deaths in East and Southeast Asia during World War II (b). **285 Alamy Stock Photo:** Geopix (b). **288 Getty Images:** Ullstein Bild (bl). **289 Alamy Stock Photo:** NG Images (br). **290 Alamy Stock Photo:** Pictorial Press Ltd (tr). **292 Getty Images:** Bettmann (br). **293 Alamy Stock Photo:** Associated Press (br). **Getty Images:** Gamma-Rapho / Reporters Associes (tl). **295 Alamy Stock Photo:** Science History Images (cr). **297 Alamy Stock Photo:** CPA Media Pte Ltd / Pictures From History (tr). **Getty Images:** The Chronicle Collection / Dick Swanson (bl). **299 Alamy Stock Photo:** GRANGER - Historical Picture Archive (tr); Süddeutsche Zeitung Photo / AMW (bl). **301 Getty Images:** Hulton Archive / Keystone (br); Picture Post / Bert Hardy (tl). **303 Alamy Stock Photo:** Abaca Press (tc); Keystone Press / Keystone Pictures USA (bl). **304 Alamy Stock Photo:** Mauritius Images GmbH / Starfoto (bc). **308 Alamy Stock Photo:** CPA Media Pte Ltd / Pictures From History (bl). **309 Alamy Stock Photo:** World History Archive (tr). **310 Alamy Stock Photo:** Associated Press / Jerome Delay (br); Süddeutsche Zeitung Photo / Rainer Unkel (tl). **311 Palestinian Central Bureau of Statistics (PCBS):** Number of the Palestinian Population by Country of Residence (tl). **312 Getty Images:** Hulton Archive / Robert Nickelsberg (bc). **313 Alamy Stock Photo:** Everett Collection Inc (br). **315 Shutterstock.com:** Everett Collection (tr). **317 Alamy Stock Photo:** Mirrorpix / Trinity Mirror (cr). **319 Alamy Stock Photo:** Sipa USA / Piero Cruciatti (tl). **320 Alamy Stock Photo:** UPI (bl). **Getty Images:** Anadolu (tc). **321 Getty Images:** Anadolu (br).